AIDS and Business

Routledge Advances in Management and Business Studies

For a full list of titles in this series, please visit www.routledge.com

7. HRM, Technical Workers and the Multinational Corporation
Patrick McGovern

8. The Internationalization of Small to Medium Enterprises
The interstratos project
Edited by Rik Donckels, Antti Haahti and Graham Hall

9. Neo-Industrial Organising
Renewal by action and knowledge formation in a project-intensive economy
Rolf A Lundin, Hans Wirdenius, Eskil Ekstedt and Anders Soderholm

10. Perspectives on Public Relations Research
Edited by Danny Moss, Dejan Vercic and Gary Warnaby

11. Resources, Technology and Strategy
Edited by Nicolai J Foss and Paul L Robertson

12. Telecommunications Regulation
Culture, chaos and interdependence inside the regulatory process
Clare Hall, Colin Scott and Christopher Hood

13. Rethinking Public Relations
The spin and the substance
Kevin Moloney

14. Organisational Learning in the Automotive Sector
Penny West

15. Marketing, Morality and the Natural Environment
Andrew Crane

16. The Management of Intangibles
The organization's most valuable assets
A Bounfour

17. Strategy Talk
A critique of the discourse of strategic management
Pete Thomas

18. Power and Influence in the Boardroom
James Kelly and John Gennard

19. Public Private Partnerships
Theory and practice in international perspective
Stephen Osborne

20. Work and Unseen Chronic Illness
Silent voices
Margaret Vickers

21. Measuring Business Excellence
Gopal K Kanji

22. Innovation as Strategic Reflexivity
Edited by Jon Sundbo and Lars Fuglsang

23. The Foundations of Management Knowledge
Edited by Paul Jeffcutt

24. Gender and the Public Sector
Professionals and Managerial Change
Edited by Jim Barry, Mike Dent and Maggie O'Neill

25. Managing Technological Development
Hakan Hakansson and Alexandra Waluszewski

26. Human Resource Management and Occupational Health and Safety
Carol Boyd

27. Business, Government and Sustainable Development
Gerard Keijzers

28. Strategic Management and Online Selling
Creating Competitive Advantage with Intangible Web Goods
Susanne Royer

29. Female Entrepreneurship
Implications for education, training and policy
Edited by Nancy M. Carter, Colette Henry, Barra Ó Cinnéide and Kate Johnston

30. Managerial Competence within the Hospitality and Tourism Service Industries
Global cultural contextual analysis
John Saee

31. Innovation Diffusion in the New Economy
The Tacit Component
Barbara Jones and Bob Miller

32. Technological Communities and Networks
International, National and Regional Perspectives
Dimitris G. Assimakopoulos

33. Narrating the Management Guru
In search of Tom Peters
David Collins

34. Development on the Ground
Clusters, Networks and Regions in Emerging Economies
Edited by Allen J. Scott and Gioacchino Garofoli

35. Reconfiguring Public Relations
Ecology, Equity, and Enterprise
David McKie and Debashish Munshi

36. The Pricing and Revenue Management of Services
A Strategic Approach
Irene C. L. Ng

37. Critical Representations of Work and Organization in Popular Culture
Carl Rhodes and Robert Westwood

38. Intellectual Capital and Knowledge Management
Strategic Management of Knowledge Resources
Federica Ricceri

39. Flagship Marketing
Concepts and Places
Edited by Tony Kent and Reva Brown

40. Managing Project Ending
Virpi Havila and Asta Salmi

41. AIDS and Business
Saskia Faulk and Jean-Claude Usunier

AIDS and Business

Saskia Faulk and
Jean-Claude Usunier

Taylor & Francis Group

New York London

First published 2009
by Routledge
711 Third Avenue, New York, NY 10017

Simultaneously published in the UK
by Routledge
2 Park Square, Milton Park, Abingdon, Oxfordshire OX14 4RN

First issued in paperback 2014

Routledge is an imprint of the Taylor & Francis Group, an informa business

© 2009 Taylor & Francis

Typeset in Sabon by IBT Global.

All rights reserved. No part of this book may be reprinted or reproduced or utilised in any form or by any electronic, mechanical, or other means, now known or hereafter invented, including photocopying and recording, or in any information storage or retrieval system, without permission in writing from the publishers.

Trademark Notice: Product or corporate names may be trademarks or registered trademarks, and are used only for identification and explanation without intent to infringe.

Library of Congress Cataloging in Publication Data
Faulk, Saskia, 1966-
   AIDS and business / Saskia Faulk and Jean-Claude Usunier.
      p. ; cm.—(Routledge advances in management and business studies ; 41)
   Includes bibliographical references and index.
   1. AIDS (Disease)—Economic aspects.   I. Usunier, Jean-Claude.   II. Title.
   III. Series.
   [DNLM: 1. Acquired Immunodeficiency Syndrome—economics.   2. HIV
Infections—economics.   3. Developing Countries—economics.   4. HIV Infections—
prevention & control.   5. Organizational Case Studies.   6. Public Health—economics.
WC 503 F263a 2009]
   RA643.8.F38 209
   362.196'9792—dc22
   2008041944

ISBN13: 978-1-138-87945-4 (pbk)
ISBN13: 978-0-415-45463-6 (hbk)

Contents

Preface		ix
Foreword		xi
Acknowledgments		xiii
List of Tables		xv
List of Figures		xix
List of Boxes		xxi
1	A Medical Anthropologist in Morocco: Social and Cultural Factors and HIV/AIDS	1
2	Addressing a Global Cause in Local Contexts: Country Case Study of HIV/AIDS in Brazil	48
3	Mexicom Designs a National Public Health HIV/AIDS Campaign	81
4	Ross IVD: Global Marketing Issues for HIV Testing Products and Services	101
5	Protectom: Selling Condoms, a Complex Business	127
6	Global Pricing and Ethics of Marketing HIV/AIDS Drugs	141
7	RealSource India: HIV/AIDS in the Back Office to the World	184
8	WinThai: Initiating HIV/AIDS Action in a Reborn Epidemic	194
9	Woolworths South Africa	211
10	Designing a Company HIV/AIDS Program	220
Glossary		249
Notes		261
Index		319

Preface

As educators working in an international business context we uncovered a need for a book that has broad coverage of issues around HIV/AIDS and business. To fill that need, we developed *AIDS and Business* to be of use in analyzing the interplay between business and the HIV/AIDS pandemic for three primary types of readers. Firstly, it is useful for business people who need to learn more about the commercial impact of HIV/AIDS worldwide and the roles that business plays in the epidemic. Secondly, students enrolled in upper-level courses in business-related disciplines are frequently called upon to analyze emerging factors in the global business environment, macroeconomic factors, and the ethical dimensions of business policies—all of which are impacted by HIV/AIDS. Thirdly, educators and other nonsubject area specialists in the fields of business, economics, political science, law, ethics, public health, communications, and the social sciences may want or need to incorporate the study of the spread of HIV/AIDS into their course or training offerings. In addition, *AIDS and Business* could be of interest to the public health or social activist as well as the general reader seeking an understanding of one of the major social phenomena of our time: the HIV/AIDS pandemic.

It would be irresponsible to attempt to put the broad and complex study of the HIV/AIDS epidemic and its interactions with economics and commerce in "a nutshell." Yet between the covers of this book we have assembled a unique range of tools useful to the reader in beginning to understand the epidemic, designed from the perspective of economic actors.

The case study format was selected because it is one that is often used in business education and in-house company training programs. Case studies are efficient, effective, thought-provoking learning tools that can be used in different ways according to the learning objectives of instructor or trainer. The case studies are grounded in research findings. They are brought to life by protagonists that readers can identify with, who face compelling decision situations.

The book may be used as a resource on HIV/AIDS and business, a set of case studies, or a training tool. For those conducting research or interested in learning more, radiating from the book's notes are links to websites that

x *Preface*

provide information from experts around the world, and a wealth of resources about many aspects of the syndrome relevant to the business sector.

Countries covered throughout the volume include: Brazil, India, Mexico, Morocco, Russia, South Africa and other sub-Saharan African countries, Switzerland, and Thailand. We offer ten perspectives about the complex interplay between AIDS and the world of companies dealing with significant issues such as the following:

Developing an international perspective on HIV/AIDS epidemics (Case Studies 1, 2, 3, 7, and 8)

Improving the manager's understanding of the economic, political, and sociocultural factors that contribute to the spread of HIV/AIDS (Case Studies 1 and 2)

Voluntary testing and counseling (Case Study 4)

Communications for HIV/AIDS prevention and education (Case Studies 3 and 5)

The pricing and marketing of AIDS drugs, testing equipment, and intellectual property issues (Case Studies 4 and 6)

Marketing and social marketing of condoms (Case Study 5)

Workplace, ethical, and human resources issues (Case Studies 7, 8, and 9)

How to design a workplace policy (Case Studies 9 and 10)

Corporate social responsibility (Case Studies 6, 8, 9, and 10)

The case studies are based on real companies and situations, however, with the exception of the Woolworths South Africa case, names (of companies, locations and people) have been changed. Thus, any resemblance with existing people or organizations is unintentional and purely coincidental. The cases were designed to depict a decision situation for the purposes of learning through discussion and debate, not to demonstrate a "right" or "wrong" course of action.

Foreword

Twenty-five years into the epidemic, AIDS has become a make-or-break challenge for humanity. Like climate change and globalization, it is one of the defining issues of our time.

Over the past quarter-century, well over sixty million people in every country in the world have been infected with HIV. Some twenty-five million of these have died of AIDS. There have been some promising developments in the global response to AIDS in recent years, such as increased access to treatment. Nevertheless, the number of people living with HIV continues to grow, as does the number of deaths due to AIDS. A total of 39.5 million people were living with HIV in 2006—2.6 million more than in 2004. And almost half of people living with HIV are women. Sub-Saharan Africa is home to two-thirds of all people living with HIV. However, the most dramatic increases in infection rates are now taking place in Eastern Europe and Central Asia.

In many regions of the world, new HIV infections are heavily concentrated among young people (15–24 years of age). Thus, AIDS kills people in their most productive years, which makes AIDS impact on families, communities, and the society as a whole quite exceptional.

In recent years, the business sector has started to observe evidence of the direct and indirect impact of the AIDS epidemic. Companies operating in highly affected countries such as South Africa, but equally in lower prevalence countries such as China or India, have begun to experience spiraling costs due to absenteeism, the need to recruit and train new staff to replace those too ill to work or those who have died, increased insurance costs, early pension payouts, not to mention loss of productivity.

This has triggered an upsurge in business' interest in AIDS. Initiatives such as the Global Business Coalition on HIV/AIDS have been key to raising international awareness of the business responsibility in the AIDS response. They and others are also beginning to lead a more meaningful engagement of the private sector—both in terms of financial contributions to the wider AIDS response and in providing HIV prevention and treatment services to employees. A number of big multinational mining

xii *Foreword*

companies, banks, pharmaceutical companies, transportation industry as well as media companies are also taking steps to provide support to staff.

Nevertheless, a wide gap remains between the potential of business to respond to the AIDS epidemic and what is actually happening. One reason for this is a lack of understanding of the full complexity of the epidemic, the scope of its impact, and what can feasibly be done.

This book is a welcome step, supplying business with user-friendly information about AIDS. It outlines problems and solutions, through a practical case study approach. The studies themselves present some key elements of the AIDS epidemic. Each study illustrates a realistic situation where a decision needs to be made and looks at some of the different perspectives—human resources, marketing, social and cultural factors—that need to be factored into a company's response to AIDS.

AIDS will be with us for generations to come—affecting people in almost every walk of life, all over the world. In many regions, its impact on business is likely to grow.

This book offers a timely opportunity for business to scale up its involvement in local and global AIDS strategies—an involvement that will be critical to the success of our collective effort to respond effectively to the epidemic—both now and in the longer term.

Dr. Peter Piot
Executive Director
UNAIDS

Acknowledgments

The authors thank all those who contributed in different ways to the making of this volume, to include Laura Ciaffi, Roderick Duncan, Ann Robinson Faulk, W. Page Faulk, Katy Hayes, Franz B. Humer, Ted Karpf, Marco Lalos, Tobias Meier, Peter Piot, Pedro Marcos de Castro Saldaña, Edward Vela, Vincent Vandersluis, and Christian Viladent, among others.

SF is grateful for the inspiration that J, A, and A provide.

Tables

1.1	HIV Prevalence and Mode of Transmission/At-Risk Populations in Middle East and North African Countries in 2005	3
1.2	High Prevalence Regions of Morocco as a Percentage of National HIV Cases	7
1.3	Selected Cultural Aspects of Sexuality Relevant to the Study of the Spread of HIV	15
1.4	Socioeconomic Groups Vulnerable to HIV/AIDS	27
1.5	Summary of Poverty-Related Factors that Increase Vulnerability to HIV/AIDS	32
2.1	Health Summary: Brazil	50
2.2	Estimated Proportion of People Receiving Antiretroviral Therapy of Populations Who Need it. Regional Data from Low- and Middle-Income Countries, December 2003–June 2006	57
2.3	Comparison of Government Estimates and Other Expert Estimates (Selected Countries)	62
2.4	Critical Factors in the Success of Thailand's Response to AIDS	76
2.5	Factors Often Cited in the Success of Uganda's Response to AIDS	77
3.1	Informal Notes on Barriers to HIV/AIDS Social Marketing in Mexico	82
3.2	Possible Needs Identified for HIV/AIDS Infections Reduction Campaign	83

xvi *Tables*

3.3	Potential Target Audiences Identified in Informal Study	84
3.4	Noninclusive Survey of Communications Ideas Implemented in Other Countries	85
3.5	Potential Partners for the HIV/AIDS Campaign	88
3.6	Potential Media Channels to be Used for HIV/AIDS Awareness Programs	90
3.7	Characteristics of Models Commonly Used as Bases for HIV/AIDS Programs	95
4.1	Basic Information about Commonly Used Types of HIV Tests	111
4.2	Some Cultural/Social Psychological Aspects of HIV/AIDS Testing and Treatment	115
A.1	Quick Reference Facts on HIV Test Kits. SIMPLE and/or RAPID HIV TEST KITS	120
A.2	Quick Reference Facts on HIV Test Kits. ENZYME-LINKED IMMUNOSORBENT ASSAY (ELISA) TEST	121
B.1	WHO Bulk Procurement Scheme 2004 Specifications of HIV Test Kits: SIMPLE/RAPID, ELISA, AND CONFIRMATORY ASSAYS	122
5.1	Estimated Male Condom Needs and Donor Supply	133
6.1	Macroeconomic Impacts of HIV/AIDS	144
6.2	Summarized Major Ethical Bases of HIV/AIDS Treatment Policies	151
6.3	WHO Estimates of People Aged 0–49 Years Receiving Antiretroviral Treatments in Low- and Middle-Income Countries, Compared with Estimated Number of People Who Need Them	152
6.4	Pharmaceutical Industry Stance on Patent Issues, and Rebuttal for Each	167
6.5	Benefits of Equitable Pricing, or Differential Pricing	173
6.6	HIV/AIDS Drugs Marketing Activity by Roche	181

Tables xvii

7.1	Comparative View of India and Selected Countries Incidence and Prevalence Rates	192
8.1	Company Benefits for Initiating an HIV/AIDS Marketing Communications Program	201
8.2	An Overview of Selected HIV/AIDS Company Programs in Africa	208
10.1	Some Direct Impacts on Business of HIV/AIDS	221

Figures

2.1	A representation of the individual within two types of risk environments.	59
10.1	HIV/AIDS prevalence rise effects on businesses in low-income countries.	223

Boxes

1.1	Spotlight on the Psychological Roots of Stigma	17
1.2	A View from the Field: Pedro Saldaña: HIV/AIDS Prevention in Brazil and the So-Called ABC Model	18
1.3	Spotlight on Discrimination: The Case of People with Disabilities	19
1.4	A View from the Field: Dr. Laura Ciaffi: The Experience of Médecins Sans Frontières in Adherence to Antiretroviral Drug Therapy in Resource-Poor Settings	24
2.1	A View from the Field: Procurement Policies for the Government-Supplied Antiretroviral Program	60
2.2	A View from the Field: WHO's Ted Karpf on Nationalization and Health Emergencies	64
2.3	The Guiding Objective and Agenda of the World Health Organization	66
2.4	A View from the Field: MSF's Dr. Laura Ciaffi on the Availability of Funds to Pay for Antiretroviral Treatments	67
2.5	A View from the Field: The Complementarity Between Government and Business in the HIV/AIDS Fight in Brazil	69
2.6	A View from the Field: WHO's Ted Karpf on the "Ugandan Miracle"	78
3.1	A View from the Field: How Does Brazil Keep its HIV/AIDS Message Fresh and Appealing, and Avoid "Safe-Sex Fatigue"?	94

xxii *Boxes*

4.1	A View from the Field: What Can be Done to Encourage More People to be Tested and Who Could be More Active in this Area?	107
4.2	An In-Depth View: Testing Issues and Pregnant Women	114
6.1	Is Business Involvement in the Fight Against HIV/AIDS Pandemic Mere 'Enlightened Self-interest'?	154
6.2	A View from the Field: Ranbaxy Laboratories Limited Satement	160
6.3	A View from the Field: Brazilian Generic Manufacturers of Antiretroviral Drugs	174
6.4	A View from the Field: Replies to Our Questions from Dr. Franz B. Humer	179
8.1	A View from the Field: How Some Companies Make a Difference With Their HIV/AIDS Policies	197
8.2	A View from the Field: Challenges Facing Companies Starting HIV/AIDS Programs	205
8.3	A View from the Field: Coca-Cola's Work in the Area of HIV/AIDS	207
10.1	A View from the Field: PRODUCT (RED): A New Branding Approach to HIV/AIDS Fundraising	227
10.2	A View from the Field: The GBC's Dr. Neeraj Mistry on Corporate HIV/AIDS Programs	237
10.3	A View from the Field: Winners of GBC's "Outstanding Business Action on HIV/AIDS" in 2006	243

1 A Medical Anthropologist in Morocco
Social and Cultural Factors and HIV/AIDS

Dr. Mouna Benamour considered the streaks of color under the blue sky as her taxi swished from one lane to another along one of Rabat's busy avenues. "This won't be easy," she thought, as she considered her mandate to get a closer view of the HIV/AIDS epidemic in Morocco. She had grown up as an only child in Paris, with Spanish and Moroccan parents. Now, as a medical anthropologist and AIDS activist with a Spanish HIV/AIDS advocacy organization, she was in the country of her grandparents for six months to use her language skills and anthropological and cultural knowledge to understand the roots of the epidemic. Her organization was worried: some recent studies had identified warning signs of a hidden or potentially serious future epidemic in Morocco (Robalino, Jenkins, and El Maroufi, 2002; Obermeyer, 2006).

Mouna had become interested in HIV prevention and treatments during her first posting in southern Spain during the 1990s. At the time, Spain had the worst HIV epidemic in Europe and the highest number of injecting drug users in Europe with HIV/AIDS.[1] In 2004, Spain had the biggest cumulative number of AIDS cases in Europe.[2] Things had improved in Spain since then, thanks to effective interventions targeted at injecting-drug users, men having sex with men, and female sex workers as well as the introduction of antiretroviral medication in 1996.[3] In 2005, there were an estimated 140,000 people with HIV/AIDS in Spain and 2,000 who had died.[4] However, Mouna observed that the conditions for localized epidemics still existed there. There were, for instance, high figures among male sex workers in nineteen Spanish cities—12 percent of whom were HIV positive (Belza in UNAIDS, 2006). There were also large numbers of migrant workers from Morocco and other African countries employed by farms exporting Spanish produce to Europe. The workers often had little access to health care services, and tended to live in clusters of improvised housing close to the fields and orchards. In addition, a growing stream of impoverished migrants was reaching Spanish shores from sub-Saharan Africa, bringing with them the social and health vulnerabilities suffered by poor migrants everywhere.

Although HIV/AIDS prevalence levels are relatively low in the region (at 0.2 percent[5]), there is still a lack of accurate statistics upon which to make reliable estimates of prevalence. Morocco and other countries in North

2 AIDS and Business

Africa and the Middle East are characterized by factors thought to increase the spread of HIV/AIDS (Robalino, Jenkins, and El Maroufi, 2002).[6] In addition, high levels of sexually transmitted diseases in the region point to unprotected extramarital sexual activity, according to Obermeyer (2006).[7] The economic, social, and cultural factors specific to these countries include the following:

1. Low-income countries with wide income disparities.
2. High levels of labor migration, where living and work conditions that increase HIV risk.
3. Large proportion of youth are unemployed.
4. Where tourism increases, more commercial sex or drug use is likely.
5. When there are security threats or instability, government priorities may shift away from HIV prevention and treatment.
6. Strong stigma prevents people at risk from coming forward for prevention education, testing, or treatment.
7. Inadequate broad-based HIV/AIDS information is provided.
8. Wide disparities between males and females on education and income place women at increased risk.

Basic facts were available about HIV in Morocco, partly because Morocco is one of the few countries in the region that compiled information on the epidemic. HIV prevalence in the country was relatively low, estimated at 0.1 percent in 2005 by UNAIDS (or 19,000 Moroccans living with HIV). The estimate range is between 12,000 and 38,000 Moroccans.[8] Other estimates of HIV prevalence in Morocco were as much as 0.2 to 0.3 percent higher than official estimates according to the analysis of Jenkins and Robalino (2003).[9] The Middle East and North Africa region as defined by UNAIDS and the WHO is characterized by a steady advance of the epidemic, although reported prevalence levels are relatively low except for Sudan.[10] In order to provide a broader perspective, Table 1.1 shows the HIV prevalence and HIV-related concerns of UNAIDS about countries in this region. UNAIDS reports consistently emphasize that there is a lack of information on the roles of men having sex with men and commercial sex in spreading HIV in the region. This is one of the reasons it is difficult to craft an effective strategy to slow the spread.

WORRYING TRENDS IN MOROCCO

HIV prevalence in Morocco more than doubled between 1999 and 2003 among women reporting to antenatal clinics, and prevalence increased particularly among young people.[11] The Ministry of Health characterized the numbers of HIV cases as "a considerable increase" in the number of cases over five-year periods since 1986 (Ministry of Health, 2006, p. 7).[12]

A Medical Anthropologist in Morocco 3

Table 1.1 HIV Prevalence and Mode of Transmission/At-Risk Populations in Middle East and North African Countries in 2005

Country	Adult HIV prevalence in 2005	Mode of transmission or at-risk populations
Algeria	0.1% HIV cases doubled in 2004; notable increase among women; HIV epidemic "inadequately surveyed" (UNAIDS 2005, p. 71)	Unprotected sexual intercourse, particularly among sex workers
Bahrain	< 0.2% "Very little is known about the spread of HIV . . ." (UNAIDS, 2005, p. 72)	Mainly injecting-drug use
Egypt	< 0.1%	Mainly unprotected heterosexual intercourse
Iran	0.2%	Mainly injecting-drug users using nonsterile equipment; prisons
Iraq	< 0.2%	
Israel	< 0.2% "Slight but steady increase" (UNAIDS, 2004a)	Some cases came from countries with high prevalence
Jordan	< 0.2% "Very little is known about the spread of HIV . . ." (UNAIDS, 2005, p. 72)	
Kuwait	< 0.2% "Very little is known about the spread of HIV . . ." (UNAIDS, 2005, p. 72)	Mainly injecting-drug use
Lebanon	0.1% No systematic surveillance (UNAIDS, 2004b)	Mainly unprotected heterosexual intercourse
Libyan Arab Jamahiriya	< 0.2% On the increase. HIV prevalence in Tripoli prison was 18% in 2002	Mainly injecting-drug users using nonsterile equipment
Morocco	0.1% On the increase, notably among women	Mainly unprotected heterosexual intercourse; higher prevalence among sex workers (2.3%) and prisoners (0.8%)

continued

4 AIDS and Business

Table 1.1 (continued)

Country	Adult HIV prevalence in 2005	Mode of transmission or at-risk populations
Oman	< 0.2% "Very little is known about the spread of HIV . . ." (UNAIDS, 2005, p. 72)	Mainly injecting-drug use
Qatar	Very little information is available	
Saudi Arabia	< 0.2% HIV surveillance data is "insufficient" (UNAIDS, 2005, p. 71)	Most male HIV infections from paid sex; most female infections from husband
Somalia	0.9% On the increase	
Sudan	1.6 % The only country in the region with a generalized epidemic	Highest HIV infection rates in unstable south and among internally displaced persons
Syrian Arab Republic	< 0.2%	Despite testing a number of demographic groups, very low levels were found
Tunisia	0.1%	Increase in sex work and drug use may herald an increase in HIV
Turkey	< 0.2%	Commercial sex work drives the epidemic (Ministry of Health, 2006)
United Arab Emirates	< 0.2%	
Yemen	< 0.2% "Very little is known about the spread of HIV . . ." (UNAIDS, 2005, p. 72)	Mainly commercial sex

Source: Adapted from UNAIDS (2005) *AIDS epidemic update*. Geneva: UNAIDS; UNAIDS (2006) *AIDS epidemic update*. Geneva: UNAIDS; UNAIDS (2006) *Report on the global AIDS epidemic*. Geneva: UNAIDS. Ministry of Health, Turkey. (2006). *UNGASS indicators country report: Progress indicators*. Retrieved May 30, 2007, from http://data.unaids.org/pub/Report/2006/2006_country_progress_report_turkey_en.pdf. UNAIDS. (2004a). *Epidemiological fact sheets: Israel*. Retrieved May 30, 2007, from http://data.unaids.org/Publications/FactSheets01/Israel_EN.pdf. UNAIDS. (2004b). *Epidemiological fact sheets: Lebanon*. Retrieved May 30, 2007, from http://data.unaids.org/Publications/Fact-Sheets01/lebanon_en.pdf.

In addition, sexually transmitted infections (STIs)—which are normally correlated with HIV prevalence—continue to occur at very high levels.[13] More than three quarters of HIV cases stemmed reportedly from heterosexual activity.[14] The proportion of people using contraceptives, including condoms and other methods, was 50 percent in 2005.[15] UNAIDS pointed out in its report that "very little" is known about how many people are HIV positive in the Middle East and North Africa, and what the typical spread patterns are (UNAIDS, 2006, p. 50).[16] Mouna was in Morocco to fill some of those gaps.

An auxiliary reason for her trip was to conduct a preliminary investigation into the HIV/AIDS situation in Western Sahara, an area formerly known as Spanish Sahara. It was annexed by Morocco in 1975 after the discovery of phosphates deposits,[17] and still has an uncertain status today. For a time it was disputed among Morocco, Algeria, Mauritania, and the local fighters of Frente Polisario. Since the UN-brokered cease-fire in 1991, Morocco administers the area, which also contains a small United Nations peacekeeping force.[18] Mouna was fascinated to learn that no one was watching HIV/AIDS there, for example, the fact that the UNAIDS Epidemiological Fact Sheet on the country was empty![19] UNAIDS and many aid agencies all made the same declarations about the region: there was little or no data about it. "Rather surprising for a geographic area covering an area more than half the size of Morocco itself," she thought. It was well known that factors putting people at risk for contracting HIV included poverty and migration, and she knew that Western Sahara was poor and full of migrants. She wondered what she would observe there—if anyone let her in at all.

She had noted in her first few days that Morocco was indeed a land of contrasts: vibrant cities flourished while surrounded by rural areas seemingly frozen in time. Many urbanites looked, acted, and spoke like the Parisians Mouna knew. She noticed that they interacted comfortably with child beggars, wizened old women, and modest street sellers of various wares. Elegant hotels with wireless Internet may have as neighbor a decrepit block of flats. Some of the slums they called "bidonvilles" were as squalid as those she had seen south of the Sahara, and she knew that 14.3 percent of the Moroccan population lived on less than two dollars per day.[20]

She wondered what was the influence of the Muslim religion on the spread of HIV. The vast majority of Moroccans were Sunni Muslims. Did Islamic marital codes potentially increase HIV risk when four wives are permissible per man? Was it possible that the new *mudawana* family code instituted in Morocco in 2004 reduced HIV-related risks? She had heard—and read—countless times that sexually conservative Muslim values protected people from STIs. Some people told her they believed that the Muslim requirement to wash oneself after sex could remove any viruses. In a multivariate analysis of countries in sub-Saharan Africa with substantial Muslim populations, Gray (2003)[21] argued that the prohibitions on sex outside marriage, if followed, may have HIV-protective value. Previous studies had found lower HIV prevalence rates among Muslims in the countries being studied. Irrespective of the Muslim prohibitions and rituals, however, Gray concluded that lower HIV rates among Muslims may be the result of circumcision alone. Circumcision is a Muslim requirement. Obermeyer (2006) noted that the Muslim alcohol

6 AIDS and Business

prohibition, if followed, may prevent certain compromising and HIV-risky sexual situations caused by alcohol-induced disinhibition.

In a recent development, fundamentalist Muslims in Morocco expressed in the national press their disagreement with the promotion of condoms as a means of preventing the spread of HIV, calling for "fidelity to religion and marriage" to fight the "divine punishment" of AIDS.[22] In the Middle East and North Africa, many people believed their countries to be relatively safe from HIV due to the protective values of the Muslim religion. Governments assumed that adultery, sex work, homosexuality, and injecting-drug use do not occur—or occur at low levels—in Muslim societies.[23] Yet UNAIDS (2007)[24] stated that injecting-drug use is the primary HIV transmission route in Afghanistan, Iran, Libya, and Tunisia. In Algeria, Morocco, and Syria, drug use is a contributing factor to the epidemic. "A dangerous blind spot?" mused Mouna.

She knew that approximately one-third of the population in Morocco was aged 15–29, as was the case in Egypt and Jordan.[25] Such a demographic structure implied that there would be large numbers of people who were not yet married, but who were likely to be sexually active. Mouna had heard that women were contemplating marriage later in order to complete their education and that marriages generally took place at later ages. In addition, it was expected that young couples should be economically prepared to start their household, but many were unable to do so because of unemployment and economic uncertainty. It was therefore not surprising that some researchers had found young Moroccans to be accepting of premarital sex.[26] Compounding this risk was the fact that there was little HIV/AIDS information and medical outlets for this age group, given that most "family planning" efforts were for married couples.[27] Such behaviors were likely to result in increased spread of STIs and HIV. To complicate matters, the number of health threats in Morocco may make HIV diagnosis difficult: malaria, tuberculosis, and other diseases have symptoms similar to those that accompany early stages of symptomatic AIDS.

In neighboring Algeria there was a localized HIV epidemic in the south, where the country bordered Libya, Mali, Mauritania, and Niger. Hundreds of thousands of migrants came through the border points, on their way to Europe or seeking work locally, creating demand for sex workers in the area and bringing HIV prevalence among pregnant women to 1 percent in 2000.[28] Did Morocco's geographic proximity to sub-Saharan countries with higher HIV prevalence have an effect through migration or cross-border interactions as it did in Algeria? Were there vestiges of European cultural values that lingered from the country's colonial past that would influence sexual behavior? Did returning migrants from France, Spain, and elsewhere have different norms of sexual behavior? What were the cultural beliefs and values particular to Morocco that may protect from or increase vulnerability to an HIV epidemic?

The outward signs of contrasts observed by Mouna were not just economic or cultural; they were clearly visible in the country's HIV statistics. Of Morocco's sixteen regions, only five contained the majority of Moroccans with HIV. These five were heterogeneous, as is visible on the following Table 1.2.

It was puzzling to Mouna how such contrasting places could figure together as having a high HIV prevalence. Obviously, this was not purely an urban phenomenon because big cities like inland city Fez (pop. 1,185,000),[29] Straits of Gibraltar entry-point Tangiers (pop. 782,000),[30] and former Portuguese and Spanish port city El-Jadida (pop. 1,102,000)[31] did not report such high HIV prevalence. Nor was it related to being a port city, a factor related to HIV prevalence in some places due to a high concentration of transport workers and transient populations, because Marrakech (quite high HIV prevalence) and Taroudant (very high HIV prevalence) were inland cities. It was known that of the cities, Tangiers had more injecting-drug users and

Table 1.2 High Prevalence Regions of Morocco as a Percentage of National HIV Cases

Moroccan region and description	*Percent of national HIV cases*
Souss Massa Draa (central region; capital is port city Agadir, pop. 494,000), population: 3,113,653. The city with one of the highest levels of HIV, Taroudant, is here.	23
Grand Casablanca (northwest region; capital is port city Casablanca, pop. 3,389,000), population: 3,631,061	17
Marrakech Tensift Al Haouz (central region; capital is Marrakech pop.1,068,000), population: 3,102,652	15
Rabat Sala Zemmour Zaër (northwest region; regional capital is also national capital and port city Rabat, pop. 673,000 and adjacent city Salé, pop. 880,000), population: 2,366,494	9
Doukkala Abda (west-central region; capital is port city Safi, pop. 906,000), population: 1,984,039	8

Table compiled with data from:
Kingdom of Morocco, Haut Commissariat au Plan. (2004) *Rencensement générale de la population et de l'Habitat.*
Kingdom of Morocco, Ministry of Health. (2006). *Implementation of the declaration of commitment on HIV/AIDS, 2006 National Report.*
UNAIDS. (n.d.). *Morocco: Regions countries.*
UNSTATS. (2003). *Population of capital cities and cities of 100,000 and more inhabitants: Latest available year.*[1]

8   AIDS and Business

Marrakech more men who have sex with men (MSM) with HIV/AIDS.[32] There were complex social, cultural, and economic factors at work, thought Mouna, which I need to investigate.

THE HISTORICAL CONTEXT OF MOROCCO

The original people of Morocco historically were the Berbers, principally composed of three major tribes, each with its own version of the Berber language. The name *Berber* was given to them by the Arabs, who used it to refer to those they categorized as "non-Arab."[33] Phoenicians, Carthaginians, and Romans passed through the region in ancient times, and some of their legacy—mostly Roman—is still visible.[34] Following the invasion of the Arabs and the establishment of the first Islamic state, the Almoravids dynasty began their rule, which was to include most of what today is Spain. Later, when thousands of Arabs and Jews were expelled from Spain, many settled in Morocco.[35] For hundreds of years Morocco and the rest of North Africa, or the *Maghrib*, was composed of a number of ethnic and religious communities as eloquently described by Ibn Khaldun, the fourteenth-century historian, statesman, and resident of Fez.[36] The Maghrib describes much of northern Africa, a region that has a shared Berber and European past, and still today the countries share some cultural similarities. However, Algeria, Morocco, and Tunisia have distinct political traditions.[37] During the past two hundred years, Morocco has lived under the shared protectorate of France and Spain, gaining independence only in 1956. The French played a strong historical role in the country, and even today the French language remains despite the imperial abuses of the colonists in the region as documented prophetically by George Orwell in his essay "Marrakech."[38] In sum, the influences on Moroccan history, thought, and culture are Arab, Berber, French, Portuguese, and Spanish, and the vast majority of the population are Muslim.

Since gaining independence from France in 1956, Morocco gained the reputation of being a relatively "open" society in the Muslim world. This reputation continued to be bolstered by allies such as the United States, under the reign of King Mohammad VI. In support of this view, the king pushed through the parliament in 2003 a family code (*mudawana*) that ranks among the most modern in the Muslim world, granting men and women equal status in marriage, raising the legal age for marriage to 18, codifying divorce in a legalistic and unreligious way, and reducing the legal possibilities for polygamy.[39] However, female adult illiteracy may reach 90 percent in rural areas while overall female illiteracy is 62 percent,[40] making it difficult for women to be aware of their human rights, contraceptive possibilities, and HIV/AIDS protective measures. Only 12 percent of Moroccan women in 2005 knew how to prevent HIV.[41] The general literacy rate is 52 percent.[42]

To external observers, Morocco seemed to do without extremist Islamic movements until the terrorist attacks in Casablanca in 2003.[43] The alleged involvement of Moroccans and other nationals of Moroccan origin in the terrorist bombings of trains in Madrid in 2004[44] and implications in other terrorist activities (such as the attacks on the World Trade Center in 2001) made Mouna question the appearance of stability emanating from Morocco. There is much bubbling beneath the surface, Mouna knew, with the Western Sahara dispute going back almost one thousand years and not going away soon. There was also a vocal Islamist opposition party, which was officially banned, the Al-Adl-wa-l-Ihsan,[45] and widespread disapproval of the former king's decision to send troops to Saudi Arabia in 1991 to contribute to the Gulf War.[46] The King has increased opportunities for democracy; however, he remains the "maker and breaker in the political system" (Richani, 2002, p. 8).[47] In addition, there were a number of popular riots, some of which were deadly, two failed military coups over the past three decades, and continuing media censorship.[48]

Because of its geographical location as a buffer between Africa and Europe in a region not known for its stability, thought Mouna, Morocco was bound to be complicated. The country of thirty-three million inhabitants[49] is located just one hop over from Spain on the other side of the Straits of Gibraltar, and shares its longest border with Algeria, where there has been civil unrest for decades. The rest of its border is shared between Mauritania and the Western Sahara region. Economically and demographically, also, there were contentious societal issues in the country, such as the fact that more than half the population are under the age of twenty-five,[50] there was an increasing gap between rich and poor, rising immigration from sub-Saharan Africa, and worsening demographic imbalances between the cities and the countryside caused by urbanization. Already 57.4 percent of the population lived in cities, and the proportion was growing fast.[51] Mouna reflected that these were statistics which one could almost literally see with one's own eyes, once the visitor looked beyond the colorful charm of Morocco.

HIV/AIDS IN MOROCCO[52]

While HIV/AIDS remains at relatively low levels in the North Africa and Middle East region, the epidemic is growing in Algeria, Iran, Libya, and Morocco, according to UNAIDS (2006). In 2003, 2 percent of Moroccan commercial sex workers had HIV/AIDS, making them a significant factor in the spread of HIV.[53] In the early stages of the epidemic, HIV was diagnosed mainly among men having sex with men, but women have accounted for more than 40 percent of people with HIV in Morocco since the year 2000.[54] It is therefore essential to understand the situation of women in Morocco in order to identify specific factors that place women at risk for contracting HIV. An official report conceded that lower literacy rates among women prevented them from using medical services (UNAIDS, 2006).[55] In other countries, child marriage and marriage of young women to older men is a known

10   *AIDS and Business*

HIV risk factor for women. In Morocco it is likely that the *Mudawana* family law of 2004 protects some women by prohibiting marriage to those under the age of 18.[56] However, an age differential typical of the region between older men and their younger wives remains a risk in that older men are more likely to be infected (Obermeyer, 2006).[57] Yet, men may be protected by the Muslim practice of circumcision.[58] The social construction of femininity requires that young women be "innocent," thereby discouraging them from seeking HIV-prevention information, evaluating their risks realistically, or raising the topic with their partners (Obermeyer, 2006).[59] Female genital mutilation, known to carry HIV risks among many others, is carried out on at least 130 million women in Northern, Western, and Eastern Africa as well as some Gulf states.[60] Despite the country's geographic and cultural context, female genital mutilation is not thought to be practiced in Morocco.[61]

There is a taboo on discussing sexuality in public forums in Morocco, likely stemming from the Muslim majority culture. Commercial sex, homosexuality, and extramarital sex are condemned by Islamic law, increasing tensions on Muslim leaders who publicly acknowledge that these practices exist in Morocco.[62] There are high levels of discrimination against men thought to be homosexual, and stigma is attached to people known to have HIV.[63] Commercial sex work is illegal. It is a subject that is not openly discussed and sex workers are marginalized. One exception to this, according to D'Adesky (2006), was certain Berber female sex workers, who did not consider themselves to be marginalized by their own Berber community because they were seen to follow an ancestral profession.[64]

Because of this lack of openness in discussing sexual matters, it has been particularly important in Morocco that the government is seen to make an effort to publicly affiliate itself with HIV-prevention efforts. The King, H. M. Mohamed VI, and figures from the Ministry of Habous and Islamic Affairs have made statements on the topic and visited people with AIDS in hospital. A government-funded program trains imams and journalists on HIV/AIDS in an effort to galvanize these two conduits of social dialogue to HIV/AIDS causes. An antistigma campaign runs during Ramadan, a time when a spirit of "solidarity" reigns (Royaume du Maroc, p. 26).[65] The mass media has broadcast hundreds of public service announcements on television and radio in four dialects as well as an outdoor billboard campaign and a mobile unit that traveled the country. The messages promoted abstinence and fidelity and the promotion of condom use.[66] One government program trained peer educators to provide prevention education among female laborers and sex workers. HIV-prevention campaigns targeted at young people were carried out by Programme SIDA and partners at music festivals and civic activities such as beach cleanups. In an effort to reach out to women and young people as well, a number of plays have been performed with HIV as a topic by traveling actors, and films are also used.[67] Using a strategy common to countries with similar religious contexts, the Moroccan government has encouraged nongovernmental organizations (NGOs) to service illegal, marginalized, or stigmatized populations vulnerable to HIV.

A Medical Anthropologist in Morocco   11

THE SITUATION OF MEN AND WOMEN AT RISK IN MOROCCO

Sex between men is illegal, carrying a prison sentence of three to six months under the Moroccan Penal Code Section 489, which specifies same-sex to be "lewd or unnatural acts."[68] MSM have been subjected to forced testing and harassment by police, and carrying a condom may be considered as evidence that one is a sex worker.[69] In one study, Moroccan male sex workers stated they were very unlikely to use a condom (57 percent had never used one) and frequently had anal sex[70]—a dangerous combination because of the known vulnerability for contracting HIV in this manner. Male sex workers stated that it was difficult to negotiate condom use with clients.[71] Researchers found many barriers to using condoms among MSM in Morocco and northern Africa including cost, fear that a police officer or family member might find the condom, and the belief that STIs and HIV may be transmitted even when a condom is used.[72]

In addition to specific groups who may be more at risk for contracting HIV, married women are most at risk. There are two types of risk for women from their husbands: women who marry men older than themselves (Himmich in D'Adesky, 2004)[73] and women married to men who also have sex with men. The age-differential risk reflects similar findings in a number of other countries, because older men may be statistically more likely to have contracted HIV. One direct risk to women is that condoms are not generally used in marital sex, partly because of the importance of producing babies, particularly boys.[74] This exposes them to all the infections the husband may have contracted over time, including during commercial sex.

In Morocco there is a common belief that women are risky partners and the originators of STIs, known collectively as *berd*, which means "cold." Such a belief maintains social status quo and saves face for men who contract infections: they are considered to be victims. This also relieves men of the responsibility to protect against such infections, although interestingly they have more information about HIV and STI prevention than do women. [75]

Because it is a norm to marry and procreate, many men whose sexual orientation is towards males are also married with children, making them a "bridge" population between MSM groups practicing high-risk behaviors and the general population—their wives and children. Men who have sex with men may not consider themselves to be "gay" in Morocco.[76] This means they do not receive the messages directed at "gays" or do not perceive them to be relevant, thereby placing their female partners at risk.

QUESTIONS TO BE ANSWERED ABOUT HIV/AIDS IN MOROCCO

Mouna's perspective was, to use the words of another medical anthropologist, that "Disease epidemics are social processes" (Schoepf, 2001, p. 336).[77] Were there old tribal cultural factors still at work? Was it possible that the ancient cleavage between Berber and Arab existed in HIV prevalence

12   *AIDS and Business*

differences today? What were the gender-related or ethnic differences that might help or hinder HIV-prevention programs? What role was played by injecting-drug users? By prisoners? By sex workers? By men having sex with men? What was the effect of sub-Saharan migration on the spread of HIV? What about returning expatriates, mainly from France and Spain: could they play a role in increased or decreased spread of HIV? She determined to visit the high-prevalence cities to conduct some interviews with local activist organizations and local residents, as well as those cities which puzzled her because they did not have high HIV prevalence.

CASE BACKGROUND: SOCIAL AND CULTURAL FACTORS AND THE PREVENTION OF HIV/AIDS

> *HIV/AIDS is not purely a medical problem, but a complex socio-economic and societal/cultural phenomenon*
>
> UNESCO/UNAIDS report (2001, p. 25).[78]

According to the authoritative UNAIDS report (2006), almost forty million people worldwide are living with HIV and half a million are newly infected each year,[79] higher numbers than predicted by epidemiologists ten years earlier.[80] In 2005 alone, 2.8 million people died of AIDS-related causes.[81] From its beginnings as a disease of men who have sex with men, the epidemic increasingly affects women. In some sub-Saharan African countries there are three young women with AIDS to each man with AIDS.[82] In Latin America the number of women with HIV has risen by 10 percent in just three years, while in Western Europe the proportion of women to men with HIV has remained stable at 25 percent.[83] In the United States, HIV is again on the rise after two decades of decrease among MSM.[84] According to some estimates (see Epstein, 2004),[85] life expectancy has been halved after half a century of increases in a number of sub-Saharan African countries due to adult AIDS deaths. Because of AIDS, the estimated average life expectancy at birth in 2005 was on average fourteen years lower in a dozen sub-Saharan countries than it would have been without the AIDS epidemic. Before the end of the next decade, life expectancy in some African countries will fall to thirty years due to AIDS, bringing it back to where it was in the early 1900s. Outside of Africa, life expectancies are expected to fall in Asia, the Caribbean, and Latin America; in Guyana and Haiti the effects of HIV/AIDS on life expectancy are already being felt, according to Epstein.

Worldwide, most people with HIV/AIDS live in poverty, which bars them from accessing high-cost therapies and even diagnostic tests. For this reason, medical advances, such as the continuing quest for an HIV vaccine, cannot be considered as a means to slow the epidemic. Rather, international organizations and businesses have placed the emphasis on prevention and awareness campaigns and primary health services, as well as the consideration of structural adjustments that reduce HIV/AIDS risk. Such approaches assume an understanding of cultural, social, and economic factors that underlie the spread of HIV. As argued by Benatar (2002), it is essential to study the "profound social forces and human behaviour" (p.170) that allow the propagation of disease. Today, policymakers seeking effective responses to the HIV/AIDS epidemic increasingly take into account the economic and social development factors known to play a role in the spread of the disease (Parker, 2002). This is due to a recognition that HIV is a behaviorally mediated infection due to the contexts within which the virus is transmitted from one person to another.

In a world where television and radio have penetrated even the most isolated mountain villages, some people may be surprised at the amount of ignorance about HIV/AIDS and simple protective behaviors. Even when people are aware of HIV/AIDS, UNESCO (2001) researchers noted that many do not know how to protect themselves—or cannot do so. Similarly, although people may know on an intellectual level how to protect themselves from contracting HIV, they are behaviorally and physically unable to do so, often due to cultural or social factors. For instance, where people live in an environment characterized by multiple health threats in addition to HIV such as malaria, tuberculosis, malnutrition, and cholera, it may be difficult for people to prioritize protecting themselves from one threat over others. This may be exacerbated by the presence of massive and immediate survival threats such as war, drought, famine, and displacement.[86]

Epidemiologists commonly study the proximal causes of disease such as diet and other habits, and have identified specific risk factors for HIV. HIV is primarily spread through heterosexual intercourse and secondarily by men having sex with men[87] and injecting-drug use. Sexual behaviors that are most risky for contracting HIV include sex without a condom, violent sex, anal sex, having multiple sexual partners, and having a sexually transmitted infection. Being born vaginally ("vertical" transmission) or breast-feeding may spread HIV to babies whose mothers carry the virus. Exposure to HIV-contaminated blood is another route of infection, whether through transfusions, blood donations, injections, tattooing and skin perforations, and unsterilized medical instruments.[88] Each country has distinctive patterns of HIV spread due to different contexts of risk generated by an interaction of cultural, social, and economic factors. For example, in Russia, the country with Europe's biggest epidemic,[89] intravenous drug use is thought to be responsible for an estimated 80–90 percent of HIV infections.[90]

Since the earliest HIV/AIDS cases became known in the 1980s, the body of social-sciences research on the spread of the epidemic has grown and changed in focus. Once the proximal causes of HIV spread were established, researchers began to consider the distal causes which are social and economic (Link and Phelan, 1995). Regardless of the context of infection, it is striking that HIV is mainly spread through the most intimate of human interactions. These interactions are regulated by powerful norms, values, traditions, and motivations which are within the realm of social psychology, sociology, and cultural studies. For many researchers,

14 AIDS and Business

the wider economic and political context should also be considered (Castro and Farmer, 2005; Gaffeo, 2003; Marmot, 2002; Farmer, 2001; Farmer and Connor, 1996, among others). Factors cited in the literature as playing a role in increasing the risk of HIV transmission include poverty, low-level national economic growth, national culture, government policies, gender relations, and social factors such as social class, discrimination, and stigma. It is through these lenses that the spread of HIV will be examined in the following pages.

Cultural values, beliefs, and traditions may encourage or even mandate behaviors that place people at risk for HIV infection. Conversely, such aspects of culture may encourage or require behaviors that protect people from contracting HIV (Taylor, 2006).[91] Therefore, it is vital for policymakers, business leaders, HIV/AIDS advocates, and others planning HIV/AIDS interventions or communications campaigns to have an understanding of cultural and social determinants of behaviors that may foster the propagation of HIV/AIDS. A United Nations Special Session report (2006) emphasized the importance of poverty reduction, women's empowerment and gender equality, the reduction of stigma, the promotion of respect for human rights, the improvement of social and medical infrastructure, and increased funding for communication campaigns, testing, treatment, and care.[92]

AIDS, SEX, AND CULTURAL FACTORS

Culture is not easily defined, and yet most would agree that culture structures our thoughts, our lives, and our societies. Culture describes the values, customs, and norms that are shared by a number of people over time. These people are likely to share the same affiliation to a generation, a region, or other demographic variables and consider themselves to be different from people with other affiliations according to gender, class, race, religion, language, or ethnicity.[93] Because of their culture, people are likely to exhibit similar attitudes, beliefs, and behaviors in the sexual sphere as in other spheres of social interaction.

As the HIV/AIDS epidemic increased in importance as a subject of study, researchers began to advocate that, in order to understand the direction of the epidemic, an understanding of cultural meanings was vital. This was a reaction to the primarily biomedical approach used, without much success, to structure preventive programs at the beginning of the epidemic. Unfortunately, due to alarm over the spread of HIV/AIDS in Africa, much of the focus of HIV and sex-related research was on the "specificities" of the continent, resulting in what some have considered to be a racist analysis (see Gausset, 2001, for an example of these arguments). Table 1.3 summarizes some aspects of human sexuality that are strongly influenced by culture, which may inform at the design stage of HIV/AIDS interventions.

A Medical Anthropologist in Morocco   15

Although there are some similarities across cultures in human sexuality and, more broadly, in gender roles, among the world's cultures there exist broad differences in each of the aforementioned aspects. One's culture will to a large degree determine who is a possible sexual partner, under which circumstances, when, how, and with which desired outcomes is sex undertaken.[94] One example is the cultural value of virginity until marriage, which is common across cultures. Yet cultural values and acceptable behavior may have paradoxical results. For example, in countries where virginity is highly valued, such as Brazil, young unmarried women may be likely to

Table 1.3   Selected Cultural Aspects of Sexuality Relevant to the Study of the Spread of HIV

Cultural representations of sex
Desired outcomes of sexual contact
Meanings of sexual behaviors
Defining a range of acceptable practices
Power differentials between sexual actors and their relative negotiating power
Who are desirable sexual partners
Determination of what constitutes risky behavior
Number of partners and types of partners
Extent to which one's sexual behavior is controlled
Extent of control which one may exercise over the sex partner's personal life
Circumstances under which sex acts should take place
Range of roles which one may play in sexual situations
Determination of who can and who should initiate a sexual encounter
Culturally sanctioned practices and rituals carried out on sex organs, such as female genital mutilation, genital scarification, and circumcision, among others
Wider societal gender roles and stereotypes which develop as a result of biological sex (male or female)
Wider societal attitudes to—and the social status of—youth, women, and girls
Acceptance of condoms and other protective or contraceptive devices
Willingness or openness to receive messages about sexual behavior, and to talk about sexual issues
Determination of what is acceptable "male" or "female" sexual behavior

Table compiled based on readings in:
Parker, R. (2001). Sexuality, Culture, and power in HIV/AIDS research, *Annual Review of Anthropology*, 30: 163–79;
Schaller, M., & Crandal, C. S. (eds.) (2004). *The Psychological Foundations of Culture*. Mahwah, NJ: Lawrence Erlbaum Associates.
Wood, W., & Eagly, A. (2002). A cross-cultural analysis of the behavior of women and men: Implications for the Origins of Sex Differences. *Psychological Bulletin* 128(5), 699–727.

16 AIDS and Business

practice anal intercourse. The reason for this is to protect the hymen—the proof of virginity—until marriage.[95] Of Brazilian women in a national survey, 50–60 percent reported practicing anal sex,[96] possibly placing themselves at substantial risk for contracting HIV.

However, it would be simplistic to state that culture alone determines sexual behavior, because culture's influence is moderated by economic, political, and structural factors[97] such as power relations. Cultural factors thus may assist in spreading HIV/AIDS, or reduce it. It has been clearly established that disruption or collapse of cultural value systems, such as during war, migrations, or economic crises, cultural sexual barriers may dissolve, leading to risky behaviors and increased vulnerability to contracting HIV/AIDS.

The ease with which sex is discussed within a local culture may either assist or abbreviate public discourse and education about the disease. In China, when a controversial topic like homosexuality or extramarital sex is discussed in the media, official censorship may result. Therefore, many journalists self-censor their writing before having it published, ensuring the impossibility of popular debate or even of awareness.[98] In contrast, in Japan, where sexually explicit material is relatively commonplace, and the sex industry is growing (worth 2.3 trillion yen in 2001, not including receipts from e-commerce porn sites and the forty thousand sex hotels),[99] an open discussion of biomedical sex issues, such as sexually transmitted diseases, is very unusual. Recently, Dr. Peter Piot of UNAIDS personally warned Japanese policymakers that without education, Japan's constantly rising but still relatively low prevalence rate would rise to levels in comparable nations.[100] Talking about sex and societal debate about sex are not the same thing.

The Role of Stigma

People thought to have HIV/AIDS may suffer enormously from stigma. Stigma communicates public disapproval,[101] and in some places may be so strong that people with the syndrome prefer to die silently rather than bring shame upon their entire family. It builds on existing inequalities in society, such as those based on gender, class or caste, tribe, ethnic group, religion, or race. It grows from preexisting prejudices, like those entrenched against sex workers and men having sex with men. People who are stigmatized may be physically and socially isolated from others, insulted, and may be deprived of their independence and human rights.[102] People who have HIV/AIDS may experience chronic stress as a result of social stigma.[103] "People living with AIDS have reported that the stigma of HIV/AIDS is far worse than the disease itself. In addition to its devastating effects on the morale of those living with HIV and AIDS, stigma represents one of the primary obstacles to achieving change in social norms and individual behavior" (McKee, Bertrand, and Becker-Benton, 2004, p. 285).[104]

Social fears are generally related to the suspected "causes" of HIV/AIDS, which are surrounded by a complexity of norms and taboos: primarily sex (extra- and premarital, homosexual, with or as sex workers) and drugs (mainly illegal and socially unacceptable injected drugs). HIV/AIDS-related stigma may be more intense than that associated with other diseases, such as malaria, because the disease itself is perceived to be the result of one's own behavior.[105] People who are stigmatized are perceived as guilty for themselves causing the condition that invokes the stigma.[106] In this respect, the difference between HIV/AIDS and the recent outbreak of severe acute respiratory syndrome (SARS) in Southeast Asia is illuminating. Although some governments were unwilling initially to disclose the state of SARS at home, there was an almost immediate global response to this imminent threat. Many people feared contracting the disease and everyone felt concerned—in contrast to the "moral judgments" commonly made about people with HIV/AIDS.[107] Perhaps the most terrible aspect of stigma is that people who may be infected do not get tested, and thus continue to infect many others until serious opportunistic infections set in. When seeking treatment or testing, people living in areas where HIV/AIDS-related stigma is strong will likely travel away from local clinics and physicians to a more anonymous location, such as a city clinic.[108]

In places in India where stigma is strong, people with HIV may be labeled "immoral" and "worms from the gutter"; children who are found to have the virus may be abandoned in the streets; hospital staff may refuse to treat people with HIV.[109] In collectivistic societies, entire families may be stigmatized by association with the one family member who has HIV/AIDS.[110]

Box 1.1 Spotlight on the Psychological Roots of Stigma

Pryor, Reeder, and Landau (1999) summarized three social psychology issues surrounding HIV/AIDS-related stigma. First, a number of associative connections—which are often negative—may come to mind when AIDS is evoked. Second, the fear of social contamination from people with HIV, however indirectly, may be a very real issue for many people. Third, there may be two psychological steps in HIV/AIDS stigma of which the immediate one is an "automatic" reaction which subsequently becomes more reasoned and controlled.[111] In their examination of reactions to stigmatized people (such as people with HIV/AIDS), they found that reactions to stigmatized people were moderated by the observer's perception of the degree to which stigmatized people were responsible for their own misfortune, such as having HIV.[112] Stereotypes tend to grow up around stigmatized activities and groups, and serve to reassure people who are not from these groups and who do not participate in these activities that such a misfortune as HIV is not likely to happen to them.[113] The stigma of homosexuality may impede MSM from identifying with this stigmatized group:[114] they may not want to consider themselves possibly able to contract HIV/AIDS. As a result, they may not want to get tested, or even consider the possibility of doing so. Thus, they may continue to spread the virus to others.

18   AIDS and Business

The stigma associated with HIV/AIDS is often based on misinformation about how the disease is spread, and this is made worse by the long incubation period: HIV may be present for many years before the appearance of symptomatic AIDS, making people unsure whether apparently healthy individuals might be sources of infection.[115] Resulting discrimination against stereotypes considered likely to have the disease (such as homosexuals, drug users, commercial sex workers, and so on) can culminate in refusal of employment, housing, education, marriage, basic hospital care, and human rights.[116] People have reported that they suspect anyone who is thin may have the virus.[117]

The Role of Discrimination

People who publicly have HIV/AIDS are likely to experience discrimination, most significantly at the workplace. Discrimination and stigma are social

---

Box 1.2   A View from the Field

Pedro Saldaña: HIV/AIDS Prevention in Brazil and the So-Called ABC Model

The Brazilian policy on HIV prevention is based on information and interventions aimed at vulnerable groups. Therefore, policy does not follow the so-called "ABC" model (abstinence, being faithful, or consistent condom use). Among the interventions promoted by the Brazilian Government, the advocacy of consistent condom use is of utmost importance. Through the promotion of condom use, including the distribution of condoms by the Government, the Brazilian Programme on HIV/AIDS could avoid in the last eight years the appearance of almost 60 thousand new cases of AIDS. With the dissemination of condom use, it is not necessary for the Government to promote specific behaviours, such as "abstinence" or "being faithful", which would mean unnecessary interference in the individual's private life.

Prevention policy is based on the assumption that everyone is free to choose one's sexual expression without discrimination or stigma. Therefore, as a priority, the Brazilian AIDS Programme needs to provide a sufficient amount of condoms to the more vulnerable groups and the population in general to promote and support safer sex practices. Since 2000, condom distribution is also being made available directly at schools for the students aged 13 and older.

Source: Information provided by Mr. Pedro Marcos de Castro Saldaña, Second Secretary, Permanent Mission of Brazil, Geneva, Switzerland.

Link to Brazil National Program for AIDS and sexually transmitted diseases: http://www.aids.gov.br.

processes with psychological elements often discussed in the literature but rarely empirically tested. Labor-market discrimination may explain the persistent income inequalities of certain racial, ethnic, and other groups (Jonsson, 2001). Discrimination may be indirect, resulting in exclusion from networks and assistance; or direct and based on prejudice and imperfect information that excludes people from employment, housing, or other resources (Elliott and Smith, 2004).

Medical doctors treating people with HIV may themselves discriminate based on race, gender, social class, or other attributes. In one study it was reported that doctors are hesitant or do not prescribe antiretroviral drugs for women who are perceived as stereotypically low status white, black, or Latino because doctors perceive such people to be unreliable or irresponsible.[118] Discrimination thus remains a social force to be addressed in workplaces, governments, and other institutions like hospitals and places of worship, both for ethical and legal reasons.

The Role of Religion

Religious issues influence the spread of HIV/AIDS. For instance, during his past career as Cardinal Joseph Ratzinger, Pope Benedict made clear his stance against homosexuality, calling it "an intrinsic moral evil" and describing Catholic opposition to gay marriage and adoption of children by gay couples as "a moral duty."[119] The Vatican's opposition to contraception has been an obstacle to the promotion of condom use in certain Catholic

---

Box 1.3 Spotlight on Discrimination

The Case of People with Disabilities

One process behind discrimination that may be particularly relevant to understanding behavior towards people with HIV/AIDS was described in the work of Katz and Glass (1979) on the topic of ambivalence response amplification (ARA) theory and people with disabilities. The researchers researched the ambivalence felt by people without disabilities towards those "less fortunate" than they are. When confronted with a person with disabilities (or a person thought to have HIV/AIDS), people free of disease and disability feel aversion as well as concurrently feeling sympathy. Such incompatible feelings threaten self-esteem and typically result in a strong response that justifies one feeling at the expense of conflicting feelings. This response may explain overfavorable assessments of people with disabilities on the one hand, and on the other, exaggeratedly negative responses to unfavorable behavior displayed by people with disabilities, surmised Colella and Varma (2001) in their organizational leadership simulation and field work. In the earlier work of Katz and Glass (1973), experiments with white subjects and black "victims" had similar outcomes.

20   AIDS and Business

countries.[120] The Vatican officially denounced the use of condoms for safe sex in its 2003 publication *Lexicon on Ambiguous and Colloquial Terms about Family Life and Ethical Questions*. The book denounced governments that promote condoms as serving their own commercial interest, then stated that condoms do not work 10 percent of the time.[121]

An ideologically motivated policy example is that of then-U.S. President George W. Bush, who, on the first day of his presidency in 2001, reinstated the Mexico City Policy, also known as the "Global gag rule," in order to block U.S. federal funds from going to any organizations operating worldwide that offer abortion-related services, including counseling. This affected organizations like International Planned Parenthood Federation[122] that are committed to reducing abortion for health and safety reasons, and primarily work to increase the use of condoms worldwide as a contraceptive option.[123] The policy was to be extended to HIV/AIDS funds.[124] Any U.S. government funds going to the United Nations Population Fund or international family planning organizations, for example, may not be used to support condoms as a preferred means of protection against HIV/AIDS and other sexually transmitted diseases, having as an effect reduced counseling about sexual health and fewer available condoms.[125] Coexisting American cultural values of diversity and extreme conservatism have bred a powerful right-wing social conservative lobby that works to impose abstinence from sex, strict monogamy, fidelity, and "partner reduction" at home and around the world. The policy has become an obstacle for those working worldwide to stem the tide of HIV/AIDS.

In most religions there are official condemnations of men having sex with men. In an extreme example, Malaysia, a primarily Muslim country, a recent trial of an allegedly homosexual act by a politician ended up with a nine-year prison sentence for sodomy[126] although the possibility exists that this was politically rather than morally motivated. According to the head of education and research at Malaysia's Islamic Affairs Department, Abdul Kadir Che Kob, homosexuals are "shameless people" and homosexuality is a "crime worse than murder." The Islamic Affairs Department has the latitude of a police department, and regularly arrests people in Malaysia doing "immoral" acts.[127] At the other end of the spectrum, however, during the same year a film was released in Malaysia by director Osman Ali, titled "Bukak Api," that showcased transsexuals, injecting-drug users, and commercial sex workers in Kuala Lumpur. The film graphically showed safer sex with condoms, and realistically portrayed various aspects of sex workers' lives.[128] This short example demonstrates that, while religion may play a strong role in defining morality, people continue to conduct themselves in ways that go against that morality—despite the threat of censorship, imprisonment, and terrible social shame. The relevance for HIV/AIDS prevention and treatment is that, in such an environment, people who may be most at risk for contracting HIV may not come forward for testing and therefore continue to spread the virus over a long period.

The Role of Circumcision

The practice of surgically removing the foreskin of the penis, known as circumcision, is a very old and widespread practice. It is known that some ancient Egyptians practiced circumcision, and since then, Judaism and Islam have advocated this genital alteration. Circumcision remains common worldwide because it is required by religious authorities, has become a ritual, a rite of passage, or is simply considered to be hygienic.[129] In some places peoples living in close proximity have opposite views on the topic, such as the Kikuyu and Luo, both Kenyan tribes, who demonstrate that HIV prevalence is lower among the circumcised Kikuyu than among the uncircumcised Luo. For more than a century, physicians have observed that circumcised men tend to contract fewer sexually transmitted diseases than those who are not circumcised.[130] A large number of studies have linked circumcision with lower HIV rates.[131] Researchers are concerned about how to realistically, ethically, and in a culturally sensitive manner advocate or mandate circumcision, and have concerns that newly circumcised men would reject previously acceptable safer sex practices because they feel safe.[132]

The Role of Culture in Adherence to Treatment Regimens

Cultural issues also color the health management of HIV-positive people and those with AIDS. There are different cultural approaches to health, life and death, fate, and responsibility. A fatalist perspective on life encompasses the belief that one has little control over one's future. This is often related to powerlessness. Individuals suffering from AIDS-related stigma are likely to be more fatalistic.[133] People living in countries with very low life expectancy are also likely to be more fatalistic due in part to their short time horizon.[134] An economist's perspective on this in Oster (2005) explains that people with a shorter life expectancy (as in Africa) are likely to make smaller changes to their sexual behavior as HIV/AIDS rates rise because they will "lose" fewer years if they contract HIV compared with a person with a longer life expectancy (as in the United States and Europe).[135] To compound matters, in "developing" countries, medical science and its accompanying institutions may be bound by the local population's perceptions that are formed from a neocolonialist, or conspiratorial perspective.

Cultural and social factors influence the relationship between patient and caregiver and may influence the subsequent success or failure of HIV/AIDS treatments. Distrust of public health officials may be a significant barrier to communicating with risk groups in the United States, for instance (Reif, Lowe Geonnotti, and Whetten, 2006).[136] Poor members of ethnic groups and people living in poverty perceive government agencies as attempting to direct their lives, and may feel that the only area of their lives over which they have control and power is in intimacy and sex. "Safer sex" messages—particularly when given by people or groups with authority—are resented when they are perceived to invade the private realm.[137]

22   AIDS and Business

Time orientation, a concern controversially raised by Bush Administration officials at the turn of the century, may be only a small part of a mosaic of cultural and economic factors that influence adherence to drug regimens. Cultural differences in the perception of time may affect the success of HIV/AIDS medical regimens. Examples of this in the research include monochronic or polychronic time orientations first set out by Hall (1990)[138] or the long-term/short-term orientation devised by Hofstede and Bond (1988).[139] Antiretroviral drugs commonly need to be taken according to a strict time schedule, and usually for the remainder of the patient's life. When taken incorrectly, at inexact doses, or at inconsistent times, they are not only less effective, but may result in the patient becoming resistant to treatment with specific medications. Additionally, antiretroviral drugs can cause unpleasant and sometimes debilitating side effects which may result in poor adherence. Despite these difficulties, good adherence to drug regimens has been observed on the ground as discussed in the Médecins Sans Frontières box.

The person living with AIDS is likely to experience severe stress related to this complex medical condition. In addition to stigma, likely depression, and crushing expenses, one faces the likelihood of an early death, frequent opportunistic infections ranging from diarrhea to tuberculosis to cancer, and complications from the inevitable interactions of AIDS medications and those prescribed for opportunistic infections. Each pill in the "cocktail" of treatment may need to be taken with certain foods or on an empty stomach in order to avoid the crippling side effects, such as constant diarrhea. In addition, the different drugs have specific storage requirements, often requiring refrigeration.

Treatment of the inevitable opportunistic infections may require large doses of wide-spectrum antibiotics that also require specific storage, dosage, and side effect prevention measures. The education and long-term perspective necessary to understand and carry out the complicated drug regimen may not be present in many patients. Patients may have difficulty following specific time-related instructions, and may not have access to a refrigerator.[140] According to Ciaffi (2005), Médecins Sans Frontières has found these issues to be unfounded. However, the specific foods recommended to accompany each dose in order to combat side effects may not be available.

In countries lacking in infrastructure and health-related funds, local solutions have been found to increase adherence to the rigorous drug regimens that must be followed by people with HIV and particularly by those with AIDS in order to maintain functional health. In the conference report of the International AIDS Conference (2002), many examples were given of drug access programs in poor countries that boast of high adherence and survival levels. Médecins Sans Frontières, the medical group that ran many successful pilot projects, reported that such programs share several of the following features, which are grounded in the local cultural environment, and are therefore more likely to be effective:[141]

- People are enrolled in the program after months of counseling.
- Presence at appointments is recorded.
- One or more family members are trained to help the treated person.
- Community groups offer ongoing support, including visits by a volunteer at regular intervals to observe the patient taking the medications.
- Local governments strongly support the projects.

In countries where victories were declared in the early stages of the epidemic, today one is often faced with complacency and ignorance among young, sexually active adults. It is difficult to isolate which factors were indeed those that changed people's behavior in Thailand and Uganda in a way that protected them from contracting HIV. There is still no cure, nor is there a vaccine. Taken as a global trend, heterosexuals in the general population (as opposed to risk groups) are increasingly spreading the disease, while some risk groups, such as men who have sex with men in high-income countries, are more likely to ignore "safer sex" messages. According to the Netherlands Development Assistance Research Council (RAWOO, 2001), social-science research is urgently needed in order to understand which behavior change interventions are effective and which are not. The very complexity of HIV/AIDS pleads for more social-scientific research into behavioral communication, the measurement of sexual behavior changes, and characteristics of risk groups.[142] In summary, until more is known about human behavior in addition to human biology, AIDS may continue unabated.

It has been well documented that a culturally specific case management system will result in improved adherence to medication schedules, hence improved survival. In the United States, when HIV positive immigrants from Latin America were supported by a culturally and linguistically compatible peer group, drug adherence improved, as opposed to the usual model whereby a randomly assigned health care worker counsels the AIDS patient.[143] To resolve the difficulty of adhering to the strict medication regimen in Botswana, a "buddy system" was developed whereby people with HIV/AIDS are delegated to check on each other's medication schedules and provide help and encouragement with it.[144]

The Role of Fatalism

Fatalism may play a role in the transmission, voluntary testing, and treatment of HIV/AIDS. In Fanon's (1965) writings about medicine, there is a lucid description of the fatalism he observed in the poor of Algeria and the "disinherited in all parts of the world, who perceive . . . life not as a flowering or a development of an essential productiveness, but as a permanent struggle against an omnipresent death" (p. 128). He described how the poor often refused medical treatment until their illness was unbearable.

24   AIDS and Business

Box 1.4   A View from the Field

Dr. Laura Ciaffi: The Experience of Médecins Sans Frontières in Adherence to Antiretroviral Drug Therapy in Resource-Poor Settings

I am in charge of HIV projects and consultant at MSF's HIV projects medical department. We currently run 12 HIV projects at different stages in the following countries: Cameroon, Mozambique, Angola, Myanmar (Burma), Laos, Guatemala, Honduras, and Sudan—12 projects not 12 countries. These are patient care projects that also have a prevention component. We do focus on the prevention component for people coming to the clinic who are HIV positive, and for education and promotion for those coming to the hospital. We are less active in the community, for which reason we try to liaise with existing structures and organizations. Our energy really goes to helping patients, taking care of opportunistic infections, providing antiretrovirals, and so on.

It is often said that patients in resource-poor settings do not follow their treatments properly, but that is not true. In some cases there are better results on our studies than those of clinical trials in northern Europe. The reason for this is that our patients have never taken medical treatments before so they are less likely to have drug resistances. The problem with patients in the northern hemisphere is that many who are on triple therapy have already been on other antiretroviral treatments, so drug resistance levels are much higher. Our patients in the southern hemisphere have—in the main—never taken any medications, and so respond better to treatment and have fewer drug resistance cases.

We do a lot to improve adherence to drug regimens as part of the regular follow-up on treatment. We take the time to prepare the patients, to follow them through, to bring in a family member for support. They also know that ours is the only chance they will have to receive care. For these reasons, they follow their medication regimens carefully and we have good outcomes.

One of the reasons that access to antiretroviral therapy was delayed in poor countries was the generally held opinion that Africans did not take their medications regularly, that they are not used to medicines and so on. However, our experience proves that this view is wrong—as do our patients' very good HIV monitoring test results.

Every so often there is someone who will not take their medication correctly, and usually there will be social reasons behind the behavior. In Cameroon we had patients complete a questionnaire and found that when people do not take their medications correctly it was because there were too many side-effects, they hated taking pills, or they were not feeling well—all elements in the patient-treatment relationship. In Cameroon, the main reason people gave for missing a dose of medication was "I changed my routine, I was in the house with someone who does not know my HIV status, I have problems with people around me." These are more social relationship issues rather than individual issues. The main obstacle for patients is the fear of disclosure, due to living in a house where others do not know one's HIV status.

continued

A Medical Anthropologist in Morocco   25

Box 1.4 (continued)

According to our questionnaire findings, the majority of people do tell others they are HIV positive, but only to one or two people in their families. Most African households include more than just the nuclear family members so there is always someone who does not know. For this reason, there is very little private space and life is a collective matter so when someone does not know that a family member is HIV positive it is difficult to keep all the medications secret. At first we had big compartmentalized pill boxes to organize which pill to take when, on which day. Patients asked us how they could possibly explain such a thing if family members caught sight of it! We learned from that so now there are no more pill boxes. Instead we give them the antiretrovirals in their packages just like any other medicine. Fixed-dose combination therapy drugs are good because patients need only take one in the morning and one at night. Otherwise you need at least three boxes of tablets, each with a different dose, one in the morning, one at noon, one at night, one with food, one on an empty stomach . . . it is very complicated.

According to our statistics, of 100 patients who start antiretroviral therapy with us, between 5–7 percent die, mainly during the first three months in the case of patients arriving at later stages of AIDS. Let us say that 7 percent die, 10 percent disappear and we do not know if they live or die, and the rest continue their antiretroviral therapy.

Source: Information provided by Dr. Laura Ciaffi, HIV/AIDS specialist, Médecins Sans Frontières, Geneva, Switzerland.
Link to Médecins Sans Frontières site: http://www.msf.org.

After consulting a doctor they tended not to take medications, or did so erratically. This behavior was, he posited, due to an attitude towards death that was derived from their attitude towards life as well as their view of medical science, introduced at the same time as colonialism, racism, and humiliation.[145] Similarly, in her extensive interviews with Southern African miners and sex workers, Campbell (2003) often heard respondents echo the theme of powerlessness. Miners felt powerless in front of the risks and unpredictability of working in the mines. They felt powerless to complain about their unpleasant living conditions: far from home, isolated from families, and living in an all-men's hostel. They also felt powerless to protect their health from diseases. "While mineworkers may be aware of the dangers of unprotected sex with multiple partners, such behavior may be beneficial at a range of other levels in the stressful and socially impoverished living and working environments of the mines" (Campbell, 2003, p. 35).[146] In Kenya, young people felt that there was not much point trying to protect themselves from HIV/AIDS: their attitude was fatalistic.[147]

The Role of Belief Networks

Belief networks tend to grow up around the disease, as people strive for control and understanding of this phenomenon that strikes close to home and is so new to their culture. Where the facts are scarce, or where cultural values downplay "official" or "scientific" information, myths develop around the disease.[148] For political reasons, certain HIV myths may be developed or fostered about a particular group in society. A commonly reported myth about AIDS in some countries is that one cannot contract the disease during sex with a virgin or a child, and that such an act may even cure AIDS.[149] Among African American men, HIV/AIDS prevention efforts are commonly seen through the lens of conspiracy beliefs, constituting a veritable barrier to HIV/AIDS prevention programs.[150]

Among Southern African miners there were competing beliefs about HIV, such as the belief that HIV/AIDS may be cured by traditional healers, such as shamans, faith healers, and herbalists, combined with "Western" doctors, chemists, and alternative medicine. HIV/AIDS and other diseases are thought to be caused by an enemy's curse. A traditional healer may restore the social harmony that caused the problem. Traditional healers may dispense preventive medicine that one may drink before sex in order to avoid using condoms.[151] In the words of Campbell (2003), "Health education messages are not simply passively accepted by their audiences, but must compete with alternative beliefs, experiences, and logics that may be more compelling than the information that the health educator seeks to impart" (p.25).[152]

SEGMENTING THE POPULATION IN TERMS OF VULNERABILITY TO HIV/AIDS

A person's vulnerability to HIV/AIDS is often related to cultural issues that play a role in determining that person's status, profession, or place of residence. In most countries where AIDS has been studied, certain groups are more at risk than others. Generally, at-risk groups include the poor, females, and young people. An example that highlights the infection risk faced by the poor is that of a study in India that found only 2 percent of illiterate women were aware of the existence of HIV/AIDS.[153] In the United States, the epidemic is becoming increasingly prevalent among economically disadvantaged populations, including ethnic groups.[154] Perhaps the clearest message about HIV/AIDS and poverty comes from this: 95 percent of new HIV infections are among populations in low-income countries.[155] Table 1.4 sets out the main socioeconomic groups considered to be vulnerable to contracting HIV/AIDS, organized into three groups.

Table 1.4 Socioeconomic Groups Vulnerable to HIV/AIDS

Underprivileged populations	Culturally destabilized groups	Other specific risk groups
The poor	Disintegrated families	Segregated groups
Women and girls	Unemployed	Men who have sex with men
Young people	Refugees/displaced people	Commercial sex workers
People lacking in schooling	Domestic/foreign migrants	Intravenous drug users
Mobile workers	Prisoners	Armed forces

Primary source: UNESCO/UNAIDS. (2001). A cultural approach to HIV/AIDS prevention and care: Culturally appropriate information/education/communication elaboration of delivery and care. *Methodological Handbooks,* Special Series, Division of Cultural Policies, UNESCO, No. 1.

Gender: Women and Girls

According to Kofi Annan, former director-general of the United Nations, practices that empower women are the only "vaccine against HIV."[156]

There is cause to take a gendered view of the epidemic. Being female is considered to increase the risk of contracting HIV for physiological, social, economic, and cultural reasons. Once a disease associated with gay men, HIV is taking on an increasingly feminine face. In 2006, one million more women than in 2004 had HIV/AIDS. In sub-Saharan Africa, there are fourteen women with HIV for every ten seropositive men (UNAIDS, 2006). South African women accounted for three-quarters of all women worldwide with HIV/AIDS.[157] An increasing number of researchers and policymakers are recognizing the economic, social, and cultural factors tied to gender (see Chacham, Maia, Greco, Silva, and Greco, 2007; Dunkle et al., 2004; Dworkin and Ehrhardt, 2007; Elliott and Smith, 2004; Gupta, 2002; among others).

Differences in the behavior of men and women have been observed in all societies. A number of disciplines have attempted to explain these, as summarized by Wood and Eagly (2002). According to their summary, an evolutionary psychology perspective views gender differences as a result of differential male and female investment in parenthood. A social anthropological explanation is that gender-based differences are determined socially according to local contexts. Like anthropologists, sociologists eschew a biological basis for sex differences and have a variety of perspectives to explain them, including social role theory. Similarly, for psychological constructionists gender differences are maintained by gendered language and social relations. Wood and Eagly developed a biosocial model that combines the sociologist's interest in roles that are perpetuated and reinforced by sex-based stereotypes, with a recognition of the physical differences between men and women, to include hormonal and body strength differences.

28   AIDS and Business

Gender theory, which researches why men and women behave in their respective ways, has been used in female-targeted AIDS-prevention programs and is increasingly used to answer the questions "what makes a man?" and "what makes a woman?" Many values associated with masculinity put men at risk for HIV/AIDS, while those associated with femininity place women and their children at risk also. Gender-based attitudes depend on local, religious, ethnic, and national cultures. Across cultures, perceptions of masculinity tend to be associated with independence, bravery, strength, and sexual activity. Femininity tends to be associated with chastity, fidelity, and fertility. According to the UNAIDS world AIDS campaign, 2001, men are often in a stronger position in their relationships with women for social, cultural, and economic reasons. Men tend to decide when and where to have sex, and whether or not to use condoms.[158] Women with low levels of educational attainment are less able to negotiate protective measures and are more likely to contract HIV. Women and girls tend to be ignorant about sex due to social norms that hold sway in many cultures. In a recent survey conducted by MEASURE and UNICEF, more than half the women in many less affluent countries did not know three ways to prevent contracting HIV (UNAIDS, 2004). This was the case of more than 80 percent of women in Moldova, Ukraine, and Uzbekistan. Their ignorance of prevention methods means in practice that these women cannot protect themselves from contracting HIV.[159]

Women comprise 70 percent of the world's one billion people living in extreme poverty (under one dollar a day), thereby becoming concurrently members of two groups at higher risk for HIV: females and people living in poverty.[160] In the United States and other affluent countries, men having sex with men still drives the epidemic; however, the proportion of women with HIV is rising.[161] The sociocultural construct of gender needs to be better understood in order to communicate with young people of both sexes in a manner that can get them internally motivated to protect themselves from HIV/AIDS.

Cultural expectations of marriage and reproduction may affect women's ability to protect themselves from contracting HIV, as do cultural institutions and their variations such as polygamy, prostitution, and rites of passage.[162] When pregnancy is socially desirable, condoms may be viewed unfavorably. In sub-Saharan Africa, for example, there may be such an emphasis on female fertility (particularly as it relates to sons) that many women may believe that the benefit of potential pregnancy outweighs the risk of contracting HIV/AIDS during sex. In cultures like many in Africa, much value is placed on ancestry, descent, and fertility—concepts stopped in their tracks by condom users.[163]

Women are exposed to a higher HIV risk when there is civil strife, sectarian violence, war, or simply massive insecurity. Even in the absence of declared or open conflict, when there is heightened personal and human insecurity, women are at risk.[164] This risk may take many forms. For example, rape may

A Medical Anthropologist in Morocco   29

be used to terrify a group of people, and demonstrate symbolically the victory of one group over another. It is well documented that military personnel tend to have higher HIV rates than the general population.[165] There is also an assumption that soldiers need to be given an outlet for their sexual impulsions. In cases of extreme instability, women may undertake transactional sex in order to bargain for their lives or those of their families, or in order to attempt safe passage. Women who are widowed during a conflict are in some places forced to remarry, usually another man selected by her family, her late husband's family, or a person of authority.

A culturally sanctioned practice that increases women's exposure to HIV is female genital mutilation (FGM). This is the cutting, burning, or removal of part or all of the external female genitals in the belief that it is a good tradition, that the girl will be more easily married, or that the religion demands it.[166] Some definitions of FGM include the insertion of herbs or other substances into the vagina to narrow it.[167] An estimated 100 to 150 million women have undergone FGM, which is sometimes erroneously referred to as "female circumcision," primarily in Egypt (97 percent of women), Mali (92 percent), and northern regions of Sudan (90 percent).[168] In addition to being practiced in approximately forty countries in Africa and on the Arabian peninsula, FGM is increasingly done in Western Europe, North America, and other countries where these populations have migrated.[169] FGM is a traditional practice that puts women at risk for contracting HIV in several ways. First, the procedure itself may spread HIV through unhygienic instruments such as broken glass or scissors used on several cases without sterilization.[170] Second, the procedure often results in lifelong scarring and painful intercourse for the woman, which may contribute to tearing of tissues and increased vulnerability to HIV. Third, because the birth canal may be obstructed—particularly in the most extreme form of mutilation known as infibulation—there may be obstetric complications leading to loss of blood and blood transfusions that may not be properly screened for HIV as the woman gives birth, as well as increased medical procedures surrounding the birth of a child which in some places have their own HIV transmission risks.[171]

Cultural values that place a premium on many sexual partners for males ensure the perpetuation of sexual politics in a manner that places both sexes at risk for spreading HIV/AIDS.[172] In the case of men in high-risk occupations like mining, sex played important roles in the men's lives, such as companionship and as part of their masculine identity that helped them to cope with the difficult realities of daily life. Such men preferred mainly "flesh to flesh" sex without a condom.[173] Where men adopt "macho" values, often they are supposed to have multiple sex partners, increasing the HIV/AIDS risk for everyone concerned.[174] There are particular concerns about the wives and female partners of men having sex with men. Such women are often not aware of their husbands' sexual activities with men. In a Bangladeshi study, men agreed that even if their wife were to find out,

30   AIDS and Business

she would be unlikely to tell anyone because people would blame her for not sexually satisfying her husband, thereby forcing him to seek satisfaction elsewhere, and she would feel great shame. [175]

In the case of poor, young men, particularly those lacking in education and a sense of opportunities for the future, sex may be the only affirmation in life. A young man from the Ivory Coast told researchers that "around here there is only football, drink and sex. When it is dark there is only drink and sex. And when the drink runs out, there is sex" (Scalway, 2001, p. 13).[176] In Campbell's (2003) study of South African miners living in workers' quarters, miners commonly expressed a sense of powerlessness over their lives, where one of their few spheres of power was in sex, particularly with prostitutes, and often without condoms.[177] Where men believe that violence against women and forced sex is desirable or normal, more women risk contracting HIV/AIDS. Half of all new HIV infections in Thailand originated from sex within marriage, the husband generally considered to have been a current or former user of commercial sex workers.[178] Such a fact may be exacerbated by high levels of domestic violence in Thailand. In one study, more than 40 percent of Thai women said they had been sexually or physically abused by their husbands.[179] In a study conducted by the Asia Pacific Network of People Living with HIV, women were significantly more likely than men to experience HIV-related discrimination such as physical assault, eviction, exclusion, and loss of financial support from family members.[180] In countries where there is civil unrest or open warfare, calculated mass rape may be used as a "weapon of war," according to Amnesty International, referring to Darfur, Sudan, Democratic Republic of Congo, and Colombia, among others.[181]

In Amnesty International's report on women, HIV/AIDS, and human rights (2004), a number of societal, political, and legal factors conspire to place women at greater risk than men for contracting HIV. Women experience violence in the home, community, and at the hands of government employees such as police, prison guards, and soldiers. Worldwide, it is estimated that one in five females has been physically or sexually abused, and violence against women causes more deaths than traffic accidents and malaria combined. A United Nations Development Program (UNDP) report defined sexual violence as "the deliberate use of sex as a weapon to demonstrate power over, and inflict pain and humiliation upon, another human being" (section 1).[182] Other factors that increase the HIV/AIDS risk for women and girls may not explicitly include violence and include early marriage, female genital mutilation, wife inheritance, economic dependence, lack of access to schooling, and discrimination, among other factors. Marriage to very young women and girls brings a number of dangers for the young wife who is subordinated in a powerless situation, often with a husband who is much older (and more likely to have HIV). For these reasons, the presence of so-called ABC programs (where sexual abstinence is prioritized) do not protect women.[183] Such programs may only make women aware of the risks that they tragically cannot avoid taking.

People Who Live in Poverty

A strong determinant of HIV risk is membership in a poorer socioeconomic group. Poverty is often considered to be such a determining factor that some activists call the disease "Acquired *Income* Deficiency Syndrome" (as opposed to *Immune*). It is significant that 95 percent of all infections occur in low- and middle-income countries.[184] Poverty in and of itself may not be a driver of HIV. Rather, World Bank (1997) research showed that countries with an unequal distribution of income had higher rates of HIV/AIDS.[185] Poor regions, such as some in sub-Saharan Africa, are characterized by low levels of literacy, malnutrition and poor health care, employment-related as well as forced migration, and lack of access to basic services.[186]

People who are poor may have lower immunity resistance due to fewer possibilities to eat a sufficient quantity of nutritious foods, likely reducing their body's ability to fight HIV. People with lower education levels are less likely to have received any form of sex education and may be ignorant about HIV/AIDS prevention measures. They are unlikely to be able to afford to prolong their lives with costly antiretroviral treatments.[187] In poorer countries, women may suffer disproportionately from a gender disadvantage that reduces their health care possibilities, nutritional support, and elementary education.[188] When treating patients already at a social and economic disadvantage, doctors need to take the time to explain how they must follow their treatment regimen and why nonadherence will compromise their ability to improve under antiretroviral therapies. However, because of preexisting discrimination they may not do so.[189] Table 1.5 summarizes the ways in which people's lack of resources places them at heightened risk for HIV.

Even within high-income countries, such as the United States, poorer socioeconomic groups are more at risk for contracting HIV. Similar characteristics as those described in Table 1.5 apply to disadvantaged socioeconomic groups in high-income countries, particularly in the case of racial or ethnic minorities, rural or isolated populations, recent migrants and refugees, and "inner-city" poor. According to a World Bank assessment, "international evidence suggests that sustainable growth and a more equal distribution of income are factors that contribute to diminishing the spread of HIV" (Garcia, Noguer, and Cowgill, 2003, p. 50).[190]

Young People

Young people are more likely to indulge in HIV-risky behaviors for reasons related to culture, politics, and economics. In addition, risk-taking behavior may be more common among adolescents due to developmental changes going on in their brains.[191] Young people are in a life-cycle stage where they are living the conflicting pressures of independence and dependence, peer pressure and individualism—and their knowledge of sexual situations may

32   AIDS and Business

Table 1.5   Summary of Poverty-Related Factors that Increase Vulnerability to HIV/AIDS

People who are poor are less likely to have knowledge about HIV/AIDS and how to protect themselves because they tend to be less educated.

Poor people may be geographically isolated in areas lacking proper infrastructure for health and communications.

People with fewer resources, especially women, may not have other income-generating possibilities.

When experiencing income squeeze, crop failure, forced migration, departure of spouse and breadwinner, women may have little choice but to resort to sex work for survival.

Women doing sex work for survival may not feel free to demand that their clients wear condoms.

Negotiating power in the so-called condom negotiation is very low for sex work done by men, women, or children who are fighting to survive.

People living in poverty may not know about the protective benefits of condoms, and even if they do, may not consider the benefit worth the cost.

Poor men may need to delay marriage for long periods in order to amass some income, and during that time may have multiple casual partners, increasing the likelihood of contracting HIV.

People who are poor are more likely to have to migrate to earn a living, thereby placing the entire family at higher HIV risk if they all follow, or placing the two members of the couple at risk as the migrant male seeks sex as "companionship," and the commonly at-home wife may be forced into sex work until the husband returns.

People living in poverty have less healthy lifestyles due to insufficient nutrition and nutrients, sporadic meals, difficult access to mediocre or ineffective health services, and are more exposed to environmental pollutants and health hazards, weakening their immune system.

Resource-poor governments may not be able to provide vaccinations, essential nutrients to pregnant and lactating mothers, and other necessary health and sanitation services. A weak immune system is less capable of fighting off HIV and other infections, such as sexually transmitted infections, parasites, tuberculosis, and hepatitis, to name a few.

Information compiled from: Garcia Abreu, A., Noguer, I., & Cowgill, K. (2003). *HIV/AIDS in Latin American countries: The challenge ahead*. Washington, DC: The World Bank; Gillespie, S. (ed.) (2006). *AIDS, poverty, and hunger: Challenges and responses*. Highlights of the International Conference on HIV/AIDS and Food and Nutrition Security, Durban, South Africa, April 14–16, 2005. Washington, DC: International Food Policy Research Institute; Hunter, S. (2005). *AIDS in Asia: A continent in peril*. New York: Palgrave Macmillan; Jenkins, C., & Robalino D. A. (2003). *HIV/AIDS in the Middle East and North Africa: The costs of inaction*. Washington, DC: The World Bank.

be far from complete. As observed by McKee, Bertrand, and Becker-Benton, "The very nature of adolescent relationships increases their risk of HIV infection" (p. 111).[192] Of the five million people who contracted HIV in 2002, half were under the age of twenty-five.[193] In a rising trend in the United States, most new HIV infections are among young people aged thirteen to nineteen.[194] Young women are particularly under pressure with regard to their sexual conduct. There are low rates of reported condom use for heterosexual anal intercourse, a matter for concern when this form of sex puts people at a much higher risk for contracting HIV. UNAIDS estimates that fewer than 50 percent of young people worldwide have comprehensive knowledge about HIV,[195] placing more than half the world's young people at risk.

Men Who Have Sex With Men

Most studies and official documents have eschewed the term *homosexuals* in favor of *men who have sex with men* or *MSM*. This is intended to signal the wider relevance of male same-sex sexual acts, rather than the sociocultural construct of homosexuality as a choice or a lifestyle or even a subculture shared with others in a social group. An example of the value of this broader perspective is that in the United States in 2003, MSM accounted for one-third of male HIV infections; however, only 5–7 percent of Americans identify themselves as MSM.[196] Many men who have sex with other men do not consider themselves to be homosexuals, and have sexual relations with women as well. Some even eschew the term *bisexual*. Several sources have documented this attitude. For example, men in Morocco, Lebanon, and other countries believe that they are not "homosexual" if they are the "active" partner in the sex act. India is thought to have five hundred thousand to one million "hijras," or male transsexuals, with whom sex is not considered to be a male-to-male sex act.[197] Thus, men who do not see themselves to be homosexual may not perceive and comprehend messages aimed at warning the "homosexual" audience about HIV risks. Such men may even perceive such messages as distasteful in addition to being irrelevant to themselves.

The issue of MSM identity may be confused by another source of identity, such as a nationality or membership in a subculture. In the United States, for example, African American and Hispanic MSM are likely to live in neighborhoods identified with their ethnicity or origin, so they will not be exposed to much of the communications efforts aimed at MSM and conducted in and around "gay" neighborhoods. Hispanic men in the United States may be less likely to view themselves as MSM because of a number of cultural values commonly shared by Hispanic males, such as *machismo* (an assertive expression of masculinity), *simpatia* (belief that it is important to maintain harmony in relationships and avoiding conflict), and *familismo* (being the close involvement of the family in most aspects of life).[198]

Male-to-male sex may be a more covert act in societies where a high value is placed on virginity, marriage, reproduction, and families. Men who feel attracted to men may attempt to stifle this aspect of their sexuality in response to negative religious doctrine on the subject or social pressures. Marriage may be necessary for social reasons, making more likely the risk of "crossover" from HIV/AIDS risk groups (men having sex with men) to the general population (their wives and children). Where a large

34   *AIDS and Business*

number of males live together, men having sex with men is reportedly more common. Prisons, armed forces, migrant workers' camps, and others are examples of the primarily male environments where sex between males may take place.[199]

Men having sex with men as a group already encountered stigma in most countries before the arrival of HIV/AIDS. They face difficulties even in more permissive countries where same-sex marriage is allowed, such as Sweden.[200] Homosexuality is classified as a crime in seventy countries, including Romania, Puerto Rico, and Jamaica.[201] Men who have sex with men have been sentenced to death, hard labor, or long prison sentences in several countries over the last decade, including Egypt (including the so-called Cairo 52), Saudi Arabia, and Iran.[202] In the United States, gay, lesbian, bisexual, and transgendered people are commonly beaten, sexually abused, insulted, and harassed by police.[203] Under such conditions it is difficult to communicate "safer sex" behavior to men who have sex with men, and similarly it would be dangerous for an individual to make a request for testing or treatment. UNAIDS estimated that in 2005 only 9 percent of men having sex with men worldwide received any HIV prevention services.[204]

In the United States, HIV among MSM decreased over the first two decades following the first explosion of HIV/AIDS cases. Affluent gay communities in affluent countries rapidly understood the threat posed by HIV, and organized an effective response.[205] Recently, however, the number of HIV positive MSM has started to rise again. According to the U.S. Centers for Disease Control, there have been reports of increasing unprotected anal sex among MSM. Reported research on the topic yielded a number of likely reasons for this increase:

- There is increased incidence of drug use, including ecstasy, gamma hydroxybutyrate (GHB), ketamine, methamphetamine (known as "crystal meth"), and nitrate inhalants (known as "poppers").
- People may have the perception that HIV is a chronic but manageable condition due to dramatic and visible improvements in treatment.
- Increased ease of seeking sex partners using Internet "communities" of men with similar sex interests who can conveniently arrange sexual encounters.
- Age is a factor: young MSM are less likely to practice safer sex, most likely because they did not see firsthand the devastation wreaked by AIDS in the 1980s.[206]

Prison Populations

Prisoners are often cited as risk groups for HIV/AIDS, partly because these people may experience other risk factors, such as poverty, sex work, drug use, being a migrant, and so on. People in prison may contract HIV, often from shared hypodermic needles, but also from unprotected sex. Other health threats commonly coexist with HIV in prisons, such as tuberculosis and hepatitis, complicating prisoner health issues.[207] Released prisoners and prisoners on leave are likely to spread HIV and other health problems to their families and home communities upon liberation. This process has been well documented in Russia during frequent prison amnesties.[208] In the United States, HIV prevalence in prisons is six times that of the general population. In France, HIV prevalence in prison is ten times higher than that of the general population.[209] In Brazil, an estimated 17 to 20 percent of prisoners are HIV positive.[210]

Injecting-Drug Users

Injecting-drug users as a group face stigma, cultural breakdown, depression, and multiple life stresses. In Russia and some neighboring countries, drug use is the primary method of infection.[211] In the Ukraine, 70 percent of people with HIV/AIDS inject drugs.[212] In Iran, 65 percent of recorded HIV cases were injecting-drug users in 2001 (a figure that more than doubled since 1998).[213] In Spain and Portugal, the main route of HIV/AIDS transmission is injecting-drug users. In the United States, drug users make up 14 percent of reported HIV diagnoses,[214] and sex with an injecting drug user was the first source of HIV infections among heterosexuals.[215]

People who inject drugs may contract HIV from contaminated needles shared with others, from having unprotected sex in exchange for drugs or money to buy drugs, and from becoming vulnerable to risky sex while in an uninhibited "high" imparted by drug use. A source for concern relative to HIV/AIDS is that consumption of illicit drugs is rising worldwide. Such drugs include cocaine (injected or snorted), heroin, crack, and psychotropic medicines that are crushed and injected. A relatively new concern is synthetic drugs that are not injected but cause sexual people to lose sexual inhibitions, such as methamphetamine, a drug commonly cited because of its use by North American men having sex with men. The strong social stigma attached to illicit drug use in some countries, such as the Middle East and North Africa, effectively prevents many drug users from becoming conscious that they have a problem and that they should seek help.[216]

Armed Forces

> "There's no Khmer Rouge, now we have HIV."
>
> Dr. Om Khantey of the Preah Ket Mealea military hospital in Phnom Penh.[217]

According to one estimate, the armed forces have a rate of infection for sexually transmitted diseases that is two to five times higher than the civilian population. During armed conflicts, the rate may rise to fifty or more times

36   AIDS and Business

higher.[218] Armed forces include the police, national service conscripts, soldiers, sailors, rebel military groups, and armed militias. Data collection of HIV prevalence in military contexts is difficult. The peacetime prevalence of sexually transmitted diseases among military personnel is thought to be higher than among the general population. According to UNAIDS and National Intelligence Council (U.S.), the estimated HIV prevalence in African militaries, for example, ranges from highs of 40 to 60 percent (in Angola and Democratic Republic of Congo) to lows of 10 percent in Eritrea.[219] In Namibia and Zambia, the leading cause of death in the military and police forces is HIV/AIDS-related diseases.[220]

Military personnel, including peacekeeping personnel, may be more likely to contract HIV than the general population because they are often isolated from their families and are geographically mobile. They are likely to be relatively affluent[221] and are likely to have sex with multiple partners over a large geographic area—thereby contracting and spreading sexually transmitted diseases. Troop movements may be followed closely by local professional and casual sex workers, particularly in places where conflict and instability have resulted in scarcity of needed goods.[222] An atmosphere of competition and an ethos of risk taking tends to characterize military culture, including drug and alcohol consumption, and sexual prowess—a combination of values likely to reduce condom use.[223] Violent sex acts, as have been well documented in the Congo, Bosnia, and elsewhere, add to the risk factors for military personnel.

Migrants and Mobile Populations

According to UNESCO, other groups who may be vulnerable to conduct risky behaviors include "culturally destabilized" ones like migrants who experience cultural breakdown, disintegrated families where some members may themselves have been killed by AIDS-related illnesses, and newly urbanized groups and certain urban subcultures.[224] In the Philippines, for instance, 30 percent of the very few AIDS cases in the country were Philippine nationals working in other countries, where strong cultural norms that protected from risky behaviors at home are not supported in foreign environments.[225] People engaged in professions that require traveling, such as truck drivers, may be more likely to conduct risky behaviors. In many cases, a person considered to be "vulnerable" and at risk for contracting HIV may concurrently be a member of several groups.

Migrants generally fall into a number of categories:

- Economic migrants seeking a better life in a city or another country
- Migrant workers who leave home and family to work far away or in another country
- Refugees or internally displaced persons seeking safety from civil unrest, sectarian violence, war, or government repression

A Medical Anthropologist in Morocco   37

- Trafficked people, usually women and girls smuggled across borders or into cities for forced sex work
- People who work in industries with high levels of mobility, including travel and tourism, trucking, shipping and transport, and traveling entertainment and exhibitions

Because of these and other factors, it is not surprising that port cities worldwide are "hotspots for AIDS transmission," according to Singhal and Rogers (2003, p. 131). Culture shock remains an important obstacle to prevention education and safer sexual or drug-taking behavior. The severe cultural disorientation of many newcomers to the world's burgeoning cities is indeed a shock. Shock may be exacerbated when rural and often uneducated young women and children are forcibly taken from their homes and forced into sex work, estimated by the United Nations to number two million per year.[226] The most common destination countries reported for trafficked people are Belgium, Germany, Greece, Israel, Italy, Japan, Netherlands, Thailand, Turkey, and the United States. Most reported incidences of trafficked people come from Albania, Belarus, Bulgaria, China, Lithuania, Republic of Moldova, Nigeria, Romania, Russian Federation, Thailand, and Ukraine.[227]

Trafficked people forced into sex work are likely the most vulnerable for contracting HIV because they cannot insist on condom use, have no access to medical counseling or care, and have no rights or freedom to escape from their situation.[228] In one example, described by Ainsworth, Beyrer and Soucat (2003),[229] such a sex worker may be an illegal immigrant working illegally in a brothel, who may be threatened with deportation if she approaches local health workers, and is not accessible to HIV/AIDS prevention workers or messages. Even if these were available, there would be communication difficulties based on lack of language skills. Because of her lower social status than clients due to her gender and origin, she would not be able to successfully demand that her clients wear a condom even if she was aware that a condom would protect her from contracting HIV. She demonstrates how economic disadvantage places women, and particularly migrants, at high risk for HIV. Over time she may be shuffled through brothels in different locations, thereby contributing to the spread of HIV from high prevalence areas to ones with low HIV prevalence, as described by Dworkin and Ehrhardt (2007).[230] The importance of such incidents for businesses is that they are often tied to the sex tourism market, which is growing by all accounts and has well-documented negative social and economic effects on host communities—as well as increased transmission of HIV and other sexually transmitted diseases (see Omondi, 2003; O'Connell Davidson and Sanchez Taylor, 1995; Cabezas, 2004).

When there is a drought or famine, so-called ecological migrant families may head for urban centers. Upon arrival in the city they are immersed in

38   AIDS and Business

an urbanized world of unemployment, fierce competition for jobs, little or no housing, widely available drugs, and few cultural resources left to create meaning in the daily struggle to survive.[231] Where basic survival is one's preoccupation, protection from HIV/AIDS may not appear to be a priority—drug taking and prostitution may be the only options left to meet one's needs. HIV/AIDS is thus a likely outcome.

Displaced women may be at particular risk for contracting HIV. They may have lost all their possessions and wealth and may be left with nothing to generate income or buy food. In addition, they may have lost their supportive social networks.[232] Commercial sex work may be the only solution for survival of the woman and her family. When displaced women become refugees, they may face a new risk of rape in refugee camps as they search for water or wood, or use the camp's public toilets.[233]

A category of migrant workers that received ample attention in the literature was that of men working in the travel and transport industries. Indeed, the protagonist of the popular myth about the initial spread of HIV/AIDS into the United States, "Patient Zero," was an airline employee.[234] Truck drivers in India, Africa, and elsewhere are described as being at special risk for HIV/AIDS due to their solitary occupation away from family, their unpredictably long waits in sleazy border towns and truck stops, and norms facilitating sex as payment for hitchhikers, who are often poor rural women taking their wares to market.

MASS COMMUNICATION, EDUCATION, AND INFORMATION DISSEMINATED ABOUT HIV/AIDS

National educational systems and the mass media are crucial for disseminating information, education, and communication about the spread of HIV/AIDS. A UNESCO report has concluded that, up until 2001, school systems have generally been unable to bring up the issue in an effective manner, particularly with regard to risk groups excluded from schooling, while the mass media have been more effective. Further, the report states that unless cultural factors are taken into account, the current conditions of misunderstanding and limited knowledge will continue unabated—as will the AIDS epidemic.[235] HIV/AIDS awareness programs need to be offered to children, going against the value of "purity" or "innocence" commonly ascribed to childhood. One-third of American boys and one-quarter in the Dominican Republic have had sex before the age of fifteen, and similar (and some more frequent) figures may be revealed around the world, suggesting that children need HIV/AIDS knowledge at younger ages than commonly thought.[236]

Outside official educational systems, some traditional rituals help to instill a sense of sexual responsibility in young people. The *luskewane* ceremony practiced in Swaziland is an example of encouraging a young man to abstain from sex until marriage by linking his behavior with the honor of his family and his area. During the ceremony, young men are led on a long walk to cut a sacred shrub and, on the way, receive information on how to grow up in a responsible manner, as well as abstain from sex. The consequences of not doing so are powerful and could bring shame on the boy's family and region.[237]

Television, radio, and the press can help people protect themselves from HIV by providing them with information and awareness that may motivate them to modify their behavior in ways that could protect them from contracting HIV. The media can raise awareness about traditional cultural practices and norms that intensify the spread of HIV or which may protect from the spread of the disease. Sony Entertainment Television India has stated its commitment to provide HIV/AIDS information within its programs, including pop-reality show Indian Idol, hospital show Ayushman, and CID, a detective series. Other television channels are actively participating.[238] Illiterate Indian women who watched television at least once per week or went to the cinema at least once per month were much more likely to be aware of HIV/AIDS than those without access to such media.[239] In some countries public demand may drive the mass media to provide more information about HIV/AIDS. In Russia, for example, where 1–2 percent of adults are estimated to have HIV, more people rely upon and trust the television for information about HIV than medical establishments, according to a 2005 national opinion survey. Survey findings included the belief by 73 percent of respondents that the mass media plays a "vital role" in the fight against HIV/AIDS.[240]

There is a real difficulty in creating a sociocultural environment that is conducive to safe sexual practices. For example, in Thailand's remarkably successful campaign to encourage 100 percent condom use among sex workers and their clients, a far-reaching and free independent news media played an important role. In Senegal, an African HIV/AIDS success story, 61 percent of young people claimed the media were their primary source of HIV/AIDS information.[241] The media reflect how a society views HIV/AIDS, and at the same time the media shape the attitudes of society's members and institutions in dealing with the disease.[242] In many Asian countries, journalists and others in the mass media feel pressure to respect traditional sexual norms, thereby sacrificing clarity to euphemism and metaphor. Where journalists fail to censor their own work, government or religious organizations step in to do so, resulting in muted public debate about HIV/AIDS. In China, online pornography laws have been invoked to censor or close down websites that offer HIV/AIDS awareness and prevention information for men having sex with men, or even generally sexually explicit HIV/AIDS material. Another channel for disseminating HIV/AIDS information—the workshop or

40 AIDS and Business

conference—has also met with censorship in China, where a law forbidding illegal assemblies was invoked.[243] When there is a lack of primary information and the mass media do not support safe sex in its depictions of sex acts, the risk of HIV rises. In Japan, for example, where there is a very low level of sex education at schools, in the mass media and public debate, HIV is on the increase. In fact, Japan is the only G7 country where that is the case.[244] Widely disseminated pornographic materials such as SIMS-type games where the player manipulates on-screen characters, mangas, and films overwhelmingly depict actors without any consideration for safe sex. Indeed, this is not only the case in Japan but in most countries.

Cultural barriers delay much-needed action on an international basis. One example of this was the refusal by the United States, the Vatican, and several Islamic nations to use explicit language in international documents, such as the United Nations "Declaration of Commitment" on HIV/AIDS. So-called explicit language condemned by these countries at the United Nations in 2001 included terms such as *men-to-men sex, intravenous drug-users*, and *sex workers*. After considerable debate, subsequent approved language was *sexual practices, drug using behavior*, and *livelihood*, respectively. Cultural barriers against explicit references to sex were so strong among these countries that this declaration, among many others, creates obstacles to a necessary international consensus on HIV/AIDS action and restricts fruitful debate.[245]

Where school systems, government and nongovernmental programs, and media campaigns have failed to raise HIV/AIDS awareness or change behavior, the private sector has often stepped in. Companies large and small have initiated AIDS committees, distributed materials from nongovernmental organizations like comic books, brochures, condoms, and posters. Drama and songs with a local or regional flavor may also be common features of company HIV/AIDS programs. Some companies provide voluntary counseling and testing, treatment, or comprehensive medical care to employees with HIV. TATA Tea in India provides free treatment of sexually transmitted infections as well as opportunistic infections, among other measures.[246] Volkswagen South Africa extends HIV/AIDS expertise to its more than one thousand suppliers, mainly small and medium-sized companies.[247] In some companies, medical coverage extends to family members with HIV. In other companies, action is limited to human resources policies such as "reasonable accommodation" for employees with AIDS who are not well enough to perform their tasks fully. Many companies must stop at simple measures for budgetary reasons, such as the Kenya Tea Association's "Mama Condom" and "Baba Condom"—trusted female and male workers, respectively, who have been trained to provide condoms and advice at work. In-depth discussion of company responses to the epidemic will be discussed in detail in other sections of this book.[248]

QUESTIONS FOR FURTHER DISCUSSION

1. Consult a report showing HIV infection rates worldwide and locate your own region/country rates. Then, based on your readings, list the main cultural and social factors that favor the spread of HIV/AIDS in the specific social and cultural environment of your own region/country. You can base your search on the *UNAIDS/WHO epidemiological fact sheets* per country or the *UNAIDS epidemic updates* to be found at http://www.unaids.org, a site that provides authoritative worldwide statistics on HIV/AIDS.
2. Outline how cultural and social factors may impact in different ways the prevention, testing, and treatment of HIV/AIDS.
3. As a top company executive at regional level in a multinational corporation who is concerned about growing numbers of people with HIV/AIDS working in the company and buying the company's products, which cultural and social factors would you consider to be relevant in order to gain an understanding of the epidemic situation? What kind of information would you need to make a decision about how to design a strategy to address the problem? In order to understand the potential impacts of the epidemic on your company in the short, medium, and long term, what kinds of further research would you need to have done on the topic?

ADDITIONAL RESOURCES ON THE TOPIC

Web Sites and Campaigns

National Black HIV/AIDS Awareness Day. Awareness campaign for black people in the United States. Available at: http://www.blackaidsday.org/.

Films

Dispatches: Living with Illegals. (2006). Filmed in various countries, a documentary that follows African illegal migrants from Morocco to the UK and makes clear the kinds of risks they run. Available at: http://www.insightnewstv.com/store/.

Raja (2003). Drama by French filmmaker Jacques Doillon about a powerless young Moroccan woman's experience of sexual exploitation and manipulation at the hands of a wealthy Frenchman.

Bukak Api (2000). Film by Malaysian filmmaker Osman Ali about sex workers, transvestites, and drug users at risk for contracting HIV in Kuala Lumpur, Malaysia. May be viewed in parts on http://www.youtube.com.

42   AIDS and Business

Suggested Further Reading on Cultural and Social Factors, and the Spread of HIV

Abu-Raddad, L. J., Patnaik, P., & Kublin, J. G. (2006). Dual infection with HIV and malaria fuels the spread of both diseases in sub-Saharan Africa. *Science* 314(5805), 1603–6.

Adari, J. S., Moghadam, M. R., & Starnes, C. N. (2007). Life expectancy of people living with HIV/AIDS and associated socioeconomic factors in Kenya. *Journal of International Development* 19, 357–66.

Agadjanian, V. (2005). Gender, religious involvement, and HIV/AIDS prevention in Mozambique. *Social Science and Medicine* 61(7), 1529–39.

Ainsworth, M., Beyrer, C., & Soucat, A. (2003). AIDS and public policy: The lessons and challenges of "success" in Thailand. *Health Policy* 64(1), 13–37.

Airhihenbuwa, C. O., & Obregon, R. (2000). A critical assessment of theories/models used in health communication for HIV/AIDS. *Journal of Health Communication* 5(Suppl.), 5–15.

Allen, T. (2004). Why don't HIV/AIDS policies work? *Journal of International Development* 16, 1123–27.

Allen, T., & Heald, S. (2004). HIV/AIDS policy in Africa: What has worked in Uganda and what has failed in Botswana? *Journal of International Development* 16, 1141–54.

Arrindel, W. A., Eisenmann, M., Oei, T. P. S., Caballo, V. E., Ezio, S., Sica, C., Bagés, N., Feldmann, L., et al. (2004). Phobic anxiety in 11 nations: Part II. Hofstede's dimensions of national cultures predict national-level variations. *Personality and Individual Differences* 37(3), 627–43.

Arrindel, W. A., Steptoe, A., & Wardle, J. (2003). Higher levels of state depression in masculine than in feminine nations. *Behavior Research and Therapy* 41(7), 809–17.

Bandura, A. (1994). Social cognitive theory and exercise of control over HIV infection. In R. J. DiClemente & J. L. Peterson (eds.), *Preventing AIDS: Theories and methods of behavioral interventions*. New York: Plenum Press.

———. (1997). *Self-efficacy: The exercise of control*. New York: Freeman.

———. (2004). Health promotion by social cognitive means. *Health Education and Behavior* 31(2), 143–64.

Barnett, T. (2004). Postscript: HIV/AIDS—How bad does bad have to be before we believe it is bad? How can we translate words to deeds? *Journal of International Development* 16, 1181–84.

Barnett, T., & Whiteside, A. (2001). The world development report 2000/01: HIV/AIDS still not properly considered! *Journal of International Development* 13, 369–76.

Basabe, N., Paez, D., Valencia, J., Gonzalez, J. L., Rimé, B., & Diener, E. (2002). Cultural dimensions, socioeconomic development, climate and emotional hedonic level. *Cognition and Emotion* 16(1), 103–25.

Benatar, S. R. (2002). The HIV/AIDS pandemic: A sign of instability in a complex global system. *The Journal of Medicine and Philosophy* 27, 163–77.

Bredstrom, A. (2005). "Love in another country"—"Race," gender and sexuality in sexual education material targeting migrants in Sweden. *Sexualities* 8(4), 517–35.

Cabezas, A. L. (2004). Between love and money: Sex, tourism and citizenship in Cuba and the Dominican Republic. *Signs: Journal of Women in Culture and Society* 29(4), 987–1015.

Caldwell, J. C., Caldwell, P., & Quiggin, P. (1989). The social context of AIDS in Africa. *Population and Development Review* 15(2), 185–234.

A Medical Anthropologist in Morocco   43

Campbell, C. A. (1995). Male gender roles and sexuality: Implications for women's AIDS risk and prevention. *Social Science and Medicine* 41(2), 197–210.

Campbell, C., Foulis, C. A., Maimaine, S., & Sigiya, Z. (2005). "I have an evil child at my house": Stigma and HIV/AIDS management in a South African community. *American Journal of Public Health* 95(5), 808–16.

Castilla, E. J. (2004). Organizing health care: A comparative analysis of national institutions and inequality over time. *International Sociology* 19(4), 403–35.

Castro, A., & Farmer, P. (2005). Understanding and addressing AIDS-related stigma: From anthropological theory to clinical practice in Haiti. *American Journal of Public Health* 95(1), 53–59.

Chacham, A. S., Maia, M. B., Greco, M., Silva, A. P., & Greco, D. B. (2007). Autonomy and susceptibility to HIV/AIDS among young women living in a slum in Belo Horizonte, Brazil. *AIDS Care* 19(Suppl. 1), 12–22.

Clark, S. (2004). Early marriage and HIV risks in sub-Saharan Africa. *Studies in Family Planning* 35(3), 149–60.

Deaton, A. (2003). Health, inequality, and economic development. *Journal of Economic Literature* 41(1), 113–40.

Devine, P. G., Plant, E. A., & Harrison, K. (1999). The problem of "us" versus "them" and AIDS stigma. *The American Behavioral Scientist* 42(7), 1212–28.

Dunkle, K. L., et al. (2004). Gender-based violence, relationship power, and risk of HIV infection in women attending antenatal clinics in South Africa, *Lancet* 363(9419), 1415–21.

Dworkin, S. L., & Ehrhardt, A. A. (2007). Going beyond ABC to include GEM: Critical reflections on progress in the HIV/AIDS epidemic. *American Journal of Public Health* 97(1), 13–18.

Eberstadt, N., & Satel, S. (2004). Health, inequality, and the scholars. *Public Interest* 157, 100–18.

Elliott, J. R., & Smith, R. A. (2004). Race, gender and workplace power. *American Sociological Review* 69(3), 365–87.

Fitzgerald, T., Lundgren, L., & Chassler, D. (2007). Factors associated with HIV/AIDS high-risk behaviours among female injection drug users. *AIDS Care* 19(1), 67–74.

Forsythe, S., & Rau, B. (1998). Evolution of socioeconomic impact assessments of HIV/AIDS. *AIDS* 12(Suppl. 2), 47–55.

Freedman, J., & Poku, N. (2005). The socioeconomic context of Africa's vulnerability to HIV/AIDS. *Review of International Studies* 31, 665–86.

Fuhrer, R., Shipley, M. J., Chastang, J. F., Schmaus, A., et al. (2002). Socioeconomic position, health, and possible explanations: A tale of two cohorts. *American Journal of Public Health* 92(8), 1290–95

Gaffeo, E. (2003). The economics of HIV/AIDS: A survey. *Development Policy Review* 21(1), 27–49.

Gausset, Q. (2001). AIDS and cultural practices in Africa: The case of the Tonga (Zambia). *Social Science and Medicine* 52(4), 509–18.

Gillespie, S. (ed.) (2006). *AIDS, poverty, and hunger: Challenges and responses.* Highlights of the International Conference on HIV/AIDS and Food and Nutrition Security, Durban, South Africa, April 14–16, 2005. Washington, DC: International Food Policy Research Institute;

Groenewald, P., Nannan, N., Bourne, D., Laubscher, R., & Bradshaw, D. (2005). Identifying deaths from AIDS in South Africa. *AIDS* 19(7), 744–5.

Gupta, G. R. (2002). How men's power over women fuels the HIV epidemic: It limits women's ability to control sexual interactions. *British Medical Journal* 324(7331), 183–84.

44 AIDS and Business

Hall, E. T. (1990 reissue). *The silent language*. New York: Anchor Books.

Hall, E. T., & Hall, M. L. (1990). *Understanding cultural differences: Germans, French and Americans*. Yarmouth, ME: Intercultural Press.

Haller, M., & Hadler, M. (2006). How social relations and structure can produce happiness and unhappiness: An international comparative analysis. *Social Indicators Research* 75(2), 169–216.

Hampton, N. Z., & Marshall, A. (2000). Culture, gender, self-efficacy and life satisfaction: A comparison between Americans and Chinese people with spinal cord injuries. *Journal of Rehabilitation* 66(3), 21–29.

Härtel, C. E. J., & Härtel, G. F. (2005). Cross-cultural differences in emotions: The why and how. *Social Science Information* 44(4), 683–93.

Harvey, P. W. (2006). Social determinants of health—why we continue to ignore them in the search for improved population health outcomes! *Australian Health Review* 30(4), 419–23.

Herek, G. M. (1999). AIDS and stigma. *The American Behavioral Scientist* 42(7), 1106–27.

Hofstede, G. (1998). *Masculinity and femininity: The taboo dimension of national culture*. Thousand Oaks, CA: Sage.

———. (2001). *Culture's consequences: Comparing values, behaviours, institutions, and organizations across nations*. Thousand Oaks, CA: Sage.

Hofstede, G., & Bond, M. H. (1988). The Confucian connection: From cultural roots to economic growth. *Organizational Dynamics* 16(4), 4–21

House, R. J., Hanges, R. J., Javidan, M., Dorfman, P. W., & Gupta, V. (2004). *Culture, leadership, and organizations: The GLOBE study of 62 societies*. Thousand Oaks, CA: Sage.

Jarama, S. L., Kennamer, J. D., Poppen, P. J., Hendricks, M., & Bradford, J. (2005). Psychosocial, behavioural, and cultural predictors of sexual risk for HIV infection among Latino men who have sex with men. *AIDS and Behavior* 9(4), 513–23.

Jonsson, P. O. (2001). Networks, culture, transaction costs and discrimination. *International Journal of Social Economics* 28(10–12), 942–59.

Katz, I., & Glass, D. C. (1979). An ambivalence-amplification theory of behavior toward the stigmatized. In W. Austin & S. Worchel (eds.), *The social psychology of intergroup relations* (pp. 55–70). Monterey, CA : Brooks/Cole.

Katz, I., & Hass, R. G. (1988). Racial ambivalence and American value conflict: Correlational and priming studies of dual cognitive structures. *Journal of Personality and Social Psychology* 55(6), 893–905.

Katz, I., Wackenhut, J., & Hass, R. G. (1986). Racial ambivalence, value duality and behavior. In J. F. Dovidio & S. L. Gaertner (eds.), *Prejudice, discrimination and racism*. New York : Academic Press.

Kreuter, M., & Haughton, L. T. (2006). Integrating culture into health information for African American women. *The American Behavioral Scientist* 49(6), 794–812.

Lahelma, E., Martinkainen, P., Rahkonen, O., Roos, E., & Saastamoinen, P. (2005). Occupational class inequalities across key domains of health: Results from the Helsinki Health Study. *European Journal of Public Health* 15(5), 504–10.

Link, B. G., & Phelan, J. (1995). Social conditions as fundamental causes of disease. *Journal of Health and Social Behavior* 35(Extra issue), 80–94.

Liu, J. X., & Choi, K. (2006). Experiences of social discrimination among men who have sex with men in Shanghai, China. *AIDS and Behavior* 10(4 Suppl.), 25–33.

Luchetta, T. (1999). Relationships between homophobia, HIV/AIDS stigma, and HIV/AIDS knowledge. In L. Pardie & T. Luchetta (eds.), *The construction of attitudes toward lesbians and gay men.* Binghamton, NY: The Haworth Press.

Marmot, M. (2002). The influence of income on health: Views of an epidemiologist. *Health Affairs* 21(2), 31–38.

Maznevski, M. L., Gomez, C. B., DiStefano, J. J., Noorderhaven, N. G., & Wu, Pei-Chan. (2002). Cultural dimensions at the individual level of analysis: The cultural orientations framework. *International Journal of Cross-Cultural Management* 2(3), 275–95.

Mboi, N. (1996). Women and AIDS in south and South-East Asia: The challenge and the response. *World Health Statistics Quarterly* 49(2), 94–105.

McIntosh, W. A., & Thomas, J. K. (2004). Economic and other societal determinants of the prevalence of HIV: A test of competing hypotheses. *The Sociological Quarterly* 45(2) 303–24.

McLaughlin, L., & Braun, K. L. (1998). Asian and Pacific Islander cultural values: Considerations for health care decision making. *Health and Social Work* 23(2), 116–26.

Missildine, W., Parsons, J. T., & Knight, K. (2006). Split ends: Masculinity, sexuality and emotional intimacy among HIV-positive heterosexual men. *Men and Masculinities* 8(3), 309–20.

Moffic, H. S., & Kinzie, J. D. (1996). The history and future of cross-cultural psychiatric services. *Community Mental Health Journal* 32(6), 581–92.

Morgan, D., Mahe, C., Mayanja, B., Okongo, J. M., Lubega, R., & Whitworth, J. A. G. (2002). HIV-1 infection in rural Africa: Is there a difference in median time to AIDS and survival compared with that in industrialized countries? *AIDS* 16(4), 597–603.

Ortiz-Torres, B., Serrano-Garcia, I., & Torres-Burgos, N. (2000). Subverting culture: Promoting HIV/AIDS prevention among Puerto Rican and Dominican women. *American Journal of Community Psychology* 28(6), 859–81.

Oyserman, D., Kemmelmeier, M., & Coon, H. M. (2002). Cultural psychology, a new look: Reply to Bond (2002), Fiske (2002), Kitayama (2002) and Miller (2002). *Psychology Bulletin* 128(1), 110–17.

Parker, R. (2001). Sexuality, culture, and power in HIV/AIDS research. *Annual Review of Anthropology* 30: 163–79.

———. (2002). The global HIV/AIDS pandemic, structural inequalities, and the politics of international health. *American Journal of Public Health* 92, 343–6.

Pliskin, K. L. (1997). Verbal intercourse and sexual communication: Impediments to STD prevention. *Medical Anthropology Quarterly* 11(1), 89–109.

Pryor, J. B., Reeder G. D., & Landau, S. (1999). A social-psychological analysis of HIV-related stigma. *The American Behavioral Scientist* 42(7), 1193–1211.

Pryor, J. B., Reeder G. D., Yeadon, C & Hesson-McIness, M. (2004). A dual-process model of model of reactions to perceived stigma. *Journal of Personality and Social Psychology* 87(4), 436–52.

Rahman, M. R., & Hashem, F. (2000). The state of health determinants in Bangladesh. *The International Journal of Sociology and Social Policy* 20(8), 33–54.

Rhodes, T., & Simic, M. (2005). Transition and the HIV risk environment. *British Medical Journal* 331, 220–23.

Rhodes, T., Singer, M., Bourgois, P., Friedman, S. R., & Strathdee, S. A. (2005). The social structural production of HIV risk among injecting drug users. *Social Science and Medicine* 51(5), 1026–44.

Rodgers, G. B. (2002). Income and inequality as determinants of mortality: An international cross-section analysis. *International Journal of Epidemiology* 31, 533–38.

Romero, L., Wallerstein, N., Lucero, J., Fredine, H. G., Keefe, J., & O'Connell, J. (2006). Woman to woman: Coming together for positive change—using

46 AIDS and Business

empowerment and popular education to prevent HIV in women. *AIDS Education and Prevention* 18(5), 390–405.

Rosen, S., Simon, J. L., Thea, D. M., & Vincent, J. R. (2000). Care and treatment to extend the working lives of HIV positive employees: Calculating the benefits to business. *South African Journal of Science* (July). Retrieved November 30, 2006, from http://sph.bu.edu/images/stories/scfiles/cih/Businessbenefitsofcareandtreatmentsajs.pdf.

Rosen, S., Vincent, J. R., Macleod, W., Fox, M., Thea, D. M., & Simon, J. (2004). The cost of HIV/AIDS to businesses in Southern Africa. *AIDS* 18, 317–24.

Schaller, M., & Crandal, C. S. (eds.) (2004). *The psychological foundations of culture*. Mahwah, NJ: Lawrence Erlbaum Associates.

Soskolne, V., & Shtarkshall, R. A. (2002). Migration and HIV prevention programmes: Linking structural factors, culture, and individual behaviour—an Israeli experience. *Social Science and Medicine* 55(8), 1297–1307.

Sternberg, P. (2000). Challenging machismo: Promoting sexual and reproductive health with Nicaraguan men. *Gender and Development* 8(1) 89–95.

Subramanian, S. V., & Kawachi, I. (2006). Being well and doing well: On the importance of income for health. *International Journal of Social Welfare* 15 (Suppl. 1), 513–22.

Tangwa, G. B. (2002). The HIV/AIDS pandemic, African traditional values and the search for a vaccine in Africa. *The Journal of Medicine and Philosophy* 27, 217–30

Taylor, B. M. (1995). Gender-power relations and safer sex negotiation. *Journal of Advanced Nursing* 22, 687–93.

Taylor, J. J. (2006). Assisting or compromising intervention? The concept of "culture" in biomedical and social research on HIV/AIDS. *Social Science and Medicine* 64(4), 965–75.

Turmen, T. (2003). Gender and AIDS. *International Journal of Gynecology and Obstetrics* 82(3), 411–18.

Turner, D. (1996). The role of culture in chronic illness. *The American Behavioral Scientist* 39(6), 717–29.

UNAIDS. (1999). *Communications framework for AIDS: A new direction.* Retrieved March 27, 2007, from http://data.unaids.org/Publications/IRC-pub01/JC335-commFramew_en.pdf.

———. (2001). *Comparative analysis: Research studies from India and Uganda. HIV and AIDS-related discrimination, stigmatization and denial.* Retrieved April 13, 2007, from http://data.unaids.org/Publications/IRC-pub02/JC650-CompAnal_en.pdf.

———. (2002). *A conceptual framework and basis for action: HIV/AIDS stigma and discrimination.* Retrieved April 13, 2007, from http://data.unaids.org/Publications/IRC-pub02/JC891-WAC_Framework_en.pdf.

———. (2005). *HIV-related stigma, discrimination and human rights violations: Case studies of successful programmes* (UNAIDS Best Practice Collection). Retrieved April 13, 2007, from http://data.unaids.org/publications/irc-pub06/JC999-HumRightsViol_en.pdf.

———. (2006). *2006 AIDS epidemic update.* Retrieved March 27, 2007, from http://www.unaids.org/en/HIV_data/epi2006/default.asp.

United Nations Global Compact. (2003). *HIV/AIDS everybody's business.* New York: The Global Compact Learning Forum.

Veenstra, N., & Whiteside, A. (2004). Economic impact of HIV. *Best Practices and Research Clinical Obstetrics and Gynaecology* 19(2), 197–210.

Whiteside, A. (2001). Demography and economics of HIV/AIDS. *British Medical Bulletin* 58, 73–88.

Wood, W., & Eagly, A. H. (2002). A cross-cultural analysis of the behavior of women and men: Implications for the origins of sex differences. *Psychological Bulletin* 128(5), 699–727.

World Health Organisation. (n.d.). *Violence against women and HIV/AIDS information sheet*. Retrieved March 25, 2007, from http://www.who.int/hac/tech-guidance/pht/en/InfosheetVaWandHIV.pdf.

Zhang, H. X. (2004). The gathering storm: AIDS policy in China. *Journal of International Development* 16, 1155–68.

2 Addressing a Global Cause in Local Contexts

Country Case Study of HIV/AIDS in Brazil

The Brazilian HIV/AIDS program is widely considered to be an international best practice.[1] According to a World Health Organization (WHO) publication, "Brazil has the most advanced national treatment program in the developing world" (WHO, 2004, p. 1).[2] The World Bank called the program an "international model."[3] Brazil has led a feisty and public fight on the international stage for the protection of its citizens with HIV/AIDS. It was in 2005 one of the few countries that offered its people free access to antiretroviral treatments. The others to do so were Botswana, Ethiopia, Tanzania, Thailand, Senegal, and Zambia.[4]

In 1981, several affluent and educated urban gay men were diagnosed with AIDS. Two years later, a woman was diagnosed, and a child contracted HIV from a blood transfusion.[5] Then, from a concentrated epidemic among injecting-drug users, HIV spread gradually to the general population. By 2002, the ratio of men to women with HIV was 2:1.[6] More recently, the heterosexual mode of transmission has become the most prevalent, with women increasingly contracting the virus.[7] National HIV prevalence in pregnant women has remained stable at less than 1 percent over recent years.[8]

When faced with the biggest epidemic in the Western Hemisphere in 1990, the Brazilian government determined that antiretroviral treatment should be available free of charge through the public health system. At that time, the World Bank estimated that there would be 1.2 million people with HIV in Brazil by the year 2000.[9] In fact, in 2006 there were a little over one half that estimate with HIV/AIDS.[10] This is in stark contrast with South Africa, which is by economic standards a similar country. In the early 1990s, Brazil and South Africa were at a similar stage in adult HIV prevalence: approximately 1.5 percent. However, by 1995 South Africa's prevalence had "begun to explode" (Okie, 2006, p. 1977),[11] while Brazil's had declined significantly. What was so special, then, about Brazil?

Brazil is a country with multiple challenges. Although in 2004 the economy grew by 4.9 percent, and in 2005 GDP growth was 2.3 percent, long-term economic growth improvements are necessary.[12] The adult literacy rate was 88.4 percent in 2003, which is close to the Latin American and Caribbean average of 89.6 percent.[13] In 2003, 22.4 percent of the population was living on under $2 a day.[14] Public health expenditure per capita was 3.6 percent of GDP, which was comparable with that of the Russian Federation (3.5 percent), and below that of Bolivia (4.2 percent), Jordan (4.3 percent), Turkey (4.3 percent), and Zimbabwe (4.4 percent).[15] Some key indicators of health are summarized in Table 2.1.

The averages depicted on Table 2.1 mask socioeconomic crevices between regions, states, races, and social classes. In terms of income inequity, Brazil ranked higher than South Africa.[16] The illiteracy rate ranged from 6.3 percent in Santa Catarina (a relatively affluent southern state) to 33.4 percent in Alagoas (a relatively poor northwestern state). Similarly, life expectancy in Brazil was lowest in Alagoas at 63.16 years and highest in Santa Catarina at 71.34 years.[17] The contrast between poorer north and richer south was again visible recently when President Luiz Inácio Lula da Silva was reelected. Many of the votes for President "Lula," as he is simply called, came from the poorer northern states.

The population of Brazil was 181.4 million in 2003 and growing fast.[18] Brazil accounted for half the population and land mass of the entire Latin American and Caribbean region.[19] Brazilian urban areas grow at the rate of 2 percent per year, and 82 percent of all Brazilians were urban dwellers in 2001.[20] There are thirty-two million Brazilians between the ages of ten and nineteen years, in terms of numbers alone a massive group with HIV/AIDS information and awareness needs.[21] Brazil is the biggest Catholic country on the planet, although 15.4 percent of Brazilians are Protestants (approximately twenty-six million people)[22] and 7.4 percent profess to not have a religion. The number of Catholics in Brazil fell by 15.4 percentage points between 1980 and 2000, many of which defected to Protestantism.[23]

Portuguese explorer Pedro Álvares Cabral claimed Brazil for Portugal in 1550. The country is composed of different ethnic groups, including the indigenous peoples, African slaves, Germans, Italians, Japanese, Jews, Lebanese and Syrians, and Spanish, among others.[24] Between the sixteenth and nineteenth centuries, Brazil imported approximately four million slaves from Africa.[25] In 1864 there were 1,715,000 slaves working in Brazil.[26]

In the economics and health literature, Brazil is often referred to as one of the BRIC countries (Brazil, Russian Federation, India, and China)—emerging economies of the developing world. Brazil is member of Mercado Comun del Sur (MERCOSUR or MERCOSUL), a customs union formed in 1991 comprised of Argentina, Brazil, Paraguay, and Uruguay.[27] In 1999, MERCOSUR was the fourth largest economic area in the world and accounted for 50 percent of Latin American GDP.[28]

THE HIV/AIDS FIGHT IN BRAZIL[29]

With 620,000 Brazilians living with HIV/AIDS in 2005, more than one-third of Latin Americans with HIV are in Brazil, but this fact is due more to the huge population of the country than government policies. There are 1.7 million people living with HIV in the region and of these two-thirds live in

Table 2.1 Health Summary: Brazil

Health and economic factor	Brazil measure	Comparison measure with:		
		Russia	China	India
GDP per capita (US$) 2003	2,788	3,018	1,100	564
Percent of population living under US$ per day (1990–2003)	22.4	—	46.7	79.9
Public health expenditure (% of GDP, 2002)	3.6	3.5	2.0	1.3
Public health expenditure per capita at purchasing power parity US$, 2002	611	535	261	96
Contraceptive prevalence rate 1995–2003 (%)	77	73	84	48
Population undernourished (%) 2000–2002	9	4	—	21
Population with sustainable access to improved sanitation (%) 2002	75	87	44	30
HIV prevalence rate ages 15–49 and estimate ranges (UNAIDS, 2007)	0.5 [0.3–1.6]	1.1 [0.6–1.9]	0.1 [0.1–0.2]	0.36 [revised]
Tuberculosis cases per 100,000 people, 2003	91	157	245	287
Female life expectancy at birth (years) 2003	74.6	72.1	73.5	65
Male life expectancy at birth (years) 2003	66.6	59	69.9	61.8

All data from the United Nations Development Programme (2005). *Human development report 2005* and UNAIDS/WHO (2007).[30] AIDS epidemic update.[31]

Argentina, Brazil, Colombia, and Mexico. Much HIV transmission in Latin America happens within a similar context: urban and rural divergence in knowledge about the prevention, poverty, migration, and homophobia.[32] In 2005, adult HIV prevalence in Brazil was 0.5 percent (similar to Malaysia, lower than the United States, and at the same level of average prevalence for the Latin America region).[33] Smaller countries like Belize and Honduras have much higher prevalence rates than Brazil, exceeding 1.5 percent of the adult population.[34] It is estimated that half of Brazilian HIV infections are sexually transmitted (UNAIDS, 2007).[35]

HIV/AIDS and tuberculosis are two major health threats in Brazil; however, they are not alone. Diseases and conditions that take root in extreme poverty are present such as schistosomiasis and malaria.[36] In addition, there are health problems typical of affluent countries, such as diabetes.[37] One of the major challenges facing Brazil is the sheer immensity of the country, heralding a communications and treatment gap between urban and rural areas. There are many isolated villages without regular access to health care and where, consequently, not much is known about HIV prevalence. In addition, there is a population of 7 to 8 million street children at high risk for contracting HIV due to unsafe sex and drug-taking.[38] Another challenge is the trend towards increasing number of sex partners, and having first sex at an earlier age.[39]

ACHIEVEMENTS IN BRAZIL

HIV/AIDS in Brazil is fought on two fronts: prevention and treatment. Today, the Brazilian response to the AIDS epidemic is termed "commendable" by UNAIDS (p. 42)[40] and has the "most comprehensive" antiretroviral therapy provision in the world. Between 1998 and 2005, condom use among Brazilians increased by nearly 50 percent.[41] Injecting-drug users make up at least half the AIDS cases in some areas but effective harm reduction programs drove prevalence down very swiftly in some cities. HIV prevalence among drug users in Salvador fell from 50 percent to 7 percent between 1996 and 2001.[42] The government offered antiretrovirals to 113,000 patients by 2002, thereby improving their quality of life and productivity, and reducing the need for costly hospitalizations. The antiretroviral drug Zidovudine is offered free of charge to pregnant women with HIV in Brazil, along with formula for feeding and psychological and social support, thereby averting many HIV infections in children.[43]

Since 1996, the rate of HIV-related infections fell by about 80 percent, AIDS deaths have been reduced by 70 percent, and 358,000 AIDS-related hospital admissions were avoided.[44] The WHO estimates that more than US$1 billion have been saved by reducing hospital admissions and lower spending on the treatment of opportunistic infections, including tuberculosis.[45] The government asserts that it has saved more than US$2 billion

52 AIDS and Business

in health care costs because of the rapid provision of free antiretrovirals.[46] Yet, a number of challenges remain, such as the standard of tuberculosis care (a number of people with HIV/AIDS are likely to be coinfected with tuberculosis), which is allegedly rather low.[47]

GENDER ROLES IN BRAZIL AND MSM

There is a strong norm for virginity among young women, which has the effect of depriving them of practical information about sexual matters early on in life[48] and making them ill-equipped to protect themselves from HIV and sexually transmitted infections. Similarly, a set of values termed *marianismo* (derived from the Virgin Mary) means that women should be passive, sexually innocent, and yet receptive to the sexual advances of their male partners.[49] Another female value is *ediquetta*, to cultivate one's sexually attractive appearance while maintaining virtue.[50]

A man tends to be judged by others according to his claimed number of sex acts and partners (*machismo*), as well as by the perceived virtue of his wife, girlfriends, sisters, and so on.[51] Pronatalism describes the expectation that young men and women are expected to produce children, a value which is compatible with the Catholic proscription of contraception and abortion.[52] More important than the distinction whether it is men or women having sex with men in Brazil is the concept of giving and receiving. The sex partner who "inserts" (*comer*, or "to eat") into the other is contrasted with the one who is "receptive" (*dar*, or "to give").[53]

THE ROLE OF THE GOVERNMENT

Article 196 of the Brazilian constitution of 1988 and Act 8.080/90, articles 2 and 3 stipulated that health care is a "right of all and the duty of the state, guaranteed by means of social and economic policies aimed at reducing diseases and injuries and through actions and services for promotion, prevention, and rehabilitation."[54] The government established in 1990 the national health system *Sistema Unico da Saúde*, offering free and universal health care. The government mandates AIDS education in primary schools, distributes condoms, supports condoms and manufacturing of pharmaceuticals, designs mass media safer sex campaigns,[55] and maintains an attractive website.[56]

Per year, the Brazilian government spends US$395 million on HIV treatments, of which two-thirds are branded drugs.[57] Between 1996 and 2002, the government spent US$1.8 billion on antiretroviral drugs.[58] The country has earned a reputation as a tough negotiator on HIV drugs pricing, having threatened pharmaceutical companies with patent violation when they do not get a low price offer on HIV/AIDS drugs.[59] The government's threat of

Addressing a Global Cause in Local Contexts 53

compulsory licensing lowered the prices of three HIV/AIDS drugs in 2001, two from *Merck* and one from *Roche*, by approximately half.[60] The government's recent negotiations with the pharmaceutical company Abbott for its drug Kaletra (lopinavir-ritonavir) culminated in a price almost half that originally offered. The government commonly seeks voluntary licenses that would allow them to manufacture patented medicines in Brazil.[61]

The generics law was passed in 1999, permitting manufacture of generic medications, which in 2006 comprised 11.6 percent of all drugs made in Brazil.[62] Brazil has played a very active role in international intellectual property negotiations since 1830, when the country passed its first patent law and was one of the first signatories of the Paris convention for the protection of industrial property rights. Brazil frequently takes on a leadership role in intellectual property debates in the context of the World Trade Organization (WTO) and the World Intellectual Property Organization (WIPO).[63]

In May 2007 the Brazilian government broke with their reputation as tough negotiators who always manage to push through a last-minute compromise. After long negotiations to lower the price on Efavirenz (Sustiva), an antiretroviral sold by Merck, the Brazilian government finally utilized the ultimate weapon to lower drug prices. They issued compulsory licensing of the drug. By declaring Efavirenz to be "in the public interest," Minister of Health Mr. José Gomes indicated that Efavirenz could now be manufactured in Brazil or purchased from a generic manufacturer abroad. At the same time, a small royalty would be offered to Merck. The decision followed in the wake of Thailand's recent compulsory licensing of three antiretrovirals, and specifically that Brazil was seeking the same price level as was granted to Thailand.[64] Efavirenz is the most utilized imported HIV/AIDS drug (38 percent of Brazilians with AIDS, or 87,000 patients, take it). Describing his view on the matter, Brazilian president Lula called the price difference for the drug between Thailand and Brazil as ethically "grotesque."[65] The Brazilian STD and AIDS offices justify the government's decision with the claim that compulsory licensing will save the Brazilian government a total of US$236.8 million by 2012, when Merck's patent expires.[66]

THE PHARMACEUTICAL INDUSTRY IN BRAZIL

In 1993, a Brazilian company, *Microbiologics*, began manufacturing AZT. The following year, government laboratories were producing the drug for provision to public health system patients free of charge.[67] In 1996, free and universal access to antiretroviral treatments began.[68]

In 2005 there were 551 private companies operating in Brazil's pharmaceutical industry (Intercontinental Medical Statistics in Chamas, 2005); however, most pharmaceutical products consumed in Brazil are made

54 *AIDS and Business*

by multinational corporations. There are also eighteen public laboratories, some of which have earned prominence. The most notable example is probably the state-owned *Farmanguinhos*, which grew precipitously in the 1990s. Public laboratories fulfill approximately 10 percent of the government's procurement needs.[69] The government's assigned priority in its procurement policies was to purchase generic medications. This helped to foster the local industry: in 2004 there were 1,033 generic medicines registered in Brazil.[70] Today, the Brazilian health service treats approximately 160,000 people free of charge with seventeen antiretroviral drugs, eight of which are manufactured in Brazil.[71]

The provision of medications and health care is only one aspect of the government's program. A comprehensive prevention strategy has been key in keeping down the number of new infections, including a range of condom promotion and distribution programs.[72] Condom sales quadrupled in the years between 1993 and 1999 (UNAIDS, 2000).[73] The government distributes approximately twenty million condoms per month, and 50 percent more than that are distributed during carnival time.[74] Extensive and constant social marketing campaigns remind people to use their *camisinha* ("little shirt," slang for condom).[75] In order to raise prevention awareness and capabilities among injecting-drug users, a high-risk group, needle-exchange programs have been implemented in Brazil.[76]

THE ROLE PLAYED BY RELIGIOUS ORGANIZATIONS IN BRAZIL

The Brazilian Catholic church has "liberation theology" as part of its history. This uniquely Brazilian brand of Catholicism endorses helping people in poverty and those who are oppressed, thereby allowing the church to carry HIV messages to virtually all sectors of Brazilian society.[77] This has enabled people of Catholic orders to become public advocates and private helpers of the oppressed and the ill. The church has not consistently upheld this approach, however. There has been sporadic church grumbling about condom distribution in particular. In 2004, a bishop's conference released a statement alleging that condoms were not as safe as many people thought. In response, the government designed a campaign still being echoed today with the statement "nothing gets through a condom" (Starmer-Smith in Human Rights Watch, 2004).[78] In 2007, Brazilian church leader Cardinal Geraldo Majella Agnello stated that "the condom encourages people to have inconsequential and irresponsible sex. We cannot agree with the use of the condom."[79]

THE ROLE OF THE BRAZILIAN PRIVATE SECTOR

A number of companies have shown leadership in offering HIV/AIDS prevention, awareness, and care initiatives. However, according to Bendell

(2003),[80] only half of Brazil's largest companies have workplace HIV/AIDS policies, perhaps as a result of the proactive government stance on the issue. Often-cited examples of the most active companies include Volkswagen Brazil, an automobile market leader and one of Brazil's biggest employers. The company paid for employees' medications until the government took responsibility for medication costs for all Brazilians. Since then, ethical concerns regarding confidentiality and protection of employees with HIV/AIDS have driven activities.[81] Like Volkswagen, Nestlé Brazil developed its workplace program before the Brazilian government started the national program. The Nestlé program offers voluntary counseling and testing, HIV/AIDS prevention education, and other related services to its fifteen thousand employees in the country. Over its two decades of operation, the company saw HIV-risky behaviors among its employees drop by half from preprogram studies to monitoring measurements.[82] Also active very early in the epidemic was Varig, one of Latin America's biggest airlines. The company was particularly concerned about HIV risks to its flight attendants due to their work-led lifestyle and the interrupted sleep patterns inherent to their jobs. Varig offers voluntary testing and counseling as well as treatment and care on-site for employees with HIV/AIDS and other sexually transmitted diseases at their three outpatient clinics along with a range of other services offered through its foundation.[83]

THE ROLE PLAYED BY NGOS IN BRAZIL

Nongovernmental organizations (NGOs) have quite free rein to conduct their campaigns in Brazil, and there are many of them. In 2007 there were six hundred NGOs active in the area of HIV/AIDS; in the year 2000, Brazil had five hundred NGOs, up from 120 in 1992.[84] NGOs are considered to be more effective in reaching groups at high risk than the government. The World Bank has lent support to a number of NGOs in Brazil, conferring upon them a sort of societal legitimacy in their prevention efforts with prisoners, sex workers, and drug users.[85] One program that has won praise is Estudios y Comunicación en Sexualidad y Reprodución (ECOS), a pioneering sexual education program aimed at changing male perceptions about sexuality that uses discussion, role playing, and videos.[86]

Project Hope has been often cited as an NGO that uses "best practices" such as using a range of motivators for its volunteers, who provide support and assistance to people living with HIV/AIDS as well as the orphans of the epidemic; and because of the organization's use of NGO, government, and international partnerships.[87] Arco Iris is an advocacy NGO for the gay and lesbian communities and has many partnerships with government agencies and official endorsements.[88] In one of their projects, Arco Iris peer educators go to nightclubs, saunas, and other places popular with gay men in Rio de Janeiro to distribute condoms and HIV/AIDS

56 AIDS and Business

prevention and awareness information.[89] As stated by Ana Paola Prado of AIDS NGO Arco Iris, "We do not have the best model in the world, but our model answers the demands from Brazil" (p. 41).[90]

CONCLUSION: LESSONS LEARNED FROM BRAZIL

Certain factors intimately related to the history and unique context of Brazil cannot be transposed as a "lesson learnt" to any other country. Yet there is value in teasing out other factors that may serve as lessons for other developing countries.[91] For the purpose of analyzing successful elements of Brazil's scheme, it is useful to distinguish between "hard" capacity such as health infrastructure and health care providers, and "soft" capacity such as governance, economic, social, and institutional factors. Many have argued for the importance of the soft capacity factors in the success of Brazil's program (see notably Oliveira-Cruz, 2002).[92] One soft factor relates to the historic situation in the 1980s and early 1990s, when the epidemic was gathering steam. With the country mired in a difficult political transition from a military regime, a new relationship between people and their government fostered a new concept of participative and active citizenship, while a sense of solidarity defined by respect for human rights was growing. These two soft factors took shape in the sanitary reform movement, which advocated for and received recognition for health as a human right in the Brazilian constitution.[93]

Other factors commonly pinpointed about the Brazilian response include coordinated government response action, strong civil society participation, and mobilization of the private sector, education, and health services, among others.[94] Specific and targeted prevention campaigns are carried out with commercial sex workers, injecting-drug users, and men having sex with men.[95] Legislative support also helped: in 1988, the government passed a law guaranteeing equal rights for employees with HIV on par with those who have other disabilities.[96] Such a law reduces fear about HIV and encourages people to take an HIV test. The free press and its role in publicizing the open confrontation of HIV/AIDS and homosexual stigma by leading activists and public figures similarly lowered barriers to those considering getting tested or informing potential sex partners about their HIV status.[97]

BACKGROUND TO THE CASE STUDY

Marketing a Global Cause: HIV/AIDS in Local Contexts

Over the past twenty-five years or so, many governments and other organizations have committed themselves to educating and motivating people to adopt safe and healthy behaviors, particularly in the case of HIV/AIDS.

Addressing a Global Cause in Local Contexts   57

Social marketing of condoms and testing services are prominent examples of this type of commitment. The outcomes of these programs have been variable, and in some cases it is possible to identify key success factors in the areas of policy and social marketing.

Despite the multiple sources involved in HIV/AIDS prevention, treatment, and care, there is a severe and constant shortage of funding that blocks efforts to slow the spread of HIV. According to a UNAIDS (2006) estimate, it is thought that over two years HIV/AIDS prevention programs worldwide will need almost US$30 billion; treatment and care will need US$12.3 billion; and, combined with other HIV/AIDS programs, US$55.1 billion will be needed in total. However, only US$10 billion was estimated to be available, resulting in inevitable funding shortfalls.[98] One common result of a funding gap is a failure to provide antiretroviral therapy—the treatment of choice for HIV/AIDS—to all those who need it. For figures that demonstrate this failure, see Table 2.2.

In this section we will examine structural political, institutional, and economic elements that may help or hinder HIV/AIDS interventions. As stated by the International HIV/AIDS Alliance (2002) in their report: "No one person, organization or sector can ensure effective action on HIV/AIDS on their own" (p. 24).[99] Accordingly, the following sections will analyze the roles played by governments, international organizations, nongovernmental organizations, public-private partnerships, and faith-based organizations and advocacy organizations.

Table 2.2   Estimated Proportion of People Receiving Antiretroviral Therapy of Populations Who Need it. Regional Data from Low- and Middle-Income Countries, December 2003–June 2006

Geographical region	Estimated number of people needing antiretroviral therapy in 2005	Percentage of people needing antiretroviral therapy who actually receive it
North Africa and the Middle East	75,000	5
Europe and Central Asia	190,000	13
East, South, and Southeast Asia	1,440,000	16
Sub-Saharan Africa	4,600,000	23
Latin America and the Caribbean	460,000	75
TOTAL	6,800,000	24

Source: World Health Organization. (2006). *Towards universal access by 2010: How the WHO is working with countries to scale-up HIV prevention, treatment, care and support.* Retrieved June 30, 2007, from http://www.who.int/hiv/mediacentre/universal_access_progress_report_en.pdf.

58   AIDS and Business

The Role Played by Governments in Fighting HIV/AIDS

Governments play a central role in the HIV/AIDS epidemic. Government initiatives, planning, and coordination had results in initially stemming the tide of the epidemic in Brazil, Senegal, Thailand, and Uganda. Senegal was one of the first cases in Africa where the government's response was immediate and effective due to a taboo-breaking involvement with churches and mosques. This was combined with a multisectoral approach including social marketing of condoms that increased condom use from 1 percent to 68 percent in a decade.[100] UNAIDS defines social marketing as the use of commercial marketing techniques to further social causes through behavior change, educating people about the protective value of condoms, and making them available to people who need them.[101] Social marketing may be carried out by international organizations, nongovernmental organizations, governments, and others. Yet it is national and local government support that is needed for a social marketing program to be successful.

Researchers commonly identify two types of environments that increase or decrease HIV risk: the micro environment, which is individual decisions and prevailing local norms and beliefs, and the macro environment, which is composed of economic conditions, legal/regulatory factors, military activities, and cultural factors.[102] These environments are depicted graphically in Figure 2.1. When governments are unstable or in transition, as in the case of a number of governments in Eastern Europe and Central Asia after the fall of the Soviet Union, ensuing economic and social changes may create environments propitious to the transmission of HIV by fostering informal economies that result in bigger drug and sex markets. Such transition may also lead to a collapse of health infrastructure, lower social cohesion, reduction in drug law enforcement, and other factors that aggravate HIV risk conditions in the micro and macro environments.

Governments commonly provide preventative education, testing (which may be obligatory for some members of risk groups, as in Russia), and many provide treatment directly or through nongovernmental organizations or independent health care organizations. In countries where access to government health services is not equally available to all segments of the population, HIV/AIDS tends to concentrate in populations who lack easy access, such as the poor and the socially marginalized. In the United States, for example, which rates badly on deaths from preventable conditions, racial and ethnic minorities and the poor are more likely to die from AIDS than more wealthy or nonminority citizens.[103] Governments may be the only source of purchasing power in poorer countries to negotiate with pharmaceutical companies. Those countries which, like Brazil and Thailand, go so far as to petition for compulsory licensing for AIDS drugs, or directly purchase the drugs to distribute to their people, do so with the conviction that economically, long-term benefits outweigh costs.

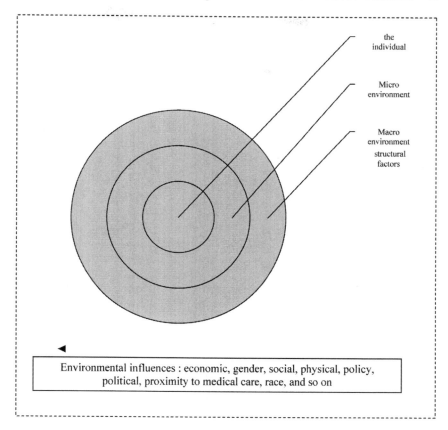

Figure 2.1 A representation of the individual within two types of risk environments.

Governments also have a role in tracking and reporting HIV/AIDS cases. However, there are different measurement criteria and statistic models, as well as varying definitions, to be interpreted. Other factors may enter the equation to make HIV/AIDS case tracking unreliable, as discussed in the following section.

REASONS WHY OFFICIAL HIV/AIDS DATA MAY NOT BE ACCURATE

In July 2007, the National AIDS Control Organization of India surprised the world by releasing figures on HIV/AIDS estimates for the country that were lower by six million than previously thought. These figures received the backing of the World Health Organization (WHO) and UNAIDS. The new lower estimates did not reveal Indian success in beating the epidemic; however, they did reveal weaknesses in compiling data on HIV prevalence

60 *AIDS and Business*

Box 2.1 A View from the Field:

Procurement Policies for the Government-Supplied Antiretroviral Program

Drug procurement is usually carried out once a year and complies with the Brazilian laws governing public bidding. The suppliers are both public and private manufacturers. In the private sector, Merck and Abbott are currently among the suppliers to the Brazilian national program. Deliveries are usually divided in three to four consignments.

Patients receive ARV drugs in the Units Dispensing AIDS Drugs, which usually are the pharmacies of HIV/AIDS outpatient services. Currently there are 424 such units throughout the country.

In order to guarantee a continued flow of distribution of ARV, the AIDS Drugs Logistic System was implemented. Still, to rationalize the costs and to facilitate this logistic control, the National Program on STD/AIDS developed the SICLOM (Computerized System for the Control of Drug Logistics), which has as objective the control of the supply and the supply to the patients; improvement of the supplying system; bigger guarantee of the continuous supply of medicines; and enhancement of management activities. The system also presents the following main characteristics:

- Nationwide patient register
- Registration linked to the individual drug dispensing unit
- Validation of the register and dispensation, using Ministry of Health criteria.
- Computerization of the dispensing units
- Certification of the ARV prescription through a magnetic card
- Patient information on the appropriate use and storage of drugs
- Daily transfer of data to the National AIDS Program by telephone data transmission

It is important to highlight that while the federal government is responsible for ARV drugs, the procurement and distribution of drugs for treating opportunistic diseases are decentralized to the states and municipalities.

Source: Information provided by Mr. Pedro Marcos de Castro Saldaña, second secretary, Permanent Mission of Brazil, Geneva, Switzerland (2005, 8 September). Personal communication.

---

and incidence, highlighting the fragility of HIV/AIDS estimates. Because it is neither possible nor desirable to test everyone for HIV, governments and international organizations must develop estimates on the topic that are as realistic and accurate as they can be.

WHO (2006) states that "weak monitoring and evaluation systems are an obstacle to increased funding and more effective implementation" (p. 49).[104] According to UNAIDS (2004), "All HIV estimates need to be assessed critically" (p. X). Oster (2005)[105] and Barnett and Whiteside (2002), among others, assert that HIV/AIDS data provide conservative estimates of the true amplitude of the epidemic. One reason for this is the HIV data sources in high-prevalence countries, which are often based on the number of HIV-positive pregnant women attending antenatal clinics. This number is extrapolated onto the population as a whole, a problematic process due to uncertainty about the number of sexual partners per individual as well as the fact that the proportion of women attending clinics is variable between regions and countries (UNAIDS, 2004). This method may omit entirely male injecting-drug users and men having sex with men, thereby skewing downwards the estimates for the population as a whole.[106] Also contributing to lower estimates may be falling fertility rates of women who have HIV and therefore do not attend antenatal clinics, or become pregnant more infrequently.[107] However, some argue that, to the contrary, this method may overestimate the number of people with HIV because it excludes those women who use contraceptive methods correctly and have fewer or no children.[108]

Another reason to consider HIV data as conservative estimates is that new HIV infections and cause-of-death information may be skewed downwards by death and case reporting systems. In many countries, government disease data are based on voluntary or compulsory reporting by physicians and antenatal and sexually transmitted disease clinics. People who are in dire poverty may never attend a clinic and therefore may never be identified as HIV positive. The poor tend to attend clinics where they may be identified as HIV positive and subsequently enter the reporting system. However, the middle class and the affluent tend to go to private physicians or go abroad for testing and treatment. Private physicians may yield to social pressure and avoid official reporting of the HIV status of patients. They may, for example, report the fatal opportunistic infection as the cause of death or cite "natural causes"—not the underlying AIDS condition. According to Jenkins and Robalino (2003), this cause-of-death practice is likely quite common, particularly in countries or regions with high levels of stigma. Other factors may explain low reporting rates. One example is that tuberculosis may be an indicator that a person has HIV because it is a frequent opportunistic infection; however, doctors may prefer due to bureaucratic reasons to list the cause of illness or death to be tuberculosis only.

In a South African example, when a doctor declares HIV/AIDS as the underlying cause of death, the family's life insurance or funeral benefits may be invalidated. Motivated by compassion, some doctors in South Africa choose not to mention HIV/AIDS as a cause of death, reporting instead the opportunistic infection (Groenewald et al., 2005).[109]

National population-based surveys are another source of HIV/AIDS data. These are done house to house, and are considered to be reliable; however, it may precisely be the household members absent at the time of the survey who may be more likely to have HIV/AIDS—the migrant worker and the family member whose whereabouts are unknown (UNAIDS, 2004). Another problem with household research is that by its nature it cannot include households that have been eradicated by HIV/AIDS (Barnett and Whiteside, 2002). In poverty-stricken regions or conflict areas, local

62   AIDS and Business

resources may be so minimal or so isolated that diagnostic tests may be unavailable. In that case HIV/AIDS cases may remain hidden or recorded as other diseases commonly observed in the area.[110]

Some have argued that HIV/AIDS estimates in sub-Saharan Africa are high rather than low (Oster, 2005).[111] The news of massively reduced HIV/AIDS estimates in India in 2007 illustrated the difficulties of estimating the number of people infected, particularly when these are thought to be overestimates.[112]

It is clear that a number of factors complicate the issue of determining the extent of the epidemic, and may lull the government and its constituencies into complacency when figures are inaccurately low. Table 2.3 demonstrates the margins between government estimates and estimates made by other experts, such as UNAIDS. The figures highlight the difficulties of pinpointing the correct number of people with HIV/AIDS at a given time in any given country.

When HIV prevalence rates stabilize or even decrease, there may be little cause for celebration. As resumed by Epstein (2004),[113] "HIV prevalence is a function of AIDS mortality and new infections" (p. 8). Therefore, if HIV prevalence remains stable at a high level, behind the numbers there may simply be a large number of new people newly diagnosed with HIV that replace an equally large number of people dying of AIDS-related causes.

Governments of some countries influence responses to AIDS in other countries by offering financial and technical assistance. The governments of Australia, Canada, France, The Netherlands, United Kingdom, and the United States have been noted in this regard. In the case of the United States, several reports have discussed the "national security" and geopolitical interests of the U.S. government as linked to a humanitarian stance on health security worldwide.[114] In response, government agencies like

Table 2.3   Comparison of Government Estimates and Other Expert Estimates (Selected Countries)

Country	Government estimate of number infected with AIDS (millions)	Expert estimate of number infected with AIDS (millions)	2010 Government projection of number infected with AIDS (millions)	2010 Expert estimate of number infected with AIDS (millions)
Russia	0.18	1–2	5–8	6–11
India	4.00	5–8	3–4	20–25
Ethiopia	2.70	3–5	7–10	19–27

Source: National Intelligence Council (2002). The next wave of HIV/AIDS: Nigeria, Ethiopia, Russia, India, and China. *Intelligence Community Assessment* 2002–04, September, 2002, p. 6.[115]

the Centers for Disease Control and Prevention (CDC),[116] U.S. Agency for International Development (USAID),[117] and the National Institutes of Health (NIH)[118] have become internationally involved in the global surveillance and management of epidemics like HIV/AIDS and tuberculosis.[119] Yet, the links between national security and HIV/AIDS epidemics are not as obvious as depicted in some government reports (Barnett and Pryns, 2006).[120]

In wealthy countries and in some poorer countries with national treatment programs like Brazil and Thailand, HIV/AIDS treatments do not lack. However, there may be no health worker to dispense the drugs or provide vital information about how to take the drugs effectively, nor to follow up with further medical care for patients. There is one national and one international migration reason for this. In resource-poor regions, doctors and nurses with rural origins are likely to migrate to the city, where there may be higher wages and better working conditions. In addition, doctors and nurses from resource-poor countries are likely to migrate to more wealthy countries for the same reasons. As was eloquently argued by Dare, Kim, and Farmer (2006), in addition to working to retain doctors and nurses, countries with a health worker shortage should create a new category of health worker. Those in this category would be paid a salary and would be rooted in the community where they serve. They would receive ongoing training and be supported by doctors and nurses in their primary care work, thereby reducing pressure on professional medical staff and the health services sector in countries with lower and mid-income levels.[121]

Governments that did little to help people with AIDS in their countries saw HIV/AIDS cases increase, as was notably the case of South Africa, with one of the world's worst epidemics. Some criticized Nelson Mandela, who was silent about AIDS until 1998. However, his successors did little better. The South African administration that followed Mandela—the government led by Thabo Mbeki—adopted the initial position that the AIDS drug AZT was too expensive. Then, following the drug manufacturer's offer of a much lower price, President Mbeki claimed it was too toxic.[122] In 2003, South African organization Treatment Action Campaign (TAC) brought legal action against the ministers of Health and Trade by equating their inaction on HIV/AIDS with human rights abuse and manslaughter since they allegedly had the legal duty and power to prevent hundreds of AIDS deaths daily in the country.[123]

A frequently used HIV/AIDS prevention approach, which is currently favored by the Bush administration, is Abstinence (to abstain from sexual intercourse and increase age at first sexual intercourse), Be Faithful (mutual monogamy and reduction of number of partners) and use a Condom, simply

64 AIDS and Business

Box 2.2 A View from the Field:

WHO's Ted Karpf on Nationalization and Health Emergencies

Another example of business involvement is in the development of drugs. This is a story about what the pharmaceutical business has done and not done. There are now about 40 million patients worldwide. In an early example with AZT pricing in 1987, it took the threat of Senator Kennedy and Senator Hatch to say to the pharmaceutical company Burroughs Wellcome,[124] that according to the 1935 Public Health Service Act the US government could nationalize the pharmaceutical industry in a public health emergency we can do that, and we will charge the price that we think it's worth. The next day the drug price collapsed. Up until that point federal programs were paying higher prices through federal assistance grants.

This is perhaps why the President of South Africa would not announce a national emergency. It would have meant that anything and everything that had an impact could be nationalized—and that's not good for business. Such an action could curtail competitiveness and attractiveness in a business environment. A health emergency could force all sectors to coordinate and work together. While there had been an acknowledgement that there was a health "urgency", which was President Mbeki's chosen term, all sectors could operate individually. This is how government doesn't work when you give it a chance.[125]

There were thousands of AIDS orphans created in South Africa because of lack of treatment. Legal guardians or foster parents could receive an assistance grant to care for a number of orphans. However the grant did not include school fees because it was not coordinated with the Department of Education. So basically they could not go to school, they were being subsidized to eat, and people who only know how to eat and know nothing else do not go far later on. Then this aid comes to an end when the child reaches 16 years of age. So children at the most vulnerable age of contracting HIV or passing HIV on to someone else, were turned out onto the street with no means to take care of themselves.

We began to discover that, given the laws in South Africa, it was better to not reform the laws rather resort to the use of bridge funding to create support systems for those with disabilities and function from that perspective. The system was actually rewarding people for contracting AIDS, because only when they were infected and sick they would qualify for all sorts of support. If not infected and sick, the government was not going to save you. And this was particularly true if you were a child.

As you can see from my passion this issue of nationalization is very dear to me because when a health emergency is declared, all these sectors have to come up with formulas that one does not preclude the other. You get a joint, collective strategy at country level with the agencies of government. You do not get that response routinely anywhere because HIV is often

Addressing a Global Cause in Local Contexts   65

Box 2.2 (continued)

reduced to merely a health matter. That's why you don't hear business and industry talking about HIV other than as a risk management question: it poses risks for investment and profit. A provocative question to get my hands around because it moves on me and unless you have all the sectors together in one room it gets really messy.

Source: Ted Karpf, director of partnerships, WHO HIV Department, WHO, Geneva, Switzerland (2005, 27 June). Personal interview.

---

known as ABC.[126] The assumption of this approach is that individuals can protect themselves from HIV by making decisions relating to safer sex practices. Many HIV/AIDS advocates and nongovernmental organizations have criticized government emphasis on abstinence, citing the available data that show clearly that many women are more at risk from HIV/AIDS in their own monogamous marriage than in unmarried sexual relationships. Marriage may be more of an HIV risk for women because condom use is rare among married couples. In addition, men are likely to be older than their wives and therefore more likely to have HIV;[127] in many cultures men are allowed or encouraged to have sex outside marriage, which makes them likely "bridges" of HIV to their wives. Dworkin and Ehrhardt (2007)[128] argue that the weakness of ABC is its inability to take into account the lack of "relationship power" that negates or reduces women's ability to make safer-sex decisions in many cultures. Making matters worse is the fact that condom use is not as high as it should be, particularly among young people, due to lack of awareness, misinformation, lack of availability, and inaccessibility.[129]

The Role Played by International Organizations in Fighting HIV/AIDS

At the beginning of the epidemic, it was assumed that the World Health Organization (WHO) and the United Nations (UN) would be able to slow the spread of HIV. Yet it soon became clear that the budgets and capabilities of the UN and related organizations were not sufficient. In 1996, the United Nations Joint Program on AIDS (UNAIDS) was born, and was composed of the following organizations:

- United Nations Children's Fund (UNICEF)
- United Nations Development Project (UNDP)
- United Nations Education, Scientific and Cultural Organization (UNESCO)
- United Nations International Drug Control Program (UNDCP)
- United Nations Population Fund (monitoring and reporting) (UNFPA)
- World Health Organization (WHO)

66 AIDS and Business

Box 2.3 The Guiding Objective and Agenda of the World Health Organization

The objective of the World Health Organization:

WHO's objective, as set out in its Constitution, is the attainment by all peoples of the highest possible level of health. The Constitution defines health as a state of complete physical, mental and social well-being and not merely the absence of disease or infirmity.[130]

The six-point WHO agenda:[131]

1.   Promoting development, to include attainment of relevant Millennium Development Goals.

2.   Fostering health security: strengthened defence against outbreaks of "emerging and epidemic-prone diseases"

3.   Strengthening health systems by increasing their reach, human resources, financing, data collection, technology and vital pharmaceutical products.

4.   Harnessing research, information and evidence to monitor and report, develop standards and formulate policy.

5.   Enhancing partnerships with UN agencies, international organizations, donors, civil society, and the private sector, among others.

6.   Improving performance through effectiveness, efficiency and results-based management.

The World Health Organization (WHO)[132] with UNAIDS is playing a most active high-profile role in monitoring the epidemic, evaluating progress, and reporting. The WHO monitors pricing for HIV/AIDS medications, provides technical assistance to countries and protocols for testing and treatment.[133] The WHO formulates strategic directions for reducing the spread of HIV/AIDS and scaling up treatment, such as the "3 by 5" program[134] launched with the target of gaining access to antiretroviral treatment by three million people in low- and middle-income countries before 2005.[135] Other UN and related international organizations have become active in response to the spread of HIV, including the United Nations General Assembly Special Session (UNGASS) and the United Nations Development Fund for Women (UNIFEM), among others. The International Labor Organization (ILO)[136] developed workplace policies and best practice educational materials for employers about HIV/AIDS, and monitors the response of businesses to the HIV/AIDS threat.

The Global Fund to Fight AIDS, Tuberculosis and Malaria[137] has created a mechanism for fund raising and fund allocations. The Global Fund works as a partnership between civil society, donors, the private sector, and communities affected by HIV/AIDS, tuberculosis, or malaria. It is a financial mechanism that works to leverage funds, not implement programs.

Addressing a Global Cause in Local Contexts 67

Box 2.4 A View from the Field:

MSF's Dr. Laura Ciaffi on the Availability of Funds to Pay for Antiretroviral Treatments

The aim of MSF is to provide antiretroviral therapy to the majority of patients, because it is known that this saves lives. Despite the efforts being made, MSF estimated in 2004 that approximately 24,000 patients receive antiretroviral therapy out of six million or so who are in need of it. That is very few so far but MSF sees itself as a catalyst, guiding other players in the epidemic to provide antiretrovirals. That is one driver that makes our work worthwhile. When MSF started providing antiretroviral treatments, policymakers generally were not convinced that was necessary. Now, most are convinced of the necessity of antiretrovirals and are committed to providing them. Cost is not such a big issue because there is funding available. The problem for national health systems is how to manage the funds, and how to put in place the requisite drug logistics processes. The biggest problem of all is the lack of medical personnel. In Mozambique, for example, there are only 600 doctors and most of those have no training on antiretroviral therapy and management of HIV.

MSF wanted to demonstrate that it was possible to treat people with antiretrovirals. For this reason, the organization at first used massive resources to make antiretroviral treatment programs work. Today, the focus is on simplification: MSF aims to attain the same outcome with fewer resources.

The work of MSF France in Chiradzulu, Malawi, was documented in the WHO/MSF report *Surmounting challenges: Procurement of antiretroviral medicines in low and middle income countries—The experience of MSF.* The treatment program, which treated 3,000 patients in 2004, is small compared to the need. However, by being active in the field MSF can put pressure on governments and other organizations, form a network of partnerships, and gather data. Experience has shown that a broad-based approach is necessary: social, economic, family, health, and social networks need to be taken into consideration. For this reason, organizations working in different fields need to work together in order for a treatment program to be effective.

Source: Dr.Laura Ciaffi, Medical Advisor, Médecins Sans Frontières, Geneva, Switzerland (2005, 27 June). Personal interview.
*The full report is available at: http://www.msf.fr/documents/came/msf-whoaids2003.pdf.

The World Bank[138] provides loans, grants, and expertise at the governmental and community levels all over the world in the areas of HIV/AIDS prevention, care, and impact mitigation. The bank also conducts research and provides analytical and advisory services with the goal of supporting economic development for countries in need. A stated goal of the World Bank is to strengthen health systems.[139] The World Economic Forum (WEF) and the International Monetary Fund are similar examples.

68 AIDS and Business

The Role Played by Nongovernmental Organizations (NGOs) in Fighting HIV/AIDS

There are a large number of nongovernmental organizations (NGOs) dedicated to, or involved with HIV/AIDS. Such NGOs range from tiny community- or faith-based initiatives to organizations of global reach like OXFAM, to the billion-dollar worldwide initiatives of the Bill and Melinda Gates Foundation. For the purposes of this chapter, only two contrasting organizations will be discussed: Médecins Sans Frontières and the Bill and Melinda Gates Foundation. Médecins Sans Frontières (Doctors Without Borders)[140] has worked on preventing the spread of HIV/AIDS, and caring for those who have it by supplying needed medications and by opening free clinics around the world, most recently in China. The Nobel Prize–winning organization leads a campaign advocating for "Access to Essential Medicines," much of which is devoted to increasing the affordability and access of HIV/AIDS drugs. According to a Médecins Sans Frontières (MSF) report on medicine access, at the close of 2002 only 300,000 people in the developing world were receiving antiretroviral treatment for HIV/AIDS, half of whom live in Brazil, where there is universal access to the drugs (see related section). The World Health Organization notably failed to meet its own goal of providing antiretroviral treatment to three million people by the end of 2005 (3 by 5 initiative). Yet, a relatively small organization like MSF can provide treatment to 4,472 AIDS patients in twenty-three countries. Their commitment to people with HIV/AIDS is just one of many projects run by the organization.

The Bill and Melinda Gates Foundation[141] has made global health a primary focus, as the cofounder of Microsoft, Bill Gates, told the international community with emotion. In a speech given to UN delegates he stated that he and his wife were "stunned" to discover the medical wrongs and negligence suffered by children around the world.[142] The Bill and Melinda Gates Foundation works to maximize the utility of the organizations currently working on any particular project, partly by parceling out its US$24 billion funds donated by Bill and Melinda Gates. The foundation works uniquely through existing programs and organizations, for example, by financially scaling up programs that the World Health Organization cannot fund alone. The Bill and Melinda Gates Foundation with its partners provided AIDS treatment for 8,000 people within eighteen months in Botswana, one of Africa's hardest hit countries, a rare success of speedy delivery.[143]

THE ROLE PLAYED BY PRIVATE SECTOR AND PUBLIC-PRIVATE PARTNERSHIPS IN FIGHTING HIV/AIDS

The private sector has made important strides towards helping the work of governments, international organizations, and nongovernmental organizations. Around the world, the global work force has lost at least twenty-eight million people as a result of AIDS—a figure likely to

> **Box 2.5** A View from the Field:
>
> *The Complementarity Between Government and Business in the HIV/ AIDS Fight in Brazil*
>
> In Brazil, treatment programmes are sponsored by the government and are free of charge. Accordingly, there is no need for companies to pay for their employee's treatments. In terms of prevention, there are companies that are quite active in the promotion of prevention/awareness programmes within their work environment.
>
> The Brazilian Programme on HIV/AIDS works closely with the national and international Business Council to promote prevention policy implementation within the businesses and draw guidelines and set up regular campaigns. The most important Brazilian and multinational companies form part of the council. Also on state level the Brazilian Programme is promoting the foundation of business councils and specific action plans for prevention at the work place. These initiatives are directly linked to the health services to assure access to treatment and care. The Brazilian Branch of *Volkswagen*[144] is seen as a good example for the work it has been implementing on the field of prevention and care.
>
> Source: Information provided by Mr. Pedro Marcos de Castro Saldaña, second secretary, Permanent Mission of Brazil, Geneva, Switzerland
> Link to Brazil National Program for AIDS and sexually transmitted diseases: http://www.aids.gov.br.

increase to seventy-four million people by 2015.[145] Examples of private organizations that are prominent in HIV/AIDS work include the World Economic Forum's Global Health Initiative,[146] Global Business Coalition on HIV/AIDS, and certain private firms that have taken leadership on AIDS-related initiatives.

The Global Business Coalition on HIV/AIDS (GBC)[147] was founded in 1997 to "fully engage the private sector and recognize business as an important partner in ending the HIV/AIDS pandemic" (GBC, p. 9).[148] One line of argument contends that the business skills inherent in most companies could be most effectively used to prevent HIV/AIDS and to work for AIDS care. For instance, corporate expertise in communications and marketing could benefit AIDS prevention programs, particularly in the area of behavior-change programs. An example of this was the production by Viacom[149] network MTV of the television show *Staying Alive* in conjunction with UNAIDS and the World Bank, using its unique and powerful way to communicate with young people. Nelson Mandela was on the show for his eighty-fifth birthday, reaching more than two billion people worldwide via MTV.[150] GBC contends that private sector expertise in human resources could benefit HIV/AIDS prevention and care programs by training and motivating the program's paid staff and volunteers. Private sector expertise in logistics could benefit HIV/AIDS programs by ensuring

70   AIDS and Business

that medical supplies are procured and delivered promptly, even in remote areas. Coca-Cola's Africa Foundation program is an example of this, using the company's logistics and distribution skills to bring HIV/AIDS-related materials, such as condoms, to places where they are needed in Kenya and Zambia.[151] The GBC counted two hundred member companies worldwide in 2006, including many multinational corporations.[152]

A more recent arrival in the HIV/AIDS fight was the Global Fund to Fight AIDS, Tuberculosis and Malaria,[153] which made its first call for proposals in January 2002. The Global Fund is an independent public-private partnership dedicated to reducing the six million deaths caused each year by these diseases, and emphasizes a country-based approach.[154] Sponsors include the World Bank and seven other major organizations. The fund calls itself a "financial entity" as opposed to an action/implementation entity. It leverages financial contributions and awards grants based on an independent assessment process.

The Role Played by Activists in Fighting HIV/AIDS

Activist organizations sprang up in wealthy nations at the beginning of the epidemic, and continue to spread around the world. A common premise of AIDS advocacy is that the epidemic was avoidable and a consequence of negligence. In their "Global manifesto," initially published at the HIV/AIDS Conference in South Africa, the American organization AIDS Coalition to Unleash Power (ACT UP)[155] demanded that the United States and European governments allow looser patent rules and offer developing countries health infrastructure help. They demanded that international organizations like UNAIDS do more than "publish statistics," and they asked researchers to work harder and faster to cure AIDS.[156]

Organizations seeking better HIV/AIDS care commonly act on four levels:

1. Individual: this includes providing assistance to individuals with AIDS, such as accompanying them to a clinic;
2. Community: to advocate for more information about AIDS treatment and access to treatments;
3. National: to press the state or national government for more free or subsidized drugs, and demand better quality care for people with HIV/AIDS;
4. Global: to lobby regional and international organizations and trade bodies on global issues such as compulsory licensing and parallel importing of HIV/AIDS drugs, and lower drug pricing.[157]

COUNTRY EXPERIENCES IN PREVENTION AND TREATMENT

The Countries of Sub-Saharan Africa

Sub-Saharan Africa is the world's most impoverished region, comprised of extremely diverse countries and cultures intersected by a multitude of

Addressing a Global Cause in Local Contexts   71

languages and political and social structures.[158] There is therefore no one "African" epidemic, but rather a variety of different epidemics that reflect the differences between countries, and even within countries. Overall, HIV/AIDS prevalence remains extremely high in this part of the world: southern Africa is home to one-third of all people with HIV/AIDS worldwide.[159]

There appears to be evidence that prevention programs and increased government spending have been effective in changing people's behavior to reduce HIV risk in three countries on this continent: Kenya, Uganda, and Zimbabwe. The same is thought to be true for urban areas of Burkina Faso.[160] Uganda will be discussed at the end of the chapter. In Kenya, campaigns urging people to reduce the number of sexual partners and increase condom use are thought to have been effective. In Zimbabwe, most significant in reducing HIV prevalence was increased condom use, as well as reduction in the number of sexual partners. According to a Southern African Development Community[161] expert think tank, key drivers of the HIV/AIDS epidemic were the following:

- Multiple sex partners
- Lack of consistent condom use
- Low levels of male circumcision

The think tank reported that a number of factors underlie these key drivers, particularly the following:

- Gender-specific attitudes and behaviors
- Sex between partners from different generations
- Gender-based and sexual violence
- Stigma and lack of openness about sexual matters
- Untreated sexually transmitted diseases that increase vulnerability to HIV.

Further, the think tank argued that southern African social and structural drivers were at the basis of the factors and drivers listed previously, to include high levels of population mobility, wealth inequality, and gender inequality.[162]

A number of studies found that, for many Africans, condoms signify distrust and unfaithfulness. In Kwa-Zulu Natal (South Africa), men considered that condoms were useful for limiting family size, but they considered condoms otherwise to be associated with promiscuity and having sex with a partner they did not trust. Couples did not consider that sex was an appropriate topic of discussion between men and women.[163] Nigerian university students believe it is unseemly for a young woman to buy and carry a condom with her.[164] A study conducted in Burkina Faso, Ghana, Malawi, and Uganda highlighted the need for adolescents to receive HIV/AIDS and sexually transmitted disease education due to a number of misconceptions about contracting diseases through sex, and the difficulties encountered by young women trying to negotiate condom use.[165] In cultures where polygamy

72 AIDS and Business

is prevalent, as it is in Uganda, condom use may be low due to the competition among wives to have the most children. The number of children each wife has determines the size of her family property allotment. During the 1980s, just over one-third of married Ugandan women reported that their husbands had other wives. In addition, more than half Ugandan women during the same period reported a desire for more than six children, conditions that did not bode well for condom promotion.[166] Such aspirations are likely to be common in other countries where polygamy is practiced.

Another practice that may increase vulnerability to contracting HIV in sub-Saharan Africa is women's use of bleach and other means to dry out the vagina's natural secretions, due to the perception that these natural secretions indicate infidelity. The drying process causes inflammations that are receptive to HIV and removes the lactobacilli that protect against sexually transmitted diseases.

The economic status of women in most low- and middle-income countries in southern Africa tends to be legally and culturally tied to that of men in their family. One practice that illustrates this dependence is "sexual cleansing," where a woman whose husband has died must have intercourse with a man in the community to be "cleansed" of the evil forces that caused her husband's death.[167] More frequently, however, when a man dies of AIDS, his wife or wives may lose their access to credit, and often the rights to their house, land, and livestock. The subsequent increase in food insecurity may force the children to migrate to overcrowded urban centers to look for work, or exchange sex for food. The climate of social disintegration in millions of families creates conditions propitious to the spread of AIDS. Such vulnerability caused by poverty and dependence of women upon men makes clear the link between culture, poverty, and AIDS.[168]

In contrast to the culturally based analysis outlined earlier, some have argued that the spread of HIV cannot be explained by cultural phenomena (Gausset, 2000). Rather, according to this argument, the problems underlying the HIV transmission are universal and "what is common across cultures is more important to AIDS prevention than what is different, even if it is still important to adapt our message to the local cultures" (p. 16). Gausset takes his argument further: the main cultural problem at stake was not African: it was the "prejudice" of Western HIV/AIDS prevention programs. His view was that "exotic" African beliefs and sexual practices like dry sex, female genital mutilation, wife inheritance, polygamy, and so on are not inherently risky in terms of HIV transmission and should therefore not be targeted for eradication by Western HIV/AIDS campaigns. Rather, these beliefs and practices are functional in the creation and maintenance of identity, and should thus be protected but made safer.

In African countries such as the Congo or Rwanda, where war-related rape has spread HIV/AIDS, economic insecurity forces women and children into sex work. In such countries the demobilized soldiers may take the disease home to their families far from the conflict zone, and children and

Addressing a Global Cause in Local Contexts 73

orphans of these situations are likely to remain poor, perpetuating the risk factors for contracting and spreading AIDS.[169]

UNITED STATES AND OTHER AFFLUENT COUNTRIES

In the United States, as in other rich countries, medical interpretation of the disease has become one of chronic illness,[170] in contrast to representations of a deadly epidemic common in the 1980s. This is mainly due to the perception that drug regimens and antiretroviral cocktails prolong life to the degree that living with AIDS is considered to be "manageable" for many. Some commentators have implied that certain groups of people with AIDS may have a well-defined "lifestyle," particularly in big cities with sizable gay communities. Several publications are expressions of this lifestyle, of which a prominent example is POZ (short for "HIV-positive"; on the Web at www.poz.com).[171] Until the official recognition of HIV/AIDS by the Reagan administration in the 1980s, the gay press was primarily supported by advertisements for "poppers," amyl nitrate in capsules, intended to be inhaled for its muscle-relaxant and euphoric properties.[172] Since then, however, advertising in gay publications has become devoted to AIDS, with condoms, drugs, and a myriad of disease-support items and services (books, dietary supplements, bereavement counselors, and so on) taking up most of the advertising space in the major publications. Yet, substance abuse— whether methamphetamines (also known as "crystal meth"), alcohol, or other drugs—was still an independent risk factor for contracting HIV.[173]

In 2008 there was concern that HIV was again on the rise, particularly among young gay men. Between 2001 and 2006, HIV infection among young gay New Yorkers rose by 32 percent.[174] Reports of new diagnoses among young men aged thirteen to nineteen doubled during that time. Similarly, in Australia, a sexual behavior survey started in 1996 mapped a continued trend towards more unprotected sex among homosexuals, and increasingly negative attitudes towards condoms.[175] This may be partially explained by official government policies, and explained by Altman (2006):

> While epidemiological figures support the argument that HIV is largely spread through heterosexual intercourse, and that young women are increasingly vulnerable in many parts of the world, this is only one part of the overall pattern. The constant stress on HIV/AIDS as a disease of women and children allows governments to pass over realities they find less acceptable: injecting drug use, commercial sex and homosexuality. In a sense we have gone full circle: when the epidemic first emerged in western countries in the 1980s there was concern that depicting it as 'a gay disease' would both foster homophobia and obscure other forms of transmission. Today the emphasis on heterosexual spread means that those most likely to be ignored in prevention programmes are men who

74   AIDS and Business

> have sex with men, who are often not mentioned at all in official pro-
> grammes and policies. (p. 261)[176]

In the United States and other high-income countries, there is popular cur-
rency in a "post-AIDS" epoch. A number of scientists from otherwise repu-
table institutions have claimed that HIV does not exist. They commonly
claim that AIDS describes conditions brought on by a multitude of factors.[177]
Factors cited to support such arguments include drug use, particularly those
associated with urban gay communities such as methamphetamines; malnutrition in poorer countries; and even AIDS medications themselves.[178] In
8the United States, researchers found that blacks and Latinos, particularly
females, were likely to have conspiracy theories about the origin of HIV.
Some of these theories were "genocidal" in nature, and reduced their likelihood to use condoms or take other protective measures.[179] Some point out
that black Americans have tended to distrust the U.S. government, due to
historical factors such as the Tuskegee Syphilis Study (1932–1972), where
scientists left black subjects untreated in a longitudinal study.[180]

Some allege that, rather than negating the existence of HIV/AIDS, a
small gay subculture embraces it by organizing their sexual behavior
around their desire to risk contracting HIV.[181] Websites, chat rooms, private
parties, and e-mail mailing lists dedicated to unprotected sex ("barebacking") have emerged, some of which extol the virtues of intentional infection
with AIDS.[182] This phenomenon may be viewed as males indulging in risky
behavior, similar to extreme sports or gambling, and as a backlash against
"paternalistic" bombardment with safe-sex messages. Unsafe sex practices
are more likely among younger men who are unlikely to have experienced
the illness and death of friends with AIDS in the 1980s.[183] There is a new
element also: the growing use of methamphetamines, which are directly
linked to HIV risk—and may be linked to double the risk—because of the
physiological changes that take place in the drug user, and because of the
reduction of "safer sex" inhibitions that it causes.[184]

Such behavior should also be viewed in the light of a certain acceptance
of HIV/AIDS in media discourse and a different social environment. For
instance, big pharmaceutical companies have come under fire for unbal-
anced antiretroviral advertising when they portray sexy male models sail-
ing, climbing mountains, and throwing javelins. In the context of a society
where many people take a large number of medications for the smallest to
the biggest ailment and another load of pills as diet supplements, the need
to follow a complex drug regimen for HIV/AIDS perhaps did not seem
to be too unusual.[185] While some argue that "the face of AIDS" should
be healthy-looking in order to give hope to people with the disease and
to reduce stigma from the general public, others claim that the advertisements amount to a glamorization of AIDS. Giving AIDS a tinge of glamour
could encourage young people to believe that they have nothing to fear
from unsafe sex practices—a suggestion corroborated by the San Francisco
Public Health Department study on the topic.[186]

Despite some highly visible AIDS awareness campaigns, about 50 percent of Americans believe that AIDS may be spread by sharing a glass, and almost half believe that a cough or sneeze could transmit the virus (significantly more than a decade earlier). About one-third would not buy from a supermarket owned by an AIDS patient. Up from a decade earlier, 25 percent of Americans believe that those with AIDS got what they deserved.[187]

Thailand

In Thailand, a government committed to stemming the tide of AIDS actually changed social norms about sex. The Thai response to AIDS is considered to be one of the few successful interventions in the history of the epidemic.[188] Until the onset of the AIDS epidemic, Thai men visited commercial sex workers with the apparent understanding of their wives. Sexual initiation of young men by prostitutes was often encouraged and paid for by older men. Although Buddhism considers male sexual desire to be unsound or even a sin, Thai Buddhists believe that overcoming sexual temptation is singularly difficult for men. Hence, male sexual expression was given a relatively free rein in Thai society until the government anti-AIDS campaigns in the early 1990s.[189] For more on Buddhism and AIDS, visit: www.buddhanet.net.

In the early 1990s, AIDS was the number one cause of death in Thailand, with 31 percent of sex workers infected (with infection rates as high as 44 percent in the northern Chiang Mai Province) and 4 percent HIV-positive army recruits in 1993. The government considered the epidemic a threat to the national security of Thailand. The government's response was suitably serious. The prime minister led a multisectoral attack on risky sexual behaviors, comprised of a massive education campaign through the media, NGOs, and government and a campaign for 100 percent condom use in commercial sex transactions.[190] The campaign was very successful in many regards over its first decade, the most significant perhaps being the modification of behavior due to the government's intervention in changing social norms. In a few years, visits to commercial sex workers were reduced by half, infection among army conscripts was reduced by half, condom use was increased, and sexually transmitted diseases were dramatically reduced. Substantially fewer new AIDS infections were reported.[191] HIV/AIDS prevalence among sex workers fell from 28.2 percent in 1996 to 12.27 percent in 2002.[192] Relatively new sexual norms in Thailand include the view of brothel patrons as "bad" or "dangerous," particularly if they are married; women no longer tolerate the practice by their husbands. A prominent Thai researcher characterized the rapid behavior change as "phenomenal."[193]

Certain elements of the Thai response to AIDS are considered to have contributed to the success in Thailand. The government's leadership on the issue and visible commitment of politicians, starting with the prime minister, was vital and was probably facilitated by the unelected nature of Anand Panyarachun's provisional government. Well-established epidemiological systems were

76 AIDS and Business

vital in raising and maintaining awareness. The public sector created partnerships with NGOs to promote respect for human rights and nondiscrimination. Programs were initiated, ranging from the local level through to national levels, including scholarships for disadvantaged girls to complete their schooling. Broadcast media were mandated to provide one minute per hour of AIDS-related information. On a cultural level, the World Bank report credits Thai culture with the success of AIDS initiatives. The report cites the strong institutions and traditions of Thailand, a robust civil society, the country's tradition of basing policy decisions on evidence, a strong tradition of volunteerism, and institutional factors such as a preexisting network of NGOs and sexual health and family planning organizations. Table 2.4 summarizes the factors commonly cited as vital to the success of Thailand's HIV/AIDS programs.

The power of the HIV/AIDS program became apparent when its funding was reduced, following an economic crisis in the mid-1990s and complacency driven by earlier successes that seemed to have set in.[194] The number of infections rose among the general population, including mother-to-child transmission, as well as among high-risk populations.[195] A representative sample of young men believed that one may contract AIDS from a sex worker, but not from one's girlfriend who is not in a risk group.[196] Intravenous drug users and non-Thai-speaking tribespeople disproportionately fall victim to HIV/AIDS.[197]

Uganda

"Only a thin piece of rubber stands between us and the death of a continent," stated Janet Museveni, first lady of Uganda, at an AIDS meeting in 2002, but she went on to say that mixing family values and religion with AIDS education was crucial to slowing the spread of the disease.[198] During the 1990s, Uganda mapped a significant decline in adult HIV/AIDS rates: in 1992, prevalence of the disease exceeded 30 percent in some cities, and declined to 5 percent overall in 2001, although these figures are disputed by Allen and Heald (2004) and others.

In 1986, President Yoweri Museveni was the first African leader to openly discuss AIDS, thereby lifting the pall of silence from his country.[199] As in Thailand, where an unelected leader was able to speak out freely

Table 2.4 Critical Factors in the Success of Thailand's Response to AIDS

Government/infrastructure factors	*Cultural factors*
Visible commitment, leadership by politicians	Strong traditions and institutions
Effective epidemiological systems	Strong civil society
Partnership with NGOs	Solid policy decisions
Local/national programs	Volunteerism tradition

Source: Adapted from World Bank, Thailand. (2000) Thailand response to AIDS success and confronting the future. *Thailand Social Monitor*, November 3, 2000.

Addressing a Global Cause in Local Contexts 77

against the disease, Museveni could take leadership on AIDS unimpeded by the fetters of a fully functional democracy.[200]

Uganda is made up of many ethnic, religious, and tribal groups, with some ongoing serious conflicts at home and across its borders. These factors complicate the process of crafting and delivering an effective, culturally tailored message. In one effort made to address the diversity of perspectives, the Ugandan Islamic Medical Association designed a training program whereby Muslim religious leaders, the imams, delivered AIDS protection training from their mosques.[201] Imams and their assistants were provided with bicycles in order to give them the mobility to visit people in their homes. In 1989, the mufti (leader of the Uganda Muslim Supreme Council) declared a "Jihad" on HIV/AIDS—a holy struggle of sorts—for the 20 percent of Uganda's population that was Muslim. The spiritual leaders at the local level, the imams, received training from the Uganda Medical Association and used their social status and HIV knowledge to motivate people at the grassroots level.[202] Islamic scholars say that the Uganda experience is one that proves the power of faith-based education programs. The Ugandan AIDS program also took traditional healers into account, giving them HIV/AIDS training and allowing them to act as educators in the communities that respect them. Factors in the Ugandan response to the epidemic are summarized in Table 2.5.

USAID spins a moralistic slant in its report that AIDS education programs will only work, as in Uganda, if they encourage a Judeo-Christian

Table 2.5 Factors Often Cited in the Success of Uganda's Response to AIDS

Government/infrastructure factors	Social and cultural elements of Uganda's programs
Innovative programs of prevention, diagnosis, and treatment; one of the first voluntary, same-day testing programs and counseling regardless of the result	A highly visible, demonstrated commitment to social mobilization led by President Yoweri Museveni, Janet Museveni, and other political and celebrity figures such as later signer Philly Lutaaya[203]
Multisectoral, decentralized initiatives, with strong leadership by the president	Open and effective communication was a stated goal from the outset
Condom social marketing as an important, but not a central, element of campaigns.[204] A controversial element, often raised today, is considered by some as a success factor: deliberate limiting of condom supplies	Education initiatives channeled through tribal, ethnic, and religious organizations, including traditional healers[205]
Community based, culturally adapted, and simple safer sex messages such as "zero grazing" encouraged people to be faithful to their sex partner[206]	Attempts to reduce stigmatization of people with HIV and AIDS

Primary source: U.S. Agency for International Development (2003). *Country Profile HIV/ AIDS: Uganda*. USAID Bureau for Global Health, June, 2003.[207]

78 *AIDS and Business*

Box 2.6   A View from the Field:

WHO's Ted Karpf on the "Ugandan Miracle"

The "Ugandan Miracle" as it was once called appears to have been the result of the will of the political leadership. And the fact is, and we keep avoiding this fact, that in a country immediately following a civil war which had already decimated the civilian population in Uganda, there was an effective multi-sectoral, multi-national multilateral approach, using vast amounts of resources. It was in the government's interest, clearly, to declare a national emergency. It forced a high level of collaboration and also, because so much happened so fast, you had a lot of entities putting a lot of things in there all at the same time. No one really knows what strategy worked best or why because everybody was doing something. The other thing that happened, though, is that workforce had been decimated by this thing. They lost up to 19 per cent of the population between 1986 and 1993. In seven years, the country shrunk and all that was left were grandmothers and infants, small children who today are becoming sexually active. And guess what's happening now? HIV is once again increasing in Uganda!

The shift away from condom social marketing in Uganda is not that simple. The government is refocusing its efforts. People are AIDS-exhausted and denial is always a part of this thing. It's not just condoms which are not being discussed as I said earlier. A variety of interventions are being abandoned or dismissed for now. There was a time when you could drive from Entebbe to Kampala and see billboards for condoms and AIDS all along that road. Today you can drive on that road and see nothing, not even a Red Ribbon.

In order to find out what people are thinking, when I was last there I asked the taxi drivers where I can have sex, and, what about AIDS? "Well, it's gone", said the taxi driver. Then I asked, "What about condoms?", "You don't need them", said the taxi driver. I find this upsetting in as much as we can see that real penetration of critical or core messages have failed to reach the target. And, the President, with his abstinence policy, is only speaking to a small audience. Let's be fair about that. Abstinence really does work: you can't get a virus if you're abstinent! It's just that not everybody practices it. Always. And often.

And that's a different issue. What broke down in Uganda is the multi-sectoral and multi-focal strategy. Where everybody had a stake in this outcome and was highly motivated, there was a significant opportunity to reach everyone with any of a variety of messages. Part of the challenge with HIV, if you think about it in the history of diseases, is that we're asking people to stay in a state of constant awareness and readiness for two or more decades, and people get tired. So it seems pretty clear that you have to come up with new social marketing and new ideas. This is where business can make a huge difference. For example from the marketing world of business. Have you ever wondered how makers of peach preserves sell these products year in year out? You have to come up with a new gimmick every now and then.

Source: Ted Karpf, director of partnerships, WHO HIV Department, WHO, Geneva, Switzerland (2005, 27 June). Personal interview.

model of sexual restraint including no pre- or extramarital sex. According to USAID, the most important factor in reducing AIDS prevalence in Uganda was the "social revolution" that resulted in significant partner reduction (fidelity) and later age of first sex. One important element in this "revolution" was new programs aimed at empowering women and girls.[208] In her groundbreaking study, Oster (2007)[209] used Uganda as a case study to test her thesis that HIV/AIDS increases with cross-border trade, because of increased numbers of economic migrants, transport workers, and other travelers. Her findings were that, as cross-border trade decreased—namely, in the form of coffee—HIV/AIDS rates decreased correspondingly. Viewed in that light, Uganda's track record may be viewed as rigged by an exogenous event, and not by effective prevention programs.

Following the gains made in the 1990s to slow the spread of HIV/AIDS, in recent years, indicators point at least to a stabilization (no improvement) at least and a renewed rise at most. AIDS still is the leading cause of death in Uganda, and one million people currently live with AIDS in the country. In 2005 Ugandan women reported higher numbers of sex partners than in past years[210] and there were higher reported rates in some rural areas. Increasing numbers of rural men reported having more than two casual sex partners within the past month.[211] Government health official and designer of early AIDS communications programs Sam Okware believes that the original fear-based messages have been diluted in efforts to conform to international guidelines—and rendered ineffective.[212] A prominent Ugandan HIV/AIDS activist, Beatrice Were, places the blame for a newly nascent epidemic mainly with the "abstinence until marriage" approach increasingly advocated by U.S.-backed programs to the detriment of condom promotion.[213] This ideological model has, according to some, resulted in a shift away from the social marketing, education, and provision of condoms to a new model centered on abstinence. For this reason, critics contended in 2006, there was a shortage of condoms in Uganda.[214]

QUESTIONS FOR DISCUSSION

1. One may wonder why it seems to be more difficult for governments as well as international organizations (governmental and nongovernmental) to change people's behavior in certain cultures than in others. Is cultural resistance (or cultural facilitation) the key issue in the fight against HIV/AIDS?
2. Why such differences in the efficiency of country HIV/AIDS policies? Compare successful countries to unsuccessful countries in the fight against HIV/AIDS and selling this cause to their citizens. What are the main obstacles in such a social marketing strategy? What were the key success factors for countries that reached significant outcomes?

80   *AIDS and Business*

3. What are (could be?) the objectives of social marketing campaigns in regards to HIV/AIDS?
4. Is the fight against HIV/AIDS primarily a market or a nonmarket issue? Is HIV/AIDS a matter to be left to the free market by letting manufacturers sell commodities (condoms, antiretroviral drugs, and so on) to responsible and informed consumers? Or is it mainly a nonmarket issue where governments and not-for-profit organizations should play the leading role? What are the advantages and disadvantages of each solution?

Additional Film Materials Relevant to the Topic

Brazil: Winning against AIDS (2002). Filmed in Brazil. A documentary set in Brazil highlighting the government and NGO action on treatment and prevention. Available at: http://www.bullfrogfilms.com/catalog/clbraz.html.

Cidade de Deus (2002). Brazilian drama by Fernando Meirelles about growing up in a favela (slum), eloquently demonstrating the preoccupations that may be perceived as more important than HIV prevention.

Dispatches: Living with AIDS (2005). Filmed in Zambia. A documentary by Sorious Samura, who films his work as a nurse in a hospital where most patients have AIDS. Available at: http://www.insightnewstv.com/store/.

Paying the price (2002). Filmed in Uganda. A documentary film about HIV/AIDS epidemic in Uganda, and the price-related difficulties of providing treatment to those living with HIV. Available at: http://www.bullfrogfilms.com/catalog/clpay.html.

Tsotsi (2006). Psychological drama set in Soweto, a South African township. Like *Cidade de Deus*, the film depicts the fight for survival that may make long-term threats like HIV/AIDS seems insignificant.

3 Mexicom Designs a National Public Health HIV/AIDS Campaign

It was late when Pilar Quiñones returned to her office after a meeting with the communications director of the Centro Nacional Para la Prevención y Control de VIH/SIDA (CENSIDA), the Mexican Health Ministry's official HIV/AIDS organization. *Muy difícil*, she thought, looking at the mass of paperwork on her desk. UNAIDS reports and campaigns, Pan American Health Organization charts, internal CENSIDA statistics, and scientific journal clippings occupied the space normally taken by glowing product reviews, color-coded consumer research reports, and shiny product samples.

Quiñones, vice president of Mexicom, a large Mexican advertising agency, had just agreed to design a national HIV/AIDS awareness campaign. At first, she had resisted the idea, arguing that the government should design its own AIDS programs because an advertising agency does not have the specialized public health knowledge that is needed. Dr. Perez-Bustamante of CENSIDA eventually persuaded her by saying that many governments that had successful communications campaigns on HIV/AIDS used advertising agencies. After all, was not a leading advertising agency working with the Global Coalition Against AIDS?

AIDS IN MEXICO[1]

As Quiñones worked on the project over the next few days, her interest deepened. She personally had never known anyone with HIV/AIDS. However, she had heard of friends of friends with the syndrome and had read about several high-profile cases in the media. Mexico's HIV/AIDS prevalence rate among adults was relatively low at 0.3 percent in 2006, the same as Canada's and much less than neighboring Guatemala (1 percent), Belize (2.5 percent), and the United States (0.6 percent).[2] Despite this low infection rate, Mexico was third highest in the Americas after the United States and Brazil.[3] HIV/AIDS cases were estimated at about 180,000 in 2005, being the sixteenth leading cause of death in Mexico and fourth leading cause of death among young men.[4] UNAIDS (2006) reported that the epidemic is concentrated among men having sex with men, sex workers and clients, and injecting-drug users.[5] Among MSM, the HIV prevalence rate has been estimated at 15 percent and among drug users at 6 percent.[6] Policy documents commonly referred to *machismo* as being a factor in male sexual risk taking, putting themselves

82   *AIDS and Business*

and their female partners at risk. Yet, there was an openly gay, HIV positive director at CENSIDA nowadays. The very poor, of which nine million were children living in absolute poverty, were unlikely to have access to information, testing, or antiretroviral treatment for the disease.[7] Infection rates were not stabilizing and more worrying, the raw data on infections were probably underrepresenting reality, reflecting a mobile population, highly dissuasive stigma, corruption, and an inefficient health recording system.

Why was the vast majority of drug-related AIDS cases in Veracruz and in the northern state of Baja California,[8] close to the U.S. border? How could Tijuana, also next to the border, have an HIV infection rate three times more than the Mexican average?[9] Why were women taking up more and more of the AIDS burden? Why were homosexuals again starting to practice unsafe sex like they were in the United States? Quiñones jotted down a list of "barriers" to communication that appeared to be quite significant in Mexico, presented in Table 3.1.

Since stigma is such an important factor in AI DS prevention and treatment, what would be the best way to reduce it? Quiñones sat back in her steel-framed chair, pondering the realization that her campaign should create social norms for less risky behaviors as well as less stigma. To reduce stigma

Table 3.1   Informal Notes on Barriers to HIV/AIDS Social Marketing in Mexico

Language: campaign in Spanish and some major native languages, such as Mayan or Nahuatl? There are 62 indigenous languages and many varieties of these. Indigenous peoples make up 13 percent of Mexicans, living primarily in the following states (in ranked order): Yucatán, Oaxaca, Quintana Roo, Chiapas and others.[10] Just over the border to the south, in Guatemala, Mayan-speaking indigenous peoples were disproportionately affected by HIV—in addition to other major health problems. HIV prevalence may not be correctly diagnosed or reported, to make matters worse. HIV/AIDS has tended to establish itself among the dispossessed, the poor, and marginalized groups in other countries.

Literacy: Although Mexico has relatively high levels of literacy of 97 per cent,[11] there are some areas and demographic groups with lower literacy levels. We need a message that sounds powerful when said on radio/tv, looks powerful when represented in image form, and can be expressed simply. Health literacy is another issue.

Religion (primarily Catholic): the Pope has frequently condemned the use of condoms, and former First Lady Marta Sahagun Fox was publicly attacked by bishops for exhorting Mexicans to use condoms (their stated view was that condom use was an invitation to depravity).[12]

Demographic: massive undocumented flows of migrants (how to reach them?)
-From south to north, some in transit from Central America en route to the US.
-Mexicans leaving for temporary, usually agricultural, work in the US or manufacturing work on the northern border.
-Jobless or dispossessed farmers leaving the countryside to go to cities.
-Migrants returning from the US, usually to homes in rural areas.

Cultural: male value of *machismo* whereby men should be seen as invincible, not sick, and not seeking help; also, the idea that to be homosexual is not to be a "real" man[13] (how can we break through that?).

Mexicom Designs a National Public Health HIV/AIDS Campaign   83

in a Catholic country where homosexuality is widely considered to be a sin was not going to be easy. It had been tried, when a director of CENSIDA launched an antihomophobia campaign that ignited many controversies. Aren't all advertising campaigns like that, though, to create or encourage a social norm for product adoption and evaluation behaviors? she mused. To get people to value a particular brand is not so different from getting people to value safer sex practices. So, what is the need here? In any case, other countries had implemented antistigma campaigns, such as Brazil.

The policymakers at the Ministry of Health VIH/SIDA office had simply said that Mexicom's mandate was to raise awareness about HIV prevention nationally and reduce new infections. She would need to quantify those goals in order to measure the success of the campaign later on. She started making another list, influenced by her discussions with HIV/AIDS experts earlier, to be discussed later with the research department and the creative people within the agency. The list of "needs" that should be satisfied by the country's HIV/AIDS program is represented in Table 3.2.

Quiñones wondered whether to differentiate the campaign geographically to reflect the large cultural differences between the northern states, the central cities, and the south. On the other hand, it would be important to mirror the large differences in the urban and rural attitudes and access to testing, information, and treatment. There were also specific groups with shared values and behaviors in different geographic areas, such as MSM. In

Table 3.2   Possible Needs Identified for HIV/AIDS Infections Reduction Campaign

Simply to reopen public dialogue about HIV/AIDS: A study in Peru (a country with some cultural similarities to Mexico) found that teachers and parents needed help to bring sexual issues out into the open. Doctors at CENSIDA said that many rural Mexicans have never heard of the disease, partly because it is so difficult to openly talk about sex.

Reduce stigma: There is anecdotal evidence that stigma is so strong in rural Mexican contexts that people refuse to be tested, and do not even tell their spouses if they suspect they have the disease for fear of reprisals by neighbors on their entire family.

Get Tested: Pregnant women who visit clinics are tested, and in the private sector there are cases of employers who force their employees to be tested for HIV. Many young people believe that HIV/AIDS only happens to prostitutes, sexually promiscuous people, and homosexuals and, for this reason, are unlikely to request an HIV test. Another reason that people may avoid testing is that there is little publicly known about treatment options available even for low-income patients. Yet, Mexico was commended by UNAIDS for having made progress in providing antiretroviral drugs to those who needed them.[14] As long as resource-poor people think their likelihood of receiving treatment is low, they will assume that testing is a useless exercise.

Behavior Change Communication (BCC): Encourage men to use condoms. Condom use is dangerously low for a number of reasons but one being related to the strong value of risk taking and invincibility associated with masculinity.[15] In one study, only 9 percent of Mexican men with sex partners outside marriage used condoms at the last intercourse.[16]

84 AIDS and Business

fact, the agency might have specialized research done in the past on MSM because affluent urban gay communities had often been targeted by the ad agency in the past. Some advertising agency clients viewed them as a small but lucrative market for travel and luxury goods. She opened a new page on her laptop to list the ever-growing questions posed by this HIV/AIDS campaign, one of the major ones being who are we trying to reach? Potential targeted audiences are identified in Table 3.3.

Table 3.3   Potential Target Audiences Identified in Informal Study

Residents of the big cities? Mexico City accounted for most of reported HIV/AIDS cases in 2007; other big cities had a smaller but still significant share. Urban residents tended to be affected by advertising "clutter," with omnipresent billboards, jingles on the radio, and many ads on television. Now that advertising-rich environment was copied on the Internet. The agency would need to find a message format that would get people's attention through humor, sophistication, or controversy that would inspire lots of publicity: "guerrilla marketing" might be the key because it includes all these. Ideally, an event should be designed to raise the profile of the ad campaign launch.

Men having sex with men? A recent study made clear that men having sex with men (MSM) were 109 times more likely than the general population to have HIV.[17] Because of their large social networks, MSM might be good candidates for viral marketing, whereby they "pass on" messages to each other using Web messaging, e-mail, SMS, or MMS.

Rural populations? HIV spreads much faster in rural areas than in cities,[18] yet there is less awareness, testing, and information about the disease, and more stigma related to it in the countryside. In rural areas, women comprise 21.3 percent of those with HIV/AIDS, while in cities the percentage is closer to 14 percent.[19] Rural populations may require a more conservative format for the message.

Age segments? A particularly vulnerable group was street children, who are estimated at two million by the Mexican government.[20] Some are likely to be exploited for commercial sex and pornography, and therefore at risk for HIV in addition to other sexually transmitted diseases.[21] According to Casa Alianza, street children's NGO, children in areas close to the U.S. border were most at risk for sexual exploitation. About 90 percent of such children are addicted to glue and solvents,[22] and also suffer from a low literacy level. Child sex tourists increasingly seek out children on trips to Mexico (U.S. Department of Justice, 2007).[23]

Gender segments? Women comprised one-sixth of AIDS cases, whereas in the 1980s, they comprised one-twentieth. In some southern states (with high concentrations of indigenous peoples), heterosexual transmission is the predominant mode, implying that women are increasingly victims of the disease.[24]

Migrants? Mexico is a major crossing point for migrants in transit from neighboring countries with higher rates of the disease. An estimated 30 percent of all HIV/AIDS cases in Mexico are people who contracted the virus while in the United States.[25] Epidemiologists point to the migrant loneliness and seeking of comfort in sex; poverty leading to "survival sex"; vulnerability of migrant women to rape, among other factors. Migrants often return to rural areas where there are little or no HIV/AIDS public health communications.[26]

Intravenous drug users? These make up a relatively small portion of HIV/AIDS cases. If targeted, one geographic factor to be accounted for was that the vast majority were in states bordering the United States.

Mexicom Designs a National Public Health HIV/AIDS Campaign 85

Table 3.4 Noninclusive Survey of Communications Ideas Implemented in Other Countries

Country/organization	Communications idea
European Commission	*AIDS: Remember me?* Public awareness campaign culminating in an awards-style show featuring HIV/AIDS awareness commercials where anyone can vote online or via SMS for the best. See http://www.aids-remember-me.eu/.
UNICEF, UNAIDS 2003–2006	*Unite for Children. Unite Against AIDS* campaign with the then-secretary general of the United Nations, Kofi Annan. Spike Lee, Alyssa Milano and a number of global celebrities were seen during the campaign's film festivals, photo exhibitions, workshops, and televised events. See: http://www.uniteforchildren.org/.
Several African countries	*ABC: Abstain, Be faithful, Condomise*: Simple reminder (billboard) *Graze close to home* with cattle image: nonoffensive allegory (billboard).
United States	Sharon Stone is a vocal, high-publicity campaigner for Amfar (American Foundation for AIDS Research). She is a spokesperson, fundraiser, and awareness-raiser, notably at big international meetings like the G8.[27] PSI's YouthAIDS[28] public service awareness announcements and documentaries on U.S. channel VH1 featuring India.Arie, Adrien Brody, Ashley Judd, Avril Lavigne, and other celebrities; high-profile galas, and campaigns like *kick me!* and *Fashion against AIDS.* Jamie Foxx and Queen Latifah joined the National Basketball Association (NBA) to promote HIV testing. This was made possible by a partnership between the two stars, the NBA, HBO, the Global Business Coalition, and the Kaiser Family Foundation, thereby securing the campaign with multiple publicity outlets.
Various countries	Famous football players play in matches co-organized with UNICEF or other similar organizations, which may be combined with awareness-raising events, distribution of information materials, and condoms. For an Indian example, see http://www.unicef.org/india/hiv_aids_3184.htm.
South Africa	*Soul City*, award-winning "soap opera" type edutainment series based on television episodes, supported by radio shows, press discussions of issues, and high quality booklets.[29] LoveLife, a more recent initiative, uses branding strategies to create an identity for a range of HIV prevention campaigns, initiatives like the LoveTrain, and events with celebrities such as cricket stars.[30]

continued

86   AIDS and Business

Table 3.4 (continued)

Country/organization	Communications idea
Brazil	Condom-use promotion: Condoms emblazoned with football team emblems; carnival-themed campaigns during carnival; *Be in the know* campaign using fashion models, among others. Significant integration of social issues and HIV awareness on TV Globo programming—a national Brazilian channel with access in most homes.
Switzerland	A billboard campaign was devised targeting migrants with provocative yet culturally sensitive HIV prevention messages in twenty-one languages most commonly spoken by migrants in Switzerland—and none in Swiss national languages! Recent campaigns included controversial billboards urging people to get tested and giving specific prevention behaviors.[31]

Her assistant knocked at the door with his results of searching for ideas in other campaigns from around the world. He tabulated his preliminary findings in Table 3.4.

Quiñones was impressed by the range of social marketing strategies implemented in other countries, and particularly by the work in the area of international organizations and advocacy groups. The World Health Organization (WHO) provided a good example of this. Using a historical perspective in the publication *Mobilizing for Healthy Behavior*, for instance, there was a comprehensive social marketing model named with its acronym: C.A.U.S.E. (celebrity, activity, unexpected event/story, symbol, event). This model was inspired by the anti-apartheid movement in South Africa, the fight for civil rights in the United States, and the struggle for independence in India.

Quiñones thought it would be useful to roll out as many elements of C.A.U.S.E. as possible, including:

- Celebrity (such as Bono against poverty)
- Activity (such as rallies or MTV-sponsored competitions like *Agente de Cambio*)
- Unexpected story/event (such as media reports on contaminated blood)
- Symbol (such as a flag, ribbon, or logo)
- Event (such as World Aids Day; International AIDS Conference)[32]

From her experience with product launches and media campaigns, Quiñones knew that more research was needed. There was no need to reinvent the wheel, as much effective work already had already been done in other

Mexicom Designs a National Public Health HIV/AIDS Campaign   87

Latin American countries. For example, the output of groundbreaking activist communicators "Calandria" in Peru included many ideas in media planning and products for social marketing of health and development programs (see www.accionensida.org.pe).

The information she needed in order to design the campaign was of three types:

1. Profiles of targeted segments of the population. The advertising agency had many such profiles; however, none that looked at sexual behavior and attitudes. Quiñones would need a clear view of who these targeted audiences are, what they believe about HIV/AIDS, and what are the themes that resonate with them that would help her get the message across.
2. Review and summary of HIV/AIDS-related behavioral change intervention research. There have been many critical analyses of AIDS behavioral change programs. Ideally, each time such a program is carried out, the results are monitored, results that could be useful to Quiñones in designing her campaign. Because much of this work is conducted by nonprofit organizations and charities, it is easily accessible and will not bite too much out of the budget. A good resource to begin with is www.comminit.com (the Communication Initiative).
3. The final type of information that would be helpful to Mexicom in designing the campaign is a survey of current and past campaigns such as education-entertainment programs produced by organizations like PCI Media (http://www.population.org) from around the world. Surely, Quiñones and her creative team could find some inspiring ideas, particularly ones that already have proved their effectiveness in other settings, such as those presented in Table 3.4.

Quiñones was aware that an isolated program would get few results. It would be imperative to partner with a highly visible organization or company. It would also be necessary to support the campaign with other marketing communications activities, such as developing a credible, targeted website that communicated more effectively than the rather drab current official website, www.salud.gob.mx/conasida/. Other marketing communications channels should be used to support the campaign, such as public relations and publicity in particular. She made a short list and handed it to her assistant to solicit ideas from other executives for cause-related marketing efforts, as detailed in Table 3.5.

In order to understand the best ways to reach the targeted audiences, Quiñones drew up a list of possible media and supporting vehicles to carry the message, and a quick note about the kind of information Mexicom needed, as portrayed in Table 3.6.

88 *AIDS and Business*

Table 3.5 Potential Partners for the HIV/AIDS Campaign

Potential partner	*Quick summary of top advantages/ disadvantages*
Mexican film industry	Less reach over certain target audiences than television, possibly more impact on public relations; many possible spokespeople, although costly.
Family Health International http://www.fhi.org	As one of the primary female reproductive health providers, it is well entrenched at local/community levels around the country.
Mexican NGOs like Casa Alianza (www.casa-alianza.org) or Aproase or Ave de Mexico	Prize-winning charity working with street children in Mexico and three other countries. Their "Luna Project" focuses on HIV and AIDS. May be useful in subcampaign targeted at street children. Aproase works with commercial sex workers primarily. These experienced organizations may imbue campaigns with more credibility than a program run by the Ministry of Health.
Vete sano, regresa sano	Go Healthy and Return Healthy. Health program targeted at migrants by the Migrant Health office at the Ministry of Health.[33]
U.S. Agency for International Development http://www.usaid.gov and other similar organizations	USAID is a highly visible, credible, and financially powerful organization. It is the largest donor on HIV and AIDS to Mexico, well known for social marketing of condoms. However, with Mexicans having such high levels of "national pride," it would be better to keep the project as local as possible.
Mexican stars	A well-known singer, Tania Libertad, has been active in promoting AIDS-related causes, notably with Frente Común in Oaxaca. A Spanish group, Mecano, was used in a Mexican HIV/AIDS-prevention campaign. These are "aging" stars, however, and if we are targeting young people we need to do more research to find out what music stars or other celebrities they would listen to and consider to be credible.
Radio stations	A multitude of radio stations, already well segmented in terms of audiences, are listened to as background noise all day by many Mexicans. May lack the attention-getting power for a long message; however, may be effective for education-entertainment (or "edutainment") formats.

continued

Mexicom Designs a National Public Health HIV/AIDS Campaign   89

Table 3.5 (continued)

Potential partner	Quick summary of top advantages/disadvantages
MTV	MTV has a well-established track record in AIDS activism,[34] to include its current cosponsorship of Staying Alive at www.staying-alive.org/es/home and other initiatives.
Mexican passions	Football (everyone but mainly males), bull-fighting (mainly older males), and *telenovelas*, soap operas or social dramas (mainly females of all ages, and some gay men). A spokesperson may be found from one of these areas, or sporting events may be used to educate the "captive audience."

For an idea of the type of vehicle Quiñones might decide to use as one part of Mexicom's HIV/AIDS campaign, go to the following sites:

Media For Development International (mainly films): http://www.mfdi.org.

Avert's collection of awareness posters: http://www.avert.org/poster-shist.htm

Center for Communication Programs (Johns Hopkins Bloomberg School of Public Health and USAID); fully fledged programs of different types: http://www.jhuccp.org/.

The Communication Initiative Network, which houses a collection of international case studies, campaigns, and reviews of these, along with communications theories and other information: http://www.comminit.com/en/hiv-aids.html.

CASE BACKGROUND

HIV/AIDS Communication and the Theories that Drive it

Cognitive Dissonance and Communication for HIV/AIDS

HIV/AIDS public health communication, like any communications campaign, should catch the attention of targeted audiences and carry a limited number of specific messages. Potential messages include the following:

- Increase awareness of the consequences of contracting HIV.
- Inform people how to reduce their exposure to HIV risks.

90   *AIDS and Business*

Table 3.6   Potential Media Channels to be Used for HIV/AIDS Awareness Programs

Media	Supporting vehicles and information type
Radio	a. Advertising spots/public service announcements. b. Programming including music/talk/interviews/*radionovela* (social dramas).
Printed media	Opinion pieces, regular features, even cartoons could be used. Need to know: readership (target audience) of newspaper, magazines, and frequency of exposure.
Internet	a. Dedicated sites for health, sexually transmitted infections, and public health through government and NGO sites, such as slick, detailed, and targeted Venezuelan site www.sidainformate.org. b. Online presence through media releases to dedicated sites and online publications for men, women, youth, men having sex with men, and so on. c. Weblogs (blogs) in youth, "gay," and women categories. Videologs (vlogs) may be an expanding category with potential (see www.staying-alive.org/vlogit). d. The possibility to advertise (using click-through banner or pop-up ads) in online versions of publications and on sites. e. Presence in online forums by paid participants. f. Presence sought after in virtual social communities (such as Facebook) and why not a dedicated campaign page or participation/listing on the Facebook "causes" page? See www.facebook.com. g. Direct marketing via e-mail, possibly with a viral component (inciting the receiver to send the message on to friends). h. Internet games: e.g., online game in Swahili targeting East African adolescents titled "what would you do?" available at: http://www.unicef.org/media/media_36371.html. Information needed: access to the Internet, frequency of use, type of use for target audiences; electronic mail (e-mail): access to and frequency of use, attitudes towards direct marketing on e-mail.
Television	a. Advertising spots/public service announcements. b. Media releases that are timely and exciting for news and talk shows. c. Edutainment/information-entertainment show on the lines of *Heartlines*, an 8-week television series from South Africa which had measurable results in prevention and reducing stigma. d. Insertion of HIV/AIDS issues and situations into *telenovelas* (social dramas), comedies, reality shows, or talk shows Locate a credible celebrity spokesperson or advocate with a good media profile and frequent TV appearances.
Mobile and fixed-line phones	a. New hotline for young people, women, or men having sex with men. b. SMS and even MMS (short and media messages) to phone users, perhaps as a game. c. Viral marketing, inspiring users to forward the message to a number of their friends.

continued

Mexicom Designs a National Public Health HIV/AIDS Campaign 91

Table 3.6 (continued)

Media	Supporting vehicles and information type
Public transport	a. Minibus: the minibus being a most common means of transport, stickers could be distributed in the vehicle or by the driver. Short message ads could be displayed inside or out, such as a hotline number. b. Similar uses could be made of buses, metro, train system, and the surrounding infrastructure, e.g., bus stations and other places frequented by migrants.
Leaflets	a. Leaflets may support television, radio, and Internet efforts and featured as online content. b. These may be distributed to students and other audiences at rallies, film festivals, concerts, and so on. c. Leaflets may be distributed through schools, labor unions, companies, and women's organizations.
Merchandise	Logo T-shirts, caps, pens, condoms, to be sold online and other designated locations, such as vending machines or retail outlets.[35]
Youth mobilization program	Music and film festivals, street theatre, street football, beach volleyball, skate parks, competitions, popular songs, online and video games, Internet sites, blogs, vlogs, viral marketing activities.

- Adopt modified attitudes, such as stigma.
- Change specific behaviors, such as the adoption of condom use or risk reduction tactics for injecting drug users.
- Incite people to seek HIV testing.

Advertising is the most prominent tool of marketing communications, although not their sole instrument. Sponsoring and public relations also play an important role in communicating messages to audiences. Originally marketing communications were a feature of market-oriented actors, mainly companies selling products or services to consumers and/or trying to promote their corporate image toward their shareholders, the financial markets, or the general public. However, marketing communications have been progressively adopted by the not-for-profit sector, including governments, public agencies, NGOs, and other noncorporate organizations, in order to promote social causes, donations, responsible behavior, and more generally private investment in public goods based on moral altruism (Jenks, 1990).

The efficiency of marketing communications, especially advertising campaigns for condoms or more generally ways to protect oneself from contracting HIV, is a business communications issue surrounding HIV/AIDS. Traditional models of communication effect (such as the AIDA model) assume a linear sequence, also known as hierarchy of effects

92 AIDS and Business

(Grover and Vriens, 2006),[36] where people with a message to send, such as an HIV/AIDS-prevention message, need to design materials that go through the following stages:

- Catch people's attention before they receive information.
- Develop an interest (a cognitive stage).
- Build a desire (for a product, a service, a solution, an affective stage).
- All this to culminate in a decision (action).

However, viewers need some involvement to be ready to process information; furthermore, they may try to unconsciously avoid information about an undesirable phenomenon, such as developing cancer because of chain-smoking. Persuasive processes for such sensitive topics generally cannot follow a linear and purely rational approach, where people would first learn, then appreciate the solution, and finally act accordingly.

One key issue of HIV/AIDS campaigns being attitude change, it is likely that a number of obstacles will impede information processing and acceptance of the message, the main one being cognitive dissonance.[37] To reduce cognitive dissonance, people have two main solutions:

1. To modify their attitudes
2. To change their behavior

Changing attitudes is much easier than behavioral adaptation (Cooper and Croyle, 1984).[38] Typical strategies for reducing cognitive dissonance by changing attitudes are denial and substitution. In this case one can find the available information within those particular clues that help maintain the legitimacy of a behavior or choice while discounting unfavorable information clues. As a consequence, we tend to search for information which is in line with our beliefs, preferences, and chosen behavior. This tendency is also known as selective exposure.

Everything that is known about mass communications and behavior change suggests that marketing communications for HIV/AIDS campaigns need to be properly designed, targeting specific audiences in terms of age, sex, socioeconomic status, and ethnicity. They should have specific and achievable communication objectives, for instance, raising awareness about specific issues. Measurement of effectiveness should be built in to any campaign, with regard to the determination of what "effectiveness" means and how to measure it. Messages should also be crafted with the understanding that cognitive dissonance may deprive them from all desired influence.

Theories and Models of Communication

"People running community programs in various countries and contexts frequently repeat the same mistakes, or have to reinvent the wheel again

Mexicom Designs a National Public Health HIV/AIDS Campaign 93

and again owing to the lack of a conceptual framework for formulating and sharing lessons and findings from previous experiences" (Campbell, p. 10).[39] One reason for making the same mistakes is that there is no body of globally accepted theories or frameworks that underpin HIV/AIDS prevention and/or awareness programs. Another reason is that the literature is vast and complex, and wracked by disagreements between theorists.

A broad range of theories and models coexists in the field of HIV/AIDS activism, communications, and relevant social-science research. The theory perspectives range from individual/psychological, such as Bandura's (1997) social cognition theory; social; cultural; morality/faith-based; to the social change model that acknowledges the social, community, psychological, structural barriers and enablers for health behaviors. There are also a number of specialized theories/ideas/opinions related to health communications and behavior, which have risen to prominence along with the realization that providing information is not enough: millions of people need to be supplied with the motivation to change their attitudes and behavior. Each theory and model has limitations, for instance, some of those commonly used in HIV/AIDS prevention programs were designed to predict health behavior, not change it. Examples of health communications models are provided and explained in Table 3.7.

The Ambiguous Effect of Fear Appeals in Communication

Still commonly used in HIV/AIDS-prevention programs are fear appeals. The literature on fear appeals[40] in communication shows that there are different models to explain how messages can influence the decision to quit a dangerous behavior, of which a selection follows.

- An inversed U-Curve Model (Janis and Mann, 1965; Janis, 1967):[41] there are arousal thresholds below and above which a prevention campaign is unsuccessful. Below a certain level of fear, people are not really concerned and no motivation for self-protection is generated by the message. Above a certain level, people develop defensive mechanisms in line with the reduction of cognitive dissonance. Consequently, efficiency is at its maximum between the two thresholds.
- The Protection Motivation Model (Rogers, 1975; Keller and Block, 1996; Floyd and Prentice-Dunn, 2000)[42] is based on the idea that people are motivated to protect themselves from danger when this motivation is properly aroused by both the seriousness (degree of gravity) and the probability of occurrence of a particular threat. A message will be all the more efficient if people are *also* given concrete solutions on how to avoid the danger.
- The Extended Parallel Processing Model is an extension of the Protection Motivation Model, which better accounts for the emotional

94 AIDS and Business

Box 3.1 A View from the Field:

How Does Brazil Keep its HIV/AIDS Message Fresh and Appealing, and Avoid "Safe-Sex Fatigue"?

The Brazilian government has specific campaigns aiming at the delivery of the message of HIV prevention to young people. Basically, the national program on HIV/AIDS works in two different areas: with children and young people who are at social risk (street children and children that work) and with children and young people who are at school.

In the first group, the government works in partnership with NGOs and at community level and has been implementing measures that include information dissemination, distribution of condoms, and the promotion of the so-called intimate visits to young people who are in internment units.

In the second group, the government action is based in the formation of the so-called multipliers through three different measures: (a) capacity building of teachers through distance learning; (b) formation of "multiplier adolescents"; and (c) capacity building of teachers and students through learning in the field.

In what is referred to as "safe-sex fatigue," each year the Brazilian society has the task to inform millions of adolescents and young people as they start to be sexually active. Brazilian society is young, and there is an urgent need to assess less provided regions and hard-to reach-populations with adequate information and means to prevent the HIV transmission (condoms, good quality prenatal care including HIV testing and prophylactic treatment for HIV-positive mothers and their children as well as the distribution of harm-reduction kits to avoid transmission through unsafe drug use). There is still no "safe sex fatigue." This might also be due to the fact that the prevention policy is not based on prescriptive behavior change models but the idea to offer the necessary supplies and information to the population to make safer sex a possible option.

Source: Information provided by Mr. Pedro Marcos de Castro Saldaña, second secretary, Permanent Mission of Brazil, Geneva, Switzerland, June 27, 2005.
Link to Brazil National Program for AIDS and sexually transmitted diseases: http://www.aids.gov.br.

---

reactions of subjects (Tanner, Hunt, and Eppright, 1991).[43] In this model, fear is a mediator of the evaluation of possible solutions to the danger. When fear emotions become too intense, the process of monitoring fear (an inner defensive mechanism) takes precedence over the rational action process to avoid danger (an action strategy that results in behavioral changes). Subjects may develop a rejection/denial of the message content in order to decrease their emotions of fear.

Mexicom Designs a National Public Health HIV/AIDS Campaign 95

Table 3.7 Characteristics of Models Commonly Used as Bases for HIV/AIDS Programs

Theory/model/framework	Description	Example (if known)
Health belief model (Rosenstock, 1974)	Attitudes, expectations, and beliefs will explain a person's likelihood of adopting a less risky behavior. The nature and relevance of the threat (susceptibility and severity) and perceived ability to avoid the threat (perceived benefits and barriers) are key concepts in the model.	Commonly used in the development of national public health programs, such as HIV/AIDS prevention. The health belief model helps researchers to understand sexual behavior, particularly to identify perceived benefits and/or barriers about which communication programs may be designed.
Theory of reasoned action and planned behavior (Fishbein & Ajzen, 1975)	A group of theories that attempt to explain behavior (assumed to be rational and controllable) by analyzing beliefs, attitudes, intentions, and behavior.	Used in the design of HIV/AIDS interventions by identifying through research which are the behavioral and normative beliefs that influence people's intentions to behave in a specific (desirable) manner.
Stages of change (also known as transtheoretical model) (Prochaska & DiClemente, 1983)	Originally developed for smoking-cessation programs, this model is comprised of five stages theorized to be necessary for behavior change. Progression from one stage to the next is facilitated by viewing a model who can demonstrate skills necessary for progression.	The use of drama, talk shows, and role playing may help people to acquire skills such as condom negotiation.
AIDS risk-reduction model	A three-stage theory based on the Health Belief Model and social cognition that was developed to recognize the specific nature of HIV/AIDS as a health threat. Individuals must recognize themselves as being at risk, commit to reducing risky behavior, and action that is appropriate.	Used in television or radio dramas.

(continued)

96   AIDS and Business

Table 3.7 (continued)

Theory/model/framework	Description	Example (if known)
Hierarchy of effects	A series of theories, commonly used in marketing, based on the assumption that consumer behavior progresses through specific stages—commonly from information through to adoption.	Typically used in campaigns structured around advertising.
Diffusion of innovations	Diffusion of innovations theory (Rogers, 1995) examines the communications processes involved in the adoption of behaviors by a population. People progress through a number of stages before they implement a new behavior. In order for a behavior to become widespread, opinion leaders should model or display it first.	The STOP AIDS program first made available to gay men in San Francisco during the 1980s.
Social marketing	The use of business marketing principles, applied to social problems.	The use of marketing "branding" principles for condoms distributed free of charge or at marginal cost.
Social cognition (to be discussed next) (Bandura, 1986)	Behavior is considered to be an outcome of perceived self-efficacy, social, and environmental factors.	Many entertainment-education programs, which meld entertaining content with deliberate educational messages using role models showing desired behaviors. Examples include *Soul City* (S. Africa), *Sexto Sentido* (Nicaragua), *Jasoos Vijay* (India).

It is important to make a clear distinction between how subjects exposed to a risk react as compared with nonexposed subjects (e.g., smokers and nonsmokers in antitobacco messages; Leventhal and Watts, 1966; Keller, 1999).[44] The defensive reaction being small or nonexistent with nonexposed subjects, motivation for protection when faced with fear-arousing messages paradoxically is stronger with nonexposed than with exposed subjects. Smoking-cessation literature has been used by communications planners to model HIV/AIDS-prevention programs.

The Role of Perceived Self-Efficacy as Driver of Behavior

Social cognitive theory has been considered particularly useful to underpin HIV/AIDS communications efforts due to its recognition of the importance of the social interaction of individuals. Because sexual behavior constitutes a part of interpersonal relationships, interpersonal efficacy will be required to change this sexual behavior[45]—quite a different proposition than simply targeting behavior change as a goal. According to Bandura (2004), only social cognitive theory offers "principles on how to inform, enable, guide, and motivate people to adapt habits that promote health and reduce those that impair it" (p.146).[46]

Perceived self-efficacy has a primary role in behavior change, particularly in the domain of health. Self-efficacy is widely perceived as crucial to behavior change, a concept gradually adapted to "collective efficacy."[47] Self-efficacy is the belief that "one can exercise control over one's health habits" (Bandura, 2004, p. 144). According to him, several determinants of health promotion and disease prevention apply, in addition to self-efficacy (2004):

- Knowledge of the health risks and benefits of health behaviors.
- Outcome expectations: perceived costs and benefits of likely outcomes.
- Health goals: health-related outcomes people set for themselves and how they plan to attain them.
- Perceived facilitators and impediments to attaining the desired changes: social and structural limitations that may prevent whole or partial success.

In relation to the aforementioned points, the modus operandi of the HIV/AIDS virus has in effect made it difficult for people around the world to learn how to avoid infection even though they may understand the epidemiology and prevention methods. It is difficult for people to evaluate their *risk* status for contracting HIV/AIDS from their partner because this knowledge is necessarily incomplete: the complete and honest revelation of both sexual partners' history of sexually transmitted diseases, drug use, and sexual partner networks is constrained by social norms and potential premeditated deception, this compounded by the fact that a partner may not be aware of the risks inherent in his/her own behavior. According to Bandura (1994), people tend to evaluate the risk of contracting HIV/AIDS by using a potential partner's physical appearance and perceived social status as guidelines. Because HIV/AIDS can be asymptomatic for a decade or more, the HIV test based on appearance is very risky and conforms blindly to stereotypes (e.g., she looks chaste and educated, therefore she probably does not have AIDS). The *outcome expectations* of practicing safer sex, (i.e., using a condom and avoiding HIV/AIDS transmission) are dependent on that wholly unreliable process.

98   *AIDS and Business*

Critics of social learning theory and other individual models of behavior change have pointed to other factors that urgently need to be considered in HIV/AIDS-prevention communications, including the often unplanned and emotional nature of sexual encounters, the use of recreational drugs and/or alcohol leading up to the sex act, sex used as a form of violence against an individual or a targeted group (as in war), and the likelihood of inequality in the power status of two or more partners. Power differences (and thus differences of negotiating power) are mainly codified in gender role definitions, but may fall equally under the roles of sex buyer versus sex seller, or the power and deference commanded in many societies by age that is often gender-determined in terms of older man–younger woman. In line with these criticisms, UNAIDS declared in 1999 that, according to the research, individual behavior change communications are likely to be ineffective. UNAIDS set out its own communications framework[48] in its report *Communications Framework for AIDS: A New Direction*. In the report, UNAIDS (1999) stated that "Seeking to influence behavior alone is insufficient if the underlying social factors that shape the behavior remain unchallenged" (p. 23).[49] Reporting on the shortcomings of approaches used at that time, UNAIDS summarized the typical inadequacies of the assumptions that underpinned communications programs:

- There is no "linear relationship" between people's knowledge, attitude, beliefs, and their actions, particularly when cultural, political, and socioeconomic differences are considered.
- People are not always in control of their own behavior, which itself may be determined by gender or cultural contexts.
- Sexual behavior is a realm where rational thinking about HIV/AIDS may be less applicable than emotions.
- Condom promotion should be part of a holistic prevention strategy, rather than an end in itself that ignores cultural and social contexts.
- Men should be targeted as much as women regarding issues such as condom use.
- Condom promotion alone may not be effective without "addressing the importance and centrality of social contexts, including government policy, socioeconomic status, culture, gender relations, and spirituality" UNAIDS, 1999, p. 26).

QUESTIONS FOR DISCUSSION

1. In order to have the biggest impact, what should be the primary target audiences of the Mexicom-designed HIV/AIDS campaign?
2. How should sensitive messages about AIDS issues be conveyed to a Mexican audience given the cultural and social characteristics of

Mexicom Designs a National Public Health HIV/AIDS Campaign 99

Mexico described in this case study? What do you propose is the best strategy: direct or indirect? Emotional or rational? Informative or persuasive? Make propositions regarding the copy strategy and media planning of the campaign.

3. Which potential partners would you approach for this campaign? Do you recommend that Quiñones use sponsoring and other forms of marketing communications? How would you design an integrated marketing communications plan?

4. Go to three of the sites listed in the "Further Resources" section following. Make note of what you think would be effective and ineffective in reaching the audiences you intend to target in Mexico.

Further Resources

Associación Tan Ux'il (Guatemala)

A partnership of New York–based PCI Media Impact with NGO Tan Ux'il located in Petén. This includes a radio show, condom distribution, and other activities targeted at adolescents. Available at: http://www.pci-mediaimpact.org/programs_latin_case_study_2.shtml.

Government of Mexico Ministry of health television spot campaigns for HIV/AIDS (in Spanish). Available at: http://portal.salud.gob.mx/contenidos/sala_prensa/sala_prensa_campanas/condon/condon.html.

Haath se Haath Milaa (Let's Join Hands)

Long-running television series, album, and video clip where "Bollywood" stars meet people who have successfully raised HIV/AIDS awareness. Available at: http://www.bbc.co.uk/worldservice/trust/whatwedo/where/asia/india/2008/03/080229_india_hiv_project_hshm.shtml.

Live With It

This is an award-winning campaign sponsored by Gilead Life Sciences and designed by Incendia Health Studios. The campaign features a series of short animated hand-drawn films that focus on the life of a person living with HIV/AIDS. Using the Live With It cartoon characters as a basis for discussion, there are message boards, information, and an HIV support online community. Available at: https://www.livewithit.com.

Mo Kexteya Project

Designed with the aim to reduce stigma and discrimination, the project features, among other activities, a photojournal—an online set of richly photographed biographies of Mexicans living with HIV/AIDS titled "De frente a la vida." Available at: http://www.policyproject.com/MoKexteya.cfm.

100 *AIDS and Business*

National HIV testing resources.

National HIV Testing Day campaigns on television, radio, and podcasts. Available at: http://www.hivtest.org/press_files/subindex.cfm?FuseAction =spotlight.psa.

Panos London: Reporting AIDS case studies

The report analyzes in depth the use of media in five southern African countries as regards HIV/AIDS. http://www.panos.org.uk/?lid=291.

4 Ross IVD
Global Marketing Issues for HIV Testing Products and Services[1]

Stefan Weiss, marketing manager at Ross IVD, just read an e-mail from Dr. Carola Chabari, a prominent scientist he had recently met in Kenya. What he read made him sit back and think cautiously about what she offered to the company. Dr Chabari, a researcher at the Kenya Medical Research Institute, had proposed a new, less costly HIV testing method. She wrote that she had not sent this information to anyone else in the in vitro diagnostic industry, although her findings were to be published in a medical journal soon.

Chabari had written in her message: "I was impressed by your CEO's speech at the WHO (World Health Organization) meeting. He seemed truly interested in a solution to develop a more affordable HIV test. It seemed to be a personal commitment of his." An innovative researcher, Chabari had discovered a way to simplify the CD4 T cell count—a means of monitoring HIV patients. She had named the procedure *Simplex*, and believed that it had the potential of making testing more widely available because it cost less than other methods and was slightly less complicated to use.

The chief executive officer of Ross IVD, Dr. Harry Knowles, had publicly stated his readiness to support global efforts to offer affordable HIV monitoring tests for developing countries. His statement to the media came after a contentious meeting at World Health Organization (WHO) headquarters in Geneva on the topic of HIV/AIDS tests pricing. "Find a way to make these lower-cost tests happen, Stef. I know if anyone can, you can," had said Knowles, slapping Weiss confidently on the shoulder before flying out to a President's Emergency Plan for AIDS Relief (PEPFAR)[2] meeting in Washington, DC.

Weiss reread a passage from the e-mail Charabi had written: "As a Kenyan, I know the situation 'on the ground'. I can vouch that from a human resources perspective *Simplex* makes sense because it renders HIV monitoring tests a bit easier. It is so difficult to recruit, train, and retain good people to run clinical laboratories. In the case of *Simplex*, the logistics, too, are simplified. I also know that until tests are more affordable and easy to carry out, governments in my part of the world won't be buying enough of them." Charabi's method used fewer of the reagents (monoclonal antibodies used to detect HIV antigens in biological samples) commonly used in European and North American tests, thereby reducing the costs.

102 *AIDS and Business*

Her method also had the benefit of being accurate even when blood samples had been collected as much as ten days earlier and treated with a fixative. For more details about tests please see Appendix B.

As Marketing Director at Ross IVD, Weiss had met with enough non-governmental organization (NGO) people from organizations like the International HIV/AIDS Alliance to know that time and money were serious clinical testing issues in the developing world. In the first place, it was hard enough to get people to agree to testing, especially in remote locations and small villages. For the few who agreed to be tested, testing staff had to rush down mountain tracks or perilous roads, often in searing heat, to get the blood sample as quickly as possible to the big city hospital. There were all kinds of anecdotes he had heard, about HIV testing program cars breaking down on the way back from a remote village in the African savannah, or sinking in mud on deserted mountain tracks in Latin America or East Asia . . . and the blood samples being carried in the driver's own bag as he walked and hitchhiked great distances to the hospital laboratory. As these kinds of stories illustrated, there was a human commitment to testing and monitoring which the country's infrastructure did not support in many regions. Then, after all that, someone would have to get the results back to the remote villager who agreed to be tested and often another confirmatory test[3] would be needed before treatment could begin. And that was a different kettle of fish. "Sometimes it must be like paddling upstream, working on location with an HIV/AIDS voluntary testing and counseling program," mused Weiss as he sat back in his orthopedic chair and ate a few pretzels.

Ross IVD is a leading supplier of HIV detection and monitoring systems located in Portland, Oregon, USA. The company's portfolio of products had the potential to service global HIV testing and monitoring needs. Ross IVD's line of HIV testing products represented 40 percent of the company's total business worth US$1 million worldwide. Ross IVD testing products for HIV included the following:

- Testing kits: a well-packaged all-in-one kit targeted at laboratories in primarily affluent settings.
- Reagents in bulk packaging: simple bottles containing multiple doses, targeted at governments, NGOs, and the WHO Bulk Procurement Scheme.
- Diagnostic instruments: sophisticated and sensitive soft- and hardware equipment that does cell counts (flow cytometers) and displays the results per test.
- After-sales service: training provided in testing technology, interpretation of results, the use of and troubleshooting for diagnostic instruments, and quality control and quality assurance programs.

Reagents used in tests were typically purchased from manufacturers in the United States, then assembled and packaged by Ross IVD. Components

Global Marketing Issues for HIV Testing Products and Services 103

of the diagnostic instruments were manufactured in low-cost sites across Southeast Asia, but the final assembly, packaging, and distribution were done at the Ross IVD plant outside Portland, Oregon, USA.

Concerned about the high cost of manufacturing in the United States, Ross IVD had explored licensing possibilities and offers in several developing countries for the reagents. However, the company had decided based on the precautionary principle not to proceed with licensing. "There are just too many unknowns . . . and who trusts them not to cut us out and start making their own? With their history on intellectual property I know I sure as hell don't!" had snorted the research and development director, when Weiss presented all the marketing opportunities that would arise from lower-cost licensing in key markets. Upon hearing that comment, Weiss thought it was typical of the divergence of opinion between marketing and R&D people. And that was not only true for Ross IVD! Long term, he was convinced that the benefits of licensing outweighed the risks—especially if Ross IVD was one of the first firms to do it. The market for testing was growing for the following reasons:

1. HIV is still spreading, and more people are contracting it than ever before.
2. People with HIV and AIDS are now living longer (those who receive the treatments), and so need HIV monitoring tests for a longer time.
3. The calls for widespread provision of antiretrovirals were being heard by organizations with a global impact like the Bill and Melinda Gates Foundation[4] and the William J. Clinton Foundation,[5] with the WHO doing its part with the "3 by 5"[6] initiative, which implied that the testing market was opening up. Where treatment becomes available, more people are willing to come forward for testing ("otherwise, who would want to hear their death sentence?" thought Weiss).
4. Global organizations, events, and personalities like the G8 Summit, the World Economic Forum, the World Social Forum, the Bush administration's PEPFAR, the World Bank, Bono, and Angelina Jolie, to name a few, are talking more often and more openly about HIV and AIDS, leading to increased awareness and increased funding for testing and treatment.
5. Private companies big and small as well as public sector employers and trade unions are committing themselves to action on HIV, and testing programs like "Know your Status" are spreading.

Plus, he reasoned, it was a lost opportunity to portray the company as having a sense of social responsibility.

As Weiss reflected on the problem, he loosened his tie. How on earth can he sell "affordable" HIV tests to developing countries and make a reasonable profit from it? After all, Ross IVD is not in the charity business:

104 *AIDS and Business*

our strongest responsibility is to our shareholders! Unlike country-tailored strategies for businesses, HIV has no borders: the marketing manager feared waking the sleeping bear of its wealthier western and northern customers. When they find out we give lower rates to so-called developing countries, they will have legitimate complaints . . . and I will likely have a crisis communications problem on my hands, puffed Weiss.

Weiss was well aware also that, like a spreading virus, international scientists have no borders: they regularly attend international conventions on HIV where they talk about the tests they use, and pricing inevitably comes into the discussion. Northern scientists will not fail to notice pricing differences. "Worse," thought Weiss, "there's a handful of HIV/AIDS activists who would jump on the occasion to publicize differential pricing to their fellow activists here in the US. HIV positive New Yorkers without medical insurance are going to whine about paying higher prices than people in Zimbabwe." Weiss could just imagine how that would pan out in the media.

As an experienced marketer, Weiss knew that he could divert attention by fine-tuning the product definition and its positioning. Even the packaging made a lot of difference, whether it was a "kit" or a "bulk" package. However, HIV is a sensitive business area. If HIV/AIDS patient activists came to know that a "more affordable" testing product existed, they would ask their clinical lab to switch to it and Ross IVD's profits on its HIV line would likely plummet. Weiss could feel the gray hairs coming through his scalp as he considered these different angles of the "affordable" testing idea. However, he took out a pen, a calculator, and a sheet of paper and began to write an offer for the WHO, to be presented to them in a meeting next month. The offer for CD4 count kits contained the following elements:

1. Simplex kit: set of two reagents, instead of the four usually used in affluent settings.
2. Quality control product for daily use.
3. Quantix instrument systems, new or used. (Quantix is a rather sophisticated instrument but a new simple and cost-effective instrument will be possibly developed for the resource-poor settings at a later stage, when *Simplex* takes off.).
4. Training, installation, and after-sales service.
5. Volume discount.
6. Simplified purchasing process.
7. Calculations of difference between the WHO offer and current market prices.

Weiss was concerned about the role that the WHO would play: they would become a sort of distributor if the details could be worked out. Weiss smiled at the irony of that. His smile faded as he considered the details to be worked out with the WHO. What would be the extent of competitors offering test kits under the bulk procurement scheme? To what degree

Global Marketing Issues for HIV Testing Products and Services   105

could governments have freedom to choose one brand over another in the scheme? Is delivery at airport like in the current procurement scheme to help us keep our costs down? How would the WHO promote Simplex and its peripheral products to WHO partners, affiliates, and organizations on the ground? How long would we be locked into this program?

BACKGROUND FOR THE CASE: THE MARKETING
OF HIV TESTS AND THE CONTEXT OF TESTING

On the occasion of World AIDS Day 2005, Richard Holbrooke,[7] president of the Global Business Coalition on HIV/AIDS, boldly stated that the world's HIV/AIDS-fighting strategy was wrong. He delivered a stinging critique of the status quo in HIV/AIDS programs. According to Holbrooke, "The number of people infected is still growing sharply."[8] Treatment is a "bottomless pit" and prevention programs "have failed most seriously."[9] He offered a range of arguments for increasing testing in addition to treatment and prevention because "the spread of the disease cannot be stopped, and we cannot offer drugs to those who need them, unless people know their status."[10]

Holbrooke had stated his belief that people who have been tested and know their status are more careful in their sexual behavior, and wider testing programs result in increased awareness, less stigma, and more people being treated. In his call for widespread testing, Holbrooke was sharply criticized by human rights and HIV/AIDS activists. His assumption that infected people would be more careful in their behavior to restrict passing on the virus to others may be flawed. Some have argued that altruistic motives do tend to sway people diagnosed with HIV, if they have been provided with effective counseling (Mechoulan, 2004).[11] However, there is uncertainty about human behavioral consequences of taking an HIV test. According to Philipson and Posner (1993) in Mechoulan (2004), some people who discover they are HIV positive are assumed to operate in selfish ways, for instance, by increasing their sexual encounters and thereby increasing the spread of HIV because they feel they have "nothing to lose." Meanwhile, a proportion of those who tested positive increase their protective measures and may balance out the effect of those with risky behaviors.[12] Analyses of MSM testing patterns showed that those who test negative may in fact increase their risky behavior, in which case HIV testing may in fact contribute to high-risk behavior in this high-risk population.[13, 14] There is a possibility that improved behavior—when it occurs—may be a response to the counseling received at the testing site; however, the true behavioral outcomes of voluntary HIV counseling and testing are as yet little understood.

Technology for HIV tests is fast improving, and the market is growing.[15] There are more than seventy tests available,[16] and new tests are being developed—particularly tests that provide rapid results and those that use saliva instead of blood or serum. Some newer so-called rapid tests require

106 *AIDS and Business*

only ten to twenty minutes to deliver results, as compared to older tests that required more than two hours.[17] This is a significant development because there are specific situations that require a rapid medical response, as in the case of a pregnant woman of undetermined HIV status who is giving birth and may be in need of antiretroviral drugs to prevent transmission to her baby. Time is also an important factor in the case of health workers exposed to blood of a patient who may have HIV, as in the case of a "needlestick" when the syringe needle used on a patient accidentally pierces the health worker's skin. The health worker may then be promptly offered postexposure prophylaxis to diminish the risk of contracting HIV by more than 80 percent.[18] The antiretroviral drug zidovudine (Retrovir) is commonly used for this purpose. Similarly, a person who has been sexually assaulted may receive protective doses of zidovudine if the HIV status of the rapist is known. Another issue is related to post-test counseling: when older tests were conducted in resource-poor settings, people who had been tested were often asked to return the next day or even several days or weeks later[19] for their results, which in effect meant that many would never return due to fear of public disclosure (acquaintances might see the HIV test candidate entering the testing site) or simply lack of accessibility where people must travel far on foot or through dangerous territory to the testing site. In the United States, an estimated 30 to 40 percent of those tested do not return for their results,[20] a figure which is likely to be higher in resource-poor regions. Other settings where rapid tests may be useful include combat settings and workplaces where there are particular risks of exposure.

Online, Home, and Self-Tests

Today tests are available for purchase over the Internet, by mail order, or at pharmacies for testing at home. A small minority of the tests are approved by a government medical regulatory agency, such as the U.S. Food and Drug Administration (FDA). There are many fraudulent offers of home HIV tests.[21] In a developed market like North America, an approved HIV testing procedure commonly includes the following steps:

1. Order is placed for testing kit and payment is made.
2. Testing kit is received by customer via an express mailing service.
3. A customer personal identification number (PIN) is activated to maintain anonymity when customer calls the testing service, and pretest counseling and further instructions may be provided.
4. Customer uses the contents of the test kit to prick finger to obtain a blood sample and apply sample to the sample test card that is marked with the customer PIN.
5. Sample test card is sent to the testing service via express mailing service.
6. Testing service conducts HIV test in a certified medical laboratory.

Global Marketing Issues for HIV Testing Products and Services   107

> **Box 4.1**   A View from the Field:
>
> *What can be Done to Encourage More People to be Tested and Who Could be More Active in this Area?*
>
> New ground has been established by governments such as Botswana, where people have to opt out of being tested, rather than waiting for voluntary testing to be sought. Since 2003, the government has initiated "routine HIV testing and counseling," which means all citizens of Botswana can expect to be offered an HIV test whenever they have contact with their health care system and offered counseling if they are found to be positive. This has dramatically increased the number of people receiving ARV treatment. Similar initiatives are under way in Zambia, Malawi, and Lesotho.
>
> A concerted effort by all stakeholders to reduce the stigma which surrounds HIV/AIDS in many countries is essential to increase uptake of testing. Information and education by national governments are of primary importance. But also employers have an important role to remove barriers and encourage testing by ensuring effective nondiscriminatory workplace policies are in place.
>
> Source: Information provided by Dr. Franz B. Humer, former chairman of the board of directors at Roche; former chairman of European Federation of Pharmaceutical Industries and Associations (EFPIA), Basel, Switzerland

7. Two or three days later, the customer calls the testing service and, using the PIN, retrieves the HIV test result. If the test is positive, post-test counseling may be provided, as well as a list of medical facilities in the customer's region.[22]

Issues related to home testing and self-testing include regulatory aspects which may be little understood by many consumers. For example, testing kit literature may boast of "approval" or "accreditation" by a number of official-sounding (but potentially nonexistent) entities. The quality of pre- and post-test counseling may be a serious issue, in particular for people who discover that they are HIV positive and may need more than a telephone call to understand the significance of the news. As stated in the WHO document on the topic of post-test counseling, "counseling is a relationship," and counselors need to be sensitive to the client's context, culture, and emotions. A number of complex features should be included in post-test counseling, including an assessment of who else will be affected by the result, a medical overview of HIV and AIDS, and prevention of transmission to others, which may include the client's baby and permanent or casual sex partners.[23] For many consumers, the main issue is their anonymity and the confidentiality of their results. This concern has legal implications, particularly

108   *AIDS and Business*

in U.S. states where disclosure of HIV status is mandatory and regions where stigma is high. People with HIV/AIDS may have a moral obligation to inform their sex and needle-sharing partners that they have the virus. However, privacy, autonomy, and safety issues have so far prevented the development of official "right-to-know" programs.[24] The confidentiality of medical records, particularly as it relates to HIV, is an issue of increasing importance in the United States, where the Centers for Disease Control (CDC) is encouraging all states to convert from code-based to name-based reporting and using the allocation of federal funds as an incentive. In early 2006, only nine states and the District of Columbia still used code-based reporting.[25] Such actions may reduce official reporting of HIV cases and increase the use of home testing.

Pricing of Tests

Because diagnostic tests are not medicines, they may not be included on essential drugs lists, which implies that the pricing of tests is still quite open, depending on the setting (for a detailed account of selection and procurement of HIV/AIDS diagnostics, see PAHO, 2005[26]). In most countries, especially in Europe and North America, the prices for tests are regulated either by governments or health insurance companies, or both. Another issue is that the public does not have a grasp of the nature and importance or HIV tests and their diagnostic and monitoring roles, while people can more easily appreciate the importance of treatment. For this reason, the pricing of HIV tests is not a media-friendly issue and thus not a big public relations issue. This is changing, however, with the increasing media coverage of statements like those of Richard Holbrooke about testing and those of Bill Clinton with regard to the Clinton Foundation activities in price negotiation on HIV tests.

In 2004, the Clinton Foundation negotiated price reductions on CD4 and viral load tests with five of the biggest test makers internationally: Beckman Coulter, Becton Dickinson & Co., Roche Diagnostics, Bayer HealthCare, and bioMerieux. Price reductions negotiated individually were 20–80 percent lower than comparable offerings. The strategy of the Clinton Foundation was to negotiate bulk prices that would be profitable long term for the diagnostics companies.[27] In 2006 the foundation announced that it had negotiated rapid HIV tests priced at 49 cents and 65 cents per test from Chembio Diagnostics, Orgenics, Qualpro Diagnostics, and Shanghai Kehua Bio-Engineering. Clinton stated that there are two factors that indicate the importance of testing. First, 90 percent of people living with HIV today are not aware of their status, and second, many initiatives, such as that of the Brazilian government to increase testing candidates up to seven million per year (up from three million), aim to increase testing.[28]

Particularities of Diagnostic Tests

HIV tests need careful management because they tend to have a short shelf life, require a cold chain, usually need skilled technicians to use them and interpret results, and all should be properly managed through an inventory management system. [29] Diagnostics companies are asked by activists to lower their price per test, develop simpler testing protocols, offer effective training to laboratory staff, provide after-sales service on the equipment, long-term price negotiation on the reagents needed for the tests, and other marketing issues. [30]

In the United States and other affluent settings, it is considered essential that patients take viral load and CD4 tests twice or more per year for monitoring purposes. This is necessary because, as described by Holmes (2001), once in the body, HIV evolution takes the form of an "arms race" (p. 239). The virus continually mutates in response to the body's immune responses to fight it. For this reason, when antiretroviral treatments are administered alone (i.e., not in combination with other antiretrovirals) the virus may become resistant to treatment within a period as short as several months. For the same reason, it is difficult to design an effective vaccine [31] and monitor whether treatment continues to be effective. Viral load tests provide the most effective means of determining whether the prescribed regimen is working, or whether resistance to medication is emerging. These tests are, in effect, the doctor's guide to treatment and to treat a patient without them would be considered irresponsible. In resource-poor settings the picture is different.

Doctors in resource-poor settings acknowledge the importance of viral load tests; however, they are concerned about the high price per test, the level of expertise needed by laboratory staff to conduct the tests, and infrastructure issues such as predictable supply of electricity needed to run the tests. [32] There are several types of HIV tests, each of which is more appropriate for certain situations. Some are better for screening purposes, while others are commonly used to monitor the progress, or lack thereof, of people with HIV. Table 4.1 provides a summary of the most common tests.

False positive and false negative results from tests are common, meaning that the test results may be interpreted as HIV positive when the person does not have HIV and vice versa. Because it is recommended by the WHO and other regulatory bodies to conduct multiple tests using different methods and/or reagents, HIV testing procedures are complex and costly. In many countries, for instance, in Europe, several tests using different products must be conducted before a person is considered to be HIV positive. Two common strategies for repeat testing include serial testing and parallel testing. In serial testing, a rapid HIV test is conducted on a series of samples, followed by another test on a second series

110 AIDS and Business

of samples that had a positive result. A third series may be necessary, particularly if results in the first and second series were not in agreement (discordant). In parallel testing, samples are tested concurrently using two different methods.[37]

A Variety of Reasons for Conducting HIV Tests, a Variety of Settings

There are a number of reasons for conducting HIV tests, each of which has a number of situational constraints. These reasons are outlined below:

1. Clinical diagnosis, requested or required by a physician. This is often the case when a person has recurrent infections, tuberculosis, or health problems commonly associated with HIV, such as Kaposi's sarcoma.
2. Testing of babies whose mothers are known to have HIV. This may change the mode of treatment for a number of ailments and allow the baby to benefit from targeted medical and social programs.
3. Prevention of mother-to-child transmission (PMTCT); when a woman of unknown serostatus is pregnant or in labor, it is beneficial for medical staff to know her HIV status so preventative measures can be applied to protect the baby.
4. Screening of donated blood to prevent HIV transmission through blood products, for example, transfusions, blood banks.
5. Voluntary counseling and testing (VCT) programs commonly target populations considered to be at risk for HIV.
6. Sentinel surveillance is the screening of certain at-risk populations or pregnant women at maternity clinics.[38]
7. Monitoring of HIV-positive people currently taking antiretroviral drugs is necessary to determine the effectiveness of the drug regimen in keeping down the viral load (the number of virus copies in the blood), as well as the person's adherence to or tolerance of a drug regimen.

Issues relating to these different situations include time, in the case of prevention of mother-to-child transmission for a pregnant woman in labor, and whether a return appointment is necessary to find out one's results. A serious issue in voluntary counseling and testing (VCT) relates to the return appointment, when the person who has requested the test is expected to return for the results. This is often a problem, as documented by research that shows that 20 to 40 percent of people tested do not return for their results.[39] These people may never return to the testing facility, or may go to another facility less visible to their social group. They may decide that knowing the result is too psychologically risky, particularly in settings where treatment will be unavailable in any case.

Table 4.1 Basic Information about Commonly Used Types of HIV Tests

Test type	Description	Use situation	Limitations
Simple/rapid assay	Test offers rapid results, i.e., 10–30 minutes, that can be done on-site. Staff need not be highly skilled. Useful for screening.	Well-suited to a number of use situations, including small laboratories, emergency rooms, and STD clinics.	The sensitivity of the test may vary, for instance, depending on whether the sample is whole blood, serum, or oral fluid. Quality control issues involved with the use of these tests at many test sites in resource-constrained settings.
ELISA (enzyme linked immunosorbent assay)	A very sensitive test, most commonly used. Test detects antibodies in blood serum.	Large hospitals, blood banks, or other large facilities. Useful for screening.	Need equipment and skilled personnel. May be costly if conducted on small scale.
Western Blot	The "gold standard" of HIV tests.	Often used as a confirmatory test, to confirm that an earlier HIV positive result is correct. Useful primarily in the setting of hospitals, government laboratories, and large sites	Skilled, experienced personnel needed. An expensive test.
CD4 Counts	An instrument counts the numbers of CD4 (receptor present on T lymphocyte cells, T cells being part of the immune system). When the numbers fall below 200/mm3 in an HIV infected patient, the person is considered to have AIDS. The patient is now at high risk to be infected by and die from opportunistic infections because the immune defenses are low.	Provide data to physicians to evaluate the success of a specific drug regimen. Most reliable predictor of survival.	Should be conducted 2–4 times per year, making it a costly or even a "luxury" procedure in resource-poor settings.

Sources: Family Health International (n.d.). *Issues in diagnostics for VCT.*;[33] USAID/Deliver. (2003). *Guide for quantifying HIV test requirements.* Arlington, VA: John Snow, Inc./Deliver;[34] John Snow, Inc./Deliver. (2003). *Guidelines for managing the HIV/AIDS supply chain.* Arlington, VA: John Snow, Inc./Deliver;[35] World Health Organisation Regional Office for South East Asia. (2003). *Standard operating procedures for diagnosis of HIV infection.* Guidelines on standard operating procedures for diagnosis of HIV opportunistic infections.[36]

112   *AIDS and Business*

The Social and Cultural Environment of
Testing, Counseling, and Treatment

The issue of voluntary testing and counseling plays a vital role in HIV/AIDS-prevention programs worldwide. In the United States, it is estimated that 900,000 people have HIV, and of those, one-third have never been tested and so do not know that they carry HIV.[40] It is vital to understand why people do not consider being tested if we wish to reduce their potential to infect many others. The reasons for avoiding or refusing to consider testing are manifold.

As is the case with other catastrophic diseases, the first barrier to diagnostic testing is psychological: denial may set in, an unrealistic evaluation of risk status may determine that a test is not taken, and the fear that one may be facing an incurable, gradually degenerative, fatal disease is enough to send people away from testing. This attitude is more likely for people who have no hope of ever receiving antiretroviral treatment. In poor communities where HIV testing is available, the impact of an HIV positive result may be devastating over the long term for the entire family or even the entire social group as professional and social stigma isolates them from their work, their homes, and any social networks they may have sustained in the past. For these reasons, people with HIV or AIDS tend not to get tested, and, if they do, they will not tell others of their affliction. For those who died of an opportunistic infection like tuberculosis, perhaps the family and community would have been none the wiser. That is, unless HIV/AIDS was silently transmitted to others, such as their children.[41]

The individual decision to agree to testing may depend on factors like its cost, the fear of meeting a family member or neighbor near the test site, the amount of privacy accorded to patients, and the extent to which people believe that the testing site staff will preserve their anonymity. The voluntary counseling and giving of informed consent by the person to be tested may dissuade people from even considering testing because the process takes time and requires trust between the community and medical providers. People in rural areas are known to travel great distances to cities in order to benefit from the anonymity of a city clinic versus an HIV clinic nearby.[42] Fear of disclosure is another important issue for those considering taking an HIV test. They may fear that if the test is positive, they may need to publicly explain their homosexual orientation, injecting-drug use, covert commercial sex work, or other socially undesirable practices.[43] Many factors come together to ensure a successful testing program. Table 4.2 sets out additional cultural, social, and psychological issues related to HIV testing. Further issues surrounding testing and counseling will be discussed in another section of this book.

A Chronology of the Voluntary Testing and Counseling (VCT) Process

The process of HIV testing is rather complicated. For this reason we have set out a "typical" chronology of testing for a person living in an affluent country or setting who is concerned about HIV risk.

1. A person decides to take the HIV test, or is advised to do so by a medical professional.
2. An appointment is made at a HIV testing center, a sexually transmitted disease clinic, family planning facility, local hospital, or doctor's office.
3. The person meets with a medical staff member (may be a doctor, nurse, or trained HIV counselor) for pretest counseling.
4. During pretest counseling, the patient is told that the process is voluntary, that the results will be anonymous or at least held confidentially. The counselor should develop a level of trust with the test candidate in a relatively short period of time. The test candidate is informed of the likely consequences of the test result, whether positive or negative. The impact on others is discussed, such as partners, current children, and potential future babies in the case of young women. An assessment of likely risk factors or believed HIV exposures is done with the test candidate. An attempt is made to determine with some accuracy when the patient was potentially exposed to HIV because between infection and detectable HIV status, several weeks or months may elapse. HIV tests detect antibodies to HIV in the blood; therefore, the body needs to produce a significant number of these in order for them to be detectable.
5. Decision is taken to go ahead with the test, or not. If the patient decides not to have the test done, s/he receives preventive counseling. If informed consent is received that the patient wants to have the test done, s/he is prepared for the test.
6. A sample is taken for the purposes of the test, which may be blood, oral fluid, or urine.
7. The patient is informed when to come back for the results.
8. Laboratory staff conduct tests, most commonly the EIA (enzyme immune assay) or the ELISA (enzyme-linked immunosorbent assay). If the test shows a reaction, the test is repeated using the same blood sample. In case of uncertain results, a Western blot test is conducted, which is more costly but more reliable. For more details, see Appendix A.
9. The patient returns for the test result and post-test counseling, which includes telling the test results and discussing risk reduction for the patient in the future.
10. If the results are negative (patient not known to have HIV at this time), the implications of this are discussed, for example, that this result does not imply that the partner is also negative. The discussion centers around how to stay negative.

114 *AIDS and Business*

Box 4.2 An In-Depth View:

Testing Issues and Pregnant Women

The HIV testing of pregnant women has inspired a series of debates. For some, the primary issue is the protection of babies and children. For others, the rights of the mother as an entity distinct from her fetus and offspring generally should be the focus. With proper HIV screening, prenatal health care and treatment, a short treatment with antiretroviral drugs, and protective measures such as a caesarian section, there is a 98 percent chance for women with HIV to give birth to a healthy, uninfected child.[44] The debate surrounding prenatal and perinatal testing commonly includes the following facets, some of which are issues in testing generally:

1. Is compulsory testing of mothers permissible if it is known to potentially protect an unborn child from contracting HIV but may reveal the mother's HIV status?
2. Testing of newborn babies may compromise the privacy of the mother, whose HIV status is likely to become known as a result. This may have devastating consequences for the mother, ranging from mild stigmatization to loss of her home and refusal of access to her other children.
3. Is it right to assume that women who may be illiterate or unable to understand the legal modalities of HIV testing, or simply overwhelmed by an unfamiliar medical environment, are in a position to be competent to consent to testing, that the concept of "informed consent" may apply?
4. Are the funds, human resources, counseling space, and time available for pretest counseling and post-test counseling and psychosocial support?
5. The onset of treatment may result in intolerable choices regarding who should benefit from the family's financial resources—the mother or the baby.
6. To what extent is people's privacy respected in terms of medical records? Who may have access to test results: past and current sexual partners, employers, insurance companies, fellow drug users who shared needles, courts, immigration officials, or others?
7. In the case of targeted populations considered to be "at risk," what are the arguments in favor and against their mandatory testing?
8. Breast-feeding is commonly proscribed for women with HIV, a practice which may be tantamount to a public announcement that the mother has HIV in many regions where breastfeeding is an expected, and public, occurrence. The presence or use of baby milk formula and feeding bottles in a new mother's home may be considered by visitors to be evidence that the mother has HIV. This is a common belief in sub-Saharan Africa.

Global Marketing Issues for HIV Testing Products and Services 115

Table 4.2 Some Cultural/Social Psychological Aspects of HIV/AIDS Testing and Treatment

Cultural representations of morality and sex

Perceptions of and attitudes towards medical doctors versus traditional or faith healers

Cultural value placed (or not) on accuracy, measurement, objectivity—and ultimately, on science itself

Social norms relating to health and sickness

The role of social networks to support and care for the sick

Level of stigma and discrimination towards drug users, sex workers, and men having sex with men

Fear of violence, ostracism, and forced exile may be particularly relevant to women's experience of seeking HIV testing or a positive test result

Table compiled based on readings in:
WHO. (2007). *Guidance on provider-initiated HIV testing and counselling in health facilities.* Retrieved June 30, 2007, from http://www.who.int/hiv/who_pitc_guidelines.pdf.
WHO. (2000). Violence against women and HIV/AIDS: Setting the research agenda. Retrieved March 25, 2007, from http://www.genderandaids.org/downloads/topics/VAW%20HIV%20 report.pdf.
Young, S. D., Nussbaum, A. D., & Monin, B. (2007). Potential moral stigma and reactions to sexually transmitted diseases : Evidence for a disjunction fallacy. Personality and Social Psychology Bulletin 33(6), 789–99.

11. If the results are HIV positive, the Centers for Disease Control and Prevention recommend that people be told to find a doctor, particularly one with HIV experience, even if feeling well; have a tuberculosis (TB) test done even if no symptoms are present; reduce or stop smoking, drinking alcohol, or taking drugs to strengthen the immune system; have a screening test for sexually transmitted diseases; practice safe-sex behaviors.[45]

12. For people who had HIV-positive results, typically follow-up counseling is recommended, as well as medical care referrals, emotional and social support, and legal services if needed.

This chronology was developed from the following sources: McCauley, A. P. (2004). *Equitable access to HIV counseling and testing for youth in developing countries: A review of current practice.* Horizons Program/International Center for Research on Women[46]; Sheon, N. (2004). *Theory and practice of client-centered counseling and testing,* HIV InSite Knowledge Base Chapter, June, 2004.[47]; World Health Organization (2004). *Rapid HIV tests: Guidelines for use in HIV testing and counselling services in resource-constrained settings.* Geneva: World Health Organization[48]; World Health Organisation/ UNAIDS (2004). *Scaling up HIV testing and counselling services: A toolkit for program managers.* Geneva: World Health Organisation.[49]

116   AIDS and Business

Social Marketing of Voluntary Counseling and Testing

As in the case of any health service, social marketing may be required to raise people's awareness and interest in HIV testing. According to the Global Health Council's[50] vice president of research, medical "social marketing uses surveys, focus groups, and other research strategies to understand the preferences and problems of intended audiences, test proposed intervention tactics, and monitor and evaluate whether and why behavior changed, feeding the results back into new decisions about how to organize the intervention."[51] According to AIDSMark,[52] social marketing involves the sale of branded and packaged health products and services, such as voluntary counseling and testing or condoms, motivating their use, and promoting the relevant healthy behaviors. Prices are set at an affordable level for the targeted markets and products are procured at special rates or donated to the service provider.[53]

Voluntary Counseling and Testing in the United States: An Example of Marketing Communications[54]

According to the National Association of People with AIDS[55] and the Centers for Disease Control and Prevention,[56] voluntary counseling and testing programs need to be communicated effectively. In order to do so, target audiences need to be identified. Usually these are populations at risk for contracting HIV, examples of which in the United States are the following: African Americans, who are the "single most affected group by HIV/AIDS" (p. 4); Latinos, who comprise 20 percent of people with AIDS, although their total population is only 14 percent of the U.S. population; men who have sex with men, who accounted for 57 percent of AIDS cases among U.S. males in 2003 and almost half of all AIDS cases; and women, who in 2003 comprised 30 percent of reported HIV infections.[57] Using a marketing communications approach, the Campaign 2005 document profiled issues of relevance to the specific target audiences outlined previously as follows:

African Americans

This is not a homogenous group, and should be further broken down in order that effective communication may take place. There are high levels of distrust of health services among African Americans, so trust is an issue to be actively addressed in the testing campaign. People in this group tend to delay testing.

Latinos

Because of the strong language identification of this diverse group, multilingual campaigns and service providers should be used, for example,

Global Marketing Issues for HIV Testing Products and Services 117

English, Spanish, Portuguese, and indigenous languages of Latin America. There may be high levels of fear in the group due to the strong influence of the Catholic Church and its conservative stance about sex. People in this group tend to delay testing.

Men Who have Sex with Men (MSM)

This is a very diverse group, so messages need to be formulated for the different audiences including that of men who have sex with other men but who identify themselves as heterosexual. Most MSM have a shared experience of stigma, an issue to be addressed for the viability of the testing campaign: where there is much stigma, MSM will be less likely to forward for testing and/or less likely to return for results after testing.

Women

Women are less likely to be aware of the importance of HIV testing, and may wait until symptoms appear to have a test done. They may avoid having an HIV test done for fear of physical or emotional abuse by their partner, or his withdrawal of financial support. For many women, HIV testing may not appear to have immediate priority due to their busy lives at work and at home, so testing should be offered during convenient days, times, and places where women are known to go such as schools, shops, and other locations. Childcare services should be offered while women go through counseling and testing.

In order to reduce perceived stigma for all the target audiences, people living with AIDS who are identifiable as member of the target audience should be used in communications campaigns and service provision, wherever possible. All target audiences have trust for certain community organizations, businesses, churches, agencies, and schools, among others, which should be approached as partners in the testing campaign. In the case of immigrants whether African American, female, Latino, or MSM, anonymity must be ensured to avoid legal entanglements with immigration authorities. Immigrants may suffer from multiple ills like isolation, low self-esteem, racism, poverty, and stigma in addition to fatalism and distrust.

Diagnostic Test Market Issues

Demand for tests is based on both business-to-business (i.e., clients are international organizations, nongovernmental organizations, health care agencies) and business-to-consumer segments (for home testing). Demand and prices are usually regulated by governments except for home tests. Home testing is mostly a market for developed countries. It is limited in scope in developing countries due to purchasing power

118 *AIDS and Business*

and infrastructure problems such as access to the Internet, possibility to order online, and the lack of reliable mail services for shipment and delivery. Companies selling tests are large pharmaceutical companies or companies such as Ross IVD, which dedicate their activities to testing. For instance, Roche sells both pharma drugs and tests, while Beckman Coulter sells only IVD tests. Companies may offer training for sophisticated instrument such as flow cytometers for CD4 counts. Donations of tests may also occur depending on the corporation's willingness to emphasize its corporate social responsibility. However, they usually prefer to sell tests at low prices to nongovernmental organizations and public organizations.

The role of generics for testing is almost insignificant: most tests are branded. There are in fact not many generic possibilities for lab testings; it is a too small a market for the large production scale required for low-priced generics. However, there are some "home-brew tests" made in university hospitals from bulk products which, although not branded, should not be considered as generics. Dr. Chabari's test is initially a home-brew test, that is, a test produced from reagents made in-house. Regulation and regulatory bodies such as the U.S. government's Food and Drug Administration (FDA) are relatively unimportant since tests need to be cleared with documentation that is simple compared to that required for drugs. Governments in poor settings cannot afford verification based on their own regulatory bodies and, as a consequence, tend to rely on FDA or European approval documents. Marketing channels in poor settings are usually done through distributors and agents. Logistics can be complicated due to cold chain constraints (which is often not the case with drugs) and complicated custom clearance procedures. When uninformed or unaware customs staff see "HIV test" on a parcel coming from a foreign country, they may stop the parcel and block its custom clearance. As a consequence, it is sometimes necessary to spend time and efforts clearing HIV tests from the customs for hospitals which are in urgent need of them.

QUESTIONS FOR DISCUSSION

1. How does the marketing of HIV/AIDS tests differ whether it targets individuals or organizations? Is it contingent on the type of tests presented in Table 4.1?
2. Discuss consumer behavior for HIV/AIDS tests as concerns "individual consumers," that is, people who are potentially concerned with the disease. You may envisage a number of issues (motivation to test, willingness/unwillingness to know, confidentiality, purpose of testing, purchasing power, social image issues, and so on).

Global Marketing Issues for HIV Testing Products and Services 119

3. Discuss buying behavior in the case of organizations (large international organizations such as World Health Organization, ministries of health, hospitals, health care systems, faith-based organizations, or nongovernmental organizations fighting HIV/AIDS). What are the main criteria for organizational buyers of HIV/AIDS tests?
4. Navigate on national and international websites of companies offering test kits. Assess to what extent price, confidentiality, results reliability, and access concerns may differ for different types of tests such as those done at home, in a doctor's office, at a test site, and so on.
5. Should Ross IVD decide to target the HIV-AIDS tests markets in developing countries with high HIV/AIDS prevalence? Should they do it through Dr. Chabari's new CD4 T cell count Simplex test? If so, should they sell business-to-business, business-to-consumer, or both? Which marketing mix (4Ps) strategies would you suggest?

SUGGESTED FURTHER READING

Becton Dickinson (various dates). Available at: http://www.bd.com/. Worldwide corporate site of Becton Dickinson, manufacturer of diagnostic and monitoring tests, among other products.

Cohen, J. (2004). Monitoring treatment: At what cost? *Science* 304(5679), 25 June. Available at: http://www.sciencemag.org/cgi/content/full/304/5679/1936.

Gostin, Lawrence O. (2004) *The AIDS pandemic: Complacency, injustice, and unfulfilled expectations.* Chapel Hill: University of North Carolina Press.

John Snow, Inc./Deliver (2003). *Guidelines for managing the HIV/AIDS supply chain.* Arlington, VA: John Snow, Inc./Deliver.

John Snow, Inc./Deliver (2005). *Building blocks for inventory management of HIV tests and ARV drugs.* Arlington, VA: John Snow, Inc./Deliver.

National HIV Testing resources, Centers for Disease Control and Prevention. Includes testing advice and national HIV Testing Day campaign information. Available at: http://www.hivtest.org/.

Weinhardt, L. S., Carey, M. P., Johnson, B. T., et al. (1999). Effects of HIV counseling and testing on sexual risk behavior: A meta-analytic review of published research, 1985–1997. *American Journal of Public Health*, 89, 1397–40.

WHO. (2007). *Guidance on provider-initiated HIV testing and counselling in health facilities.* Geneva: WHO. Available at: http://www.who.int/hiv/who_pitc_guidelines.pdf.

WHO. (various dates). *HIV testing and counselling.* Dedicated site with technical, training and policy documents for company, local community, advocacy, national and supranational decision makers, including current publications and e-library. Available at: http://www.who.int/hiv/topics/vct/en/index.html.

120 *AIDS and Business*

Appendix A.1   Quick Reference Facts on HIV Test Kits.
SIMPLE and/or RAPID HIV TEST KITS

Assay Name (Manufacturer)	*HIV Serotype*	*Equipment Required[1]*	*Cost/Test (USD)*	*No. of units per kit*
Capillus HIV-1/HIV-2 (Trinity Biotech)	HIV-1+2	G	1.10	100
SERODIA HIV-1/HIV-2 (Fujirebio)	HIV-1+2	D,G	JP Y 130	220
IMMUNOCOMB II BISPOT HIV-1/HIV-2 (Orgenetics Ltd.)	HIV-1+2+0	D,G	1.10	36
DIPSTICK HIV-1/HIV-2 (Pacific Biotech)	HIV-1+2	G, D optional	0.60	48, 96, 192
*Determine HIV-1/HIV-2 (Abbott)	HIV-1+2	D,G	1.20	100
HIV-1/HIV-2 Doublecheck (Orgenetics Ltd.)	HIV-1+2	G	1.35	40
HIV TRIDOT (Mitra & Co., India)	HIV-1+2	G	1.20	10, 20, 50
SERO Strip HIV-1/HIV-2 (Chembio Diagnostic Sys.)	HIV-1+2	G	1.40	30

*Determine HIV-1 and HIV-2 (Abbott) Rapid HIV Test kit can be purchased through UNFPA's Procurement Section

Global Marketing Issues for HIV Testing Products and Services 121

Appendix A.2. Quick Reference Facts on HIV Test Kits.
ENZYME-LINKED IMMUNOSORBENT ASSAY (ELISA) TEST[2]

Assay Name (Manufacturer)	HIV Serotype	Equipment Required[1]	Cost/Test (USD)	No. of units per kit
Enzygnost Anti-HIV 1 & 2 plus (Dade Behring AG)	HIV-1+2+0	A, B, C, D, E, F	0.53	192, 960
DETECT HIV I+II (Biochem)	HIV-1+2	A, B, C, D, E, F	0.43	96, 192
Biotest HIV-TETRA HIV1+2 (Biotest)	HIV-1+2	A, B, C, D, E, F	0.50	480
Recombigen HIV–1/2 EIA (Trinity Biotech plc)	HIV-1+2	A, B, C, D, E, F	0.45	192
Innotest HIV-1/HIV-2 Ab s.p. (Innogenetics)	HIV-1+2+0	A, B, C, D, E, F	0.45	96, 480
HIV-Chex (Xcyton)	HIV-1+2	A, B, C, D, E, F	0.42	96
HIV EIA (Thermo Labsystems)	HIV-1+2	A, B, C, D, E, F	0.45	96, 960
Vironostika HIV Uni-form II Plus 0 Vers 3.3 (Organon Teknika)	HIV-1+2+0	A, B, C, D, E, F	EUR 0.58	192, 576
Genscreen HIV 1+2 V2 (Bio-Rad)	HIV-1+2+0	A, B, C, D, E, F	060	96, 480
UBI HIV1/2 EIA (United Biomedical)	HIV-1+2	A, B, C, D, E, F	0.45	192, 960
HIV-1/HIV-2 GO EIA (Abbott)	HIV-1+2+0	Abbott Equip, C, D, E, F	0.85	100

(Adapted from UNAIDS Best Practice Collection—May 2001—sources and prices of selected drugs and diagnostics for people living with HIV/AIDS.)
[1]A = ELISA reader; B = ELISA washer; C = Consumables; D = Pipette; E = Power Supply; F = for large volume testing, i.e. . more than 40 samples daily; G = for small volume testing, i.e., from 1 to 40 samples daily.
[2]Using ELISA-based technology VCT clients must typically wait at least 72 hours for their results.
Source: UNFPA (n.d.). Fact sheet on HIV test kits. Retrieved June 6, 2008, from http://www. unfpa.org/hiv/prevention/factsheet2.htm

Appendix B.1 WHO Bulk Procurement Scheme 2004 Specifications of HIV Test Kits—SIMPLE/RAPID, ELISA, AND CONFIRMATORY ASSAYS

Assay Name (Manufacturer)	Company's Order Code	No. of Tests per Kit	Guaranteed Shelf Life/ Storage Temp (°C)	HIV Type[1]	Assay Type/ Antigen Type	Sample Type	Equipment Requirements[2]	Cost/ Test[3] €/¥	Cost/Test[3] US$
SIMPLE/RAPID ASSAYS									
BIOLINE HIV 1/2 3.0 (Standard Diagnostics Inc.)	03FK10	30	16 months/ 2°–30°	HIV 1 HIV 2	lateral flow/ recombinant proteins	whole blood serum/plasma	D, G		0.47
BIONOR HIV-1 & 2 (Bionor AS)	DN061	250	10 months/ 2°–8°	HIV 1+2	synthetic peptides	whole blood serum/plasma	E, G, Special Equipment		1.00
CAPILLUS HIV-1/HIV-2 (Trinity Biotech)	6048G	100	9 months/ 2°–8°	HIV 1+2	agglutination/ recombinant proteins	whole blood serum/plasma	G	€1.00	
DETERMINE TM HIV-1/2 (Abbott Diagnostics)	7D23–13	100	6–9 months/ 2°–30°	HIV 1+2	lateral flow/ recombinant protein, synthetic peptide	whole blood serum/plasma	D, G		Access countries: 0.80 Elsewhere: 1.00
DIAGNOSTIC KIT for HIV (1+2) ANTIBODY (COLLOIDAL GOLD) (Shanghai Kehua) (SEAR & WR only)	KH-R-02	50	15 months/ 4°–30°	HIV 1+2	lateral flow/	whole blood, serum/plasma	D, G		0.60
FIRST RESPONSE™ HIV 1–2-0 Card Test (Premier Medical Corp)	105FRC30	30	15 months/ 2°–30°	HIV 1+2	lateral flow/ recombinant proteins	whole blood serum/plasma	D, G		0.67
GENEDIA HIV 1/2 Rapid 3.0 (Green Cross) (SEAR & WPR only)	F3302	30	14 months/ 2°–30°	HIV 1+2	lateral flow/ recombinant proteins	whole blood serum/plasma	D, G		0.70

Product	Catalog No.	Tests/kit	Shelf life/Storage	HIV type[1]	Method/Antigen	Specimen	Equipment[2]	Price	Price[3]
GENIE II HIV-1/HIV-2 (Bio-Rad Laboratories)	72323	40	12 months/ 2°–8°	HIV 1+2	lateral flow/ recombinant proteins, synthetic peptides	serum/plasma	D, G	€2.00	
HIV 1 & 2 DOUBLECHECK (Orgenics Ltd.)	60332000	40	15 months/ 4°–8°	HIV 1+2	lateral flow/ recombinant proteins, synthetic peptides	serum/plasma	G		1.20
HIV TRIDOT (J Mitra & Co., India)	IR130010 IR130050 IR130100 IR130200	10 50 100 200	10 months/ 4°–8°	HIV 1 HIV 2	flow through/ recombinant proteins	serum/plasma	G	€1.10 €1.00 €0.90 €0.80	
IMMUNOCOMB II BISPOT HIV 1 & 2 (Orgenics Ltd.)	60432002	36	15 months/ 4°–8°	HIV 1 HIV 2	dipstick/ synthetic peptides	serum/plasma	D, G		1.30
INSTANTCHEK™ HIV 1+2 RAPID TEST (EY Laboratories)	8–1003–40 8–1003–100	40 100	9 months/ 15°–28°	HIV 1+2	lateral flow/-	whole blood serum/plasma	G		1.09 0.95
SERODIA HIV-1/2 (Fujirebio)	220658 226063	100 220	12 months/ 2°–10°	HIV 1+2	agglutination/ recombinant proteins	serum/plasma	C, D, G	¥130 ¥130	(1.19) (1.19)
UNI-GOLDTM HIV-1/HIV-2 (Trinity Biotech)	1206502	20	9 months/ 2°–27°	HIV 1+2	lateral flow/ recombinant proteins	whole blood serum/plasma	G	€1.15	

Notes: [1]Assays denoted as HIV 1 HIV 2 are able to discriminate between HIV-1 and HIV-2, those denoted as HIV 1+2 are not capable of discrimination. [2]Equipment requirements: A: ELISA reader, B: ELISA washer, C: Consumables, D: Pipette, E: Power supply, F: For large volume testing more than 40 samples daily, G: For small volume testing 1 to 40 samples daily, Special Equipment: Bionor testing station required approximate cost US$950. [3]Please note that this price does not include freight or other charges.

Specifications of HIV test kits—SIMPLE/RAPID, ELISA, AND CONFIRMATORY ASSAYS

Assay Name (Manufacturer)	Company's Order Code	No. of Tests per Kit	Guaranteed Shelf Life/ Storage Temp (°C)	HIV Type[1]	Assay Type/ Antigen Type	Sample Type	Equipment Requirements[2]	Cost/Test[3] €/¥	Cost/Test[3] US$
ELISA ASSAYS									
ANTI-HIV 1+2 ANTIBOD-IES ELISA DIAGNOS-TICS KIT (Shanghai Kehua) (SEAR & WR only)	KH-T-10	96	5 months/ 2°–8°	HIV 1+2	recombinant proteins, synthetic peptides	4520/620nm	A, B, C, D, E, F		0.27
ENZYGNOST ANTI-HIV 1/2 PLUS (Dade Behring AG) Enzygnost/TMB reagent kit	OQFK135 OQFK215 OUVP175	2 × 96 10 × 96 960	12 months/ 2°–8°	HIV 1+2 O	recombinant proteins	450/650 nm	A, B, C, D, E, F		0.99 0.75 Gratis
GENEDIA HIV Ag-Ab (Green Cross) (SEAR & WPR only)	D1305	480	15 months/ 2°–8°	HIV 1+ 2 O	HIV Ag recombinant proteins, synthetic peptides	450/620nm	A, B, C, D, E, F		0.40

GENSCREEN Plus HIV Ag- Ab (Bio-Rad Laboratories)	72375 72376	96 480	9 months/ 2°–8°	HIV 1+2 O	HIV Ag recombinant proteins, synthetic peptides	450/620 nm	A, B, C, D, E, F	€0.55 €0.50
HIV EIA (AniLabsystems Ltd. Oy)	6111011 6111012 6111013	96 480 960	12 months/ 4°–8°	HIV 1+2	synthetic peptides	450 nm	A, B, C, D, E, F	€0.40 €0.36 €0.34
MUREX HIV Ag-Ab (Abbott Diagnostics)	L/N7G79–01 L/N7G79–02	96 480	6 months/ 2°–8°	HIV 1+ 2 O HIV Ag	recombinant proteins, synthetic peptides	450/620- 650nm	A, B, C, D, E, F	1.20 0.80
UBI HIV-1/2 EIA (United Biomedical)	680328	192	14 months/ 2°–8°	HIV 1+2	synthetic peptides	492/620 nm	A, B, C, D, E, F	0.40
VIRONOSTIKA HIV UNIFORM II PLUS O (bioMérieux BV)	284017 284018	192 576	12 months/ 2°–8°	HIV 1+2 O	recombinant proteins, synthetic peptides	450/620 nm	A, B, C, D, E, F	€0.64 €0.46

Notes: [1]Assays denoted as HIV 1 HIV 2 are able to discriminate between HIV-1 and HIV-2, those denoted as HIV 1+2 are not capable of discrimination. [2]Equipment requirements: A: ELISA reader, B: ELISA washer, C: Consumables, D: Pipette, E: Power supply, F: For large volume testing more than 40 samples daily, G: For small volume testing 1 to 40 samples daily. [3]Please note that this price does not include freight nor other charges.

Specifications of HIV test kits—SIMPLE/RAPID, ELISA, AND CONFIRMATORY ASSAYS

Assay Name (Manufacturer)	Company's Order Code	No. of Tests per Kit	Guaranteed Shelf Life/ Storage Temp (°C)	HIV Type[1]	Assay Type/ Antigen Type	Sample Type	Equipment Requirements[2]	Cost/Test[3] €/¥	Cost/Test[3] US$
CONFIRMATORY ASSAYS									
HIV BLOT 2.2 (Genelabs Diagnostics)	11031–036	36	15 months/ 2°-8°	HIV 1 HIV 2	viral lysate + synthetic peptide	NA	C, D, E		10.97
INNO-LIATM HIV I/II SCORE (Innogenetics)	80540	20	2°-8°	HIV 1 HIV 2	recombinant proteins, synthetic peptides	NA	D, E	€15.50	
PEPTI-LAV 1–2 (Bio-Rad Laboratories)	72253	10	9 months/ 2°-8°	HIV 1 HIV 2	synthetic peptides	NA	C, D, E	€15.00	
NEW LAV BLOT I (Bio-Rad Laboratories)	72252	18	9 months/ 2°-8°	HIV 1	viral lysate	NA	D, E	€13.00	
NEW LAV BLOT II (Bio-Rad Laboratories)	72252	18	9 months/ 2°-8°	HIV 2	viral lysate	NA	D, E	€13.00	

Notes: [1]Assays denoted as HIV 1 HIV 2 are able to discriminate between HIV-1 and HIV-2, those denoted as HIV 1+2 are not capable of discrimination. [2]Equipment requirements: A: ELISA reader, B: ELISA washer, C: Consumables, D: Pipette, E: Power supply, F: For large volume testing more than 40 samples daily, G: For small volume testing 1 to 40 samples daily. [3]Please note that this price does not include freight nor other charges.

5 Protectom
Selling Condoms, a Complex Business

Patrick Schaller sat in his hotel room, punching his laptop keyboard and cursing the lack of ergonomics in the desk chair design. He was waiting for his business partner, Nathalie Fabre, to arrive so they could discuss a new supply contract that looked problematic for their fledgling company, Protectom. Protectom was a French company specializing in condoms for the young gay scene. Schaller himself was not young, but he had the passionate conviction that condoms saved lives. He was HIV positive. He had started Protectom in the belief that he could truly save people like himself who in the past had not thought of condoms as relevant to their lifestyle—hence the name "protect homme." He realized the limitations of the name, such as the greater share of women buyers today, increasing sophistication of competitors like Hot Rubber, and the unsexy idea of protection, but knew that the brand had grown strong fast and it was too risky to change it now.

Schaller knew that he was a success story both in terms of medical treatment and business success. He had, a few years back, one brush with catastrophe when monitoring tests showed he had become resistant to an antiretroviral drug he was taking, but a new generation drug came on the market that nursed him back to full health. To the despair of his doctors and a number of activists, Schaller always told journalists who commented on his tanned good looks and photogenic physique, "It's not the drugs alone that bring you back from the dead. My health today is more the result of a vegan diet and a scrupulous fitness regime than any drug!" Several of his friends had not been so lucky with treatments, including his closest friend who died in 1998. In terms of business success, the company he ran with Fabre was applauded in European business publications for its innovative marketing and cited by NGOs as an example to look up to, but making money was still a struggle. "And money will always be a problem," sighed Schaller as he cleaned his angular black-framed glasses.

When Fabre walked in, they went over various points of company business. She was the marketing side of Protectom, the one who knew the customers as well as her own friends—which in fact many of them were. While Schaller was getting his beauty rest (he always went to bed by ten o'clock),

128   AIDS and Business

she was out on the club circuit, going to elite parties and chatting with artists, designers, and other interesting people. She often felt that there was an emotional involvement in marketing such a product. For her, there was "big fun to work with condoms." She loved being in contact with all kinds of people, ranging from her chic friends to treatment activists; nongovernmental organizations to governments; schools to churches and many others. She had the opportunity to participate in television talk shows, online forums, and a number of public events . . . it was definitely more fun than marketing toothpaste, as she had done in her previous job. Fabre had driven Protectom beyond the obvious and towards a larger market than that of the aging gay men who had lived through the AIDS scare in the 1980s. Most of Protectom's current customers were even born after that time, and many of them were not men at all. Today's condom buyer was of all ages, both sexes, and was generally more concerned about sexually transmitted infections than AIDS. The problem with condoms, like many other consumer goods, was that the market was flooded with so many competing messages that it was difficult to cut through the clutter and get Protectom's message across.

The reason for the meeting between Schaller and Fabre today was to discuss a potential new supplier agreement. Fabre's recent trip to India had been successful, and she had several offers to supply Protectom with top-range extrasheer, superstrong latex condoms, the best of which was from one of India's biggest companies, Hindustan Latex. Then all that needed to be done at Protectom was additional quality testing, packaging of the condoms. Of course there was all the marketing and distribution to do. According to one of Schaller's famous statements, "Anybody can make condoms, it doesn't take a genius. The hard part is to add value, to get people to buy your brand, feel good about it, and actually use the damn things." In terms of marketing, Protectom directed its energy into putting its condoms within reach of everyone in France, Germany, Austria, and Switzerland who needed one. Thus, condoms were sold at its Protectom.com online shop and other online outlets, in classy vending machines at night clubs and bars, in the bowls of complimentary condoms available at gay saunas and clubs, some retail outlets such as petrol stations, pharmacies and so on, and at a number of unorthodox locations like fitness clubs, snowboard/skateboard and clothes shops as well as music stores. In order to maintain their positioning strategy, Protectom did not make its condoms available at family-planning or sexually transmitted diseases clinics. However, health workers working specifically with MSM were given free samples and samples were distributed at gay pride-type events as well as prevention campaign events—but only if they were "hip" or featured a celebrity favored by Schaller and Fabre.

Protectom had experimented with custom condoms in the past, the type that was packaged and imprinted with another company's brand and given away at trade shows and product launches, art exhibitions, cheeky designer hotels, and sports competitions. In addition, they had a brief partnership with a major top-notch European fashion retail chain to have their logo and distinctive design on the packages with condoms in matching colors. Fabre acknowledged that Protectom condoms were widely available, but she realized that the price per condom—which averaged 1.50 euros—was high. "Not that our typical customer lacks money; far from it! No: the problem is more about lowering or removing barriers to purchase by being available where needed, and then by being as attractive as possible. We are following along the theme of the Swiss Stop AIDS campaign, by positioning the condom as an essential part of making love. As if making love without a condom is as crazy as playing hockey in the nude!"[1] In fact, Protectom worked closely with the Stop AIDS campaign on a number of issues for the Swiss market, the Condoms Essential Wear[2] campaign in the UK, and the Michael Stich Foundation[3] in Germany. Recently, however, as Swiss Stop AIDS and German campaigns became increasingly controversial and shocking, Protectom distanced itself from the organizations. "There's a difference between 'thought provoking' and plain old 'bad taste'! Anyway, we've known for years that fear appeals in advertising don't work," countered Schaller when asked to justify his decision to publicly protest. Schaller's former gentlemanly but witty public pronouncements became barbed when prominent Swiss physicians recently announced that HIV-positive men, who were effectively treated with antiretrovirals, could not spread HIV to their partners, and therefore did not need to wear condoms: "I'm sorry but that is recklessly irresponsible of him. That was based on studies with pitifully small samples. It's criminal to even imply such a thing," he told a television talk-show host. Similar statements from French and international doctors and activists soon followed in the mass media.

The product line at Protectom included male latex condoms, latex oral barriers, and Protectom "Lux Lube" lubricant, which was sold in a variety of flavors. In addition, the company sold polyurethane condoms for people allergic to latex and as a more expensive, sensation-augmenting option. Protectom condoms were packaged in the typical foil package (for quality assurance reasons), but the plastic covering was imprinted with a wide range of edgy motifs and photographs in a very untypical matte finish. The outer package was designed to look like a small gourmet chocolate or deluxe coffee package—"society's other sweet little sins," as Fabre liked to say. Colored, scented, and flavored condoms were very important to Protectom's target markets, for which reason the company worked with several Swiss companies that were avant-garde in the domain of synthetic flavorings and aromas. Protectom offered in its online store the full range of unique flavors and aromas, some mimicking those of top-range food companies like "feel.pure" (green tea and gingko) and "fresh.tingle" (passion fruit and ginger). Protectom also offered more offbeat aromas, usually in limited editions with an artist's signature package such as leather jacket, new car smell, gunpowder, and freshly-cut grass. "Say we're nuts," says Fabre; "these are some of our best-selling condoms and our margin is much higher on scented/flavored condoms than it is on the other "specialty"

130   *AIDS and Business*

ranges like ribbed, studded, and special sized condoms." No Protectom condoms had spermicide added, but all were generously lubricated.

Hindustan Latex[4] was a state-owned company that produced condoms for the Indian government's family planning programs since 1969 at the rate of approximately two hundred million per year, and sold to a number of nongovernmental organizations and private companies like Protectom in sixty countries.[5] Hindustan Latex facilities were ISO9002 certified, and the condoms carried certification by CE (European), NF (France), and SABS (South Africa), and were approved by the World Health Organization and ASTM (USA).[6] The condoms were tested by SGS, a multinational company providing quality control services.[7] Schaller was pleasantly surprised when he went online to get a glimpse of their branding—for a company with such an unsexy name, he thought, they had done well to brand their condoms "Moods" and to use quite cutting-edge methods on the site. A range of animated characters personalized the site: saucy sex counselor Olivia offered real advice that was cheeky yet rang true if you took the interactive option that lets the user type in a question, and sexy Frejya told your sex fortune. The "G-Spot" offered downloads and the "MyMood Space" offered a personalized option for broadcasting one's exploits.[8] Schaller was slightly surprised to see no mention of the condom's safety, nor any health advice at all—rather as if sexually transmitted diseases did not exist.

Schaller looked again at the offer from Hindustan Latex. Their offer for male condoms was cheaper than that of Korean and Japanese manufacturers. In addition, they offered a wide range of sizes in width and length, which would allow Protectom to develop a "tailored" range of condoms similar to the They-Fit condoms available online in the United States through Condomania.[9] Fabre noted that there was a strong protection argument for Hindustan Latex "tailored" condoms: ill-fitting condom width was an important factor in slippage, a major problem associated with condom failure. In addition, customers would appreciate the personalized touch associated with sized-to-fit condoms, a factor likely to increase their satisfaction. Fabre argued also that the necessity of taking personal measurements using tools provided on Protectom's Web site would increase the customers' involvement with the company and therefore their loyalty. Fabre and Schaller did have one concern with the offer, and that was the customers' perception of India as country of origin for the condoms as opposed to "Made in Japan"—a common quality and cachet argument of top-range condoms.

Schaller reflected that all these details sometimes seemed superfluous in light of the fact that, without condoms, people were going to keep dying. As he had read in a number of studies from affluent countries recently, sexual norms were changing among MSM. In Western Europe, which was broadly Schaller's target market, thirteen countries reported a 55 percent rise in MSM HIV cases between 1998 and 2005.[10] Longitudinal studies in the UK found that gay men were more likely to have unprotected sex in 1998 as opposed to three years previously, a trend observable particularly in men younger than twenty-five.[11] In the United States, a study in New York found

Protectom   131

that new HIV diagnoses among young men aged thirteen to nineteen had doubled over a five-year period.[12] Prominent epidemiologists warned of a new epidemic among gays if these trends were to continue.

CASE CONTEXT AND BACKGROUND

HIV/AIDS Prevention as a Business and Marketing Issue

In the business marketing sense, condoms are a product like any other commercially available medical device. They are offered to potential consumers with a corporate ambition to better satisfy needs and wants than competing manufacturers. Condoms have been used throughout history and around the world, both to prevent contraception and disease and for ritual or protective (i.e., to protect from insect bites or injury in battle) purposes. Less is known about female sheaths, such as goat bladders, thought to have been used in classical Rome, than about male condoms. Today, the female condom has become an accepted product.[13]

Male condoms made of linen were known in ancient Egypt three thousand years ago.[14] Traditionally, condoms were fashioned from animal and fish intestines[15] and were often reused. The Chinese used oiled silk paper to make condoms; in Renaissance Italy condoms were made of linen; in nineteenth-century Japan they were made of leather, fine horns, or shells.[16] They were neither fully safe nor very comfortable and commerce of such items was illicit. In France, for instance, it was only with the revolution of 1789 that condoms were legalized and their manufacture and trade allowed.

The advent of vulcanization of rubber in the mid-1800s made condoms a widely available, mass-produced item. Since then, the biggest change came from the use of latex manufacturing in the 1930s, then more recently the use of polyurethane, which permitted the development of the female condom. The origin of the word "condom" is unknown: it could be a simple transliteration by the English of the word *condum* derived from the Latin word *condus* (receptacle) and from the verb *condere*, meaning to hide, to protect. It may derive from Persian *kendu* or *condu*, meaning an animal intestine used as a storage vessel. Another explanation, disputed by scholars,[17] is derived from the name of the physician of King Charles II of England, Dr. Condom, who prepared animal gut sheaths for the king.[18]

Condoms, Religion, Ideology, and Politics

Condoms are the "only technology available for protection from sexually transmitted HIV" (Population Action International, p. 4).[19] They are easy to use, are relatively cheap, have a long shelf life, may be distributed and used almost anywhere on the planet, and are effective in preventing transmission of HIV and other sexually transmitted diseases. However, condom effectiveness depends on individual compliance, which means consistent and correct use.[20] As stated simply by Altman (2006), "For almost twenty years we

132   *AIDS and Business*

have known how HIV is spread and have possessed the techniques to prevent transmission. . . . Even if one accepts that slip-ups are inevitable, as the result of human or technical failures, the consistent use of condoms and clean needles would be sufficient to slow the spread of HIV greatly" (p. 262).[21]

To complicate matters, some prominent public figures have questioned the effectiveness of condoms in preventing HIV/AIDS and more generally STDs. These include influential Catholic and other church leaders, the Bush administration, and others. This has resulted in lower belief in effectiveness and thus lower use levels among the general population. At the very least, such pronouncements have resulted in doubts as to the effectiveness of condoms. In response, an expert panel convened by the National Institutes of Health (NIH), Centers for Disease Control and Prevention (CDC), the Food and Drug Administration (FDA), and USAID (United States Agency for International Development) was asked to determine the effectiveness of condoms. An extensive review of research studies published since June 2000 was carried out. The researchers concluded that male latex condoms, when used correctly and consistently for vaginal sex, are effective for preventing HIV infection in women and men and offer statistically significant protection against other sexually transmitted infections.[22]

Barrier contraceptives generally respond to two widely different objectives for users, although both tend to be confused in people's minds:

- a means of contraception, that is, a means of enjoying heterosexual intercourse without the risk of pregnancy
- a means of protection against sexually transmitted infections, including HIV/AIDS, in any type of sexual activity.

There is a complex interplay between the two types of objectives. Where contraception is considered as legitimate behavior, the use of condoms will be facilitated. On the other hand, certain religions, especially Catholicism and Islam, tend to view condoms as an encouragement for easy, multipartner, and extramarital sex affairs. In 1826, Pope Leo XII termed the use of condoms a "diabolic" action. Condoms are also seen by the strictest religious groups as an obstacle to the divine punishment of commercial sex workers and men who have sex with men. In 2008 condoms were still condemned by the Vatican and a range of church leaders, however there are many dissenting voices in the Catholic Church, such as Catholics for Choice[23] and others who refer to a "lesser evil" in using condoms to avoid death from AIDS.

In some Latin American countries, laypeople tend to consider that condoms encourage immoral, irresponsible, and unfaithful behavior; women in these countries view condoms as good for sex workers, not "honest" women. In Jamaica, condoms are reserved for extramarital sex affairs. In contrast, most types of moderate Protestant religions tend not to separate sex and love; procreation is not viewed as a holy duty, having sex is the normal outcome of shared love, and the use of condoms is accepted behavior. There are extremists, such as the growing U.S. Quillfull movement, that go against this tolerance, however. It is important to recognize the variability of what is considered "responsible behavior."

The main ideological rival for condoms is sexual abstinence and single sexual partnering between "safe" partners, which typically culminate in the traditional, lifelong, marriage with partners coming to marriage without prior sexual experience. Exclusive abstinence advocates demand that information about safer sex—which usually includes the use of condoms—remove this element. According to a Human Rights Watch report, school educators in Uganda have been instructed not to discuss condoms in schools.[24] Yet, studies conducted in the United States found that adolescents who pledged to abstain from sex before marriage were more likely to have anal or oral sex and may be less likely to use condoms[25]—well-known means to increase vulnerability to contracting HIV.

Global Condom Demand

Due to HIV/AIDS information campaigns, one might expect that condom demand will be increasing. World Health Organization researcher Dr. Patrick Friel calculated that health programs throughout the world will need between 860 million and 2 billion condoms per year over the next decade. However, current condom use among the general population increases only about 4 percent annually, according to Catherine Taylor of major condom manufacturer London International Group. She noted that even people aware of the benefits of using condoms do not consistently use them. Condoms may be considered to be contraceptives, not a method for reducing prevalence of sexually transmitted diseases.[26] The global condom market is difficult to estimate. Global male condom needs were estimated at 314.8 million in 2000 by the United Nations Population Fund, while supplies of condoms by nongovernmental organizations and others lagged far behind, as itemized in Table 5.1.

Table 5.1   Estimated Male Condom Needs and Donor Supply

Region	Estimated total condom needs	Actual donor supply of condoms (2000)
Africa	38.0	22.3
Asia	177.7	17.5
Arab States and Europe	47.6	1.1
Latin America and the Caribbean	51.5	5.0
Total	314.8	45.9

Table adapted from UNFPA. (2002). Estimated condom requirements compared with actual donor support in 2000 (table), *Protection that only condoms provide*, UNFPA Population issues: Securing essential supplies. Available at: http://www.unfpa.org/supplies/condoms.htm.

134 *AIDS and Business*

Condom consumption is difficult to precisely assess since, in researching the matter, there are important response biases such as social desirability and courtesy biases. Respondents in surveys are often reluctant to report on intimate behavior. As a result of the arrival on the market of contraceptive pills in the 1960s, the primary demand for condoms decreased and the number of users dropped with a switch of the pregnancy responsibility from men to women. In the 1970s, some predicted the progressive disappearance of condoms as a means of contraception. However, with the advent of HIV/AIDS in the 1980s, there was a growing concern with the use of condoms as a means of avoiding sexually transmitted diseases, including HIV/AIDS. Since then, the global demand for condoms has been on the rise, although not massively.

Factors Influencing Condom Use

There are a number of factors that influence the use of condoms, and consequently consumption as a whole. The first factor is one's perception of risk to become pregnant or to contract HIV or other sexually transmitted diseases. Several studies have shown that university students feel protected by their environment and so are less likely to use condoms, as was notably the case among students in China, where HIV is on the rise.[27] Secondly, the culturally and socially determined relationship between men and women plays a role, particularly in terms of the balance of power between the two. Relative equality in status between men and women is a prerequisite for women to ask men to use a condom. In some cultures, women accept to have unprotected sexual intercourse with their male partner, in full cognizance that risks of HIV/AIDS infection are high, because pregnancy and childbearing are highly valued for a number of reasons, often so as to acquire higher status in the family and in the wider society. In this respect, condoms will be more difficult to use where it is felt that they are a definitive obstacle to fecundity, especially when this is perceived by both women and men.

Men tend to adopt condoms where it is seen as a socially accepted practice within the male group. In this sense, the issue of condom adoption (a key driver of primary demand) may be more related to male values than to the male/female relationship. A good case in point is Japan, where there has traditionally been a strong condom demand, due in particular to the prohibition of contraceptive pills up to 1999: in the early 1970s, 75 percent of contraceptive users used condoms, a high use rate in international comparison, and many were sold door-to-door by female salespeople.[28] The end result is a very low prevalence of HIV/AIDS in Japan, although some say it is largely underestimated.[29] However, Japan's health ministry announced recently that domestic shipments of condoms have declined from 737 million condoms in 1980 to 419 million in 2003—a 43 percent decline. "Since the advent of the broadband Internet in Japan,

Protectom 135

people can connect the entire night without having extra charges," said a spokesperson for Okamoto Industries, which accounts for half of Japan's condom market. "Those people who cannot break away from their computers are not able to have sex," she said. Yet it appears that some manage to do so: Japan's health ministry reported that the number of those infected with the HIV/AIDS virus exceeded 1,000 for the first time in 2004.[30]

Most condoms are sold as HIV prevention devices. It can be said that the condom business is not much about pregnancy avoidance; it is more an AIDS-related business, also more generally a business related to the prevention of syphilis and other sexually transmitted diseases. Condom brands are closely associated with disease. Therefore it is not easy to market a product with negative connotations.

CONDOM USE AMONG MSM

There is much debate as to whether condom use is stable or decreasing among groups considered to be at higher risk for contracting HIV, such as MSM. A London, England, sample of homosexual men classified into three groups (HIV positive, HIV negative, and never tested) were asked to report their high-risk sexual behavior over five years. Reported high-risk behavior with casual partners increased over five years from 6.7 percent to 16.1 percent, and over the same period unprotected anal intercourse with casual partners known to have HIV increased from 6.8 percent to 10.3 percent.[31] In Scotland, the responses of homosexual men asked about unprotected anal intercourse with HIV-positive, negative, and never-tested partners demonstrated a rise in risky behavior (inconsistent use or lack of condom use) between 1999 and 2002.[32] In one study, researchers pinpointed the age-related differences in safer sex practices of men having sex with men: younger men tended to take more risks.[33] The reasons cited for decreased condom use among a high-risk group like men having sex with men include "AIDS burnout" (years of multiple exposures to HIV prevention messages), changed perceptions about the consequences of HIV infection, and a possible dilution of targeted prevention messages to MSM as prevention campaigns target broader populations.[34]

Men seeking men online are considered to be an emerging risk environment for spreading HIV. In major cities men can contact men interested in sex with a view to meeting each other to indulge their special sex interests, such as having sex without a condom, a practice known as "barebacking."[35] A number of barebacking sites make their views clear with the tagline "no condoms allowed." Bareback.com goes further, asserting that

> you know that we are not AIDS Nazis, condom wrappers or fearful fools! What we are is a community of gay men who like the feel of raw nasty sex . . . That's why we embrace a policy of containment. What

136 *AIDS and Business*

> does that mean—It's simple. If poz [HIV-positive] boys stick to poz
> boys and neg [HIV-negative] boys stick to neg boys AIDS will be over.
> It's just that simple.[36]

Another risk environment identified by researchers is that of men with HIV
seeking other men for sex in urban centers like New York at "POZ parties"
where their HIV-positive status is not a concern for sexual partners. Sex
without a condom with several partners at POZ parties is frequent at these
parties, and scientists are concerned about the likelihood of transmitting
sexually transmitted diseases and potential HIV superinfection (reinfection
of a person who already has HIV with another strain of the virus). In one
study in New York City, three quarters of POZ party attendees had previously attended a party, suggesting a regular activity. However, by "sorting"
people as HIV-positive, these parties may reduce new HIV infections.[37]
One example of a POZ party is Hi+Five in Los Angeles, a monthly event,
a "hip social oasis where guys don't have to deal with the rejection based
on their HIV status or the stress of disclosure. Because admittedly, even
though there are totally chill Neg [HIV-negative] men who aren't freaked
out about the HIV thing, there's [sic] an equal number of guys out there
who just can't deal with a POZ man."[38]

Practical Obstacles to the Purchase of Condoms and Major Challenges

There is a well-documented reluctance in buying condoms, especially when
one has to ask for them aloud in a shop surrounded by other people. This
may be linked to religion, but also to a general sense of public decency found
across many societies. Once purchased, unlike other products that are consumed alone, condoms are used in interaction with a sex partner. In many
cultures, to ask a partner to use a condom is a sign of a lack of trust. Conversely, using a condom when not asked specifically to do it may be perceived by the partner as a sign that something is wrong with the person who
does it, such as having a sexually transmitted disease or multiple partners.

Given that users can increasingly access condoms via online purchase,
the shyness of people having to publicly request them in a store or phar-
macy may become less and less of an issue, particularly for adults. In addition to condoms, people can also easily buy a number of other sex-related
products such as lubricants.[39] Given the low attractiveness of the condom
market as such, condom manufacturers tend to diversify in related products
which are less demanding in terms of manufacturing quality, less low cost,
and therefore easier to change into profit drivers. For instance, Durex now
offers a range of erotic toys.

As underlined by the World Health Organization Web site: "Prevention is the first line of defence against HIV/AIDS and condoms have long
been a mainstay of HIV prevention programmes."[40] However, there are
a number of challenges to be overcome, not only for the global use of

condoms to increase but also for their use to be efficient in fighting the HIV/AIDS pandemic:

- Accessibility: distribution is important; dispensing machines, condoms sold in supermarkets and other relatively anonymous settings have eased the situational constraints related to the purchase context itself. A lot has still to be done.
- Price is an important challenge: it is said to be still too high for the purchasing power per capita in a number of less developed countries. However, prices have gone down (see, for instance, condom prices at: http://www.condomusa.com/4dollar.asp).
- A change in basic norms and values as concerns sexual behavior is needed, particularly to promote the perception that the use of protective products such as condoms is an example of responsible rather than irresponsible behavior. Information campaigns and health programs generally ignore the inherent ambiguity in public attitudes toward condoms and miss the key drivers for attitude change.
- Promote a product that is 100 percent safe is one of the major challenges: it is both a matter of product policy by condom manufacturers and also in relation to the purchaser (instructions for correct use).

Government and national HIV/AIDS campaigns aimed at heterosexuals often assume that men and women are equal players in sex acts, and can thus negotiate together preventive measures to be used, such as condoms. Research on gender relations has shown that this assumption is false. A number of studies have described the scripts surrounding male- and female-appropriate behavior in sexual situations, the difficulties facing people who raise condoms as an issue within their relationships, and the structural societal factors that shape many sexual encounters.[41]

The Global Condom Industry: Global And Local Players

Globally the production capacity for condoms is far above primary demand. The quality differential worldwide is considerable, as is the price gap. A condom may be priced anywhere from 0.01 euro up to 1 euro, that is, from 1 to 100. On average, manufacturing of condoms is paradoxically both a low-cost and a technically arduous operation. The industry is comprised of players that provide low-quality, low-price condoms: competition from countries such as Thailand, Malaysia, China, and India is fierce. There are also a number of companies manufacturing condoms in Japan (a major market)—however, with a much higher quality standard.[42] The Hamburg-based company BDF (Beiersdorff) also manufactures condoms and has manufacturing operations in Asia. Durex (USA) is the largest condom manufacturer in the world. Durex is a leading global condom brand with sales operations in 140 countries.[43] Other well-known brands

138   *AIDS and Business*

in Europe are Crest, Manix, Billy Boy, and Hot Rubber. The United States has a large number of condom manufacturers which receive an implicit protection, if not by customs duties, at least through the need for foreign condom manufacturers to be approved by the FDA (Food and Drug Administration), a barrier often difficult to overcome for outsiders. There have even been product liability litigation for condoms in the United States. Such litigation generally does not work in other countries where some people have unsuccessfully tried to sue condom manufacturers. It is difficult in those cases to establish clear evidence of the manufacturer's or marketer's responsibility.

As a consequence of the factors discussed previously, the manufacturing of condoms is a tough business. It is technically difficult to produce a 100 percent safe product (naturally provided that it is used properly as mentioned by the instructions for use). At the same time, it is essentially a low-cost industry. A major European condom manufacturer, Condomi, now owned by Australian conglomerate Ansell (see http://www. *Condomi*.com/) had major financial difficulties because of investment in a new large manufacturing facility, aggravated by a Brazilian default on payment.

Condom Marketing: A Swiss Example

Many companies do not manufacture condoms themselves, especially in smaller markets. For instance, the Swiss company Doetsch Grether subcontracts condoms to large manufacturers, such as Japanese company Okamoto. Value is added not at the manufacturing but rather at the marketing and distribution stage. Marketing is done through contact with public health authorities, HIV/AIDS activists, NGOs, and so on. The main purpose that these stakeholders are seeking is to cooperate for a new approach to prevention.[44] An example of this is that Doetsch Grether meets with the Swiss federal office in charge of HIV/AIDS prevention once a year in order to share information. However, the image of selling condoms is not an excellent one, and the decision to sell condoms was made by Doetsch Grether despite the fact that condoms may not be an excellent corporate image driver.

For Doetsch Grether, condoms are only a small part of their overall business. The company is a private, family business. Ms. Grether is the chief executive officer and other family members are on the executive board. The company has operations in parapharmaceuticals, candies, beauty care, and other product lines.[45] Doetsch Grether has close contacts to large consumer goods multinationals such as Hamburg-based company BDF (Beiersdorff) and American giant Procter and Gamble. Doetsch Grether does product advertising for its condom brands rather than corporate advertising. They received the Evergreen award of the Advertising Club of Switzerland in 1995 for a condom advertisement that was nominated as one of the best ads in Switzerland over the last forty years.[46] For the past ten years, sales of condoms by Doetsch Grether have almost doubled due to adequate advertising, distribution, and sales promotion.

The quality issue is extremely important for the marketing of condoms. A Swiss quality seal for condoms is provided by the organization Verein Gütesiegel für Präservative, founded in 1989.[47] Quality certification is an important marketing argument. Although selling condoms without such quality certification is feasible in Switzerland, there is much consumer awareness of the quality and safety issues, and consumers tend to buy based on quality labeling rather than price. Doetsch Grether monitors quality at every stage from manufacturing to distribution. For instance, shelf life is reduced to three years maximum and monitored so that products are not sold when being out of date. Doetsch Grether condoms are designed and subcontracted under strict specifications developed by the company. Quality control is done piece-by-piece through an electric testing process. It is not done on the basis of sampling part of the production, a common procedure elsewhere.

Condoms in Switzerland[48] are marketed through the major supermarket chain Migros (under the chain's private label), as well as in vending machines in public toilets, motorway service stations, and so on. The Ceylor brand is manufactured by Swiss company Lamprecht AG.

Doetsch Grether has two male condom brands, Crest and Hot Rubber. Crest is mostly sold in retail outlets, pharmacies, and department stores.[49] This brand was bought from Ansell (see http://www.ansell.com) more than a decade ago. The other brand is Hot Rubber, launched in 1974 with the Swiss AIDS Foundation and targeted at the gay market, with a campaign that increased condom sales by 50 percent over three years. To read more about the effectiveness of the Swiss AIDS Foundation campaign, go to: http://www.social-marketing.org/success/cs-stopaids.html.

In other countries, such as Greece, Germany, France, and Holland, Doetsch Grether condoms are sold through broad distribution networks with the local agents as intermediaries. Hot Rubber is commercialized mostly with the assistance of local AIDS federations. Doetsch Grether condoms' selling price is one Swiss franc per condom. Doetsch Grether does not sell through dispensing machines. It is a difficult retail business with about six hundred vending machines in the whole of Switzerland and small operators doing most of the job at home (filling in the packs with condoms they buy) and then servicing the vending machines. The quality of condoms sold in vending machines tends to be relatively poor; however, it is now improving and better than five or six years ago.

It is not in the general policy of Doetsch Grether to undertake social marketing of condoms on a global scale;[50] however, the company donates batches of condoms to NGOs or governments in Africa which are out of market but still usable. When governments, public authorities, or NGOs pay for their orders, viable business opportunities may emerge, but this is not always the case and such business-to-business marketing of condoms can prove dangerous with middle- and low-income countries.

140 *AIDS and Business*

QUESTIONS FOR DISCUSSION

1. Assess the main aspects of consumer behavior for condoms, especially: reasons for use, brakes at various steps of the marketing process (to search for, to purchase, to use), consumer price sensitivity as well as price-quality trade-offs, depending on their purchasing power. You should differentiate between potential condom users who are given the product for free by a public organization or a nongovernmental organization and potential consumers who pay for their condoms.

2. How would you compare the business-to-business segment of condom sales (selling to health care organizations, to nongovernmental organizations, to governmental bodies, and so on) to the business-to-consumer segment (selling direct to users through pharmacies, retail outlets, or online)?

3. How does the Internet inform potential condom users about different brands, quality levels, and features of condoms? In what ways do online condom sales facilitate condom purchases?

4. As a global marketing executive for Protectom, which economic and cultural factors do you consider as relevant for adapting marketing strategies in terms of price, retail distribution, and communication to local markets? You may find it useful to start from examples of how Durex, Ansell and other large players adapt product, price, place, and promotion to local contexts.

5. The five forces model of Michael Porter depicts rivalry between competitors within an industry based on the threat of potential entrants, bargaining power of suppliers and buyers, and threat of emerging product substitutes. Using this model, assess competition within the condom industry.

6 Global Pricing and Ethics of Marketing HIV/AIDS Drugs

The marketing of medical products in an epidemic is a complex issue. HIV/AIDS has well-documented economic, political, and sociocultural impacts on communities, economies, and entire nations. The epidemic has now reached every world region, although most of those affected live in sub-Saharan Africa.[1] These are compelling reasons to pay attention.

Ethical and legal debates cloud policymaking for HIV/AIDS treatment and prevention, often obscuring the way forward. The many different players in the epidemic complicate decision making and implementation. National governments, pharmaceutical companies, international organizations like the World Trade Organization, treatment/prevention advocates, and individual citizens with or without HIV/AIDS bring their vested interests with them, making fruitful cooperation difficult. The medications that alleviate the symptoms of AIDS are costly, patented products. Pharmaceutical multinational companies have attempted various marketing strategies to profitably make HIV/AIDS drugs available for sale to governments, organizations and individuals with low purchasing power. There is much debate surrounding patent protection of medicines and generic competition, with corporate image at stake in rich countries, and survival at stake for resource-poor people with HIV/AIDS. This case study will navigate the maze of HIV/AIDS issues, interests, and players where profits, reputations and—for some—life itself are at stake.

There is currently no cure for HIV/AIDS. Therefore, the biomedical perspective on the syndrome is to alleviate patient discomfort, prevent or treat opportunistic infections, and prolong immune system functioning, thereby prolonging life by using a combination of antiretrovirals. These are also used to prevent mother-to-child transmission of HIV (MTCT). In addition, a wide range of medications is necessary for the person living with AIDS: antibacterial, antibiotic, antidiarrheal, antifungal, antiprotozoal, antipsychotic, antiviral, and chemotherapy, among others. A person with HIV/AIDS requires a range of medical products and services in addition to medications, such as testing facilities, equipment, and personnel for the innumerable blood tests; electrolyte solution; baby milk formula (to avoid breastfeeding transmission); infrastructure for transportation and drug delivery; counseling staff; condoms; examination gloves; medical and support staff, and so on. The long-term business potential of these products and services is considerable.

142   AIDS and Business

There is a profit-generating potential in efforts to treat HIV/AIDS. The correct provision of antiretroviral therapy commonly relies on a combination of costly drugs, usually used together (highly active antiretroviral therapy, HAART). The different categories of these medicines include the following: nonnucleoside reverse transcriptase inhibitors (NNRTI's), nucleoside analogue reverse transcriptase inhibitors (NRTI's), and protease inhibitors.[2] When a combination of these becomes ineffective, a second-line therapy drug is needed.[3] People living with HIV/AIDS with access to HAART are living longer, with a 70 percent lower death rate from HIV/AIDS-related causes in the United States between 1995 and 2001.[4] During this time—which may be as long as 38.9 years for a twenty-year-old person with HIV[5] in British Columbia, Canada—they will consume a large amount and range of drugs. In contrast, in one study conducted by Morgan et al. (2002)[6] in Uganda, people with AIDS without access to treatment tended to be incapacitated for approximately nine months prior to death and on average lived just under ten years after contracting HIV.

Price differences between patented and generic medications may be very large. For instance, when a generic version of fluconazole became available in Thailand, "prices fell to 3 percent of the original level" (UNDP, p. 135).[7] However, it is not possible for many countries, especially smaller ones without local pharmaceutical companies, to make drugs accessible to people with HIV. They simply do not have the capacity to do so.

ECONOMIC, POLITICAL, AND SOCIOCULTURAL IMPACTS OF HIV/AIDS

This section will review the reasons that HIV/AIDS is considered to be a policy priority by pharmaceutical companies, national governments, multinational corporations, and activists around the world. The major impacts of HIV/AIDS have repercussions in the economic, political, and sociocultural realms of affected countries. For a start, life expectancy has seen drastic reductions over the past decade in some countries.[8] As these impacts gain momentum in the unchecked epidemics of large areas of the planet, people in high-income countries will find themselves increasingly affected.

Direct Costs of HIV/AIDS on Societies

Quite apart from the considerations of human suffering and tragedy, an economic analysis of illness usually includes consideration of direct and indirect costs on society. Direct costs include medical care of the sick, funerals, medical research and marketing, and public health prevention campaigns. The spread of HIV/AIDS has also contributed to the spread of other diseases, primarily tuberculosis, increasing the direct costs for that disease also. Tuberculosis is one of the "leading" causes of death of people with HIV.[9] In addition, it is becoming clear that people with HIV are more susceptible

Global Pricing and Ethics of Marketing HIV/AIDS Drugs   143

to developing malaria, and their viral load is increased during malarial episodes. The interaction between the two diseases is thought to have triggered thousands of excess HIV infections, higher numbers of malaria episodes, and may have aided the geographic spread of malaria.[10] People with sexually transmitted diseases (STDs) are two to five times more likely to contract HIV from sexual contact than those who do not have STDs. They are thus more susceptible to HIV because the virus may enter the body with ease through genital sores commonly caused by certain STDs. People with HIV and STDs are also more infectious and can pass on HIV more easily to sex partners than people who are HIV positive but do not have STDs.[11]

Indirect Costs of HIV/AIDS on Societies

Indirect costs of HIV/AIDS are those of a society's human assets lost through sickness and death, as measured by lost earnings and other calculations in the case of people not officially part of the workforce, such as mothers, children, and retired people.[12] The spread of HIV/AIDS has exacerbated health care shortages by impacting health workers, hospital capacity, and medical budgets.[13] In the view of World Bank economists Bell, Devarajan, and Gersbach (2003), there are three factors that make the HIV/AIDS epidemic catastrophic due to the failure of three key processes in economic growth: death of economically productive adults in their "prime" years; failure to transmit knowledge and skills from parents to offspring due to illness or death; failure of children deprived of such "human capital" to become economically productive citizens.[14]

Food Security

Food security has been deeply affected by AIDS. "AIDS has turned a food shortage into a food crisis," according to Joint United Nations program on HIV/AIDS director Peter Piot.[15] The epidemic has changed the dynamics of famine, worsening its effects by killing the members of households capable of producing food, whereas previous to HIV/AIDS, main victims of famine were dependents of the agricultural system—the elderly and children.[16] When a member contracts HIV/AIDS, families often must scale down production or sell their land in order to pay for medicines and funerals. This reduces the family's ability to feed itself, and reduces available food in the long term, which increases the risk of starvation. Subsistence crops tend to replace more labor-intensive cash crops.[17] Agricultural production per family, or per farm, is reduced as the adults who work the land fall ill or must spend time taking care of those who are ill.[18] Farmers have difficulties in finding enough workers.

In sub-Saharan Africa, women are engaged in 50 to 80 percent of food-related agricultural work; however, they also comprise the majority of those living with HIV/AIDS.[19] When productive adults sicken or die and cannot pass on their experience to children, agricultural technology is often lost

144   *AIDS and Business*

forever. This loss of know-how results in poorer crop yields, less diversified crops, and reduced resistance to agricultural pests.[20]

As discussed later in Case Study 10, businesses are severely affected by the epidemic. The World Bank points out that the young (between fifteen and forty-nine years), who are the most productive workers, are most likely to be struck down with AIDS-related illness, disability, and death.[21] Ways in which HIV/AIDS affects the economy are illustrated in Table 6.1.

Table 6.1 Macroeconomic Impacts of HIV/AIDS

Macroeconomic impact	*Description*
Reduced labor supply	Most people with AIDS are in their most productive years and may stop working temporarily or permanently due to AIDS. Cost of production may rise due to potentially higher wages.
Less spending and demand	AIDS households spend much of their income on health care and funeral costs, reducing spending on consumer goods. Survivors may never attain their former spending capacity.
Cut intellectual capital	HIV/AIDS causes the reduction or loss of valuable skills and experience of workers, resulting in higher costs for businesses and government bureaucracies as well as permanent losses to the agricultural and informal sectors.
Lower quality of education	Teachers and government outreach program administrators are often decimated by AIDS, resulting in strained educational resources. Future workers will be less well educated and, therefore, likely to form a less skilled workforce.
Reduced productivity	Workers with opportunistic infections and those tending to sick family members may not work at full capacity. Young new hires are not as productive as older ones who died of AIDS.
Less tax revenue	Less productive workers and families diverted from the work force to care for someone with AIDS result in less tax revenue for governments acutely in need of increased health resources.
Increased public spending	Increased spending on HIV/AIDS prevention and health programs cause budgetary strains and deficits.
Reduced investment by business	Businesses may relocate or reduce their investment in an area with high AIDS prevalence due to AIDS-related costs, estimated at 7% of labor costs.[22] AIDS-related uncertainty may discourage direct investment from abroad as well as local entrepreneurs.
Higher labor costs	Firms may need to hire part-time workers to cover absenteeism of workers sick with AIDS, caring for AIDS-infected family members, and attending AIDS funerals. Recruitment costs for companies operating in already reduced labor pools may be high. The costs of training new hires add to spiraling funeral and insurance spending, further reducing profit margins.

Adapted from the *Program on HIV/AIDS and the world of work*, by International Labour Organization (ILO) (2006),[23] Bell, Devarajan, & Gersbach (2004),[24] and Bloom, Reddy Bloom, Steven, & Weston (2006).[25]

Global Pricing and Ethics of Marketing HIV/AIDS Drugs   145

HIV/AIDS has lowered the gross domestic product in countries across Africa for macroeconomic reasons listed in Table 6.1.[26] In Asia, projections for 2020 view AIDS as reducing the gross national product in some countries by as much as 40 percent.[27] International Labor Organization officials point out that foreign direct investment in the economy tends to suffer as well—by 0.4 percentage points per year lost to HIV/AIDS in one sub-Saharan estimate.[28] Political destabilization may follow economic instability, as it has in a number of African countries.

"HIV/AIDS is a structural and a security issue in a world in which the links between chaos, state failure, and extranational violence are increasingly clear."[29] In its plea to the U.S. government to address HIV/AIDS, the Center for Strategic and International Studies made clear arguments to the effect that unstable governments are in no one's interest. In Africa, the report notes that military personnel and peacekeepers have HIV/AIDS infection rates two or three times that of the general population. Security personnel, such as police officers, are hard-hit by the epidemic: in Kenya, for instance, 75 percent of police deaths were caused by HIV/AIDS in 1999–2000.[30] Peter Piot of UNAIDS made the observation that HIV does to society what it does to the human body: it undermines the very institutions that are meant to defend society—its doctors, its teachers.[31] As food shortages, economic problems, illiteracy, and lowered standards of living take their toll among common people, governments will fail. Failed states create a power vacuum, imperiling regional and international stability.

Nations pay the costs of the epidemic by raising taxes, reducing savings, and increasing borrowing. Funds are often diverted from other government disease programs, resulting in higher mortality rates overall.[32] This increase in mortality is particularly true in poorer countries where malaria, tuberculosis, and diarrheal diseases thrive. Allocations for these diseases in the national health budget often total less than 1 percent.[33]

The interdependency of economic, political, and sociocultural factors is clear in the case of children orphaned by AIDS. Estimates of the number of AIDS orphans by 2010 start at twenty-five million and reach one hundred million, depending on which statistics models and criteria are used.[34] Of all children orphaned by AIDS, 90 percent live in Africa.[35] Half of all the children in Botswana will have lost their parents to AIDS by 2010, when life expectancy is projected to be twenty-seven years, down from today's forty-seven.[36] When AIDS orphans increase, education and socialization are lost, resulting in a degeneration of "social capital." These social norms, values, and levels of trust are essential for a peaceful and functional society and healthy citizens.[37] As adults, these children will be less employable due to their lack of education and socialization, and they will be more likely to contract the disease themselves. HIV/AIDS prevention and treatment are greatly facilitated by educated and aware populations. It has been well documented that those lacking in education

146   AIDS and Business

experience fewer opportunities for income enhancement. Furthermore, females lacking in education are more likely to resort to commercial sex work, thus potentially spreading the disease further, suggesting that battles against HIV/AIDS "won" today will be fought again tomorrow with the next generation, if female social status remains the same.[38] The data on orphans speak for themselves, yet there is a very human dimension to the crisis that is lost in the figures: "Orphanhood starts well before the parents have died, as they [the children] experience the grief and horror of watching parents waste away" (p. 13).[39]

ETHICAL PROBLEMS POSED BY THE COST OF HIV/AIDS TREATMENTS

An understanding of ethical and moral premises for providing access to HIV/AIDS drugs may help governments, international organizations, and corporations find the right path of action. Ethical arguments have been made for millennia to legislate the medical treatment of those who can afford to pay little or nothing. The code of laws elaborated by King Hammurabi of Babylon approximately four thousand years ago is one of the earliest examples. The code provided payment guidance according to the social rank (ability to pay) of the patient—an early form of differential or "equity" pricing.[40] Current discourse on international aspects of ethical arguments relating to HIV/AIDS often evokes a sense of responsibility. As French Minister of State Simone Veil stated in 1994, "We have a historic duty to the countries of the south."[41] Indeed, many of the arguments made in the past century for food aid and refugee policy are now used to justify wider assistance internationally for HIV/AIDS treatments.

"This is a war against humanity," stated Nelson Mandela in his plea for HIV/AIDS medications for all.[42] Treatment costs and patients' ability to pay are one of the major ethical issues surrounding HIV/AIDS. Rationing may occur when medical staff decide who should receive scarce resources like antiretroviral drugs, opportunistic infections treatments, and so on. In many places, whether a new patient should be admitted at all to hospitals with few resources is a severe form of rationing.[43]

Discrimination against people with AIDS by medical staff is a widespread problem that limits access to treatment. A particularly thorny issue is the allocation of medical funds earmarked for HIV/AIDS, in competition with other urgent medical needs. Many activists consider that treatment should be offered to everyone with HIV/AIDS because of the moral equality of all humans—an idea developed in the writings of Hobbes, Kant, and Rousseau. Social justice is often evoked to address the fact that AIDS tends to spread among society's most vulnerable members such as the poor, women and children, and those on its fringes (i.e., tribal/ethnic groups, drug users, and men who have sex with men). On

Global Pricing and Ethics of Marketing HIV/AIDS Drugs   147

an international scale, HIV/AIDS disproportionately affects the poor: more than 95 percent of the people infected with the disease live in developing countries.[44]

Public ethicists analyze the choices made by people in their professional or civic activities where they are representatives of institutions, agencies, and political or activist groups. In the case of HIV/AIDS, public ethics concerns primarily medical staff and government bureaucracies. In past epidemics, governments displayed authoritarian tendencies through quarantines, mandatory testing, compulsory treatment, and so on. Today, in the case of HIV/AIDS, governments may require that certain people— generally sex workers and injecting-drug users—be tested for HIV, may refuse entry of people with HIV (such as Armenia, China, Iraq, Saudi Arabia, Russia, and the United States),[45] and in rare cases quarantine people with HIV (as did Cuba).[46] HIV/AIDS presents particular public policy and human rights issues because it is mainly transmitted in the most private spheres of human activity. Discrimination is a common outcome. Discrimination is considered to be a human rights issue, because it eliminates or restricts the ability of certain individuals or groups to access medical care. Privacy is another issue: where physicians can legally notify spouses or unsuspecting partners of an HIV-positive result, people may be unable to seek health care.[47]

HIV/AIDS AND DEVELOPMENT

AIDS is different from other fatal diseases such as malaria, which kills more than one million people per year.[48] HIV/AIDS kills people in the prime of their lives and leaves the very young and very old to carry the load of survival, thereby severely degrading development prospects in poor countries. Moreover, by controlling HIV/AIDS, co-epidemics of tuberculosis and certain sexually transmitted diseases may also be controlled.[49]

International organizations are strongly oriented towards economic development, reflecting a moral imperative of the rich to the poor. There is a pragmatic aspect of economic development arguments that is difficult to ignore: more sick and dying people in more countries decrease both spending and demand for exports from multinational corporations based in affluent countries. Societies crippled by lack of resources to address illness, death, orphans, food supply, loss of tax revenue, and reluctance of foreign investors, among other compelling issues, may collapse. These failed societies are likely to become vulnerable targets for ideologues, dictatorships, and warlords. Humanitarian reasons set aside, economic justice may solve many problems in an interrelated, "globalized" world. Where gross inequalities in wealth, opportunities, and health exist between nations, the disenfranchised may threaten the safety of people everywhere.[50]

148   *AIDS and Business*

HIV/AIDS AND HUMAN RIGHTS

> Everyone has the right to a standard of living adequate for the health and well-being of himself and his family, including food, clothing, housing and medical care and necessary social services, and the right to security in the event of unemployment, sickness . . .
> —Universal Declaration of Human Rights (Art. 25.1)[51]

> Motherhood and childhood are entitled to special care and assistance.
> —Universal Declaration of Human Rights (Art. 25.2)[52]

The International Bill of Human Rights, elaborated in 1948, and documents and statements subsequently published by the United Nations have emphasized dignity as a foundation for "freedom, justice, and peace." Later documents and statements, published after the emergence of HIV/AIDS, took the perspective that dignity is a foundation for reduced HIV/AIDS burdens around the world. Among the first to take this view was the late Jonathan Mann, founding director of the World Health Organization's Global Programme on AIDS. His observation that "those people who were marginalized, stigmatized, and discriminated against before HIV/AIDS arrived have become over time those at highest risk of HIV infection"[53] was emblematic of his pioneering view that human rights and health were inextricably related. Unfortunately, as noted in the conclusions of the United Nations Second International Consultation on HIV/AIDS and Human Rights, the HIV/AIDS epidemic has ignited a new basis for widespread human rights abuses and curtailment of fundamental freedoms of those people living with the virus.[54]

Probably the human right most directly relevant to HIV/AIDS in the rights literature is the right to health. Similar human health rights are outlined in other international treaties, conventions, resolutions, and recommendations under the auspices of the United Nations and other international organizations, regional conventions and agreements, and national and regional law that may be codified or based on court rulings. The Council of Europe, for example, stated that authorities should provide "equitable access" to health care, and that free and informed consent is required before any medical intervention.[55]

In the United States, the "rights" orientation developed during the civil rights movement in the 1960s. HIV/AIDS emerged soon thereafter. It was in this context that people with AIDS were thought to have negative and positive rights, negative being freedom from discrimination and sanctions and positive being rights of access to services and treatments.[56] According to Gostin (2004), there are three strong relationships between health and human rights:

Global Pricing and Ethics of Marketing HIV/AIDS Drugs 149

1. Health policies of governments affect the human rights of constituents through coercive or discriminatory practices, or omissions (as in the failure to gather data on the HIV/AIDS burden of racial groups).
2. Human rights violations affect people's health in a negative manner: the violation of one's dignity and endemic discrimination may negatively affect one's health.
3. Health and human rights are interdependent: where specific groups have been denied human rights, discriminated against, and marginalized, these groups have been more likely to increase their HIV/AIDS burden.[57] Women generally are a case in point, with their increasing HIV/AIDS burden seen as a result of their lack of power in situations, such as sexual ones, that put them at risk.

For these reasons, it is vital for governments, NGOs, and the private sector to take a human rights perspective when drawing up HIV/AIDS programs and policies. For example, an HIV/AIDS policy should be researched for its potential human rights impacts prior to final drafting and implementation.

HIV/AIDS AND PUBLIC CHOICE: AN ETHICAL DILEMMA

It has been well documented that antiretrovirals improve the quality of life and survival of people with HIV/AIDS in high-income countries. In terms of ethics, do poor people in poor resource settings have a right to these new, expensive treatments? If they do have such a right, how can these costly drugs be made accessible? Is it a choice to treat AIDS when other basic health problems exist?[58] Public authorities have to make tough decisions about the allocation of government money between competing goals in terms of public health policy. Treating HIV/AIDS is a costly choice if budgets must be reduced for other diseases and health problems like malnutrition. Some tropical diseases are found only in Africa and a few countries in the rest of world, such as onchocerciasis, a parasitic disease that harms the skin and the eyes. Merck & Co., manufacturer of Mectizan, a treatment for onchocerciasis, has offered tens of millions of treatments free of charge since 1987 to these countries.[59] For a number of reasons, therefore, other diseases may appear to policymakers to be cheaper to combat than HIV/AIDS and to offer clearer results in terms of general improvement of public health.

There are strong arguments that people in poorer countries have a natural right to be treated if treatments are available. A natural right in itself is not sufficient as a basis for action: it needs to be set out in law, and embedded in legislation that can be implemented. That is the weak point, for most governments in developing countries do not want to make HIV/AIDS treatment a legal right because of economic constraints. Notably, treatment for

150 *AIDS and Business*

all would entail enormous budget increases for public health systems. Governments serious about treating everyone with HIV would have to finance costly antiretroviral and opportunistic infections treatments. The price of patented medicines is not accessible for most patients and indeed many governments in resource-poor settings. For this reason, the governments of Brazil, India, and Thailand have favored local manufacturing of generic drugs, which are much less costly. The government of Brazil has committed itself since 1996 to cover costs of HIV/AIDS treatments, as discussed in Case Study 2.[60]

Due to its effects on the labor supply and losses of productivity in manufacturing, services, and agriculture; reduction of investment and tax revenue; loss of food security, and so on, HIV/AIDS has lowered the GDP in poor countries. The drugs can for this reason be considered as "public goods." According to that argument, even if HIV/AIDS treatments are costly, they should be made available for poor countries.

The kind of ethical "choices" posed by HIV/AIDS are illustrated by dilemmas for the World Health Organization, United Nations, and governments: should we save one AIDS patient or should we save approximately nine thousand dehydrated children from death using equivalent funds? Which diseases should really be prioritized for budget allocations; why not malaria, which kills one million people per year, or an emerging health threat like SARS? Should high-income countries such as the United States send HIV/AIDS funds abroad when some people at home cannot afford to be treated? Should available funds be directed towards prevention or treatment? Almost all nongovernmental advocacy organizations believe that prevention and treatment can only work together. For AIDS advocacy groups such as ACT-UP, Oxfam, and HealthGAP, the ethical course of action would be that the United Nations buys drugs in bulk and donates them to poor nations.[61] Despite the efforts of public and private sectors and international organizations, only a few hundred thousand people in the poorest countries will receive treatment in the next few years at current rates of access.[62] Table 6.2 summarizes the main ethical perspectives on HIV/AIDS treatment policies, and provides some links for further reading.

Corporations have different ethical dimensions as legal, economic, social, and moral organizations. Business leaders may believe that the right actions are those that bring the greater good to the greatest number (utilitarianism). Some believe that the company exists purely to make a profit, and any other considerations should be disregarded, as famously expressed by Milton Friedman.[63] Profit-oriented business leaders may be the first to provide comprehensive HIV/AIDS care if they discover that prevention and treatment are cheaper long term than no program at all. Some companies have defined their area of responsibility in a large sense—to include the families of employees (e.g., DaimlerChrysler South Africa),[64] providing information technology and health information to

Global Pricing and Ethics of Marketing HIV/AIDS Drugs 151

Table 6.2 Summarized Major Ethical Bases of HIV/AIDS Treatment Policies

Major ethical bases of treatment policies	*Resources*
Equal health care for all	Global Treatment Access Campaign http://www.globaltreatmentaccess.org/
National legal framework	Inter Parliamentary Union Handbook for legislators on HIV, law, and human rights http://www.ipu.org/PDF/publications/aids_en.pdf
Social justice, discrimination, legal	World Health Organization http://www.who.int/ethics/en/ethics_equity_HIV_e.pdf
Human rights	Human Rights Watch HIV Program overview http://www.hrw.org/campaigns/aids/index.php
Humanitarian action	Overseas Development Institute review of HIV/AIDS http://www.odi.org.uk/HPG/papers/hpgreport16.pdf
Corporate social responsibility	Business and human rights resource center http://www.business-humanrights.org

communities in need (Hewlett Packard in Brazil, India, and South Africa), and providing information or treatment services to the employees of suppliers and distributors (among companies surveyed by the Global Business Coalition in 2005, 36 percent were involving their suppliers/distributors in HIV/AIDS programs).[65]

A NOTABLE ATTEMPT TO PROVIDE TREATMENT: THE WHO'S 3 BY 5 INITIATIVE

In December 2003 the World Health Organization and UNAIDS commenced the "3 by 5" initiative to help low- and middle-income countries scale up access to antiretroviral therapy to three million people with HIV/AIDS before the end of 2005. Despite the global effort, this target was not met: only eighteen countries met the target of providing treatment to at least half those who needed it. Challenges cited by the WHO included the price of antiretrovirals, which remained "unacceptably high" (WHO, p. 29) in certain countries even though the average price of first-line antiretrovirals (used when there is no drug resistance) dropped by 37–53 percent. Other serious constraints cited were procurement and supply chain management problems, weaknesses in health systems, and political commitment. By 2008, the WHO estimates that US$22 billion will be needed each year to fund treatment programs at current rates.[66]

The WHO estimates of numbers of people who need antiretroviral treatment in Table 6.3 include only those with HIV who have reached the

152   AIDS and Business

advanced stages of the disease. The estimates include people who receive treatments through private sector medical providers and their employers. Not included are those who have HIV but not yet in advanced stages, and newly infected people which together represent the majority of people with HIV. Excluded from the table are Australia, Bahamas, Bahrain, Brunei, Canada, Cyprus, Grenada, Israel, Japan, Kuwait, New Zealand, Qatar, Republic of Korea, Singapore, United Arab Emirates, United States, and the countries of Western Europe.

A number of alternatives could help to reduce the price of antiretrovirals: equitable pricing and/or price reduction, authorization of generic products, decrease or removal of the local taxes, compulsory licensing, investment from pharmaceutical companies, suppression of drug relevant patents for some countries, drugs donation programs, and public-private partnerships, among others. The WHO argues that its program to "prequalify" medicines has intensified competition among drug manufacturers. Drug prequalification ensures that medicines are independently tested for their quality, safety, and effectiveness and the manufacturing facility is inspected. In December 2005, eighty-one antiretroviral drugs were prequalified through the WHO Prequalification Project.[67] An additional problem faced by approximately half a million people is the cost of so-called second-line antiretroviral drugs—those needed by people with HIV who can no longer take the usual, first-line antiretrovirals. Second-line antiretrovirals tend to cost, in Africa, ten times more than first-line

Table 6.3   WHO Estimates of People Aged 0–49 Years Receiving Antiretroviral Treatments in Low- and Middle-Income Countries, Compared with Estimated Number of People Who Need Them

Region	People who needed treatment in 2005	People who received treatment (December 2005)	Treatment coverage (December 2005) Percent
Sub-Saharan Africa	4,700,000	810,000	17
East, South, and Southeast Asia	1,100,000	180,000	16
Latin America and the Caribbean	465,000	315,000	68
Europe and Central Asia	160,000	21,000	13
North Africa and the Middle East	75,000	4,000	5
All developing and transitional countries	6,500,000	1,330,000	20

Adapted from World Health Organization (2006). *Progress on global access to HIV antiretroviral therapy: A report on "3 by 5" and beyond.* Geneva: World Health Organization.

Global Pricing and Ethics of Marketing HIV/AIDS Drugs   153

drugs. In middle-income countries, the difference is more like four to five times more. In 2006, the Clinton Foundation announced price reductions for second-line antiretroviral drugs such as efavirenz. Efavirenz is to be produced in India by Cipla,[68] Ranbaxy,[69] and Strides Arcolab[70] and in South Africa by Aspen Pharmacare[71] for less than US$240 annually per patient, a reduction of about 30 percent or more on normal prices, depending on the market.[72]

PHARMACEUTICAL COMPANIES: MAJOR PLAYERS IN HIV/AIDS TREATMENT

It is clear that HIV/AIDS has caused serious global problems, and has already plowed a path of destruction into the future. People need medications to keep the disease under control so they can go back to work, pay taxes, and raise their children. The main source of these medications is a small number of multinational pharmaceutical companies with a business model that is dependent on the protection of patents. The history of pharmaceutical companies and the AIDS epidemic is one of significant innovative contributions to health on the one hand and the pursuit of profit on the other. At the beginning of the epidemic, the world's pharmaceutical firms were able to price their products well above cost. By some estimates, prices were ten times the manufacturing cost. At the beginning of 2000, a year's supply of a cocktail of antiretroviral (ARV) drugs used to fight HIV/AIDS could cost more than US$10,000 in high-income countries, putting it far beyond the reach of most of the developing world where income may be less than a dollar a day.[73]

According to the *IMS Review*, pharmaceutical sales worldwide continued to grow in 2002, albeit at a slower rate. Despite the generally morose business climate, drug companies' world sales rose 8 percent at US$400.6 billion in 2002. Topping the sales rankings in 2002 were, in order of importance, antiulcerants (the largest category of sales); cholesterol and triglyceride reducers; and antidepressants.[74]

A spokesperson for Aventis, a French-German pharmaceutical company, said, "We can't deny that we try to focus on top markets—cardiovascular, metabolism, anti-infection, etc. But we're an industry in a competitive environment—we have a commitment to deliver performance for shareholders."[75]

The major pharmaceutical companies are research-based, discovering and developing their own products. Research and development (R&D) is a lengthy, costly, and uncertain process. In 2002, research and development expenditure of major drug companies in the United States totaled US$32 billion, representing 18.2 percent of domestic sales. The pharmaceutical industry argues that 70 percent of their products never recoup their research and development costs.[76] The development of a new drug, starting

154 *AIDS and Business*

Box 6.1   Is Business Involvement in the Fight Against HIV/AIDS
Pandemic Mere 'Enlightened Self-interest'?

WHO is also thinking through how it can function as a health organization
and equip business to do its work better as in employee assistance, reasonable
accommodation, and occupational health in collaboration with the ILO, but
not write their agenda for them. It's a delicate line. We are looking at how
we can utilize the skills of business, not merely as employers, for example the
public relations business. . . . I think it's time to ask the question: "How can
business bring its expertise to the table?" HIV is now big enough to get everyone's attention. How to tell the story better, how to carry the message. . .

At the World Economic Forum, HIV has been on the agenda for seven
years, and keep in mind it's a competing set of agendas. That is an achievement. It's a great place to make statements and pronouncements, to appear
to be compassionate. It might stimulate the G-8 regarding debt forgiveness
and health issues and treatment. I would like to think that the WEF creates
momentum and that it has had an impact, but I don't see the evidence. People
at the WEF are very compassionate. Maybe in its day it was a great institution. Corporations today are far more in control, they are determining social
policy and government policy appears to be subservient to business.

Look at South Africa as an example. It is clear that South Africa has a
pro-business environment. Curiously, in the face of government intransi-
gence on this issue and with the risk of loss of 20-30 percent of the population, business has not insisted that people receive treatment. How can that
be good for business? I think it is short-sighted, yet on the side of economics, it appears that AIDS is solving the unemployment problem . . . It is
important to note though that there are some notable exceptions such as
DeBeers, Chrysler Corp. All have employee assistance programs.

The most interesting example is Woolworths. The Board decided to extend
benefits to part time employees. Full time employees were cared for by their
insurance companies. Part timer staff was covered by a Health Management Group, at the insistence of the Board. They extended coverage to virtually their entire staff. HIV education also is done in the workplace, at least
once a year. Health Management Groups are like HMO's, but a manager
contracts for specific services (such as specific doctors in specific practices).
This enables them to seek lowest cost in the marketplace. Additionally, there
is a cap on spending and a due diligence to keep costs down. . . . I think
Woolworth's is emblematic of a small group of entrepreneurs worldwide
who probably have thought and done the same thing. It's not a vast movement. It is one of the companies which are heavily marketing themselves all
over Africa, building an industry in the most heavily infected part of the
world, and in part building a purchasing clientele who will be with them
for a generation. So there might be some enlightened self interest in this. If
they become known as protector of family values, protector of your health,
it's to their advantage. It appears that their market strategy is focused on
the new middle class: precisely the people at risk for HIV because they have
resources, they are mobile, and their values relating to family are different.
Woolworths impressed me because they were driven by their values.

Source: Personal communication, Mr. Ted Karpf, director of partnerships,
WHO HIV Department, Geneva, Switzerland, June 27, 2005.

Global Pricing and Ethics of Marketing HIV/AIDS Drugs 155

with laboratory research and culminating in FDA approval, was estimated to take ten to fifteen years and cost around US$800 million on average.[77] Some of this cost—particularly in the case of basic research—is already covered by government funding and undertaken at public institutions such as research institutes and universities. Yet recently the big pharmaceutical companies have taken to seeking out small biotech companies with an idea that has been already researched and developed and acquiring them, rather than doing their own R&D.[78]

According to the arguments of Leisinger (2005), pharmaceutical companies, like all companies, may be viewed as a subsystem of society where each subsystem has a set of functions, rights, and responsibilities. The capacity of the pharmaceutical companies to meet challenges posed by HIV/AIDS depends not only on the companies themselves but also on the nature of the interrelationships between government, legal, education, and scientific subsystems as well as nongovernmental and international organizations. It would not be productive to impose moral norms on the pharmaceutical industry alone when other subsystems should be also attending to the health requirements of people in need. In addition, drug prices alone are not the main issue when there are immense lacunae in the infrastructure for the delivery of drugs, human resources to prescribe and instruct, and systems to encourage adherence to drug regimens in resource-poor countries that complicate the delivery of drugs—even if they were received free of charge.[79]

HIV/AIDS medications can be very profitable, thereby quickly covering R&D outlays. For example, in 2000, GlaxoSmithKline's profits on its patented AIDS drug Combivir were approximately double the combined health budgets of a group of African countries with the highest prevalence of AIDS in the world. The pharmaceutical industry estimates that a new drug incurs R&D costs of US$500 million; therefore, estimated global profits on Combivir of £300 million and growing have already permitted GlaxoSmithKline to recoup its R&D costs.[80]

The Influence of the Pharmaceutical Industry

According to the Lobbying Disclosure Act of 1995, a lobbying contact is oral or written communication with an elected or appointed government official or employee with regard to the formulation, modification, or adoption of federal legislation, regulation, executive order, appointment, program, policy, or position of the government.[81] In short, lobbying is the attempt by companies and organizations to influence lawmakers. The pharmaceutical industry spent US$91.4 million on lobbying the U.S. government in 2002, an increase of 11.6 percent over 2001, representing the most money spent by any industrial sector. In 2002, the industry used 675 lobbyists from 138 lobbying firms in order to influence legislation and policy of the U.S. government regarding issues such as prescription drugs plans for the elderly, patent enforcement for their products, and the minimization of medical litigation. Twenty-six pharmaceutical lobbyists were former members of Congress. In

156   AIDS and Business

2003, drug companies were scrambling to donate even more to further the cause of President Bush's plan to provide US$15 billion in AIDS-related aid to poorer countries. Given the amount of influence bought by tireless lobbying, it is not surprising that the U.S. government vigorously supports the efforts of pharmaceutical companies to enforce their patents.

The pharmaceutical industry is often criticized for its large sales and marketing outlays. Since 1997, it is estimated that the pharmaceutical industry spent US$100 million on issue-related advertising and marketing, speakers, sponsoring, and the creation of advocacy groups.[82] This figure is in addition to large consumer marketing budgets. Pfizer's spokesperson Brian McGlynn explains, " . . . yes, we spend a lot of money on advertising and marketing. But we don't sell soda pop. It's an enormous transfer of knowledge from our lab scientists to doctors, through those sales reps."[83] It is estimated that pharmaceutical companies provide US$12 billion in gifts and direct payments to physicians yearly in the US.[84] Per-physician payments were estimated at US$8000 to 13,000 (Drake and Ullman in Wazana, 2000).[85] These range from branded "reminders" like pens, to free samples of drugs, to pleasant meals with pharmaceutical sales representatives, to funded travel to conferences. Although gift giving is generally accepted as part of doing business and is known to be effective due to social norms such as reciprocation, it is ethically problematic in the sphere of medical care providers. [86] Physicians who accepted gifts from pharmaceutical companies reduced prescriptions of generic medications, increased prescriptions overall, prescribed newer drugs with little added medical benefit over existing drugs, and had difficulty identifying wrong claims about certain medications. However, such doctors were also more likely to identify treatments for complex ailments.[87] In the United States and New Zealand, medical advertising is permitted directly to consumers, with the effect that advertising and marketing costs of pharmaceutical companies soared as they adopted expensive media campaigns and sponsorships.[88] In 2000 consulting company IMS (in Mintzes et al., 2002) estimated that the pharmaceutical industry spent US$2.47 billion on direct-to-consumer advertising.[89] In a confirmation of industry practice, researchers found that U.S. doctors were more likely to prescribe medications advertised to consumers and requested by patients—despite their own professional ambivalence—than doctors working in Canada, where patients are exposed to very little or no direct to consumer advertising.[90] By reading POZ magazine (http://www. poz.com), a U.S. publication in English and Spanish for people with HIV, one can form an idea of the magnitude of the media presence paid for by major pharmaceutical companies.

GLOBAL MARKETS AND HIV/AIDS

Many AIDS-sensitive operations take place on a global scale. First, subsidiaries of multinationals located in regions with high HIV prevalence are often geographically far-removed from headquarters. Second, many drugs cannot be produced by local firms: either they must be imported or they are manufactured under license from the drug patent owner. Whether exporting, licensing to local pharmaceutical companies, or manufacturing in their own local subsidiaries, the AIDS drugs business is typically more global than local, even though most of the complex issues depicted following are largely at the interface of global markets and local contexts.

The distinction between multidomestic and global markets, first identified by Michael Porter (1986),[91] has been widely applied since the beginning of the 1990s. At the industry level, there has been a shift from multidomestic to global competition patterns. According to Porter, competition becomes global when "a firm's competitive position is significantly affected by its position in other countries and vice-versa" (1986, p. 18). When an industry is multidomestic, separate strategies can be pursued in different national markets, and the global competitive scene remains basically a set of largely disconnected domestic markets. There are some fundamental reasons for industries to remain multidomestic, including wide differences in consumer needs and attitudes across markets, legal barriers resulting from domestic regulations (which have long been in place in the case of banking and insurance for instance), and nontariff barriers which artificially maintain competition between purely national competitors (food and drug health regulations, for instance). Accordingly, the basic preoccupation of a global strategy is the configuration and coordination of activities, including marketing, across national markets.

Trends towards global markets differ depending on the industry. First, the influence of national regulations and nontariff barriers varies across product categories. Second, the potential for experience effects also differs across product categories: for example, there is less potential for cost reduction due to volume increase in the case of cheeses than for microchips. Third, there are different degrees of international "transportability"—the extent to which transportation costs impinge on the configuration of an industry. For instance, exporting may be the dominant internationalization pattern for easily transportable products such as semiconductors.

International trade is now heavily regulated by the WTO, especially since the Uruguay round and the emergence of global rules concerning intellectual property. Companies need to take this type of regulation into account as well as epidemiological trends such as geographical concentration, geographical spread, and patients' ability to pay. These factors, in addition to the demands of HIV/AIDS activists, negative public perceptions of companies, and the changing form of the virus itself, comprise their dynamic operating environment for pharmaceutical companies, medical products and services providers, and health care delivery systems. A survey conducted in 2004 demonstrated the many ways in which pharmaceutical companies operating in low- and middle-income countries may be active, in addition to developing and marketing medications. More than three quarters of pharmaceutical companies

158 *AIDS and Business*

developed partnerships with national health systems and implemented differential pricing in different markets to increase accessibility of their drugs. Half of the companies surveyed were active in encouraging governments to donate to the Global Fund for HIV, TB, and Malaria.[92]

The pharmaceutical and health care industries have an ambiguous status in terms of being multidomestic versus global. On the one hand, they have a number of features characterizing a global industry, such as high transportability of products (transportation costs being quite low in percentage of the product price), high potential for experience effects and economies of scale, and the emergence of global players in the pharmaceutical industry. On the other hand, consumer behavior remains largely local and it is a highly regulated industry, especially for prescription drugs but also as concerns public heath and social security systems. As a consequence, the pharmaceutical industry displays a mixed pattern: market entry authorizations for prescription drugs are still largely granted on a local basis while prices are fixed locally; however, most of this is now visible worldwide. If prices do not cross borders, information does, especially through the Internet, which is replete with provocative information on price differentials across countries for similar products. Many specialized drugs are now known worldwide and some of them can be purchased on the Internet.

Corporate Social Responsibility

As described by Porter and Kramer (2006),[93] the existence of CSR is justified in four ways: license to operate, moral obligation of companies, reputation, and sustainability, and is a concept growing in appeal among companies and, indeed, among societies generally. In order to implement CSR, companies need to decide where their most significant linkages with society are, which social issues they should address and which to ignore, and develop a system of priorities for these. When these decisions are made in a manner that is integrated with company strategy, a new competitive edge may result because what were formerly responded to as significant risks to be managed (such as social or reputation risk) are now proactively and strategically addressed.

Companies tend to attempt to cultivate a socially responsible image, in response to the expectations of their customers and the general public, and as such must be seen as active against the spread of HIV/AIDS or the treatment of those who have it. Companies are corporate citizens both at local and global levels, and as such are concerned about the wider stakeholders in their business, and the extent to which these may become affected by HIV/AIDS. Some companies contribute to the wider efforts made to increase HIV/AIDS awareness and education. Abbott Laboratories donates its Determine HIV tests to pregnant women and mothers in resource-poor settings through a partnership, the PMTCT Donations Program. Boehringer Ingelheim, through the same partnership, donates the antiretroviral Viramune to prevent transmission from mothers to babies.[94]

Global Pricing and Ethics of Marketing HIV/AIDS Drugs 159

In today's world much is expected from companies. Beyond their standard "limited liability," a concept invented in the nineteenth century to foster entrepreneurship, companies are under increasing pressure to behave "responsibly" in a broad array of corporate roles. This is partly a consequence of their increased legitimacy as social actors in a world which puts high value on market mechanisms, technical innovations, training, and human resources, all of which are often understood as being largely in the realm of private businesses. The challenges set by the HIV/AIDS phenomenon to corporate social responsibility should be considered for two different sets of companies: multinational corporations in general, irrespective of their industry, and large pharmaceutical companies which manufacture and sell antiretroviral drugs worldwide.

First, despite the inexorable fact that HIV/AIDS is a global issue of significance in the business environment, companies have a variety of perspectives on it, ranging from indifference to serious action. Yet companies present a diversity of forms and sizes, differentiated across regions and type of economy/industry, complicating the issue. A number of multinational corporations have recognized that they have a role to play in fighting HIV/AIDS at the workplace, in the community, or even on another continent in the case of donations and sponsorships. Some have expressed their concern and joined their efforts against AIDS in local, national, and regional business coalitions, and internationally some have joined the Global Business Coalition (GBC) on HIV/AIDS (www.businessfightsaids.org/). Over the last three years, the coalition has grown from seventeen companies in 2001 to include almost 180 companies worldwide in 2005.

Second, while corporate responsibility for nonpharmaceutical companies has to do mostly with the workforce and secondarily with responsibility toward society at large, there are additional issues for pharmaceutical companies. These companies can increase their profits by selling AIDS drug cocktails worldwide at relatively high prices, which provides them with much more financial resources than the mere recovery of research and development costs would imply. Pharmecutical companies that protect their property rights (trademarks and/or patents) from locally manufactured generics in developing countries by bringing them to court for infringement may be viewed as mere money makers showing no consideration for those who cannot afford their antiretroviral drugs. Obviously, then, showing an image of a socially responsible pharmaceutical company becomes is difficult. That is why pharmaceutical firms have taken some steps to alleviate the problem, following new WTO regulation about compulsory licensing that facilitates manufacturing of low-priced generics. To a large extent, pharmaceutical companies are stuck in the middle. On the one hand, they may appear to be socially responsible—and potentially lose on profit margins. On the other hand, they may appear to be defending their business rights as investors in technology development—and thus incurring the risk of spoiling their public image, not only for HIV/AIDS product lines but for their business as a whole.

Box 6.2 A View from the Field:

Ranbaxy Laboratories Limited Statement[95]

Despite significant advances made in the area of science, the world is still unable to find cures to diseases that have been prevalent for decades. To date, humankind is struggling to find solutions to malaria, HIV/AIDS, and cancer, to name a few. Being a global pharmaceutical major, *Ranbaxy* took a deliberate decision to pool its resources to fight neglected disease segments.

HIV/AIDS is among the major diseases that has impacted developing countries and is a major cause of mortality in several of them. *Ranbaxy* strongly felt that generic antiretrovirals are essential in fighting the worldwide struggle against HIV/AIDS, and therefore took a conscious decision to embark upon providing high quality affordable generics for patients around the world, specifically for the benefit of Least Developed Countries.[96] While we have already allocated sufficient manufacturing capacity to cater to several hundred thousand patients, we are committed to ramping up that capacity as and when required. The company has also made significant investments in setting up business in countries worst affected by HIV/AIDS over the last several years and these are serving as vehicles to make antiretrovirals available in some of the remote places.

Since 2001, *Ranbaxy* has been providing antiretroviral medicines of high quality at affordable prices to HIV/AIDS affected countries for patients who might not otherwise be able to gain access to this therapy. The Company's antiretrovirals have been used as mainstays in various large treatment programs, both National and NGO/Institutional with good results. In October 2003, *Ranbaxy* joined hands with The William Jefferson Clinton Foundation[97] for supply of HIV/AIDS drugs at reduced prices. The objective of the initiative was to bring antiretroviral drugs, within easy access to millions of people suffering from HIV and AIDS in developing countries. Later in October 2004, as a further means of lending support to the global fight against HIV/AIDS, *Ranbaxy* initiated filings of its antiretroviral Abbreviated New Drug Application (ANDA) with the US Food and Drug Administration (FDA)[98] under the PEPFAR program (US President's Emergency Plan for AIDS Relief).[99] *Ranbaxy* was the first Indian pharmaceutical company to initiate filings with the USFDA under the PEPFAR program. The Company has already filed a range of antiretrovirals for US FDA approvals and has begun to receive tentative approvals from the US FDA under the PEPFAR program. *Ranbaxy* also works closely with the World Health Organization (WHO),[100] Geneva, and already has a range of antiretrovirals in its pre-qualification list.

Ranbaxy's recent joint venture in South Africa, *Sonke Pharmaceuticals* (Pty) Ltd, with *Community Investment Holdings* (CIH) for marketing range of antiretroviral products in South Africa and other African markets, reflects the Company's commitment to fight this most dreaded disease of the world. We are engaged in providing international quality generics at affordable prices to the people who need it the most.

Source: personal communication with Mr. Krishnan Ramalingam, manager, Corporate Communications, Ranbaxy (17 March, 2006). For more information go to: http://www.ranbaxy.com/.

COMPULSORY LICENSING, PARALLEL IMPORTS, AND WORLD TRADE ORGANIZATION LEGISLATION

Drugs, Intellectual Property Rights, and the World Trade Organization

Intellectual property rules are now a fully fledged domain for global trade regulation by the World Trade Organization (WTO). Part of the founding treaty of the WTO was the Agreement on Trade Related Aspects of Intellectual Property Rights, including Trade in Counterfeit—commonly known as the TRIPS agreement.[101] The TRIPS agreement covered trademarks, copyrights, designs, patents, and other legal facets of intellectual property. Developing countries were given an extended time period for compliance until 2005, then prolonged until 2016. Specifically, TRIPS contains a number of rules that oblige developing countries and emergent economies to respect trademark and patent laws which some countries (such as Brazil, India, and Korea) had not fully implemented at the time of the agreement. Because costly royalties on patents and trademark generally increase the price of drugs, the implementation of TRIPS in health care is bound to limit patients' access to treatments and enters in conflict with public health policies in many countries. In recognition of this problem, a WTO ministerial declaration was adopted November 14, 2001 at Doha dealing with TRIPS and public health. Ministerial declaration paragraphs 4 and 6 stated:[102]

> We agree that the TRIPS Agreement does not and should not prevent members from taking measures to protect public health. Accordingly, while reiterating our commitment to the TRIPS Agreement, we affirm that the Agreement can and should be interpreted and implemented in a manner supportive of WTO members' rights to protect public health and, in particular, to promote access to medicines for all. . . . Each member has the right to grant compulsory licences and the freedom to determine the grounds upon which such licences are granted. . . . We recognize that WTO members with insufficient or no manufacturing capacities in the pharmaceutical sector could face difficulties in making effective use of compulsory licensing under the TRIPS Agreement.

When a government allows a local company to produce the patented product or process without the consent of the patent owner, usually in extenuating circumstances, the procedure is known as compulsory licensing.[103] Compulsory licensing has been implemented mostly in Brazil, India, and Thailand. Partly as a result of this, Indian pharmaceutical firms, such as Cipla,[104] have developed into large manufacturer of generics antiretroviral medications. The Thai government has implemented compulsory licensing for two antiretroviral drugs and three cancer treatments.[105]

162 AIDS and Business

Article 31(f) of the TRIPS agreement limits production under compulsory licensing to be predominantly for use in the domestic market and not for export. Thus, bypassing intellectual property rights cannot be extended globally by exports of generic medications manufactured under the auspices of compulsory licensing. This limitation of competition by generic drugs manufactured under compulsory licensing to the domestic markets of a small number of large and advanced "developing" countries has the effect of preventing countries with little or no pharmaceutical industry from importing cheaper generics. For instance, under such provisions Bolivia could not import Brazilian generic antiretroviral drugs. Some governments labeled "courageous" by activists creatively interpreted TRIPS provisions and issued government use orders for antiretrovirals, then licensed a local company to do the importing—such was the case of Malaysia.[106] The government of Canada used compulsory licensing to export a triple combination AIDS drug to Rwanda in 2007,[107] because like many other countries Rwanda—lacking its own pharmaceutical industry—was effectively excluded from finding a low-cost AIDS treatment solution.

The Risks of Grey Markets for Antiretroviral Drugs

A grey market occurs when "an exporter knowingly or unknowingly sells to an unauthorized agent who competes directly with the sole agent appointed by the exporter within the same territory" (Palia and Keown, 1991, p. 47).[108] Grey markets are based on parallel imports that hamper the effectiveness of a pricing strategy across various national markets. Grey markets are an issue in global markets for a large number of consumer products or industrial items (Myers, 1999).[109] They also exist for pharmaceuticals. For instance, grey markets for drugs exist in the European Union (EU), where the average price of drugs may vary widely (Chaudry and Walsh, 1995). Despite local regulations and fixation of price by local health systems in each country, the European Court of Justice generally has favored the application of Article 30 of the Treaty of Rome that provides for the free movement of goods in the EU, condemning obstacles to parallel imports. The same situation holds true in the United States, where the rights of trademark owners in grey markets changed in 1998 with the U.S. Supreme Court ruling *L'Anza Research International v. Quality King Distributors,* where judges decided that once the ownership is passed, control is lost over the resale, and the subsequent purchaser is allowed to lawfully sell the item without the authority of the rights holder (Clarke and Owens, 2000).[110]

Grey markets generally deal with branded and/or patented products of a particular manufacturer that implements very different price levels across national markets and therefore generates arbitrage opportunities. They may also develop in the case of generic pharmaceutical products. For instance, if a Brazilian generic antiretroviral drug-manufacturing company sells at a discount to a pharmaceutical distributor in a Central American

Global Pricing and Ethics of Marketing HIV/AIDS Drugs   163

country because local patients cannot afford European or U.S. price levels for antiretroviral drugs, there is a risk that the goods will be shipped back from this country to the United States and sold there through unofficial channels. Geographically proximate national markets exist not only in Europe but also in West Africa, Latin America, and Southeast Asia. Once different price levels are set in two neighboring countries, patients and pharmaceutical distributors or unofficial intermediaries may seek supplies from the cheaper source for an official, legally patented and branded drug, making the manufacturer compete with its own products (Chaudry and Walsh, 1995).[111]

Local intermediaries also may seek supplies from the cheapest sources such as Indian or Brazilian generic drugs manufacturers if the price differential is large enough to offset transaction costs. Unauthorized intermediaries (colloquially termed "smugglers") may compete with sole agents or exclusive dealers in national markets where a specific marketing strategy has been defined. They can be seen as "free riders" who take advantage of the costly R&D and marketing costs borne by the pharmaceutical company and its official distribution channels, to cut prices and margins, and build volume without participating in the overall contribution to the brand's investments (Tan et al., 1997).[112]

When corporate global price policies specify country-specific prices, unintended opportunities may arise for consumers. Country-specific price differentials across countries may be huge—as wide as a ratio of one to ten in some cases. Opportunities emerge from this situation for people with HIV as consumers of drugs, as well as distributors who may undertake arbitrage (Nyarandas et al., 2000).[113] Consumer arbitrage is often effected through holiday traveling or online ordering, and these personal imports may affect the domestic sales of pharmaceutical manufacturers in developed markets where the prices are kept high (Weigand, 1991).[114] The objective of monitoring product price positioning across markets is a difficult issue for pharmaceutical companies for these reasons. Indeed, in certain countries, local intermediaries may be forced to sell at prices lawfully dictated by the local National Health System, while in other countries, legislation may reflect the belief that such practices are contrary to effective competition. Resale price maintenance laws prohibit the imposition of prices by the producer on an agent, even though this may be required by marketing strategy. Firms then maneuver around these laws by specifying recommended retail prices, thus controlling the discretionary margin of distributors and intermediaries. An agent could potentially try to sell the medication at a discount price and come into conflict with the producer's pricing strategy.

Exclusive distribution agreements in home markets would appear to be a plausible solution to the problem of grey markets, but the implementation of exclusivity clauses is problematic. In the United States, there is some reluctance to limit competition by granting enforceable exclusivity rights to

164 *AIDS and Business*

dealers. In the United States parallel importers, competing with the authorized dealers of leading brands, were accorded an almost complete victory by the K-Mart ruling handed down by the U.S. Supreme Court.[115] Companies with well-known brands, such as Cartier and Seiko, were struggling against parallel importers, but the Supreme Court judged that they cannot prevent unauthorized importation of products bearing their brand name, since their right to control the trademark is exhausted by the sale.

Compulsory Licensing and Export to Third Countries

In 2003, WTO members agreed to remove the export prohibition associated with compulsory licensing by introducing legal changes that make it easier for poorer countries to import cheaper generics made under compulsory licensing.[116] However, there are a number of conditions for the import of generics to be allowed:[117]

- Importing countries should be unable to manufacture the medicines themselves.
- They should officially become an "eligible importing Member" by a notification to the Council for TRIPS of their intention to use the system as an importer.
- They should specify the expected quantities of drugs needed.

As expected, the system is controlled, because of the possibility—illegal but feasible—for importing countries to reexport low-priced generics to third countries, whether poor or rich. For pharmaceutical multinationals, the threat is rather large, at several levels:

- Large generic manufacturers such as India's Cipla may become low-cost competitors for a broad array of drugs including antiretroviral treatments (Cipla's products also include antidepressants, heart medications, pain medications).
- Antiretroviral generics may be (illegally) reimported from third countries which benefit from the measures taken by the WTO in 2003.
- The legitimacy (if not the legality) of property rights for drugs is partly challenged by this evolution favoring generics as a whole.

These competitive threats should be mitigated by the following facts: (1) both exports and imports of generics made under compulsory licensing are under strict control of the WTO;[118] (2) the R&D investments needed for developing new, more efficient, and more comfortable treatments will cease if intellectual property on drugs does not actually generate cash flows for reimbursing the previous investment in research and therapeutic testing, and recovering the high costs of bringing a new drug to market; (3) several large industrial countries are homes to one or several of the pharmaceutical

Global Pricing and Ethics of Marketing HIV/AIDS Drugs 165

multinationals that developed antiretroviral drugs, and they will not accept an implementation of compulsory licensing that goes too far in threatening the basic business interests of these companies;[119] (4) the high risk perceived by patients in developed countries in buying generics.

The last point is important because it may maintain a fairly high level of disconnection between local markets for antiretroviral treatments. Generally, research on evaluation of goods by consumers according to their manufacturing origin shows that consumers in developed countries tend to perceive goods manufactured in developing countries as lower in quality and reliability (Usunier, 2000).[120] Furthermore, the perceived risk is likely to be higher for pharmaceutical products, especially when sophisticated antiretroviral therapies are involved. Patients in affluent markets may not willingly transfer their trust to generic products. This is particularly likely to be true when treatment expenses are largely or fully reimbursed by the social security system or private health insurance. Then, patients in developed markets are likely to be much less price-oriented and therefore more unlikely to take the risk of buying foreign-made generics.

The Role of Patents for the Pharmaceutical Industry

Patent protection of medicines, particularly those that treat HIV/AIDS, is at the center of a worldwide ethical, economic, and social debate. Pharmaceutical companies are dependent on the strength of intellectual property because their products can be copied with relative ease, but the cost of developing them is very high. Because a pharmaceutical patent encapsulates the products themselves—unlike patents in other industries where patented processes or items are only one part of the product, such as televisions—the power of pharmaceutical companies lies in their patents. For this reason a strong local and international intellectual property framework and enforcement mechanisms are vital for the well-being of pharmaceutical companies. An inventor (individual or company) owns the patent for a particular formulation, design, or manufacturing process for twenty years. This period is less in the case of pharmaceutical products due to the specificities of medical research and clinical trials. During the twenty-year period, competitors cannot legally replicate a patented formula, also known as a proprietary medicine. This protects the patent-owning company from competition, thus allowing the company to set its own selling conditions and prices. Patent holders must apply for a patent in each country where it seeks protection.

Those who demand cheaper HIV/AIDS medications for the poor generally consider patent protection to be a barrier to access of affordable medications. Proponents of this view include Médecins Sans Frontières, Oxfam Canada, Treatment Action Campaign, Health Gap, and others. Others point out that the problem is a lack of funding to pay for drugs—patented or not.[121] Yoweri Museveni, the president of Uganda during campaigns that resulted in a reduction in Ugandan HIV/AIDS prevalence,

166   *AIDS and Business*

stated that the focus on pharmaceutical patents at trade negotiations was a "red herring" that diverted attention away from other trade issues like agricultural subsidies.[122]

Pharmaceutical companies in the United States and around the world assert that drug patents must remain intact, in the face of many poorer nations that request patent exceptions on HIV/AIDS drugs. During a period when pharmaceutical companies were under fire from some quarters on the subject of HIV/AIDS drugs for resource-poor countries, the director general of the International Federation of Pharmaceutical Manufacturers Association stated: "The international pharmaceutical industry firmly believes that the weakening or infringement of intellectual property rights as reflected in the international trade agreements amounts to a disincentive for investment and research and development, and that factors other than intellectual property rights are at the root of the problems of access to medicines."[123]

Some low-income nations, which harbor the majority of people with HIV/AIDS, cite the World Trade Organization's (WTO) Doha Declaration, which states that a nation facing a medical emergency may nullify patents for relevant drugs in order to permit generic versions of the drug to be produced domestically. This permission was intended to ease prices and shortages.[124] The stated intention of the Doha Declaration[125] was to place public health above commercial interests by lightening the restrictive international trade rules set out in the TRIPS agreement.[126] However, as discussed earlier, many low-income nations cannot produce their own drugs. The U.S. government has been frequently accused of blocking the efforts of poor countries to import generic drugs.[127] One example of this is the insistence by the President's Emergency Plan for AIDS Relief (PEPFAR) on using patented drugs to the detriment of the many cheaper generic formulations already approved by the WHO.[128]

AIDS treatment activists Health GAP Coalition summarized some of the defenses frequently used by pharmaceutical companies in patent negotiations, and their own rebuttals. According to the Health GAP Coalition, the public unthinkingly accepts the drug company line.[129] Primary defenses of pharmaceutical companies and activists' rebuttals are summarized in Table 6.4.

Patent Battles, Negotiations, and Marketing

Resource-poor governments seeking certain drugs may utilize a TRIPS-validated avenue: parallel importing, whereby a cheaper generically produced version of a drug is imported from another country.[130] Although legal, parallel importing is discouraged, as the following examples illustrate. The Common Market for Eastern and Southern Africa (COMESA) represents countries home to 70 percent of adults and 80 percent of children living with AIDS. COMESA's attempts to trade generic drugs across borders were blocked by the U.S. pharmaceutical industry, which views the issue as a cost

Global Pricing and Ethics of Marketing HIV/AIDS Drugs   167

Table 6.4   Pharmaceutical Industry Stance on Patent Issues, and Rebuttal for Each

Common justifications for strict patents	*Rebuttal by Healthcare GAP Coalition*
1. If poor countries nullify patents, R&D would stop: there would be no research incentive left.	With 80 percent of sales in rich countries, pharmaceutical companies can find enough funds to continue research. Drugs are cheaper in developing countries, adding less to profits.
2. If poor countries are given breaks on necessary medicines, they will ask for breaks on everything else.	India and others are asking for permission to produce their own cancer and heart medications. However, Indian generic drug companies are not likely to compete directly with patented products in major markets.
3. India and Brazil attempt to improve conditions for their own generics industries.	Healthy generics industries help more people be healthy, by making available reasonably priced medicines. Brazil and India understandably defend their industries.
4. The diversion risk is too great (that poor generics may be diverted for sale in rich countries).	Diversion is illegal, and strictly enforced. There is not much demand for poor-country generics in rich countries due to health insurance and perceived quality issues.

Adapted from Baker, B. K. (2002). *Four lies post-Doha*. Health GAP Coalition (December 23).[131]

issue while for African governments it is a question of public health, according to COMESA's secretary general, Erastus Mwencha.[132] He added that the HIV/AIDS epidemic was the biggest threat to regional economic development.[133] In 1997, another battle loomed when Nelson Mandela's South African government attempted parallel importing of generic HIV/AIDS medications, and was taken to court by thirty-nine pharmaceutical companies, including GlaxoSmithKline, Roche, Merck, Boehringer-Ingelheim, and Bristol-Myers Squibb. In 2001, the pharmaceutical companies withdrew their complaint after an international uproar and a public relations disaster. After a similar international pressure, the U.S. government withdrew its pressure on the South African and Brazilian governments.[134] Drug companies and the U.S. government continue to discourage parallel importing and compulsory licensing for AIDS medications, albeit in a subtle manner, using case-by-case negotiations. According to the *Wall Street Journal*, the U.S. Commerce Department is providing technical assistance to developing countries to construct strict drug patent protections that are more severe than the WTO's own rules.[135]

Pharmaceutical companies add to the legal and diplomatic pressure to protect patents by offering price reductions and AIDS drugs donations. A typical negotiating strategy includes offering company-made (patent-protected) medicines

168 *AIDS and Business*

at a discount, as long as the country agrees—in a confidential agreement—not to buy generic medicines.[136] "Systematic intimidation"[137] characterizes these negotiations, according to Oxfam's Michael Bailey, referring to the unequal bargaining power of pharmaceutical companies and needy governments.

Drug donations pose problems, although on the surface they appear to be an ideal solution. The same formulations may be available generically at lower cost long term. Donations may incur a sense of indebtedness that may cause the government to turn away from a potentially cheaper, more independent long-term solution with a generic-drug manufacturer.[138] Donations are short term, whereas HIV/AIDS drugs need to be taken consistently on a long-term basis. Because each drug has different handling and dosage requirements, donations are likely to go to waste through distribution problems and lack of patient knowledge of the drug. Donations are also likely to be seen as public relations maneuvers and may even be counterproductive for pharmaceutical companies seeking a positive image. A much more helpful program would include affordable medications, supplied consistently over time in the framework of a general AIDS management program. According to some analyses, pharmaceutical companies may donate drugs to poor countries to protect those markets from generic competition, and to enable governments to pay for medications needed for other diseases like malaria and common tropical diseases.[139]

Patents and AIDS: Recent Developments

There have been efforts to facilitate access of low-income countries to HIV/ AIDS drugs through the World Trade Organization (WTO). In November 2002 the WTO reached an agreement to make certain drugs available to poor countries before their patents expire in twenty years; however, the United States, under the influence of its pharmaceutical lobby, vetoed it. Finally, in August, 2003 the WTO members agreed to make generic AIDS drugs available in some low-income countries for the first time (see Appendix A for details). Under WTO rules agreed at Doha in 2001, many poor countries were allowed to manufacture their own versions of patented drugs.[140] However, most could not set up pharmaceutical manufacturing; therefore, the provisions effectively limited cheap generic drugs to comparatively affluent countries like Brazil.

The August, 2003 agreement was a breakthrough, and so acclaimed it was extended permanently in 2005.[141] Finally, needy WTO member countries could import pharmaceutical products made under compulsory licenses, with certain constraints. Some developed countries voluntarily opted out of the possibility of importing drugs, while others reserved the right to do so in case of a health emergency. Although there was much praise for the decision, many health care organizations and a number of countries that should benefit pointed out that the stipulations about drug

Global Pricing and Ethics of Marketing HIV/AIDS Drugs 169

appearance, packaging, and labeling were so complicated as to raise the manufacturing cost of the product—and thus the price. The pharmaceutical industry demanded such stipulations in order to reduce the risk of smuggling the drugs into rich countries.[142] Nongovernmental organization Médecins Sans Frontières (MSF) spokesperson Ellen 't Hoen criticized the agreement, saying that it was designed to provide "comfort" for Western pharmaceutical corporations, and the high prices of branded medications would continue to make access impossible for the poor AIDS patients of the world.[143] For more information and updates on negotiations, see the WTO's dedicated site on TRIPS and public health: http://www.wto.org/english/tratop_e/trips_e/public_health_e.htm.

Pharmaceutical companies may use licensing to increase access to their medications. Such was the stated goal of Boehringer-Ingelheim and Glaxo, which granted licenses to producers of generic medications in India and South Africa to manufacture antiretroviral drugs in an out-of-court settlement with activists. The companies were to receive no more than 5 percent of sales in royalty payments, and may export their drugs to other sub-Saharan countries.[144] Glaxo reached agreements to license antiretrovirals AZT and Lamivudine, while Boerhringer-Ingelheim granted three licenses for Nevirapine, an antiretroviral used primarily to prevent mother-to-child transmission.[145] Merck, with the support of Bristol Meyers Squibb, granted a royalty-free license to manufacture combination therapy drug Efavirenz to South African generic manufacturer Thembalani Pharmaceuticals.[146] At the 2006 International AIDS Conference, Gilead announced that it had granted licenses to Indian generic pharmaceutical manufacturers to make antiretroviral drugs Truvada and Viread with the capability to export the drugs to ninety-five low-income countries. Gilead President and CEO John Martin stated that the company anticipated " . . . granting additional licenses over time to help meet the needs of patients in the developing world."[147]

THE ISSUE OF ANTIRETROVIRAL DRUG PRICES: SOCIAL COSTS AND DRUG PRICES

The high prices of antiretroviral (ARV) drugs are a serious issue for governments of countries where HIV/AIDS is leaving its fatal mark. Paying for the drugs is just one of the many costs inflicted by the epidemic. Some governments have taken matters into their own hands by encouraging generic production of the drugs, sparking new competitive pressures for patented drugs. Some pharmaceutical companies have responded by changing their pricing strategies to a more equitable basis.

Antiretroviral drug prices have decreased since 2000, when pharmaceutical companies announced the first major price reductions, although they remain approximately double those of generic manufacturers. For example,

170   AIDS and Business

one generic formulation costs US$0.96 per day, versus US$2 for a patented version.[148] US$2 may be the total yearly budgeted amount per capita for all medical care in some poor countries.[149] In addition to drug costs, there are HIV/AIDS-related costs to consider when projecting the epidemic's impact, such as:

- HIV training for medical personnel and recruitment of additional staff
- Voluntary testing/counseling (often costs more than per capita medical spending)
- Patient education on drug combinations, side effects, and psychological counseling
- Prevention/treatment of opportunistic infections, and pain relief
- ARV drugs over a lifetime, their procurement and distribution
- Laboratory tests for monitoring (which currently exceed the costs of ARVs[150])
- Prevention of further spread of HIV (usually education and condom supply)
- End-of-life care.[151]

From a government's perspective, it is daunting to plan an HIV program. Treating HIV/AIDS is more complicated and costly than simply distributing pills. Prevention and destigmatization campaigns, rigorous and consistent lifelong patient follow-up, and monitoring and treating viral and bacterial changes in patients are vital to AIDS programs everywhere. Yet needs may vary greatly from one country to another. In some countries, like Cambodia, it was found that an essential element to AIDS programs was the provision of food.[152] In the Philippines, house help was considered to be important. Everywhere, basic medical supplies such as condoms, examination gloves, syringes, and laboratory tests were needed.[153]

Drug Pricing and the Contribution of Generic Manufacturers: Brazil and India

In 2002, the U.S. Congress believed that the country was threatened by a terrorist anthrax attack. It responded by demanding compulsory licensing for Cipro, a costly antibiotic produced by Bayer. The government intended to control supply and costs by legally allowing domestic competitors to produce the medication generically. As discussed earlier, this is allowed in a "medical emergency," according to principles of the WTO's Trade Related Aspects of Intellectual Property Rights (TRIPS). Bayer responded by immediately offering greater quantities of the drug at lower prices—not needed when the true scope of the anthrax "threat" was known. Critics have pointed out the inconsistency of the U.S. government's implementation of TRIPS in the face of its own perceived anthrax threat, and in the face of multiple AIDS drugs crises abroad.

Global Pricing and Ethics of Marketing HIV/AIDS Drugs 171

"Patients' rights above patents' rights" is a rallying call of the global protest against high drug prices.[154] Drug patents offer companies legal protection against competition that allows them to charge high prices: patents are temporary monopolies. Drug prices may be determined with little relation to costs due to variations between countries of profit margins, R&D costs, marketing costs, tariffs, exchange risk, fiscal burdens, and distribution costs. Price variations in the case of GlaxoSmithKline's Lamivudine were found to be approximately 20 percent higher in Africa than in ten high-income countries.[155] Médecins Sans Frontières found that Pfizer's drug Fluconazole cost considerably less in countries where there was competition from generic pharmaceuticals, such as India, Bangladesh, and Thailand.[156] See Médecins Sans Frontières (Doctors without Borders) for more information on access to medicines at http://www.msf.org.

When Brazil's Ministry of Health determined that Brazilians with HIV should be provided with free treatment in 1996, antiretroviral drugs were provided along with a social destigmatization program and awareness campaigns (see impressive resources—some in English—at http://www.aids.gov.br). Despite the considerable costs in this populous country, the ministry of health[157] boasts that the program is cost-effective, and even that it saved the government an estimated US$1 billion over five years. Annual costs of ARVs in Brazil are US$235 million, or 1.6 percent of the health budget. This cost represents half the price charged in 1997, partly due to the fact that the majority (63 percent) of the drugs were made by local generic manufacturers such as state-owned laboratory Far-Manguinhos.[158] Under budgetary pressure from the Brazilian congress in 2003, the Brazilian government again attempted to renegotiate AIDS drug prices with makers Roche, Abbott, and Merck, which supplied the majority of nongeneric drugs. A lack of agreement with the pharmaceutical companies would force the government to remove patent protection from certain medications or to turn to Indian generic drugs makers.[159]

Through real or threatened generic competition, Brazil has secured significant discounts on principal HIV/AIDS treatments. In cooperation with nine other Latin American countries, Brazil is planning to continue its fight for affordable treatment. The countries, facilitated by the Pan American Health Organization, have secured a negotiating process that puts pharmaceutical companies in direct competition with generic manufacturers. Price reductions on combination therapy secured by the process ranged from 30–92 percent.[160]

India is the second largest pharmaceutical market by volume and thirteenth in terms of value.[161] Indian generic drugs maker Cipla (www.Cipla.com) is commonly credited with breaking the combined power of pharmaceutical companies by offering an antiretroviral cocktail at less than US$1 per person per day in 2001. Cipla and an estimated twenty thousand other companies[162] produce generic ARVs legally, thanks to an Indian law that

172 AIDS and Business

permits copying a patented drug if the manufacturing process is different. The World Health Organization (WHO) and other independent bodies have officially approved the quality of Cipla medications.

Cipla uses differential pricing in the hope of recovering costs while making the drug available to as many people as possible. For instance, they may charge a "commercial" price of US$1,200, a "government" price of $600, and a "humanitarian" price of US$350 for nongovernmental organizations.[163] The company offers HIV/AIDS medications at much lower prices to poor countries like Burkina Faso than major pharmaceutical companies (e.g., US$37 per person per month versus US$150, respectively, in a 2003 offer). However, in the case of poor countries, where 45 percent of the population survives on less than US$120 per year, this may still be too expensive.[164] In addition, a Cipla executive speculated, the world's poorest governments worry that buying generic drugs may trigger the retaliation of the U.S. government.[165]

The role of generics cannot be ignored: the WHO estimates that AIDS drug prices have decreased by about 95 percent, but are still priced higher than generic manufacturers' prices.[166] Governments that implement a generic drug policy have found that generics play a vital role in bringing down the costs of private brand medicines.[167]

Competition from Generics Manufacturers Located in "Developing" Countries

There is the potential in the long term that Cipla, and Brazilian AIDS drug manufacturers, among others, may be potential competitors in developed markets for large pharmaceutical corporations. Brazil and India challenge the very notions of "Third World" and "underdevelopment," with their excellent universities, researchers, medical doctors, and pharmaceutical manufacturers. Competitors such as these who manufacture comparable—whether generic or not—medicines more cheaply raise the issue of whether AIDS medicines are not actually overpriced by large pharmaceutical corporations.

Patent legislation protects pharmaceutical companies to a degree from Indian, Brazilian, Thai, and other competitors. WTO provisions concerning the manufacturing of AIDS generic drugs in developing countries show it is now largely allowed, and the provisions of patent law are relaxed in the case of developing countries. However, this provision is limited to markets with low purchasing power. Manufacturers of generic drugs from India, Brazil, and others are neither allowed nor encouraged to compete against pharmaceutical companies in high purchasing power markets with low-priced generics that would locally infringe the legal dispositions of patent protection and market entry authorization required for pharmaceutical products. Indeed, the distinction between high and

Global Pricing and Ethics of Marketing HIV/AIDS Drugs 173

low purchasing power markets may be artificial. In Thailand, for example, medicines that are locally manufactured under compulsory licensing are not for everyone, as the former health minister makes clear the situation in Thailand:

> So we decided to try to find the generic alternative to serve these neglected people [80 percent of the population]. Actually, we never disturbed the current consumer of patented drugs—those 20 per cent of people who can afford to pay out of pocket to get access to these [brand-name] drugs. They will never change, they will never switch from the original drug to a generic drug. These are well-off people who receive their services from the private sector and pay out of pocket, and also civil servants whom the government pays for their high price patented drugs, as well as about two million foreign patients ["medical tourists"].[168]

EQUITABLE PRICING AND GENERIC COMPETITION

According to Médecins Sans Frontières, the "most powerful downward pressure on prices has been a system of equity pricing."[169] Equitable pricing and competition by generic drugs will immediately give more people access to antiretroviral drugs. Equitable pricing is particularly needed in low-income countries, where those who can afford to buy medicines do so only on a cash basis. Table 6.5 summarizes the benefits and risks of equitable pricing.

There are currently no pricing guidelines for pharmaceutical companies, which have each developed their own pricing criteria. When negotiating a discounted price for an HIV/AIDS medication, Merck considers a country's HIV/AIDS prevalence, gross domestic product, and nonincome poverty measures like the Human Development Index (http://hdr.undp.org/). GlaxoSmithKline uses a combination of least developed countries and

Table 6.5 Benefits of Equitable Pricing, or Differential Pricing

Benefits of equitable pricing	Risks of equitable pricing
Increased access due to affordability for more people	Parallel reimportation: illegal practice of reselling drugs in higher-priced market
Increased revenues from more sales made in countries that were excluded using single pricing	Possibly less profitability at the beginning

Source: Bahadur, C. (2001). *TRIPS, HIV/AIDS, and access to drugs*, United Nations Development Project, Trade and sustainable human development policy (background paper), September.[170]

174 AIDS and Business

Box 6.3 A View from the Field:

Brazilian Generic Manufacturers of Antiretroviral Drugs

Domestic production started in Brazil in 1993, with AZT, by the private sector. In the following year, AZT production in the public sector began by LAFEPE, Laboratório do Estado de Pernambuco. Domestic AIDS drugs production comprises seven ARVs: zidovudine (AZT), didanosine (ddI), zalcitabine (ddC), lamivudine (3TC), stavudine (d4T), indinavir and nevirapine, and by the association zidovudine + lamivudine (AZT + 3TC). Three ARV drugs distributed by the MoH—amprenavir, efavirenz, and nelfinavir—are under patent protection. The national production of zalcitabine and stavudine started in 1997, that of didanosine in 1998, lamivudine and zidovudine + lamivudine in 1999, and of indinavir and nevirapine in 2000.

Public laboratories manufacturing ARVs are: Far-Manguinhos/ FIOCRUZ/MoH, Fundação para o Remédio Popular/SP, Laboratório Farmacêutico do Estado de Pernambuco, Fundação Ezequiel Dias/MG, Indústria Química do Estado de Goiás, and Instituto Vital Brasil/RJ. In 2000, Far-Manguinhos provided approximately 30 percent of the ARV drugs used in Brazil, corresponding to 45 percent of the funds spent in purchases from national manufacturers. Seven Far-Manguinhos products— zidovudine capsules, didanosine tablets, lamivudine tablets, zidovudine + lamivudine tablets, stavudine capsule, indinavir capsule, and nevirapine tablet—have been approved in bioequivalence tests and thus are eligible for licensing as a generic drug.

The quality control of the antiretrovirals distributed by the ministry of health is done by: (1) mandatory statement from the competent health authority in the country of manufacture, certifying that the plant complies with the good manufacturing practices (GMP); (2) preliminary inspection of the pharmaceutical plant before the first delivery of the product; (3) monitoring of the production of the first batches; (4) in the early phases of the procurement contract, analysis of batches purchased at laboratories accredited by the National Health Surveillance Agency/MoH; and (5) starting in 2001, mandatory bioequivalence testing of all drugs purchased. Bioequivalence tests, certifying drug interchangeability, are a recent achievement of the Brazilian National Drug Policy, guaranteed by the 1999 generic drugs bill. The Brazilian bioequivalence process comprises pharmaceutical, clinical, analytic, and statistical testing. Clinical studies are carried out mainly by the quantification of the drug or its active metabolite in the circulation (most commonly in blood, plasma, or serum samples) of healthy volunteers, who receive the drugs being tested and the reference drugs at different times, in single- or multiple-dose regimens. This is a complex study and it requires the submission of a research project, experimental protocol, free and informed consent form, and approval by the Committee of Ethics in Research.

Brazil exports ARV drugs through cooperation programs. Currently these programs are being implemented with Colombia, El Salvador, Paraguay, Bolivia, Dominican Republic, Mozambique, Burkina Faso, São Tomé and Principe, Guinea-Bissau, Cape Verde, and East Timor. The government

continued

Global Pricing and Ethics of Marketing HIV/AIDS Drugs   175

> **Box 6.3 *(continued)***
>
> intends to reach ten thousand people in the abovementioned countries until 2006. The drugs that are donated must be distributed in those countries free of charge. The cooperation programs include building technical capacity for clinical management of people living with HIV/AIDS.
>
> All developing countries should be in a condition to compete in the international pharmaceutical market, not only for ARV, but also for drugs in general, if they were given the conditions to do so. The Brazilian government advocates for fair rules in the international trade. In case fair rules are implemented, a better competition in that sector would be achieved and prices would eventually be reduced, which would bring significant benefits to patients.
>
> Brazilian laboratories produce drugs with international quality and could be competitive if the necessary conditions were present. Even though they are not prequalified by WHO, the Brazilian drugs are going through bioequivalence and biodisposibility tests. Public laboratories are institutions that do not envisage profits and have as their goal supplying the needs identified in the Brazilian public health policy. Private laboratories, however, still do not have the necessary production scale to be competitive.
>
> Source: Information provided by Mr. Pedro Marcos de Castro Saldaña, second secretary, Permanent Mission of Brazil, Geneva, Switzerland (2005, 8 September). Personal communication.

sub-Saharan Africa classifications.[171] This approach has been criticized both by people with HIV/AIDS in high-income countries who cannot afford to pay for their medication and by NGOs. Recently, 65 NGOs from around the world wrote to eight of the world's top pharmaceutical companies to make two requests. First, that the companies should make their differential pricing systems more transparent. Second, that access to differential pricing should be granted to all countries except for OECD members, and all organizations including employers who provide HIV/AIDS treatments to their employees.[172]

What are the risks involved in differential pricing as concerns grey markets and parallel imports? The main risk is that low-cost—whether generic or patented—medications are legally imported in developed, affluent markets, causing unfair competition. A flood of such medicines would lower price levels and have the consequence that pharmaceutical companies would probably be unable to depreciate their R&D expenses, reducing their incentive to improve HIV/AIDS treatments. If market entry authorization for AIDS drugs is not granted in developed markets, they may also be smuggled. Drugs are easy to transport and can be discreetly conveyed by airline passengers from one country to another.

The risk of grey markets and parallel imports is largely reduced by social security systems and by market entry provisions for pharmaceuticals. The

176 AIDS and Business

sale of prescription pharmaceuticals is kept under strict control in developed markets: only medical doctors allow their purchase after examining patients. Distribution outlets are exclusive (pharmacies and hospitals) and will deliver only on prescription of a medical doctor. In developed countries, only prescription drugs that have received an official permission to be marketed (such as by the U.S. FDA) can be prescribed to patients. All effective AIDS therapies are sold only on prescription.

Moreover, people living with AIDS have three strong incentives not to bypass the public health system:

1. Their expenses may be partly or fully covered by the public health system.
2. The treatment supervised by medical doctors, often HIV/AIDS specialists, is done according to the latest guidelines.
3. A self-administered therapy is done at the risk of making major mistakes in dosage (directions for use, dosage, side effects, etc.) and suffering adverse consequences.

In addition, people with AIDS in developed countries are unlikely to buy cheaper treatments from Brazil or India. The country of origin of medicines makes a difference in the consumer decision-making process: European and North American patients may not perceive Brazil or India as countries with a great tradition in researching and manufacturing advanced pharmaceutical products.

RESPONSES OF THE PHARMACEUTICAL INDUSTRY

Alan F. Holmer, president and chief executive officer of the U.S. Pharmaceutical Research and Manufacturers of America (PhRMA), argued that the pharmaceutical industry is the "unquestioned leader in creating value for humankind."[173] He went on to state that innovation is a prerequisite for value creation, and that innovation is only possible when intellectual property incentives are strong. Because of the high cost of developing new medications, pharmaceutical companies are concerned about the power of patents to protect the products they worked to develop. They reward countries that are strict on intellectual property protection, such as Jordan, with investments and joint ventures. Similarly, any weakening of patents may slow research and development of new drugs, to the detriment of people's health and economic development everywhere. Holmer threatened a bleak future for the planet if patents were eroded. In his view, patents in the United States and around the world were under threat from an ambitious generics industry and medicines access activists. He went on to state the pharmaceutical industry's view that patents are not the major obstacle to AIDS drugs access in poor countries.

In a recent report, PhRMA asserted that poverty and the lack of spending on health care were the main barriers to AIDS drugs based on a study of

Global Pricing and Ethics of Marketing HIV/AIDS Drugs   177

the number of pharmaceutical patents in fifty-three countries.[174] A common pharmaceutical industry explanation for the numbers of untreated AIDS patients dying in poverty is that patents are not to blame; rather, it is the governments of poor countries that have yet to implement correct monitoring and healthcare infrastructure. To support this argument they cite the report's findings that 84 percent of AIDS drugs enjoyed no patent protection in Africa[175] and yet they are still unavailable due to lack of manufacturing capacity in low-income countries.[176] More information is available on the Web site of the U.S. Pharmaceutical Research and Manufacturers of America (PhRMA) at http://www.phrma.org.

In response to criticisms from activists and nongovernmental organizations, the pharmaceutical industry decided to improve on its image and performance in the area of HIV/AIDS by announcing drug donations programs, price reductions, and public-private partnerships. In addition to publicity, other reasons for donations included the protection of patents in key markets by undercutting the attractiveness of generic drugs, and helping governments economically, thereby increasing their ability to purchase other drugs from the company.[177] On the eve of the thirteenth International Aids Conference in Durban, South Africa, Boehringer Ingelheim, Bristol-Myers Squibb, Merck and Glaxo Wellcome made drug donation offers. Echoing the criticisms of other activists, Eric Goemaere of Médecins Sans Frontières South Africa suggested that donations and vague promises are not helpful to people suffering from AIDS. If generic treatments were available, however, Goemaere said sick people could start treatment "tomorrow."[178]

At times it seems that pharmaceutical companies are under siege. Activists launch vitriolic attacks at demonstrations and on Web sites. Nongovernmental organizations and governments demand lower prices. People with AIDS are taking drug companies to court. Generic manufacturers, with the help of U.S. ex-President Bill Clinton, reduced their prices to one-third of the price of a comparable patented drug.[179] Recently, shareholders joined the fray. In a rare expression of solidarity, twelve London institutional investors with investments exceeding £600 billion issued a warning that the share value of drug companies will suffer long term if they continue to block access to essential medicines in poor countries. ISIS Asset Management, Schroders, and Jupiter were among the authors of a statement that urged pharmaceutical companies to be more sensitive to "local circumstances" and to use differential pricing to increase affordability. They also urged companies to work with governments to address the "public health crisis in emerging markets" and to use their influence with affluent governments to contribute to the Global Health Fund. ISIS senior analyst Olivia Lankester summarized the concern that "continuing high-level criticism of the [pharmaceutical] sector will . . . damage its ability to operate."[180]

Large California pension fund CalPERS publicly demanded that Glaxo-SmithKline (GSK) increase access of its HIV/AIDS medications to the poor by reducing prices and reevaluating its preferential pricing policies. CalP-

178   *AIDS and Business*

ERS was estimated to hold US$850 million in GSK shares. Several weeks later, GSK complied, by practically halving the price of its leading HIV/ AIDS medicine, Combivir, from US$1.70 per person per day to US$0.90 per person per day in its preferential pricing program.[181] After GSK was fined and lost a court case in South Africa for unfair competitive practices and excessive pricing, CalPERS decided to reexamine its relationship as shareholder to GSK. AIDS Healthcare Foundation's president Michael Weinstein summarized the issue: "*CalPERS* . . . is letting *GSK* know that their business practices in the developing world are closely monitored by their shareholders . . . they will be held accountable for all their actions."[182]

In a similar development that increases accountability of pharmaceutical companies, three prominent U.S. senators have requested an investigation into the cost structure of HIV/AIDS drugs.[183] They requested an analysis of manufacturing and raw materials prices for branded and generic medications. Their request was made with a view to procuring the most economical option for the U.S. government in its plan to purchase and donate HIV/ AIDS drugs to low-income countries.[184]

CORPORATE EXAMPLES OF HIV/AIDS DRUGS MARKETING

Not many drugs companies produce antiretroviral drugs, the primary treatment for HIV/AIDS. The main six producers of patented HIV medicines are: Boehringer-Ingelheim, GlaxoSmithKline,[185] Merck, Pfizer, and Roche, as well as a growing number of generic manufacturers. The two corporate examples of companies chosen at random should illustrate the kinds of marketing strategies pursued by pharmaceutical multinational corporations for their HIV/AIDS medications.

Corporate Example 1: Roche

Roche recently made pharmaceutical history by rolling out Fuzeon, the most expensive and complex AIDS medication ever developed. Roche is a multinational pharmaceutical company based in Basel, Switzerland. It is ranked at number eight in the top pharmaceutical companies rankings 2007.[186] Roche is one of five pharmaceutical companies to have worked with UNAIDS on the "accelerating access initiative," which reduced the cost of antiretroviral medications from US$12,000 in 2000 to US$420 in 2003. However, 99 percent of people with access to retroviral medication for AIDS still live in the developed world.[187]

Like other pharmaceutical companies, Roche has sustained much criticism over its stance on medications access for AIDS. Médecins Sans Frontières claimed that Roche has not reduced the price of its HIV/AIDS drug Viracept for poor countries: Viracept may even cost as much as US$2,000 more per patient per year in Guatemala and other low-income countries than in Switzerland.[188] When Roche was asked to provide pricing information, it quoted

Global Pricing and Ethics of Marketing HIV/AIDS Drugs   179

Box 6.4   A View from the Field:

Replies to our questions from Dr. Franz B. Humer, formerly chairman of the board of directors and Roche CEO/chairman of European Federation of Pharmaceutical Industries and Associations (EFPIA), Basel, Switzerland

1. Can you give some examples of pharmaceutical companies actively involved in successful HIV/AIDS prevention programs?

Much of the work of the research-based pharmaceutical companies has been focused on increasing access to and improving treatment for people affected by HIV/AIDS. It is widely acknowledged increasing education about the disease, an area that Roche has been supporting, will ultimately help in preventing the number of new infections and the spread of the disease.

2. How do you propose to increase the numbers of people receiving anti-retroviral treatment and treatment for common opportunistic infections? Who should pay for ARV treatments in developing countries? Governments? Employers? Insurance? NGOs? Developed world? And if so, how?

Global sources of funding are now available to increase the numbers of people receiving treatment in those developing countries without local government-funded treatment programs. Such funding is sourced from developed countries via mechanisms including the Global Fund for AIDS, TB, and Malaria, the World Bank, and President Bush's PEPFAR. Many major employers in the hardest hit countries and continents are also providing employee treatment programs. Antiretroviral treatment strengthens immune systems. The greater the access is to ARV treatment, the need for treatment of opportunistic infections reduces.

3. What is your view of differential drug pricing, for example, where there are "ability to pay" criteria?

When there are so many people living on less than US$1 per day, "ability to pay" and affordability of health care and medicines will always be an issue.

Roche has tiered pricing for its HIV protease inhibitor medicines, with no profit pricing for the world's 50 least developed countries and all of sub-Saharan Africa. The tiers are based on country classifications developed and updated by UN agencies. The World Bank criteria for low- and lower-middle-income countries are based on the level of country economic wealth. We believe using such independent country classifications is the most transparent way we can offer the same level of reduced pricing for countries in the same income category.

4. How do you envision the role of business as prevention/awareness disseminators, sponsors, and partners in HIV/AIDS?

Business has a crucial role in driving awareness of HIV/AIDS amongst employees. These messages can then spread through their families and to the broader community. We are seeing businesses in the hardest hit regions rising to the challenge of HIV/AIDS care for their employees and their families.

continued

180   *AIDS and Business*

Box 6.4 (continued)

Roche is a founding member of the Accelerating Access Initiative, a public private partnership between five UN agencies and seven companies. Roche is also a member of the Global Business Coalition.

5. How do you view compulsory licensing?

Provision for compulsory licensing is made within TRIPS. After debate and discussion within the EU Parliament and consensus between commission, council and parliament, the EU will adopt very soon an EU regulation on compulsory licensing which allows—under certain conditions—granting of compulsory licensing for production and export to least developed countries and other developing countries where local production is not possible. The European industry welcomes this regulation, which is in line with the WTO/TRIPS principles and which may contribute to an improved access to medicines in least developed countries. The EU will be the fourth WTO member, after Canada, Norway, and India, to implement the WTO/TRIPS principles, which have now been made a permanent amendment to the TRIPS agreement.

Roche has a clear patent policy for its HIV medicines, which means we do not patent these medicines in the world's least developed countries or sub-Saharan Africa. This means there is no need for these poorest and hardest hit countries to obtain a compulsory license; they can manufacture generic versions locally or import generics without action from *Roche*.

Patents exist to help ensure the progression of science, without which new novel therapies such as Fuzeon would never have been developed. However, it is important to ensure that patents are not a barrier to access to all Roche medicines for those in the least developed countries, which is why the Roche policy has been developed.

6. Do you consider Indian, Brazilian, and other generic manufacturers to be competitors for branded ARV treatment? For drugs in general? At what time horizon?

From a Roche perspective, these countries can export generic versions of Roche HIV medicines to the world's least developed countries and sub-Saharan Africa. Roche sells its HIV protease inhibitors at no profit to least developed countries and sub-Saharan Africa, so we would not really regard generic manufacturers as competitors in these countries, where 69 percent of all people with HIV/AIDS in the world live.

US$3,170 for Viracept per patient per year in least developed countries. This contrasts with the offer by Merck, another major pharmaceutical company, of US$600 per person per year in the same countries. Roche's stance in Brazil was also criticized as one that may inflame the resistance to patents for HIV/AIDS drugs. AIDS activists and business observers widely felt that it was not in the interests of patients nor the pharmaceutical industry to be inflexible on pricing: Roche's inflexibility on Nefinavir with the Brazilian government cost the company its patent rights.[189]

Global Pricing and Ethics of Marketing HIV/AIDS Drugs 181

Charles Alfaro of Roche explained that their prices had already been lowered to their lowest level, and the company was spending a great deal in poor countries on training and education programs. Roche had pledged not to profit from AIDS medications in poor countries; however, research by Swiss HIV/AIDS scientists and Brazilian generic drugs makers showed that the cost of the raw materials used in Viracept (marketed by Pfizer in the United States) should enable the company to lower the price more significantly than it has to date.[190] Regarding the costly drug Fuzeon (see Table 6.6), Roche director of HIV treatments David Reddy stated that he "did not envisage" the drug to be used in Africa, where many people need it due to drug resistance problems with existing medications.[191] Several reports predicted that Fuzeon could become profitable for Roche in only three years, whereas profitability for new drugs takes, on average, sixteen years. Roche's Chairperson and Chief Executive Franz Humer stated that one factor in pricing is that Roche must share the profits with biotech company Trimeris, which developed the drug.[192] Certain HIV/AIDS drugs marketed by Roche are featured in Table 6.6

Table 6.6 HIV/AIDS Drugs Marketing Activity by Roche

Year	Marketing activity/ drug name	Properties
1992	Hivid	Roche's first HIV drug; antiviral
1995	Viracept	Marketed in the USA by Pfizer
1996	Invirase	The first protease inhibitor, awarded the Galien Prize (also marketed as Fortovase)
2002	Amplicor HIV-1 Monitor test	Very sensitive test for viral loads in HIV/AIDS patients
2003	85 percent price drop for Viracept	Roche announced poor countries could buy the drug at a discount, reducing the drug price to about US$900 per person per year. The move was praised by AIDS activists who had berated Roche in the past for not lowering prices as much as other companies.[193]
	Fuzeon	One of the most expensive and complex medications ever produced. The drug costs 18,980 euros per patient per year, twice as much as other regimens (and because it would be used in conjunction with other treatments, total cost to patients would be about double). Fuzeon has 106 production steps, more than any other drug. It is the first new approach to HIV treatment in seven years. Fuzeon is active against HIV strains that have become resistant to other treatments.[194]

182   AIDS and Business

Corporate Example 2: Pfizer

Pfizer (www.Pfizer.com) is ranked at number one among the world's biggest pharmaceutical companies,[195] with global products like Lipitor, Viagra, Zantac, and Halls. The company has used unabashed marketing and aggressive acquisitions of other companies to grow. Pfizer engineered the first hostile takeover in pharmaceutical history and has engineered megamergers, such as recently with Pharmacia. The company has been criticized for the high salaries of its executives and the large allocation of company resources towards marketing and advertising. In 2004 Pfizer spent US$16.9 billion on sales and administration, while the company's research and development budget was half that amount.[196] The company spent US$3 billion on advertising alone in 2004.[197]

Pfizer was once sole supplier of fluconazole (Diflucan), used to treat cryptococcal meningitis, an infection that commonly kills people with AIDS. When its patent ran out, a company in Thailand commenced sales of the drug at 5 percent of the Pfizer price. Pfizer made an announcement to donate the drug just before the AIDS conference in Durban, South Africa, in 2000. Donations were to continue for two years, without any discounts on the price of Diflucan, and restrictions on use (e.g., not to be used for fungal infections). In addition, donations were permitted only in certain areas, igniting the criticism of South African nongovernmental and activist agencies. Pfizer is a regular donor to the Diflucan Partnership, working with the United Nations and the World Health Organization to provide the drug in fifty poor countries.[198]

Pfizer's Viagra, approved by the FDA in 1998, has been the subject of a number of controversies. Of interest here is that in recent years Pfizer's advertising campaign positioned Viagra not so much as a curative drug for a medical condition (erectile dysfunction), but for "sexual enhancement"; as a "recreational," "lifestyle" "party drug" (AIDS Healthcare Foundation, 2007).[199] In direct-to-consumer advertising—where Viagra featured in the top twenty of the highest advertising spends in 2005[200]—a handsome forty-ish model smiled suggestively with taglines like "what will you be doing this New Year's Eve?," "Viva Las Vegas," or for Valentine's Day in the UK "Roses are red, Viagra is blue." Partly as a result, doctors were more likely to prescribe Viagra. An undesired effect was that growing numbers of MSM used Viagra to counter the negative effects on erectile performance of crystal methamphetamine—an illegal recreational drug that lowers sexual inhibition. The trend grew to the point where it became clear that there was a clear relationship between MSM using both drugs together and indulging in sexual risk behavior that results in higher rates—up to twice as high—of HIV infection, as well as other sexually transmitted diseases.[201] Hence, AIDS Healthcare Foundation's awareness slogan: "Viagra + Meth = Rx for HIV infection."[202]

QUESTIONS FOR DISCUSSION

1. Antiretroviral drugs dramatically improve the quality of life and survival of people with HIV/AIDS in high-income countries. In terms of ethics, do people in resource-poor settings have a *right* to these new, expensive treatments? If so, how can they be made accessible? Is it a choice to treat AIDS when other basic health problems exist?
2. What are the risks involved in differential pricing as concerns grey markets and parallel imports? Are HIV/AIDS patients in developed countries likely to buy cheap AIDS treatment from Brazil or India? Does country of origin matter?
3. Are Cipla and Brazilian AIDS drug manufacturers potential competitors in developed markets for large pharmaceutical corporations? To what extent does patent legislation protect pharmaceutical companies from such competition?
4. In your opinion, are drugs a standard marketable product? Do they involve particular responsibilities for the manufacturer? Present an argument about what AIDS means in terms of corporate ethics for large pharmaceutical companies such as Boehringer-Ingelheim, GlaxoSmithKline, Merck, Pfizer, and Roche.
5. Given that pharmaceutical companies sell a large array of drugs, is their position concerning AIDS drug prices in developing countries likely to damage their corporate reputation in developed markets and impact their sales of other medicines?

APPENDIX A

Low-Income Countries, as Classified by the World Bank

Afghanistan, Angola, Armenia, Azerbaijan, Bangladesh, Benin, Bhutan, Burkina Faso, Burundi, Cambodia, Cameroon, Central African Republic, Chad, Comoros, Congo (Dem. Rep.), Congo (Rep.), Côte d'Ivoire, Eritrea, Ethiopia, Gambia, Georgia, Ghana, Guinea, Guinea-Bissau, Haiti, India, Indonesia, Kenya, Korea, Dem. Rep., Kyrgyz Republic, Lao PDR, Lesotho, Liberia, Madagascar, Malawi, Mali, Mauritania, Moldova, Mongolia, Mozambique, Myanmar, Nepal, Nicaragua, Niger, Nigeria, Pakistan, Rwanda, São Tomé and Principe, Senegal, Sierra Leone, Solomon Islands, Somalia, Sudan, Tajikistan, Tanzania, Togo, Uganda, Uzbekistan, Vietnam, Yemen (Rep.), Zambia, Zimbabwe.

Source: World Bank. (2008). World Bank list of country groups by income. http://web.worldbank.org/WBSITE/EXTERNAL/DATASTATIS TICS/0,,contentMDK:20421402~pagePK:64133150~piPK:64133175~the SitePK:239419,00.html#Low_income.

7 RealSource India
HIV/AIDS in the Back Office to the World

Veera Patel watched the door softly close behind one of her Customer Care Executive managers as he stepped out on to the call center floor. Ajit had just told her, with controlled emotion, that he was HIV positive. She knew that as human resources manager, she should follow the company policy: She should immediately report him to the benefits center and the chief executive's office, and enter Ajit's HIV positive status into his personal file. For the moment, however, with no one else in the know, Veera could turn over the problem in her mind and try to find the course of action that would be right for everyone.

The real problem, she reasoned, was that Ajit was not the only one with AIDS here at RealSource Hyderabad. She personally suspected that a handful—or more—of workers had HIV. They were mostly long-term employees like Ajit. It was impossible to know for sure without a test, however. It was possible and legal to advise them to take an HIV test. However, Veera felt it was cruel to do so given the climate of discrimination in India against people with HIV. She had recently read about a research study in the *Times* that found 74 percent of employees in India would not tell their employer if they contracted HIV. In the study, Indians from six states living with HIV/AIDS reported they had been refused employment-related benefits, promotions, and loans, and some had been fired from their jobs.[1] In another study, almost 70 percent of respondents in Hyderabad said they would keep "secret" if a family member was found to have HIV.[2] People commonly thought that HIV mainly spread among sex workers and drug users—not "normal" people like those who work in call centers. Yet, she felt, the tide was changing in that respect with a highly publicized sex lifestyles survey conducted at a call center in New Delhi.[3] To make matters worse, in India there was a big social distance between managers and workers, discouraging open dialogue between them. She could understand only too well why an employee with HIV or AIDS would not want to tell her or anyone else in management.

Ajit had been with the company since before she arrived, and was now older than the average worker at 32. He had been promoted from customer care executive to customer support section manager (inbound calls); he was looking for a promotion and was on friendly terms with Veera. A few weeks back Ajit had been horrified when Veera had recommended that he take an HIV test. "I am *not* gay!" he had raged, before regaining his composure. She had responded that not only "gays" had HIV. Even as she spoke she realized that the force of a taboo was stopping her words in midair. Soon thereafter, because of his erratic ill-health, his doctor had advised him to take an HIV test. And now he had the results.

Veera knew that most people with HIV in India were heterosexual, but she also knew that the Western terms *heterosexual* and *homosexual* could not capture the wide range of male sexual experience in India. First, there was *maasti*, or "mischief" between men, which was not considered to be homosexual. Second, there were the *hijras*, effeminate men of which some were eunuchs, with whom male-to-male sex was not viewed as homosexual. To complicate matters there were other subtle variations on homosexuality and bisexuality like the *Kothis*, *Panthis*, and *Pariks*.[4,5] Third, she knew that sex before marriage was unthinkable for many young women—although less so in recent years. For young unmarried men, a quick solution was to visit sex workers.[6] Sex with commercial sex workers was generally not frowned upon although admittedly this had changed since the onset of public HIV/AIDS campaigns. In a recent study conducted among university students in Pondicherry, it emerged that Indian students had more negative attitudes towards homosexuals and people living with HIV/AIDS than their American or South African counterparts. As a result of these attitudes they were much less likely to request an HIV test or realistically assess their own HIV risk.[7]

More close to home, a study conducted in here in Hyderabad found that educated people (like call-center workers) were more aware of HIV than other sectors of the population. However, their knowledge about the specifics of HIV transmission was lacking. For instance, approximately one half thought that a healthy-looking person was unlikely to have AIDS. They also thought that people with HIV die "within a year or two." There were large age group differences also: people under the age of thirty tended to be more knowledgeable about HIV/AIDS than those who were older.[8] Given the long time it takes for AIDS to develop from HIV (which may be as long as ten years),[9] older workers like Ajit could be at greater risk. Because they missed out on HIV education at school and college, the workplace may be the only place they learn about it, thought Veera.

Ajit's declaration was quite timely for several reasons. First, her peers at competing companies were talking about this very issue at a recent conference. The NASSCOM[10] president allegedly considered advocating HIV tests for BPO (business process outsourcing) workers, which when reported in the press resulted in renewed public concern about the culture and lifestyle of BPO workers, as well as bringing the issue of HIV at the workplace to the fore.[11] Another reason for the timeliness was the launching of the Red Ribbon Express, an HIV education-dedicated train which was to reach a

186   AIDS and Business

record number of people across India. The train's inauguration was presided by Sonia Gandhi, guaranteeing front-page publicity for an issue that tended to be featured on less visible pages of newspapers.[12] In addition, and most relevant to the current climate, was the initiative by the Global Business Coalition and Confederation of Indian Industry at iEnergiser network, a New Delhi BPO. The initiative to provide education and testing and reduce stigma followed on a survey conducted by SSL International (makers of Durex condoms) among iEnergiser's four thousand young employees who, it turns out, had more sexual partners than average Indian adults, at a growing rate of unprotected sex.[13] Strangely enough, however, little was heard about that initiative since the high-publicity launch. Another example of stigma hushing good sense, perhaps, thought Veera.

Veera knew that an understanding of sexual and attitudinal details was vital to the success of HIV/AIDS campaigns. In India—as in many other cultures—a two-pronged campaign for "gays" on the one hand and "straights" on the other would never work. Unfortunately, that was what the National AIDS Control Organization (NACO) seemed to be doing. To make matters worse, sex was a very sensitive subject in India: one that was not for public discussion. At the same time, it is frequently observed that young people have an "increasingly casual attitude towards sex" (Sudha et al., p. 307).[14] To demonstrate sexual conservatism in India, Veera often used the example of Hindi films (commonly known as "Bollywood"), where on-screen kissing was not seen until the late 1990s. More recently, there was the furore over Richard Gere's public kiss of Shilpa Shetty. If one cannot publicly kiss on film or off, how can one publicly discuss the biological and anatomical details of preventing sexually transmitted diseases like HIV?

In 2001, when she attended her first board meeting soon after being hired as human resources manager at the RealSource call center, she had put HIV/AIDS on the agenda. The board members had mainly sniffed at the suggestion that there may be a potential HIV/AIDS risk for the company in Hyderabad. Being well prepared, Veera had told them that Hyderabad was located in the state (Andhra Pradesh) with the second highest HIV prevalence in India.[15] A board member retorted that most people with AIDS were illiterate truck drivers and sex workers and therefore she could not imply that educated call-center employees were concerned by HIV. She had since not raised the subject again, but was planning to hit the board with a tough report outlining her suspicions. Ajit's declaration could be the catalyst she needed.

"Poor things. They didn't know what they were getting into when they hired me!" she often joked to her friends, knowing that there was more than a grain of truth in the joke. Her Australian upbringing had given her a rough edge that Indians considered to be unfeminine, and her speaking style was woefully blunt and to the point. Needless to say, she had few friends at work but she did have the intimate satisfaction of knowing that she did her job well, and did right by her workers most of the time.

HIV/AIDS in the Back Office to the World 187

She had friends outside work: mid-career managers like her, expatriate Indians with business and technology degrees who had returned "home" to work in India. It was true that some job opportunities here could even rival those abroad, and returning expatriates did not feel too foreign—at least not at first.

Veera had attended a specialized health risk assessment seminar at university back in Australia, and had written a paper about the impact of HIV on businesses. As a result, she felt quite sure to be able to recognize typical observable symptoms in her employees. In the case of Ajit, for example, she had observed over the past year or so a pattern of unexplained absences, skin problems, tiredness, frequent trips to the toilet, and a range of minor health problems that did not seem to go away. Then there were many doctor's visits for which he had taken time off. Every so often a worker resigned whom Veera had suspected of having beginning stages of AIDS—having similar symptoms to those of Ajit. They always cited family problems as their reason for leaving, and would politely refuse further questioning. Even outspoken Veera knew not to insist in these cases. Later, when Veera asked for news of these departed workers, no one seemed to know anything about them. That in itself was strange—usually they kept in touch with each other.

Veera watched her workers like a hawk. She assumed that was part of her job, to act as a sort of mother to these young workers who converged on Hyderabad and other forward-looking cities to seek a better future with call centers and back office operations companies. These companies were also known as business process outsourcing, or BPOs.

BPOs certainly did offer improved career prospects than what Veera called the "Dad and Co." Indian companies, referring to her view that paternalistic attitudes reign in many an office on the subcontinent. In Veera's opinion, call centers tended to be managed in a progressive style, more in line with what she had learned at business school than what she had observed at other Indian companies. BPOs constantly faced a shortage of talent, and therefore had to be relatively meritocratic and had to find new ways to motivate their workers and inspire their loyalty. "Otherwise," she thought, "our young and talented staff members would simply go elsewhere to work. After all, customer care executives needed to have great interpersonal skills, be self-confident, and speak fantastic English. Who wouldn't hire them in this economy?" What was true for her call center was not true in all sectors of BPOs, she knew: some data entry employees were treated little better than factory workers, while people who worked in forms processing were like cogs on a relentless assembly line. In contrast, the little darlings of BPOs were the customer care executives, the software design people, the legal and financial experts, and other "creative" staff like those who designed advertisements and public relations campaigns for companies on other continents. It was true that burnout and employee turnover was a problem, even for these little darlings, however.

188 *AIDS and Business*

Officially, attrition was rising at 35 percent in 2006 due to difficult working conditions.[16] Yet, the BPO industry association president alleged that the real attrition rate was almost double that.[17] Job-hopping was usual practice in part because managers were tough due to constant pressure on margins, pushing employees to accomplish 100–150 calls per day, for instance, as well as working nights to reach the U.S. market. There were also limits on career advancement opportunities within BPOs.

Veera's company, RealSource, was a premier call center and BPO company in Hyderabad, with a list of clients in the banking, insurance, travel, and software industry sectors on two continents. Their clients had chosen offshore outsourcing to companies like RealSource in India because the labor costs were much lower than at home, and workers were English-speaking and highly skilled. In addition, the Indian government offered a range of incentives to companies seeking to establish their BPO services in India. The 400-strong call center at RealSource was small compared with some in this expanding market. U.S. computer maker Dell, Inc., for instance, had four call centers in India and recently announced plans to increase its capacity in one of them from 800 to 2,500.[18] Call-center services were sold mainly as part of a package of services, including other BPO and expert services. Call centers alone were simply not profitable enough long term, and customers in the United States and United Kingdom (where most client companies were located) complained about outsourcing practices. In the United States, customers were increasingly complaining about customer service staff who had foreign accents.[19] Labor unions and governments frequently expressed concern about job losses caused by offshore outsourcing. Nevertheless, outsourcing was definitely on the rise.

Veera often reflected that her workers lived in a sort of cultural and social bubble. They were away from home, some of them for the first time, in a country where "home" was the center of the universe. Some employees lived in company-owned dormitories on the outskirts of the city, and many lived in housing that had a temporary feel to it. The young men and women who could afford it preferred sharing an apartment with friends of the same sex, forming trendy new ghettos in India's major cities. These were young, single people with money to spend living alone in a culture where marriage and children, religion, and respectability were the poles of most people's lives. Many had left their network of friends behind, and had to prove themselves in a highly competitive new environment with values that were literally foreign to them. Young migrant BPO workers tended to feel rootless in their independence and aimless in their affluence. As Veera saw it, they comforted themselves by buying edgy youth fashions, getting tattoos, drinking alcoholic beverages, eating fast food, and partying. Veera thought there was drug taking also, but could not be sure. Because of these social and economic factors her employees were at risk for a range of social and psychological ills, and probably vulnerable for risky sex practices, thought Veera.

HIV/AIDS in the Back Office to the World   189

This kind of "cultural schizophrenia," as Veera called it persisted at work. Minibuses and dusty taxis brought employees to work in numbing heat. They progressed slowly and noisily along crowded streets where tiny shop fronts sold anything and everything, and zoomed through industrial zones populated by large prefabricated warehouses, laboratories, and business centers. Much call-center work was done in cavernous air-conditioned halls partitioned into grey felt cubicles, each shared by the day shift worker and night shift worker. Call-center employees followed an accent reduction training program which taught them to erase their own accent and replace it with a "neutral" accent that might be effective on the telephone with a rural Canadian or an urban New Zealander. New customer care executives were required to select a non-Indian, Western name to use with clients on the telephone. Interestingly, this name sometimes came to supplant their original Indian name in their new social circles. During their sales and order taking, up-selling and cross-selling training, budding customer care executives learned new communications styles, and a brash new way of getting what they wanted outside of work.

Veera had noticed that, compared with her own experience growing up in Australia, there was a large social distance between men and women in India. Some writers have referred to the culture as "homosocial" because in social life males have their primary relationships with males; females with females.[20] Yet here at RealSource men and women had to work closely together, side by side and at odd hours of the day and night. Veera wondered whether that was not creating potential gender relations problems, including increased HIV risk. They were under immense stress from their work lives and far divorced from the home values that may have protected them from risky sexual behavior in the past.

In addition to the necessary social adaptations, call-center employees were under massive pressure all the time. Veera conceded that this was not psychologically or physically healthy, but "that's business reality today, folks," she would say with a sigh. All calls made and received at the Real-Source call center were monitored for quality surveillance. This meant that at all times, workers had to perform at almost superhuman levels with customers who were often less than polite. There were also more recent issues relating to fraud and data theft in call centers, which had resulted in redoubled surveillance efforts. Veera had seen supervisors use recent recordings of badly managed call situations to publicly humiliate the customer care executive involved in front of the others. They were also under time pressure, with their "results" and "effectiveness" as a caller judged on the basis of how many seconds were needed to get the desired result from the client. All employee results were plotted on a screen visible to all workers, and the most effective were given bonuses. The least effective were told to attend training and refresher modules on their own time. Veera did not defend these practices, but thought they were necessary to keep people on their toes. Besides, she knew that what was going on at RealSource was not as

190   *AIDS and Business*

bad as the reality at some other companies. The high levels of employee attrition at BPOs were in many ways not surprising, given these practices.

To make matters worse, there was increasing competition in the sector, both within India, where new call centers seemed to sprout daily, and internationally, from China, the Czech Republic, Hungary, Ireland, Philippines, Sri Lanka, and Vietnam.[21] Call-center companies were poaching employees from each other, and even from other industries like the insurance, hotel, and banking industries. The field was set to become even more complex, with the arrival of knowledge process outsourcing, where Indian medical, engineering, and financial experts provide expertise to decision makers and development teams in markets like the United States.[22]

Veera thought on the one hand that if she reported Ajit's HIV status, he would be harassed by other supervisors and probably verbally teased by workers. He would not receive any medical support from the company, and Veera was not sure if the medical benefits he received would truly help towards paying for his antiretrovirals. The company was not allowed to legally fire him now, but management could make his life here so uncomfortable that he would want to leave. However, RealSource was obligated to provide him with "reasonable accommodation" on its catastrophic diseases policy originally designed for people with cancer: the capacity to leave early, arrive late, and have resting time during the day. She doubted that he would stay long, particularly if it became known that he had AIDS. On the other hand, bringing Ajit's case out into the open could open up the possibility to discuss HIV risk at RealSource. Maybe then the company could inform workers about how to protect themselves. At its most basic level, HIV/AIDS education didn't have to be costly or complex, thought Veera. RealSource could partner with an active NGO or join the Indian Business Trust on HIV/AIDS and put up a few "safer sex" posters in the toilets. Someone would come round once a year to make a speech to raise employee awareness to the HIV problem. Even if it saved just one employee, it would be a step in the right direction.

Veera summed up her thoughts: "We are operating in a talent shortage. Our employees are precious to us. We can't afford to lose even one worker—whether through sickness or going to work somewhere else. We can't stop them from leaving to work elsewhere but we *can* help them to not get sick from AIDS. And, if they have AIDS, we take care of them so they will want to stay." She thought it was wise to alert top management to the risk of lost productivity as employees became more and more ill from AIDS. Unlike other industries, call-center workers had to constantly be at their workstation, and feeling well enough to have a calm and friendly voice, in order to be productive. She suspected that there might be other business benefits from launching a workplace HIV/AIDS program.

One benefit was to be prepared for the day—which would come—when RealSource's clients would ask about their HIV/AIDS policies just as many companies nowadays asked their suppliers. She had heard of the HIV support given to supply-chain companies. However, the most publicized examples

HIV/AIDS *in the Back Office to the World* 191

were in Africa, not India. A recent World Economic Forum report highlighted the attempts by Heineken, Standard Chartered, Unilever, and Volkswagen to protect their African supply chain. In the BPO sector that was asking too much of one's clients, no matter how big they are, thought Veera. It would surely reduce their competitive advantage in a bidding process if potential clients knew we were going to ask them for HIV/AIDS workplace support—or even if they found out that we were spending money on HIV programs instead of training and development! Veera thought those arguments alone doomed her ideas for an HIV/AIDS program to failure.

If RealSource started fighting HIV/AIDS at work, the press would talk about it, but Veera was not sure whether that would constitute positive or negative publicity for the company. In any case, the publicity was likely to be local and RealSource customers were on other continents. The only other companies Veera knew of that publicized their AIDS programs were Indian behemoths like TATA Steel, Bajaj Auto, Godrej, and so on.[23] Local divisions of multinational corporations like MTV Networks India and Novartis[24] could speak openly about HIV in India because they often had their home office HIV/AIDS policies to implement. The pharmaceutical companies could bring HIV/AIDS discussions into the open, partly because of the Indian government's public commitment to provide one hundred thousand people with antiretrovirals free of charge by 2007.[25] Even the chambers of commerce had their say: the Mumbai chamber had its own workplace HIV/AIDS policy brochure. However, Veera could not think of a medium- or small-sized business that even mentioned the word *AIDS*. Certainly no BPO apart from iEnergizer had done so. Would RealSource be seen as a brave pioneer, or rather as an AIDS-ridden den of vice?

HIV/AIDS IN INDIA

There are more people with HIV in India than anywhere else in Asia. In 2005, India overtook South Africa's infamous number one position. In 2007, with the support of UNAIDS, NACO released revised HIV/AIDS incidence estimates that were lower by six million than previous estimates. According to these, 2.5 million Indians are living with HIV/AIDS. The lower estimates were due to increased surveillance and a national household survey, not Indian success in fighting the epidemic.[26] In view of the latest estimates, India's position relative to other countries with large numbers of people with HIV has changed, as presented in Table 7.1.

India's comparatively low prevalence masks vast geographic and social disparities in HIV levels. For example, one NACO study found that HIV prevalence among sex workers in Mumbai ranged from 45 to 60 percent,[27] while prevalence among women aged fifteen to twenty-four actually fell to 1.1 percent in southern India in 2004.[28]

192 AIDS and Business

Table 7.1 Comparative View of India and Selected Countries Incidence and Prevalence Rates

	People living with HIV/AIDS (millions)	Adult prevalence (percent)	Population (millions)
India	2.5	0.36	1,129
United States	1.2	0.6	301
Nigeria	2.9	3.9	135
South Africa	5.5	18.6	44
Swaziland	0.22	33.4	1.1

Sources: Compiled from Cohen, J. (2007). India slashes estimates of HIV-infected people. *Science* 317(5835), 179–81. Retrieved July 30, 2007, from http://www.sciencemag.org/cgi/content/full/317/5835/179?rss=1.
NACO. (2007). *2.5 million people in India living with HIV, according to new estimates.* NACO Press releases. Retrieved October 17, 2007, from http://www.nacoonline.org/NACO_Action/Media__Press_Release/.

The primary route of HIV transmission in India is heterosexual (85.86 percent of cases), with a larger percentage coming from injecting-drug users (IDUs) in northeastern states like Manipur, Mizoram, and Nagaland, and there are pockets of IDUs in many major cities in other states.[29] Women are increasingly contracting HIV, and the epidemic is spreading from risk-taking groups like drug users and sex workers to the general population.[30] In one study, 60 percent of women in India professed to have never heard of AIDS.[31] One high-risk group that received attention in recent years is truck drivers. India has one of the world's largest road networks,[32] and, as in Africa, truck drivers were thought to play a role in the spread of HIV. Targeted interventions have reduced risky behaviors among truck drivers, such as unprotected sex with commercial sex workers.[33]

DISCUSSION QUESTIONS

1. What action would you advise Veera to take about Ajit's (her employee) declaration that he was HIV positive? On what ethical grounds would you advise this?
2. Write up a short and punchy presentation for Veera to make to the board of directors of RealSource to convince them that the company needs to address the spread of HIV among workers by having an in-house HIV/AIDS program.
3. In addressing a young audience such as that working at RealSource (typically aged between twenty and twenty-five), the communicator often needs to be exceptionally creative. Design some examples of

online, poster, workstation, viral, and other internal communications messages on HIV/AIDS that would be attention-grabbing yet educational and in line with the professional corporate culture of RealSource.

RESOURCES FOR FURTHER RESEARCH

Confederation of Indian Industry (undated). *Business for life. Industry response to HIV/AIDS in India.* New Delhi, India: Confederation of Indian Industry.
Hunter, S. (2005). *AIDS in Asia. A continent in peril.* New York: Palgrave Macmillan.

HINDI FILMS

AIDS Jaago (2007). Four short films by award-winning directors—notably Mira Nair, who received funding from the Bill and Melinda Gates Foundation—that examine four different faces of the HIV/AIDS epidemic in India.

My Brother Nikhil (2005). Family drama shot in Goa about a swimming champion who contracts HIV and the response of his family, lover, and friends to the turn of events.

We'll meet again (Phir Milenge) (2004). A high-flying advertising executive is dismissed when she discloses that she is HIV positive, and the film portrays the legal and other battles that ensue. Featuring Shilpa Shetty, Abhichek Bachchan, and Salman Khan.

8 WinThai
Initiating HIV/AIDS Action in a Reborn Epidemic

Apapan walked down the production line for energy drinks at the WinThai plant in Bangkok after the management meeting. Coconut and peach essence tweaked her nose. She felt tired. She took an energy drink from the managers' fridge and went upstairs to her office. "We have some complex decisions to make, Mechai; take a Buffalo Power to drink and come to my office: we need all the help we can get!" she called to her assistant, glancing at the water buffalo's head on the drink can. She had called this morning's management meeting to discuss the recent rise of HIV/AIDS cases again in Thailand—and the concomitant rise in awareness that Thai businesses were not doing much to fight the epidemic. The Thailand Business Coalition on AIDS contacted her recently for a survey they were conducting with the International Labor Organization.[1] The researcher had asked what WinThai was doing about HIV/AIDS. Specifically, the researcher had asked Apapan whether WinThai, like half of all Thai businesses,[2] forced its employees to take HIV tests before they were hired or given a promotion. Apapan had been embarrassed to admit that she did not know the answer to that question. Perhaps the human resources director did that as a matter of policy. On other fronts, HIV/AIDS wasn't even on the radar screen.

During the meeting, the young managers spoke politely in very general terms about the disease and were visibly uncomfortable about discussing condoms or awareness programs. None admitted to personally knowing anyone with HIV. WinThai's founder pointed out that he knew the epidemic was a problem in countries that imported WinThai beverages, notably Cambodia, Laos, and Vietnam, making the issue even more vital for WinThai to consider.

The outcome of the meeting was that all managers agreed that WinThai had to "take action" on HIV/AIDS. Apapan, as managing director of *WinThai* and daughter of the founder, was to spearhead the program. After all, as she had summed up, it is likely that many of the company's factory workers and distributors' employees were from families and villages touched by the epidemic, "which makes us personally responsible for them." In addition, the company employed proportionally more women than men who were, as it was clear from the government reports, more vulnerable to contracting HIV than men.

Initiating HIV/AIDS Action in a Reborn Epidemic   195

WinThai was a soft drinks company founded in 1971 by Apapan's father, a Canadian-educated chemical engineer. Apapan, graduate of a well-known Canadian MBA program, was now managing director of WinThai—although her father held the real power. WinThai had a range of soft drinks and pasteurized juices destined mainly for the Thai market with some exports in the region. The company has manufactured an "energy drink," Buffalo Power, since 1998 using Japanese-manufactured base ingredients, distinctive Thai flavorings, and a good supply of filtered Thai water. The company had one bottling plant of its own; however, Apapan was considering issuing a license to a Vietnamese entrepreneur, to bottle Buffalo Power and several other WinThai drinks in Vietnam. She had even received an expression of interest in Buffalo Power from a Malaysian bottling company. WinThai managers felt proud to continue what they saw as an old Thai tradition in energy drinks, and were particularly pleased to hitch on to the shirttails of internationally known Red Bull (an Austrian company and holder of a license to produce its drink from Thai inventors). It was a tough market, however, because of the number of competitors, the fickle tastes of the youth market, and the fact that very little hinged on the quality of the drink itself: the value was mainly in the marketing activities of WinThai that added excitement to the ingredients.

Apapan called in her assistant, Mechai, and told him to take some notes. "About this AIDS program, we're not going to reinvent the wheel. Please find out what other companies have done and are doing, and report back to me." Mechai looked puzzled and Apapan realized that the twenty-odd year difference between her and her assistant was the problem: Mechai had not experienced all the HIV/AIDS campaigns and communications blitzes years back, although oddly enough he shared the name of Thailand's "condom king," who took leadership on HIV/AIDS in Thailand, Mechai Viravaidya.[3] "I will make this simple for you, then. Look at Africa as an example. Find out what Coca-Cola has done there. Remember the Coca-Cola boycott a while back? Then, we can see what they did there that we could adapt to use here—if anything. At the very least, maybe we can learn something we should be doing in some of our export markets," said Apapan.

Her interest piqued by the phone call she had received from the Thailand Business Coalition, Apapan did a quick media search to see what Thai HIV/AIDS coverage was like. She was surprised to read in the papers that 85 percent of Thai youth did not feel concerned about HIV/AIDS. She had also read that 70 percent of all new sexually transmitted diseases were reported among young Thais, signaling that they were involved in unprotected premarital sex.[4] More than half Thai male adolescents had sex with sex workers,[5] and condom use was down in a recent study on Thai army conscripts.[6] Since the Asian economic crisis in the late 1990s, the Thai government had cut the funds available for HIV/AIDS awareness and prevention campaigns. In addition, the recent changes in the government had augured for a set of new priorities, of which HIV/AIDS was not present. So

196 AIDS and Business

that meant that there was a whole generation that had missed out on about a decade of national campaigns.[7] A worrying thought.

Apapan personally believed that a partnership that would result in an association in people's minds of WinThai with a well-known NGO like Population Services International[8] (PSI) could be useful in the energy drinks sector. In this sector the target was youth, who were likely to personally know someone with HIV or AIDS. It would have to be a partnership with an organization that was appealing and credible in the Thai youth context, however. Perhaps more useful would be a partnership with YouthAIDS, a division of PSI, which had young music and film stars as "ambassadors" and edgy campaigns like "Kick me." Partner brands of YouthAIDS included Levi's and H&M, which might be appealing to well-traveled Thais, yet Apapan found the tone of the Web site was rather brash and probably not appealing to a young Thai audience.

There was not much differentiation between the energy drinks themselves, apart from marketing. The tastes were all artificial and sweet; the "energy" ingredients were basically the same. Buffalo Power contained 5 percent more caffeine than Red Bull, as well as synthetic taurine (an amino acid), Thai galangal root, ginseng, and flavorings. No one in that demographic read the ingredients label; the most important ingredient was positioning. She thought that a clever positioning of WinThai energy drinks could be at the nexus of "patriotic-responsible" and "hip."

Thai people were very proud of their country and had a deep love for the royal family and Thai heritage. For that reason, Apapan mused, it really was a shame that all the companies with attention-grabbing HIV/AIDS campaigns were foreign. Nike Thailand's workplace policy was famous, as was the company's willingness to donate articles for fund-raising by other organizations. Also famous was the business involvement of The Body Shop in Thailand and worldwide with its 2007 "Stop HIV: Spray to change attitudes" campaign in partnership with MTV,[9] thereby launching its "limited edition" Rougeberry fragrance. Japanese company Rohm Apollo had gained recognition for its workplace acceptance of employees living with HIV/AIDS in their Thailand branch. Shell made HIV/AIDS information available at their service stations throughout the country.[10] Perhaps worst of all from WinThai's point of view was the activism of a company like PepsiCo[11] in Thailand—they had received in 2006 the Certificate of Outstanding HIV/AIDS Management in the Workplace award from the Thai Red Cross and UNAIDS. PepsiCo had also sponsored all the beverages and snacks served at the International AIDS Conference held in Bangkok.[12]

Apapan considered that it should be a Thai company—not a multinational—that generates pride and zeal about such an important national issue. The company was in public view in Thailand through sponsorship of a number of edgy youth-focused activities already, such as kitesurf events and beach parties. It could use those events more effectively by bringing HIV/AIDS awareness or prevention into the program.

Box 8.1   A View from the Field:

How Some Companies Make a Difference With Their HIV/AIDS Policies

We saw some mistakes that Botswana companies were making: they eliminated HIV/AIDS projects in communities and instead focused on workplaces. The problem was that miners received condoms at work but then leave work and go out into these communities and interact with people on a nightly basis. In the evenings when they visit the brothels they don't get condoms. In other places there were treatment programs where family members, such as wives who were HIV positive and workers were going home and splitting the treatment in half. Where does that get anyone? For their work to succeed in the workplace there must be links with groups working in the community.

There are signs that some companies' HIV efforts are having an impact, but making them stick and making them more comprehensive, is a problem. There are more resources coming in but not a lot of coordination to make sense of actions. What businesses can contribute to the effort is more than money. More valuable in a sense are their basic business skills. That is our challenge: no matter who we are (whether NGO's, health workers in vulnerable groups, philanthropy) we need to attain better coordination. There are great programs with *Heineken, Daimler Chrysler,* and others. The point is to get the word out.

. . . As time goes on companies can better understand how to use linkages. Business Coalitions can help them to do that. . . . When they don't have the . . . expertise to put together the necessary documents, frameworks for action, and strategic frameworks, they liaise with companies like GTZ[13]. At first Coalitions were focusing on massive goals, to make themselves look good. Today they are working on devising workable goals, such as developing their own membership lists and training peer educators. . . . *Standard Chartered Bank* and others have settled down with a work plan that is doable. . . . We are coming towards a network of organisations.

National Business Coalitions and other forms of business membership associations are important: we want everyone to get involved in AIDS, but in some developing countries they aren't yet ready. A Chamber of Commerce, for example, can set up HIV/AIDS committees. That's what happened in Namibia. Our effort is to bring people together. We've encouraged business coalitions to work together--why don't they share their information and their networks? It's not just about coalitions, it's also about associations. We see changing needs in terms of resources that are needed, it takes time to get there. There are needs for policy guidance on different issues. Hopefully we will spend less time on coalitions because they are sustaining where they are going.

We encourage companies to do as much as they can, and we take companies where they are. For different reasons, companies might have more of an impact depending on the type of work they do, the types of workers they have, and so on. If they are only doing actions in workplace, not in

continued

198   *AIDS and Business*

Box 8.1 (continued)

communities, the impact is not so great, as we saw in the examples from Botswana. In Tanzania, we saw *Unilever* driving others to action. Another example, this time from South Africa, was that of *Standard Chartered Bank* and their fierce competitor *Standard Bank*. *Standard Chartered Bank* built the "Champions" program. *Standard Bank* saw what they were doing with their workers. At that time, 10% of the workers at any time where out, being sick and taking care of people who are sick, and attending funerals. *Standard Bank* copied *Standard Chartered Bank* programs, including the "Champions" program. The banking industry has spread these programs to other countries. The banking sector is not as impacted by HIV/AIDS as the mining sector but they operate differently.

Source: personal communication Mr. Edward Vela, External Relations Officer, UNAIDS, Geneva, Switzerland, June 27, 2005

She knew that another compelling argument for corporate responsibility was the use situations for energy drink product lines. They were drunk mainly at parties and in nightclubs, where sexual encounters were likely to occur. In WinThai focus group discussions Apapan had heard young people stating their belief that energy drinks would pep people up for all kinds of activities—including sex. Focus groups also revealed that Buffalo Power was commonly mixed with vodka or other spirits because young people felt the drink would give them a "buzz." Such attitudes and activities were not likely to lead to responsible sexual behavior, and additionally Apapan had read about several cases of abuse of these drinks that had resulted in serious health consequences. She felt that the uses made of Buffalo Power by customers invoked the company's responsibility. She knew that PepsiCo had made a decision to partner with two HIV/AIDS NGOs in India recently for the same reasons.[14]

Perhaps her strongest feelings on the topic were Apapan's personal conviction that she was personally responsible for her employees. She knew that business literature would describe her as a "paternalistic" and "authoritarian" employer, and was proud of that fact—as indeed most Thai managers would be. She took over the company from her father, who was not only authoritarian—he was an absolute monarch. She could joke about these matters, having been educated in Toronto and far from Thai family and national politics, but at heart she took them seriously.

Apapan believed that she could have an immediate and lasting effect on employees and their families by taking action on HIV/AIDS. As for customers, they were her second priority: in fact, she believed that today's young people were generally irresponsible and self-centered. If they contracted HIV because of their lack of responsibility and selfishness, it was mainly their own fault. However, the recent resuscitation of HIV/AIDS reminders by AIDS activist campaigns and the media put the virus on the agenda for youth. That could indirectly help WinThai gain publicity, and at the same time support the HIV/AIDS awareness messages of the media.

On a more practical business level, her business-to-business customers (supermarkets, kiosks, sports teams, and other distributors) would appreciate WinThai's corporate philanthropy on HIV/AIDS because it would reflect positively on their own businesses. They would be able to trumpet their participation, however indirect, in an HIV/AIDS program through WinThai. Apapan thought that WinThai should consider the power of brand association if the company became a member of the Global Business Coalition:[15] WinThai would be up there with MTV, Ford, and Coca-Cola. If we inform our customers through a dedicated advertising campaign, such a partnership could give our company a unique sheen of international corporate cool by association. Global stars like Angelina Jolie, Shania Twain, and others associated with the Global Business Coalition would shine for WinThai, thought Apapan. She made a note to find out how much membership costs. For a number of reasons, Apapan was convinced that energy drinks could benefit positively from an association with an organization that takes effective and well-publicized action on HIV/AIDS.

CHOICE OF ACTIONS

Following her meeting with the Thailand Business Coalition on AIDS delegate, Apapan was aware that HIV/AIDS programs could cover a wide range of possibilities. She knew that some Thai companies offered medical care for employees, their families, and dependents (who may be quite numerous in Thailand, thought Apapan). Others had their own awareness programs for schoolchildren and the wider community, particularly in rural and poor areas. Some companies simply made it a human resources issue. As Apapan realized, she could do all that and more: a company like WinThai that is plugged into the youth market could be a highly effective channel for AIDS messages and even for fund-raising.

Another area of personal interest to Apapan was sex tourists who prey upon the most vulnerable Thais: children living in poverty—often "hill tribe" children, orphans, and even trafficked Cambodian children and women.[16] The typical meeting place for sex tourists and sex workers was bars, restaurants, and hotels—where most likely Buffalo Power was sold. WinThai could be active in donations and sponsorships to organizations that help street children and orphans, a relatively easy way to truly help without taking a company risk, thought Apapan. The company could even partner with the government's new campaign to raise awareness about child sex tourism and feature the child sex tourism hotline on posters and flyers.

She knew that she should talk to the Thailand Business Coalition on AIDS[17] before going too much further. This organization was generally well

200   AIDS and Business

thought of in business circles because it provided consultations with member companies and training services rather than merely dispensing advice. Another simple action, thought Apapan, was to distribute condoms at the plant, even to install a distributor in the toilets. "Then would I be encouraging people to have sex at work?" wondered Apapan, "Or worse, would the wider community see it like that even if it is not true?" The worrying thought crossed her mind and she realized it was a possibility that should not be ignored. Having started on a negative vein, Apapan now continued to think of reasons not to start an HIV/AIDS workplace program, in order to anticipate the likely objections of managers:

Having a workplace treatment program would be too costly given the cost of antiretroviral drugs.

- HIV was contracted due to the employee's (or customer's) private behavior, and as a result it is not our business.
- If we provide a workplace program we will be increasing inequality in Thai society: our employees are already lucky to have a well-paid job, and now they will also receive privileged information, while other Thais who are not employed by a big, caring company will not. Therefore, it is not fair.
- HIV/AIDS awareness, education, and prevention are the government's job, so there is no reason for companies to spend on these issues.[18]

COMPANY BENEFITS OF AN HIV/AIDS PROGRAM

Apapan decided to write down her ideas of the benefits the company should enjoy after implementing an HIV/AIDS program, in order to raise the points with the Business Coalition and WinThai managers. She knew she would need to persuade the younger managers of the "business arguments" for an HIV/AIDS program. She jotted down likely company benefits, displayed in Table 8.1.

There were also risks, however. For instance, if WinThai chose a partnership with an NGO, she might be at risk of embarrassment from the NGO if they speak too much about topics considered taboo in Thai society, for example. The company's stakeholders might resent the costs represented by an HIV/AIDS program—whether corporate philanthropy or a workplace program. Might it not also place the company at a disadvantage to its competitors, who were not taking any action whatever on HIV/AIDS and might therefore be considered the more "fun" brands that do not elicit any negative associations?

She summarized the benefits and reasons, rehearsing them in her head because she knew that she would need to be very compelling in order to get more than polite agreement from managers: we must do this; it is the

Initiating HIV/AIDS Action in a Reborn Epidemic 201

right course of action. Also, WinThai is doing well despite a tight market peopled by creative local competitors and the global Coca-Cola and PepsiCo companies—both with their own energy drinks, but it could not last forever without constant repositioning vis-à-vis the competitors. An HIV/AIDS response might be just what we need to cut WinThai out of the fray and position it in front of the competition. She called in her assistant to hear what he had discovered about the Coca-Cola Company and how it had dealt with the HIV/AIDS problem in Africa. Mechai cleared his throat, shuffled through his pile of papers, and made a presentation as if he was at college.

Table 8.1 Company Benefits for Initiating an HIV/AIDS Marketing Communications Program

Company and cultural values:
Thai people are intensely proud of their nation and their language. They will admire a company like WinThai that is trying to protect the Thai people and the country from this disease.
In an unusual partnership, Thai businesspeople and antiglobalization activists were increasingly talking about Buddhist social ethics—a concept that covered the kind of corporate responsibility that interested Apapan and could propel WinThai to leadership in the field.

Business-to-business customers' benefits:
To private brand customers, e.g., sports teams and supermarkets' own brands: they would be able to claim affiliation on WinThai's programs to benefit their own brands—and at the same time through their own publicity increase peoples' exposure to HIV/AIDS messages.

Reputation in the wider region:
Because WinThai was considering widening its beverage exports to more countries in Asia, there could be a premium on reputation in the region that comes from a well-publicized HIV/AIDS workplace or corporate philanthropy program. This would be particularly true in countries with rising HIV prevalence.

Company image as leader:
In the community and the region, WinThai could be considered to provide leadership on HIV/AIDS and even CSR in general because no one else in the food or drinks sector was taking any action.

International publicity:
There was the possibility of international publicity for WinThai, for example, in case studies published by the Thailand Business Coalition, the World Economic Forum's Global Health Initiative, or other international organizations. These could bring the sort of high-level publicity needed to make such a program really worthwhile.

Public relations and brand equity:
There should be public relations benefits generally for the WinThai name and the individual drink brands, like Buffalo Power.

Protection of employees:
By initiating an internal HIV/AIDS prevention campaign, we reduce risk among our own employees and their families even if we do not spend one baht in treatment.

CASE BACKGROUND

AN OVERVIEW OF CONSUMER PERCEPTIONS OF THE COCA-COLA COMPANY

Mechai asked, "Did you know that Clare Short, former UK development secretary, said condoms should be as easily available as Coca-Cola?"[19] Coca-Cola is often considered to be the world's biggest brand.[20] The company topped the "best brands" Harris Poll in 2007[21] and in the same year was number one in the ethical consumption poll (U.S. only).[22] In recent research, Coca-Cola won the drinks category for "coolest brand" in the UK.[23] A Harris Poll conducted in 2003 found that Coca-Cola is number seven in the "best brands" ranking, which is more or less consistent with the company's position over the past five years.[24] Coca-Cola is no doubt a strong brand today; however, over the past decade it has received a beating in consumer perceptions due to rising public concern over obesity, health, and nutrition issues connected with the product[25] and some widely publicized lawsuits and unpopular corporate moves. Then there was the criticism of the company's HIV/AIDS policies in Africa. According to the American Customer Satisfaction Index, consumers were less satisfied with Coca-Cola products in 2002.

Mechai stated that it seemed Coca-Cola has few friends among environmental protection groups and health advocates. The company has come under fire for its mainly successful attempts to install Coca-Cola vending machines in schools around the United States, and its sponsorship of children's clubs and Parent-Teacher Associations.[26] The Coca-Cola Company has been subject to a variety of boycotts because of its alleged participation in hiring paramilitary killers to eliminate eight union workers in Colombia.[27] A lawsuit was filed against the company under the U.S. Alien Tort Claims Act (discussed earlier)[28] and an activist Web site, "KillerCoke," was founded to inform people of the campaign. Also contributing to Coca-Cola's recent image problems was a U.S. court case brought for alleged racial discrimination.[29]

Closer to home, Mechai noted that in India the company has come under fire from a consumer protection group, Centre for Science and the Environment (CSE), for pesticide residues in Coca-Cola. PepsiCo faced similar allegations. The campaign of CSE's charismatic leader Sunita Narain had Coke and Pepsi banned in Kerala state, resulting in a generalized debate about consumer protection and the role of multinational corporations in India.[30] The company is accused of causing water scarcity, diversion of water from local communities, and water contamination.[31]

When Coca-Cola announced it was going to launch a workplace HIV/AIDS program in 2002, there was an unanticipated response. Activists such as Health Gap and Act UP alleged that Coca-Cola was restricting access to antiretroviral drugs to employees, by excluding 60,000 employees of Coca-Cola bottler companies.[32] Coca-Cola responded that the company had covered 1,500 "direct employees" since 2001 and bottling partners were working to improve conditions for their workers.[33,34]

Activist Responses to Coca-Cola's Pronouncements and Programs

"We are watching" was the slogan of Health Global Access Project (Health GAP), a human rights and HIV/AIDS activist organization.[35] In 2002, Health GAP initiated a campaign to put pressure on a number of multinational corporations to provide treatment to their workers. Action against the Coca-Cola Company included a dedicated Web site[36] throughout the campaign, street demonstrations with activist organization ACT UP,[37,38] and a "Global Day of Action" in 2002 against the company.[39] AIDS activists held noisy protests at the International AIDS Conference in Barcelona in 2002, demanding treatment for all direct and indirect Coca-Cola employees.[40] Other companies targeted by the Treat Your Workers campaign included energy companies (Chevron-Texaco, Shell, BP, Conoco), coffee buyers (Altria/Philip Morris/Kraft, Nestlé, Procter & Gamble, Sara Lee, Tchibo), and other U.S. multinationals "with operations in the developing world."[41] Another related action targeted drinks and snacks giant in Africa PepsiCo. The Interfaith Center on Corporate Responsibility filed a resolution with the company to reveal its plans for responding to the HIV/AIDS epidemic. Similar resolutions were filed with other multinational companies operating in Africa such as Colgate Palmolive, Chevron-Texaco and Ford Motor. Resolutions were resolved at the other companies, but PepsiCo argued that its operations were too small to warrant a costly impact study to be carried out.[42]

The Coca-Cola Company in Africa

The Coca-Cola Company is one of the biggest employers in Africa, with about 100,000 employees. The company operates in all African countries except Libya and Sudan.[43] Coca-Cola Company sales volumes grew by 10 percent in Africa in 2001, and as much as 36 percent in Nigeria.[44] The company faced anti-American sentiment in some countries, and ideology-based competition from so-called Muslim colas. When Mecca Cola was launched in Senegal and Mali, for instance, Coca-Cola sales reportedly fell by 40 percent, due to the support of religious leaders for non-American products.[45]

Africa is the poorest region in the world, although there are big income differences between countries. Some are heavily indebted, some suffer from poor governance and conflicts, and there are generally high levels of

204 AIDS and Business

micronutrient deficiencies.[46] Sub-Saharan Africa carries just under one-quarter of the world's disease burden and comprises 11 percent of the world population, yet accounts for only 1 percent of global health expenditures. To compound matters, there is a shortage of health care personnel which is in part due to economic migration to more affluent countries.[47]

MARKETING COMMUNICATIONS: TELLING
STAKEHOLDERS AND CUSTOMERS ABOUT GOOD DEEDS

Perhaps not so relevant to Thailand, Mechai said, is the fact that in affluent markets such as the United States, there are increasingly low levels of trust for corporations and, concurrently, higher expectations of companies' social responsibility. People increasingly consider company CSR when making purchase, employment, and investment decisions. They are looking beyond appearances and expecting that companies have environmental and/or economic development programs that are effective. Consumer trust in the United States was so low that consumers were less likely to trust corporate social responsibility–related information from company channels, and more likely to trust the media.[48]

Coca-Cola Company and other companies with HIV/AIDS programs communicate directly with shareholders and employees via company newsletters, magazines, annual reports, and shareholder meetings. Press releases targeted at responsible investing Web sites such as Domini[49] and publications like *Ethical Corporation*[50] and *CSR-Asia*[51] may also give the reader the impression of an independent news source, thereby increasing credibility. Coca-Cola also benefited from publicity that came through the company's HIV/AIDS program partners. The company received coverage on a substantial number of UNAIDS[52] online and paper publications and reports, as it did from other partners like Population Services International. Coca-Cola published its own in-house reports and policy papers. Annual reports by nongovernmental organizations such as PharmAccess International[53] and Population Services International (PSI) emphasized Coca-Cola's social and environmental commitment, and the HIV/AIDS program documentation of policies, objectives, and monitoring is substantial.

The Coca-Cola Africa Foundation[54] has worked with UNAIDS since June 2001 to provide community AIDS education, communications initiatives, and workplace initiatives. The foundation donated billboards, airtime, transportation services, and marketing and communications expertise to HIV/AIDS prevention materials and messages.[55] The company has delivered HIV/AIDS-themed schoolbooks to school districts throughout Kenya, has developed a television commercial for the National AIDS Control Council, and supported the development of an HIV/AIDS education comic book series "Nuru."[56]

Box 8.2 A View from the Field:

Challenges Facing Companies Starting HIV/AIDS Programs

All the initiatives—from the Global Compact[57] on—have had legitimacy problems. Even the Global Reporting Initiative[58] has had problems. However, I think we begin to see groups that have broken off that are doing more substantive work, work they would not have been able to do if they did not receive this broader perspective from those global initiatives. The Unilevers[59] of the world, whether national or multinational corporations, are trying to reach back to their supply chain. We're working with National Business Coalitions, for instance in Namibia,[60] to get smaller versions of HIV/AIDS workplace handbooks that are more targeted.

It is possible that some of these multinational efforts are window dressing, but there has been a huge leap from where they were, and they are now making more substantive changes. Their potential is in outreach and advocacy. The challenge is scaling up: making it matter at country level. The Global Business Coalition[61] and the World Economic Forum (WEF)[62] are working with other organizations like the Global Fund to Fight AIDS, Tuberculosis and Malaria,[63] in investment projects to expand the business efforts at country level. I think we'll see some major outcomes.

Other companies, like Unilever, typically have supply networks they draw upon, as well as distributors. It's a huge network. The WEF has been working with companies like Volkswagen. They have been considering working with Unilever and applying what they learned to their business. When you have a larger plant subsidiary with a number of subcontractors interacting on a daily basis, the power of Volkswagen[64] or Unilever can tell them "We can show you how to start one of these programs" and help them with the capacity building. This becomes a mentoring relationship that will help the subcontractors and suppliers, which are often small or medium-sized businesses otherwise unable to take action. Business coalitions create an environment that brings companies together that can mentor others and have greater reach, greater impact.

There is criticism that the Global Business Coalition does tracking and "window dressing" to enhance their corporate image without many results. There are some good achievements, such as World Wildlife Fund,[65] and Lafarge,[66] and then you have some activists complaining about window dressing. Some independent watchdogs try to assess whether companies are seeking publicity or making changes.

Source: Personal communication with Mr. Edward Vela, External Relations Officer, UNAIDS, Geneva, Switzerland, June 27, 2005.

Coca-Cola Partners in HIV/AIDS Prevention in Africa

Coca-Cola teamed up with several organizations in its efforts to provide an effective and efficient HIV/AIDS program, the most prominent of which are PSI and UNAIDS. PSI[67] is a nongovernmental health organization that uses social marketing to deliver health products and services to people living in poverty, and motivate people to use these products while adopting a healthier lifestyle. PSI campaigns focus on delaying the onset of sexual activity, reducing sexual partners, increasing condom use, inciting people to get tested, and reducing mother-to-child-transmission of the virus.[68] By applying branding principles to low-priced health products, such as "Trust" condoms in Kenya and "Protector Plus" condoms in Togo, PSI gave itself credit for saving 500,000 people from HIV infection in 2002.[69] In Zimbabwe, a partnership was forged between Coca-Cola Africa Foundation and PSI to distribute Protector Plus condoms in rural areas, along with the drink. In Zambia, Coca-Cola distributed with Maximum condoms.[70]

Coca-Cola has worked on HIV/AIDS projects with UNAIDS since 2001, including "lending" a company marketing manager to work with UNAIDS on prevention and antistigma programs.[71] UNAIDS and Coca-Cola signed a three-year agreement to coordinate the company's provision of an HIV/AIDS education, prevention, and treatment program to Coca-Cola bottlers across Africa. The program expects to benefit from synergies in local community infrastructure, marketing resources, and human resources policies.[72]

Victory to the Activists? Coca-Cola Adopts a Comprehensive HIV/AIDS Policy

Operating in an atmosphere of corporate distrust and with soft drink sales falling, the Coca-Cola Company announced on March 31, 2003, that it would extend company health care benefits to those with HIV/AIDS. Coca-Cola chose initially to partner with Netherlands-based PharmAccess International, although the company later put a stop to it. PharmAccess also partnered with Heineken, another corporation with pan-African operations.[73] The company declared that it would commence workplace preventative education and treatment (including antiretroviral drugs) programs for its own employees, their spouses and children as well as those of its bottlers in fifty-four African countries.[74] The Global Business Coalition on HIV/AIDS particularly welcomed the Coca-Cola program because of its potential to spread preventive practices throughout Coca-Cola's far-flung distribution networks. The foundation estimated the cost of the entire program at US$11 million per year.[75]

> *Box 8.3* A View from the Field:
>
> *Coca-Cola's Work in the Area of HIV/AIDS*
>
> Yes, I've seen creative work of Coke. Procurement and supply management has gotten a boost from a company like Coca-Cola, which has mastered the art of moving products from place to place. In some places they have formed a public-private partnership with government. We have a vivid picture of Coca-Cola trucks and mules carrying Coke and related supplies in refrigerated containers. They've been doing it for years. Even to remote places. Those kinds of curious partnerships-distribution and supply chain management are a massive issue. Keep drugs coming, keep them fresh, and keep managing them. I'm not sure health agencies understand the critical and helpful role that business and particular retailers can provide about moving goods from one place to another.
>
> Source: Personal communication from Mr. Ted Karpf, director of partnerships, WHO HIV Department, Geneva, Switzerland, June 27, 2005.

There were three areas of concentration in the Coca-Cola HIV/AIDS strategy, according to a Global Business Coalition report (2003).[76]

- First, the workplace policy, which encourages voluntary testing, voluntary disclosure, and "reasonable accommodation" (continuation of work as usual) of employees with AIDS.
- Second, Coca-Cola worked on developing partnerships with local, regional, and international NGOs, mainly in the area of marketing and communications.
- Third, they extended their entire program to their bottlers.

Further afield, Coca-Cola distributed playing cards featuring HIV/AIDS information to migrant workers in China, in a partnership with the Global Business Coalition in 2007.[77] Coca-Cola's Russia/Ukraine/Belarus president, Clyde Tuggle, stated that companies are "major stakeholders" in fighting HIV/AIDS. He went on to say that Coca-Cola joined the Global Business Coalition for "selfish" reasons, emphasizing that the Coca-Cola Company is dependent for its survival upon the continued good health of the communities in which it operates, and a "successful, healthy and prosperous" Russia.[78]

For a better view of Coca-Cola's HIV/AIDS program, it is helpful to see the company in the context of multinationals operating in Africa and offering such programs. Table 8.2 provides a pan-African overview of the HIV/AIDS programs of some large corporations in the years up to 2003.

208 *AIDS and Business*

Table 8.2 An Overview of Selected HIV/AIDS Company Programs in Africa

Company name, area and sector	*Employees*	*Type of program*
Anglo American (UK) Southern Africa Metals and mining	75,000 in Southern Africa[79]	• Workplace education using peer educators[80] • Antiretroviral drugs for all employees and treatment of sexually transmitted diseases[81] • Voluntary testing and counseling drives reached 70% Southern African employees[82] • Condom distribution, mainly free, at work, in local bars, residences, and so on[83] • Zero tolerance of discrimination and stigma • Note: Similar company programs underway also in Brazil and China[84]
Heineken (Netherlands) Africa Beverages	8,000 in Africa[85]	• No discrimination policy • Employee's confidentiality maintained[86] • Partnership with Pharmaccess International • Prevention of mother-to-child transmission[87] • Voluntary testing and counseling[88] • Provide HAART for employees, a partner and children; considering extending coverage for children after 18 years • Sexually transmitted diseases treatment • Culturally appropriate programs/counseling[89]
Coca-Cola African continent except Libya Beverages	More than 60,000 in Africa[90]	• Prevention and treatment programs for employees and families, also through bottlers[91] • Sponsors or conducts community and family outreach, partnerships; uses distribution channels for materials[92] • Voluntary counseling and testing for employees and dependants • Encouragement of acceptance of HIV positive employees[93] • Note: Workplace programs now in China, India and Russia[94]
BMW S. Africa Automotive	3,000 employees and 1,800 contractors[95]	• Prevention and awareness programs, voluntary counseling and testing, treatment of sexually transmitted infections • Comprehensive treatment and support including antiretroviral drugs[96] • Multi-stakeholder HIV/AIDS committee • Specialised training for specific groups such as shop stewards • Free male and female condoms • Programs for suppliers and dealers planned[97]

Initiating HIV/AIDS Action in a Reborn Epidemic 209

Table 8.2 (continued)

Company name, area and sector	Employees	Type of program
ChevronTexaco Nigeria Extraction	More than 2,000	• Peer education, condom distribution • Community prevention, including children of employees off-site (provide male-only housing) • Voluntary testing and counselling • Prevention of mother to child transmission • Funds Nigerian government HIV/AIDS programs in schools[98] • Treatment of opportunistic infections[99] • Note: Corporation sponsors HIV/AIDS workplace programs in Russia and Ukraine[100]

QUESTIONS

1. To what extent do companies have a responsibility in the fight against HIV/AIDS, a phenomenon that is largely out of the control of business organizations? Should the social responsibility of companies go beyond caring for their own employees? What are, in your opinion, the expectations of consumers? Of NGOs and activist organizations? Of the general public?

2. How can it be explained that Coca-Cola developed a corporate program to help fight the spread of HIV/AIDS, and the public reaction was boycotts, demonstrations, and public disapproval of the company policy?

3. Public relations and corporate communications use such HIV/AIDS campaigns to improve the image of large corporations as being socially responsible. What are the dangers involved with the use of charitable actions for publicity purposes by companies that have profits as their legitimate target?

4. How do you envision WinThai taking action on the renewed HIV/AIDS epidemic in Thailand? There are a number of directions they could take. Should the company focus on workplace programs? Corporate philanthropy such as donations or sponsorships of HIV/AIDS activist organizations or NGOs? Awareness programs? HIV/AIDS cause-related marketing?

5. Design an innovative public relations strategy for WinThai that would be compatible with the target markets and corporate concerns described in the case study. Consider other elements of the marketing communications mix that could be used to support the strategy.

210 *AIDS and Business*

FURTHER RESOURCES

Coca-Cola Africa. (n.d.). *Coca-Cola Africa HIV/AIDS workplace prevention programme—community outreach manual 4.* Available at: http://www.weforum.org/pdf/Initiatives/GHI_HIV_CocaCola_AppendixE.pdf.

Ministry of Public Health, Thailand. (2005). Thailand's response to HIV/AIDS. International Poverty Center. *In Focus* (January). Available at: http://www.undp-povertycentre.org/pub/IPCPovertyInFocus5.pdf.

Revenga, A., Over, M., Masaki, E., Peerapatanapokin, W., Gold, J., et al. (2006). *The economics of effective AIDS treatment: Evaluating policy options.* Available at: http://web.worldbank.org/.

Visser, W., Matten, D., Pohl, M., & Tolhurst, N. (2007). *The A-Z of corporate social responsibility.* Chichester, West Sussex, UK: John Wiley & Sons.

World Bank. (2006). *HIV and AIDS: Thailand shows how free access to life-saving drugs can be affordable.* Available at: http://web.worldbank.org/.

Wymer, W. W., & Samu, S. (eds.) (2003). *Non-profit and business sector collaboration: Social enterprises, cause-related marketing, sponsorships and other corporate-non-profit dealings.* Binghamton, NY: Best Business Books.

9 Woolworths South Africa[1]

Nikolay Ermakov pondered the landscape as the taxi powered around the bends in the road above the sea leading to Cape Town. So different from his native St. Petersburg, where he would soon return to report to his boss, retail entrepreneur Luba Petrova, the prospects of opening a Woolworths[2] in Moscow. Rolling hills of lush vineyards rose to meet mountains of indeterminate shape, dotted with graceful white houses where, Nikolay knew, good wine was waiting for him to taste it. As Cape Town came into view, Nikolay felt his well-traveled brain struggling to position it. Almost Southern United States, but too colorful and prosperous-looking. Almost South of France, but with a colonial air and Anglo-Saxon order. Almost an English spa town, but gone wild with color and peppered with palm trees, spread out below a most extraordinary flattopped mountain. He was about to learn about the specific character of South African places and people that could only be described as South African . . .

The taxi stopped near a modernistic shopping center, where Nikolay asked directions to Woolworths. He stood for a moment, staring at the bold lettering and the inviting storefront. A cloud of doubt was pushed away and Nikolay strode into the shop, again convinced that a Woolworths franchise would work in Moscow. There was a growing class of people in the cities of Russia, made up of the diligent, upwardly mobile worker on the one hand, and of educated professionals on the other, whose debts ate up nearly all their income. Both of these groups understood quality and were sensitive to status, and yet were careful to live within their means. They wanted the material trappings they saw in the American and European television shows and the magazines they read—the clothes, home furnishings, and even food and beverages. Nikolay understood that there was a whole class of these people in South Africa also, in fact not the only similarity between Russia and this country. A shop like Woolworths could fulfill the lifestyle aspirations of hundreds of thousands of Russians, at a price they would afford.

Woolworths South Africa is a chain of retail shops consisting of full-line stores, clothing and home stores, food stores, and online shopping. Like Marks & Spencer,[3] the British retail company with which Woolworths had an ongoing relationship since 1947, Woolworths uses a "single brand"

212 *AIDS and Business*

marketing strategy. Woolworths has more than two hundred shops in South Africa, and others across Africa, in Dubai and Bahrain, many of which are run by franchisees. The Cape Town–based company owns Country Road,[4] a chain of 250 stylish retail outlets and wholesalers spanning Australia, Indonesia, Malaysia, New Zealand, and Singapore. Woolworths provides a "convenient, modern and inspiring shopping experience" (Woolworths, p. 58)[5] and prides itself on consistently offering affordable high quality as well as fostering innovation

Nikolay had several hours before his appointment with the franchise office at Woolworths headquarters, so he decided to spend them in the shop. The shop had an up-market feel, with its tasteful displays and no aisles. The stylish lighting and décor complemented the up-market impression. Nikolay noticed that the clothes were designed to conform to a distinctive style: within the realm of what one could describe as "tasteful" without being boring. In fact, the clothes he picked off the rack broadly fit with what he had observed on the streets of Moscow as being currently fashionable, and were likely to still be fashionable enough to wear again next year. "No fashion excesses committed here," he chuckled to himself. At his chuckle a puzzled saleslady approached him. "Good morning, sir, may I help you?" she said. Nikolay glanced at this tall black lady with long straight hair and stylish rectangular glasses, replied that he was seeking home decorations, and followed her directions. In the housewares department he found the same kind of design philosophy. "This is just perfect for Russians who can't afford to refurbish their home (although IKEA is doing good business there) but seek tasteful decorative accents that can follow the fashions," thought Nikolay. He noticed that Woolworths managed interestingly to do the same with their food market—supplying, in addition to basics, a line of feel-good gourmet foods like Santa red-skin potatoes, free-range eggs, organic, halal, and kosher items as well as wines.

At 11 o'clock, Nikolay strode into the office of Piet Afrikaander to discuss franchising opportunities for Woolworths in Russia. "We have a lot in common,", said Nikolay, leaning towards Piet, who was approximately his age, and like him looked studiedly casual in a sophisticated way. "I was in your central store for two hours this morning and at times I almost thought I was in Moscow. Your shoppers are the people who, in Moscow, seek value for money, but don't want to shop at 'cheap' stores like Auchan,[6] Billa,[7] or Ramstore.[8] They would be proud to go to Woolworths, which is affordable but higher status."

After a long discussion with Piet and other executives, the Russian and South Africans felt that a Woolworths in Moscow was a distinct possibility. While drinking a cup of green tea that afternoon, Nikolay almost fell off his chair when Piet asked how he thought the HIV/AIDS epidemic in Russia would affect his business long term. "Actually, I don't . . . I don't think about it, I mean. We businessmen are not concerned that a bunch of junkies and prostitutes are sick." Piet raised his eyebrows, leaned forward, and said that five years ago he did not think that HIV/AIDS was an issue relevant to businesses, but that he had now changed his mind. Then he stated what he knew about HIV/AIDS in Russia, that it was one of the world's fastest-growing epidemics, that it was known that the epidemic had crossed over from marginalized populations into the mainstream, that the number of people with the disease was vastly underestimated. "OK, but those people are never likely to become Woolworths customers anyway. It's not an issue for us," said Nikolay, forcefully.

Piet put down his teacup and gave a polite speech about the macroeconomic effects of HIV/AIDS, the reduction in household spending, the subsequent difficulty of attracting foreign investment, the lost productivity, and the specter of an orphaned generation never socialized by parents dying from AIDS. "I am speaking from experience, eh," said Piet to Nikolay's doubtful glance. "I live in the country home to the largest number of people living with HIV/AIDS. Every day in South Africa more than 600 people die of HIV/AIDS-related diseases, in fact probably many more. One in five adults here has HIV/AIDS."

Piet took a deep breath and continued, "You said earlier that we have a lot in common. We do: the growing pains of an emerging economy, infrastructure issues, a health system that doesn't reach everyone, and an HIV/AIDS epidemic. I know in Russia you are not where we are yet, but we wouldn't have such an AIDS problem here if our government had heeded calls, years ago, for action. I've heard similar calls being made to the Russian government, recently." Piet looked over to see Nikolay glance discreetly at his watch. "Even if what you say is true, I don't see what a business can do. I should go and call my partner, it's getting late," Nikolay mumbled. Piet replied, standing up, "Oh is it? We'll talk again tomorrow. Tomorrow morning I want you to meet with our director of people Zyda Rylands, and our Health and Wellness Manager Katy Hayes. After that I'll see you again. In the meantime, I have some bedtime reading for you," said Piet, handing Nikolay a glossy folder containing franchisee information and a stylish CD-ROM case titled Woolworths HIV/AIDS programme. "See you tomorrow, and don't drink too much Cape wine, eh!"

Back at his hotel and after a little Cape wine, Nikolay started reading, the sound of crashing waves and seagulls coming through the open window. In 2003, the prevalence rate for HIV/AIDS in South Africa was 21.5 percent among citizens aged between fifteen and forty-nine.[9] Woolworths considered that there was a threat emanating from its own workforce of 14,500 in its 112 South African outlets and facilities. In 2005, HIV/AIDS prevalence at Woolworths was below the national average (5.9 percent). In 2004, Woolworths management declared that they did not yet perceive an impact on absenteeism and productivity;[10] however, they recognized the threat of consumers redirecting their financial resources away from nonessential purchases to support a family member with HIV/AIDS.

Nikolay opened his laptop on the bed and went to the company's Web site www.Woolworths.co.za and noticed that Woolworths describes itself as being

214 *AIDS and Business*

"committed to the social and economic development,"[11] and "contributing to the African Renaissance."[12] That was a side of the company he knew nothing about. At home when he had researched the company as a possible franchise opportunity, he had looked at the "hard" stuff—the figures, the reports, all glowing stuff. For Nikolay this was a totally new perspective. He noted that the company runs a wide range of corporate citizenship programs, of which a number directly or indirectly addressed HIV/AIDS, to include the following:

MySchool: a loyalty and direct contribution program whereby customers designate the school they wish to receive a percentage of their expenditure at Woolworths on school clothes, bread, milk, books, and pencils.

The Woolworths Trust: a team which is representative of Woolworths employees runs the trust, which supports nutrition and ecological education and community development. It provides matching funds for monies raised by local stores.

EduPlant: run by Food and Trees for Africa, the program plants food-crop gardens at schools and trains the students and teachers in sustainable food farming techniques. The harvest is given to the schoolchildren.

The Fancy Stitch Group-Ingwavuma Women's Centre: provides employment and skills training for women in a poverty-stricken area of Zululand, where HIV/AIDS prevalence reaches 35 percent. HIV/AIDS awareness and behavior-change programs are provided as well.

The Perfect Canvas: by paying South African artists for the use of their artworks on Woolworths shopping bags, the company intends to support and stimulate South African art.

In addition to the specific programs previously described, Woolworths supports a variety of sustainable business activities in its operations and supplier agreements ranging from ecological specifications and practices, health and safety programs, human resources policies, and animal welfare standards. Woolworths is South Africa's leading seller of organic products, and has an active policy to buy from local or national manufacturers and suppliers. In 2004, the company made donations to charitable causes in excess of 120 million rand (approximately 15 million euro). The sum of these activities and programs qualified Woolworths for the Johannesburg Stock Exchange's Socially Responsible Investment Index. The Woolworths sustainability forum was set up to strategically integrate sustainability across businesses. A sustainability index reports key indicators according to the Global Reporting Initiative (GRI) index.

Nikolay raised an eyebrow, thinking these programs are all very nice here, but in Russia who really cares about these issues? Customers? The government? Perhaps such activities could help motivate Russian staff, though, he conceded.

The following day Nikolay returned to Woolworths headquarters and met with Zyda Rylands, director of people, and Katy Hayes, health and wellness manager. From Zyda he understood that Woolworths corporate values are expressed in human resources policies. These are more comprehensive than most in Africa (". . . and most in Russia!" added Nikolay). Woolworths employee benefits include access to reliable transport to and from work, paid maternity leave, and funeral cover. A far-reaching employee benefits program, the Employee Assistance Program (EAP), provides counseling services. Within the context of HIV/AIDS, Woolworths programs include notably voluntary counseling and testing and HIV/AIDS disease management (with provision of antiretroviral therapy) for all employees including flexitimer employees.

As Nikolay drank a cup of Woolworths mocha java blend coffee, he asked if the HIV/AIDS program was devised to impress customers or stakeholders. HIV/AIDS coordinator Katy Hayes patiently explained, "I'll give you some history so you can understand the rationale for the programme." The program grew out of the brand values. "Our vision," said Katy, "is that 'we aspire to being the most trusted and respected modern South African retail brand.' Tell me, who can *trust* and *respect* a company that is known not to care for its employees? We're not some big mining company or something: people come into contact with us every day, we're in their home, in their stomachs, we dress their kids . . . Then there's what we call a strategic driver of Woolworths, to 'be an actively responsible organization, focused on addressing issues unique to the environment in which we operate.'"[13] There was an expressed concern for "family structure, the community, and longer-term issues of sustainability."[14] The company first developed an HIV/AIDS policy in 1988. Some management training began in 1992. In 1997 Woolworths launched the HIV/AIDS educational programs and peer educators. They were inspired by the Zimbabwe AIDS Prevention Project, a peer education scheme that reduced workplace prevalence of HIV/AIDS by 34 percent.[15]

A study they commissioned in 1997 showed that Woolworths would feel the effects of HIV/AIDS by 2010. According to projections, 5 percent of employees would be ill with AIDS at work, 16 percent would have HIV, and there would be a 5 percent rise in mortality among employees aged thirty to forty-four by 2010. It was thought that productivity would be reduced by 2 to 3 percent—approximately as much as if a large shop was closed. Their projections were that for each rand (approximately 0.15 euro) spent on peer education annually, 10 Rand would be saved over ten years. Management believed that a comprehensive HIV/AIDS management program could reduce prevalence at Woolworths by 20 percent by 2010.[16] The business argument in favor of the workplace HIV/AIDS program was clear.

In 2003 the Woolworths HIV/AIDS steering committee was formed, sending the signal that HIV/AIDS was a company-wide issue, not just a human resources concern. The committee worked with the South African Coalition on Business (Sabcoha) and integrated elements and ideas from case studies of other companies' existing programs. The chairperson

216 *AIDS and Business*

of the Woolworths steering committee, Kevin Stanford, outlined the main aims of the program: "to create a non-discriminatory, supportive environment that minimizes the impact of HIV/AIDS on our employees and business, through sustainable interventions that address risk, focus on the prevention of new infections and prolong the health and lives of those affected."[17]

The strategic framework, as drawn up by the HIV/AIDS steering committee, contained the following elements:

1. Prevention
   - Educational and information programs and the "encouragement of safer sexual practices and personal responsibility" to include peer education, condom distribution, awareness campaigns, wellness screening.

2. Positive Living Programme
   - Fostering a supportive environment, providing support programs, and prolonging life, to include relevant elements of the Employee Assistance Program and the Clinical Management Program. The program is administered by an independent health management company, QUALSA, and includes a hotline, vitamin supplements, and access to antiretrovirals.[18]

3. Testing
   - "Know your status" campaign started in September, 2004 with tests on members of the senior leadership team. More than one-third[19] of employees had taken the test free of charge before the end of 2005.

4. Managing the business impacts
   - Internal and external risk assessment, determination and design of policies and procedures "to ensure sustainability."
   - According to the Woolworths Supplier Code of Business Principles, all suppliers are encouraged to have an HIV/AIDS policy, and if they do not, Woolworths will offer assistance in developing one
   - HIV/AIDS workplace management training module for managers, of which most have to date completed training.

5. Measurement and evaluation
   - Monitoring effectiveness.
   - Reporting according to the Global Reporting Initiative (GRI).[20]

6. Communication for education and awareness
   - An emphasis on personal responsibility in the areas of health and wellness.

Woolworths South Africa 217

In addition to this framework, according to Woolworths director of people Zyda Rylands, "Sincerity, passion, and commitment" are vital to the success of any HIV/AIDS program, as is the "full support of the most senior leadership."[21]

At first, Woolworths used a restricted number of stores in three of the largest regions to pilot the HIV/AIDS program, in particular the voluntary confidential testing (VCT) element, to determine effectiveness in light of the different demographic profiles. In order to ensure the proper levels of expertise, Woolworths contracted the testing out to Occupational Care SA, an occupational healthcare services company.[22] In a survey conducted by the University of Cape Town's Department of Public Health, Woolworths employees were more knowledgeable, had more "appropriate attitudes," and have "better practices in condom use" than employees of comparable companies.[23]

Katy looked at Nikolay, "I think you can see this is not about window dressing. In fact, many people in South Africa and in the business world don't know what we do—we don't necessarily generate publicity because we don't do this for our image enhancement. We do it for us, all of us. It is important that you understand that if you're thinking of starting a franchise. In fact, personally, I almost see it as a watershed issue: if you don't understand our values, and given the state of the epidemic in your country, maybe you're not the right person for us in Russia."

QUESTIONS

1. To what extent are Woolworths HIV/AIDS policy guidelines uniquely adapted to South Africa? Is Woolworths HIV/AIDS policy mere corporate social responsibility or does it express a broader concern of the company with both its customers and its employees?
2. Does it make sense to transfer Woolworths' HIV/AIDS policy to a country like Russia? Compare both contexts and outline key factors (consumer and shopping behavior, purchasing power, language, culture, ethnic groups, AIDS prevalence, and so on) that may or may not be in favor of transferability. What could be the likely reactions of Russian shoppers to the emphasis put by the local Woolworths franchisee on HIV/AIDS corporate policy?
3. Should Woolworths include HIV/AIDS related policy in its franchising operations? To what extent should they make it mandatory for potential franchisees worldwide to comply with Woolworths HIV/AIDS policy guidelines?

For answering the assigned questions, you should investigate similarities and differences as concerns the HIV/AIDS epidemic in South Africa and

218   *AIDS and Business*

Russia, especially by searching country information on the WHO Web site at http://www.who.int/topics/hiv_infections/en/.

APPENDIX 1: WOOLWORTHS HISTORY

Woolworths South Africa was founded in Cape Town, South Africa, in 1931 by entrepreneur Max Sonnenberg. Sonnenberg's South African Woolworths business was not affiliated with other Woolworths chains in the United Kingdom, United States, and Australasia. In the 1940s Woolworths owners, the Susmann family, associated itself with tasteful value-for-money British retail chain Marks and Spencer. A formal information agreement and specification of no competition in certain markets was agreed. This association began to dissolve in the 1960s with the concern that the Labour government in Britain might nationalize Marks and Spencer, and further damage was done with international public concerns about apartheid and subsequent boycotts.[24] Today the agreement with Marks and Spencer continues to provide access to expertise.

Woolworths is considered by different measures to be the leading retail chain in South Africa. Woolworths is commonly seen to provide merchandise of superior quality, at reasonable prices. Currently the company has two hundred shops in South Africa as well as shops and franchised outlets in Bahrain, Botswana, Dubai, Ghana, Kenya, Namibia, Nigeria, Tanzania, Zambia, and Zimbabwe. Today Woolworths is known for clothing for men, women, and children, food, financial services, cellular services, items for the home, and a range of other services. Woolworths owns Country Road, a chain of 250 stylish retail outlets and wholesalers spanning Australia, Indonesia, Malaysia, New Zealand, and Singapore.

APPENDIX 2: FRANCHISING WITH WOOLWORTHS

The information that follows comes from Woolworths franchising information available on their Web site[25]

At Woolworths we pride ourselves not only in serving our communities, but in being part of them. We believe it is the best way we can build relationships with our customers.

In order to ensure that our franchise stores meet the needs of their communities, it is vital that our franchisees have a deep understanding of the specific area in which these stores are located. It is also essential that we comply with legislation in regard to the appointment of franchisees. For these reasons, future franchise opportunities will only be advertised in local media as they arise; no general applications for franchises will be considered. These advertisements will detail our franchisee selection criteria as well as the process to be followed.

If you have already filed an application with us, we'd like to thank you for the interest you've shown. Your support and enthusiasm for our brand mean a lot to us. While we are no longer able to consider the general application you've made, you are welcome to apply again should an opportunity be advertised in your area.

Once again, thank you for your interest and support of the Woolworths brand.

For more information about Woolworths HIV/AIDS program, contact the Wellness Strategy Manager, Woolworths, PO Box 680, Cape Town 8000, South Africa.

10 Designing a Company HIV/AIDS Program

> The AIDS fight needs everything the business world can offer, from leadership to marketing, media, supply chains, organization and infrastructure, and most importantly, people.
>
> —Bill Roedy, president of MTV Networks International.[1]

Many companies currently do not have a satisfactory response to the increase in HIV/AIDS cases in the community, among customers, or among employees, and must suddenly take a reactive stance. Worse, the epidemic may not be on their radar at all. A six-year research project examining private sector responses to HIV/AIDS in sub-Saharan Africa found that the "vast majority" of businesses had a weak or nonexistent response, while many others attempted to reduce the impact of HIV/AIDS on their companies by modifying employment conditions (Rosen, Feeley, Connelly, and Simon, 2006).[2] In a survey conducted for the World Economic Forum (WEF) in 2004, it was found that only approximately one-quarter of all companies in 104 countries had an HIV/AIDS policy. However, in areas with an HIV/AIDS prevalence rate exceeding 20 percent, almost half of the companies surveyed had an HIV/AIDS policy.[3]

In the words of Dr. Kate Taylor, director of the World Economic Forum Global Health Initiative, company responses are ". . . too little, too late" (WBCSD, 2005).[4] However, there are a variety of reasons for starting a program and why large firms as well as small and medium-sized enterprises should consider doing so. As stated most powerfully by UNAIDS Secretary General Dr. Peter Piot, speaking to a group of multinational corporations, "HIV is a major threat to global economic stability and business interests."[5] The spread of HIV/AIDS is a threat for businesses tempted by the large middle-income markets of Brazil, South Africa, China, and Russia.[6] Rosen et al. (2003) argued that everyone globally will be affected by the economic fallout of HIV/AIDS—not just poor countries: "AIDS is destroying the twin rationales of globalization strategy: cheap labor and fast-growing markets" (p. 82).[7] These are threats which, if understood and planned for, may be mitigated by a strong and forward-looking company HIV/AIDS policy.

The impacts of the spread of HIV/AIDS are well documented. However, business leaders are unsure to what extent these impacts will affect them, nor how big of an impact is to be expected, and when. Due to this

Designing a Company HIV/AIDS Program 221

uncertainty, many businesses have fallen victims to policy and planning paralysis. The macroeconomic impacts of HIV/AIDS have been discussed earlier in the book, but it would be valuable to recap the major points as they directly affect business, as summarized in Table 10.1, and as discussed in detail following the table.

Table 10.1 Some Direct Impacts on Business of HIV/AIDS

HIV/AIDS-related threat	*Direct impact on businesses*
Workers may contract HIV and develop AIDS	Productivity and profitability affected as workers fall ill and become less productive, or are absent from work for health reasons.
Workers may be affected by the declining health or death of family members who have AIDS	The productivity of workers may decline and absenteeism may increase if a family member falls ill or dies, and it may be desirable for the company to extend health or counseling services to the family.
Customers may contract AIDS or a family member may do so	Consumer spending is diverted from typical consumption patterns to cover new health care costs.
Employees with AIDS need "reasonable accommodation" at the workplace	Provision of "reasonable accommodation" incurs costs that need to be planned for, particularly by small companies that suffer disproportionately when a worker is absent.
High cost of HIV/AIDS medications	The cost of antiretrovirals needed by companies who have committed themselves to treatment of employees may be prohibitively high, particularly for small and medium businesses that cannot benefit from economies of scale.
Company insurance costs may rise	Organizations may contribute to or wholly fund a range of benefits, including health, disability, life, and funeral insurance, in addition to spouse and retirement pensions. In certain contexts the funeral insurance, or funeral fund, may represent large sums.
An HIV/AIDS program may become necessary or be required by law	Costs associated with developing a program may be high, disproportionately so for small and medium enterprises which cannot incorporate HIV/AIDS planning and implementation to a dedicated human resources department.
Public funds diverted from health and development projects to HIV/AIDS projects	Governments may ask or expect companies to take on a higher proportion of health costs. In addition, workers and communities may be affected by health and development problems which formerly were in the domain of the government, and may now be within that of companies.

Table based on: Bloom, D., Reddy Bloom, L., Steven, D., & Weston, M. (2006). *Business and HIV/AIDS: A healthier partnership?* Geneva: World Economic Forum.
Rosen, S., Vincent, J. R., Macleod, W., Fox, M., Thea, D. M., & Simon, J. (2004). The cost of HIV/AIDS to businesses in Southern Africa, AIDS 18:317–24.

222 *AIDS and Business*

DIRECT IMPACTS OF HIV/AIDS ON BUSINESS ORGANIZATIONS

Businesses big and small are affected by the spread of HIV/AIDS in a number of ways. Companies of all sizes and in all sectors employ people who have, or who may contract, HIV/AIDS. Only one country exists where AIDS is mature enough as an epidemic to have run its course, according to Whiteside (2001). In every country outside South Africa, the trajectory and impacts of the epidemic are generally modeled under conditions of uncertainty. At a company level, the impacts of the disease depend on the skill levels of workers who fall ill, with urban skilled workers contributing the most impacts. On a macroeconomic level, as skilled workers become scarcer, their salaries rise (Whiteside, 2001[8]), negatively impacting employers.

Businesses are generally concerned about human resources impacts such as mortality in service, management of employees living with HIV/AIDS, health-based discrimination, work force morale, increased recruitment and training costs, and lower productivity in the case of employees with symptomatic AIDS (Rosen, Vincent, Macleod, Fox, Thea, and Simon, 2004[9]). Absenteeism and productivity are key human resources issues: employees with HIV/AIDS may be increasingly unproductive or absent from work due to chronic health conditions. Companies in Botswana and Kenya experienced a rise in labor costs directly attributable to HIV/AIDS of more than 50 percent.[10] HIV-negative employees who care for an HIV-positive family member may take time off work for that reason (Whiteside, 2001). The International Labor Organization (ILO) estimates that the number of workers affected per HIV/AIDS case at work is approximately one to one, meaning that a workplace which employs several members of the same family may be doubly affected.[11] In both cases, employers may be concerned about the long time periods involved.

A Ugandan employee with AIDS may be incapacitated by illness for an average of nine months before dying, according to a study done in Uganda.[12] On average, people lived just under ten years after contracting HIV. Those over the age of forty at seroconversion tended to live for a shorter period. Mortality in service is a consequence of HIV/AIDS. By 2010, the ILO estimates that forty-eight million workers will be lost to HIV/AIDS. The number of employees dying from AIDS may be shockingly high, as in one Malawian case where AIDS deaths increased from 4 per 1,000 workers to 23 per 1,000 workers over five years.[13] These employees need to be replaced, and their passing may impact the emotional health and/or morale for those who are left on the job. Those who die will likely be replaced by a new employee who is younger, less experienced, and who will require training. Another issue is the increase in pension benefits and sick leave payments as a result of higher payouts for HIV/AIDS-related reasons (Rosen, Simon, Thea, and Vincent, 2000[14]). The effect of the epidemic on consumers depends on demographic factors, but generally the most affected market is consumers aged twenty-five to forty-nine years because those are the most affected by HIV/AIDS (Whiteside, 2001). Last but not least, the loss of knowledge, experience, and competencies is a consequence of HIV/AIDS. Organizations are concerned that critical knowledge, experience, and competencies are lost as employees, suppliers, and distributors sicken and die. HIV/AIDS typically affects adults who have already accumulated work-related knowledge and experience, and may never be able to put these into play. The impacts of these various factors on businesses are summarized in Figure 10.1.

THE INDIRECT, MACROECONOMIC IMPACTS OF HIV/AIDS ON BUSINESS ORGANIZATIONS

Economic growth for the country overall may suffer. According to the International Organisation of Employers (2004),[15] government investment in economic development will be slowed in high-prevalence countries, as pensions, health, and social security systems strain under expenditures on sickness and death benefits, and survivors' pensions. Private parallel systems of insurance, often supported by corporate plans, will likely raise their rates in response to the strains they feel as a result of increased payouts for HIV/AIDS-related reasons.

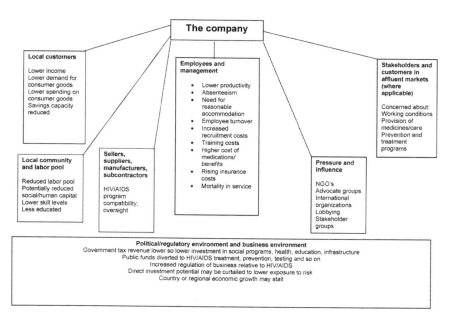

Figure 10.1 HIV/AIDS prevalence rise effects on businesses in low-middle income countries.

224 *AIDS and Business*

As succinctly stated by the ILO director general Juan Somavia, " . . . HIV/AIDS is a threat to sustainable global, social, and economic development. The loss of life and the debilitating effects of the illness will lead not only to a reduced capacity to sustain production and employment, reduce poverty and promote development, but will be a burden borne by all societies—rich and poor alike"[16] (International Labor Organization, 2004, p. V). Companies and organizations are affected by macroeconomic trends related to the spread of HIV-AIDS, such as the following:

- Economies as a whole suffer as their most productive citizens sicken and die.
- The labor supply is reduced by people with AIDS and those who withdraw from the workforce to care for them.
- The savings capacity of households is reduced.
- Lower human capital reduces the human resources potential for businesses and the public sector.
- Poverty and famine risk increase when adults die and households lose the ability to grow their own food.
- Banks become exposed as people with HIV/AIDS—unable to afford payments—default on loans, and die.
- Long term, there are fewer incentives for foreign investment in the economy.
- There is a dramatic rise in society's health-related costs caused by increased demand for health services and concurrent shortages.
- Gross domestic product (GDP) may be reduced by 0.5 to 4 percent, according to research on African countries with high prevalence rates.[17]
- A government's tax revenue is reduced as individual/household income is reduced by those with AIDS, and government services may correspondingly suffer.

Finally, it is necessary to underline the importance of stability at a societal level, and the business impact of its lack. Companies have a stake in civil society, stability, and generalized confidence in political and economic institutions. The cohesive strength of societies, cultures, and values may be eroded by young people who, because of HIV/AIDS, are impoverished, lack education and socialization, and have little faith in the future.

ROLES THAT BUSINESSES MAY PLAY IN THE HIV/AIDS FIGHT

"One of the most important trends in international development over the past two decades has been a growing awareness of the crucial role that a productive, competitive, well-diversified and responsible private sector plays, not only in underpinning economic growth and wealth creation, but also supporting other key pillars of development" (The World Economic Forum, 2005, p. 10). More than any other sector of society, businesses are uniquely positioned to take on an active role in the progression of the HIV/AIDS epidemic. Businesses play a key role in international development and, as such, may take leadership in the provision of HIV/AIDS education, awareness programs, condom distribution, and the development of an infrastructure necessary for the provision of treatments. Other sectors have been involved in the effort to hold back the tide of HIV/AIDS: governments and local authorities, faith-based organizations and traditional healers, educational systems, health systems, and local or international nongovernmental organizations.

Businesses may play a key role in increasing HIV/AIDS prevention, prolonging life for those who are infected, and helping survivors and communities to rebuild. Companies tend to play multiple roles in the economic system, and can act through these roles to spread awareness programs, prevention information, and medications widely throughout society. The various roles of business may include responsible sellers, suppliers ,and producers. Companies that sell products and services to the general public may efficiently provide HIV/AIDS information, policy suggestions, and social marketing to diverse populations in large numbers. Companies that sell to others may be an efficient channel by which to reach many client businesses with HIV/AIDS information, policy suggestions, and social marketing.

Companies may play an important role in the fight against HIV/AIDS as employers. Employment relationships have evolved over the years to include, in addition to salary and benefits, social and psychological aspects such as "trust, commitment, influence and communication" (IOE, 2004, p. 1).[18] This implies that, in order to motivate and retain workers, companies need to inspire people beyond the limits of the employment contract. Companies can influence the attitudes and perceptions of their workers in a very direct manner, and provide them with health information. Company HIV/AIDS policies, training sessions, in-house testing and counseling, condom distribution, medical services, and treatment access may directly reach all company employees and their families.

Companies may also act as lobbyists and advocates. Large businesses typically have an ongoing relationship with government officials in some capacity—they may inform or influence government decision-making and policy-forming processes. In a recent survey, it was reported that 64 percent of pharmaceutical companies worked to influence governments in developing countries to address public health problems by encouraging them to spend more on health infrastructure and education.[19] As powerful entities, companies individually and business as a collective have power in society due to their critical mass, their voice, and their spending power. In some countries, business leaders have immense personal power as individuals and can have the ear of those in power.[20]

Companies that work as distributors frequently develop effective communications and transport infrastructure in order to attain their own objectives. They may effectively work to distribute HIV/AIDS information, messages, and products (such as condoms) over a wide area—and often reaching otherwise isolated locations. Coca-Cola and Heineken are two

226   AIDS and Business

examples of companies capitalizing on their distributors and bottlers to assist in distributing HIV/AIDS care and related products.

Because they are highly skilled in influencing various publics, through advertising, sponsoring, and public relations, companies have communication expertise. Big companies and organizations may already "have the ear" of local, regional, or national audiences. Companies tend to be experienced in crafting and sending messages, and have valuable relationships with key mass media contacts. They may also have a nonnegligible bargaining power with the media for advertising placements, publicity, press releases, and so on. The work of television networks, such as Viacom, in this area has received acclaim. Large businesses typically have a developed communications and distribution infrastructure and a network of relationships that are ripe for scaling up a local, regional, or national HIV/AIDS intervention. They may have an interest in doing so but not the knowledge or experience for which a specialized nongovernmental organization could provide overnight. As agglomerations of expertise, multinational companies may benefit from the specialized knowledge and experience of subsidiaries in other countries with longer experience in HIV/AIDS policies, communications, and social marketing. As resource-rich entities, big companies may draw on their in-house experts in human behavior, health care, communications, and law in order to apply themselves to aspects of the HIV/AIDS epidemic.

REASONS FOR STARTING COMPANY HIV/AIDS PROGRAMS

One of the most basic reasons is the defense and promotion of corporate values at a broad level. Nestlé Brazil launched its HIV/AIDS program in 1986 because to do so was congruent with the company's values, and it was felt that the threat to the company and to society was so great.[21] Levi Strauss & Co., according to Stuart Burden, director of community affairs–the Americas, became involved with HIV/AIDS prevention programs because doing so was seen as "consistent with the company's values, which are empathy, originality, integrity, and courage" (Kotler and Lee, 2005, p. 200).[22] The company and its foundation reported a contribution of more than US$26 million since 1980, when it became one of the first companies to become active against HIV/AIDS.[23]

Employee morale and more generally human resource management concerns are another reason for starting HIV/AIDS corporate programs. The JW Marriott Hotel Bangkok considered that its employees were particularly at risk due to their demographic profiles and the fact that "many" employees travel regularly to their homes outside Bangkok. There also was the belief that HIV/AIDS and health programs will "increase employee morale, reduce employee turnover, and reduce employee sick leave."[24] Ford Motor Company's director of occupational health and safety Dr. Greg Stone told a conference about the beginnings of Ford's HIV/AIDS program in South Africa: "HIV/AIDS was spreading with unbelievable speed . . . We had invested enormous resources in developing our South African workforce.

Designing a Company HIV/AIDS Program   227

We could not afford to see these resources, our employees, our most valuable asset—literally perish." He continued, explaining why Ford Motor Company is expanding its HIV/AIDS program, "We face the same potential today in China, Thailand, India and Russia—all regions where Ford has a strong interest in expanding its business operations and marketing its vehicles."[25] Ford Motor Company selected China, India, Thailand, and Russia, among others, for its expanded "Workplace and Community Initiative" HIV/AIDS program based on the country's HIV/AIDS prevalence rate, rate of spread, Ford's business presence, and market opportunity.[26]

A more down-to-earth motive and a quite compelling reason for undertaking action is the lack of significant governmental AIDS policy in many countries. In response to questioning about why BIC South Africa started offering antiretroviral treatments to workers, BIC chief Errol Sackstein answered: "We're stepping in because the government isn't."[27] Siemens Limited in southern Africa estimated that workplace HIV/AIDS prevalence would increase to 13 percent by 2009 if no action was taken.[28]

Box 10.1   A View from the Field:

PRODUCT (RED): A New Branding Approach to HIV/AIDS Fundraising

In 2006, singer Bono and DATA (Debt, AIDS, Trade, Africa) chairman Bobby Shriver launched a novel branded approach to collaborative marketing for a cause: (RED). The initiative was announced at the World Economic Forum held in Davos, Switzerland. Participating companies designed a red-branded product range, launched it using considerable publicity, and committed themselves to donating a percentage of sales to the Global Fund to Fight AIDS, Tuberculosis, and Malaria. The following companies formed (RED):

- American Express[29] with a red credit card, and "REDdeals" with a number of lodging, retail, and restaurant partners.
- Apple Computer[30] with a red iPod nano special edition.
- Converse[31] with limited edition shoes and custom designs.
- GAP[32] with T-shirts made from African cotton, jeans, and other items.
- Giorgio Armani[33] with sunglasses, watches, clothing.
- Motorola[34] with a series of phones with red features and exclusive ringtones and services.

A number of other companies joined the effort later such as Starbucks, iTunes, MTV, and others. (RED) cofounder Bono explained that the color choice was guided by the red often associated with emergencies.

For more information go to:

(RED) site: http://www.joinred.com/.

DATA (Debt, AIDS, Trade, Africa) site: http://www.data.org.

The Global Fund to Fight AIDS, Tuberculosis, and Malaria http://www.theglobalfund.org.

228 *AIDS and Business*

SPECIFIC ISSUES FOR SMALL AND MEDIUM SIZED ENTERPRISES

Small and medium-sized enterprises (SMEs) have been referred to as important growth engines for economies. In South Africa, for instance, more than 55 percent of total jobs are created in SMEs, businesses which account for 22 percent of the national GDP.[35] Small and medium-sized enterprises provide employment in cities and in rural areas; they develop entrepreneurial skills, and may contribute to innovation and competitiveness.[36] OECD statistics show that significant portions of the workforce are employed in SMEs. In the United States, 56.8 percent of all companies are comprised of up to nine employees. In Turkey, that figure is 95 percent (OECD, 2002 in IOE, 2005). These figures are probably conservative because the informal economy was not considered in their calculation, which may be a considerable portion such as 29 percent of GDP in Greece, according to the ILO (2005). Another sector not included was agriculture, which includes employees working mainly in micro enterprises. Small companies tend to pay lower wages and offer fewer benefits than big companies, and typically are run by people with little time to spend on legal and community issues.

SME managers tend to be very unaware of potential impacts of rising HIV/AIDS rates (SABCoHA/BER, 2005).[37] In another study, SME managers expressed little interest in examining potential impacts and formulating a company response, while less than 50 percent of SME managers had ever raised the topic of HIV/AIDS with top managers (Rosen et al., 2006).[38] A study of 209 small enterprises in South Africa conducted by the University of Port Elizabeth found that HIV was one of the top three causes for business failure; the other two top causes were crime and insufficient management expertise (International Finance Corporation, 2005).[39] Despite their constraints, small businesses can be contributors in HIV/AIDS programs: In Ghana, hairdressers and car-repair garages were used in a pilot program to distribute HIV/AIDS information and educational materials. Because of the nature of customer contact and the reach of these companies, they were considered to be effective conduits of information.[40]

It is vital that governments and other players in the economy assist small and medium enterprises in considering the issue of HIV/AIDS in a balanced manner—both for their own benefit and for that of the wider economy. In some areas, big companies have begun to share their HIV/AIDS expertise with SMEs. In South Africa, a new initiative by the Global Health Initiative, World Economic Forum brings big companies like Accenture, Eskom, Unilever and Volkswagen together with their suppliers—often SMEs—to share their HIV/AIDS-related experiences as well as concrete guidelines for HIV/AIDS programs. In effect, this expands their own programs and bolsters their own self interest, as expressed by Eskom health and wellness manager Dr. Penny Mkalipe: "As a multinational company we see this supply chain program as a real win-win situation for us. Without our suppliers we simply wouldn't be able to function."[41]

COST-BENEFIT ANALYSES OF HIV/AIDS PROGRAMS

Many companies provide, or are considering provision of, effective HIV/ AIDS prevention education to its employees, their families, and the wider community. Often this includes basic information such as correct condom use, a behavior change component, and an awareness component designed to reduce stigma and encourage people to be tested. Companies also provide HIV/AIDS-related medical services and products at variable levels of quality and coverage. Costs are most commonly related to medical services provided by companies which include voluntary counseling and testing, and the provision of condoms, medications, and health services. TATA Tea Ltd. of India—one of India's biggest companies—provides, at great cost and great risk, medical care to all of its employees,[42] including the treatment of opportunistic infections.[43]Concerning HIV/AIDS program costs, PT Ricky Putra Globalindo (RPG), Indonesian undergarments manufacturer, conducted a cost-benefit analysis regarding HIV/ AIDS medical costs and the cost of a company-wide prevention program. Their finding was that medical costs excluding antiretroviral treatments per person would be US$2,950, while prevention for the entire workforce would cost US$2,500 if combined with existing efforts.[44] The budgeted cost per employee of Nestlé Brazil's HIV/AIDS program was US$2 per year, of which 48 percent was allocated for prevention and 52 percent was allocated for treatment.[45]

According to South African consultant Alexander Forbes Ltd., companies which conduct a cost-benefit analysis long term find that a "direct AIDS intervention" (DAI) is more cost-effective than the business-as-usual model of HIV/AIDS programs. Using a DAI, companies encourage employees to have an HIV test and, based on the result obtained, provide immediate antiretroviral treatment through their managed care plan, which results in employees being more productive and able to pay into their health insurance plan, for a longer time—a saving of US$16,750 in the case of an employee earning US$1,012 per month, assuming that an employee is kept on the job for an additional seven years and absenteeism is reduced.[46]

South African mining company AngloGold, a subsidiary of AngloAmerican, found that almost one-quarter of its 90,000 employees had HIV. Absenteeism, early pension payouts, and staff replacements have driven up costs at the company—reaching US$6 per ounce of gold.[47] Boston University School of Public Health researchers (Rosen et al., 2003) undertook a study of the impact of HIV/AIDS on six firms in South Africa and Botswana, across six different industries. They found that AIDS was costing the companies almost 6 percent of their labor costs, a figure which could almost be halved by a workplace AIDS program. Although the companies faced different prevalence levels and varying cost structures, perhaps most significant was the finding that all companies would have seen a positive return on their investment had they provided antiretrovirals free of charge to their employees.[48]

230 AIDS and Business

Some companies also cover the treatment costs of workers' families. Siemens Limited in southern Africa has designed a workplace program that incorporates awareness (using peer educators), participation in a mandatory health coverage plan that provides antiretroviral therapy for workers and their families, and encouragement for employees to seek voluntary counseling and testing through external doctors. The program costs US$13 per employee per year, and is reviewed on a yearly basis. Siemens plans to conduct knowledge, attitudes and practice surveys to measure the effectiveness of its programs, as well as researching the prevalence of HIV/AIDS among employees.[49] Benefits are there for dedicated companies: after three years in action of a comprehensive HIV/AIDS workplace program at DaimlerChrysler South Africa, results were clear, according to a GTZ[50] report (2004).[51] HIV/AIDS-related death rates among employees were reduced, tuberculosis cases were treated successfully, and as a result of a peer education program, 75 percent of employees agreed to be tested under the company's voluntary counseling and testing program.

FIRST STEPS IN DESIGNING A PROGRAM: TAKE STOCK OF THE SITUATION

It is important to assess who are at-risk employees. Indonesian manufacturer PT Ricky Putra Globalindo (RPG) determined that its factory workforce was likely at risk for contracting HIV/AIDS because their age groups corresponded with typical age groups at risk for HIV/AIDS in Indonesia. In addition, a large number of workers were young women living independently for the first time and originating from rural areas—presenting socioeconomic, gender, and situational (migration) risks for HIV/AIDS.[52] The first action a company needs to take is to find out HIV/AIDS prevalence among workers and communities in which they operate, and identify current and potential impacts of this prevalence on workers and customers.[53] Only by taking careful measurements of the current situation can a company have a baseline upon which to determine specific goals and measure success periodically.

Risk assessment instruments most commonly used by companies are the knowledge, attitude, perceptions study (KAP)—or KAP/B when it includes behavior—as well as workplace prevalence studies or prevalence estimates based on national or regional HIV prevalence data. This provides a baseline for forecasting. Conducting a KAP/B study can provide managers with insight into HIV risk levels of the workforce. A study conducted by DaimlerChrysler South Africa, for example, found that many employees believed that traditional healers and other nonmedical acts could cure people of HIV. The results also showed that employees knew they should use condoms, but often did not do so (Seitz, Staber, and Jonczyk, 2002).[54] Such information is crucial in determining specifically what a company needs to do to address the spread of HIV among its workers—such as conducting HIV/AIDS education and awareness campaigns, and condom distribution.

Designing a Company HIV/AIDS Program   231

An HIV prevalence audit may be a preferred method, when the social and regulatory environment allows it. In this case, employees may provide informed consent to take an anonymous and confidential HIV test. Post-test counseling may be provided at the work site. The test results give managers a true picture of HIV risk within the company and statistics on HIV prevalence, which is the basis most companies use. This data can be used to conduct a cost-benefit analysis for a variety of workplace interventions. However, Rosen, Simon, Thea, and Vincent (2000)[55] caution against taking prevalence as the basis for decision making due to the long latency period, which is calculated as the time that elapses from the moment HIV was contracted to the onset of symptomatic AIDS—five years in their estimation. They advocate instead that companies take an incidence (case-based) approach to HIV/AIDS measurement. By doing so, companies view HIV/AIDS incidence more realistically as future costs to the company that may be avoided. These costs can be avoided if employees are provided with antiretroviral treatment and benefit from several additional years of productive life, or new infections are prevented due to better education and condom distribution. Some companies, such as Nestlé Brazil, have relied on condom use surveys to assess employees' likely risk of contracting HIV as an indicator,[56] rather than a formal HIV testing program.

One company is considered by UNAIDS to be "a global benchmark" in terms of institutional audits—a big Botswana-based mining company, Debswana. The audit was reported to include six steps: personnel profiling with reference to the susceptibility of particular groups to contracting HIV; critical postanalysis comprising an assessment of the importance of certain employees to the organization; size of organization and flexibility of employees; liabilities determined according to the amount of employee benefits and the amount of value added by labor; productivity and absenteeism effects on output; legal and industrial relations context of the organization (Barnett, Fantan, Mbakile, and Whiteside, 2002).[57]

In a World Bank study on risk management in South Africa, Kalavakonda (2005)[58] described how to model a company risk assessment for HIV/AIDS. First, reliable demographic projection of HIV/AIDS are needed, with specifics as to location (in South Africa this was done per province), industry, class, gender, and race. In South Africa, the Actuarial Society of South Africa provided the data. Such specific data are often not available outside South Africa and other affluent countries. The average median term from HIV seroconversion to symptomatic AIDS is the next data set needed in this model. Again, such data are often not available but in South Africa the Actuarial Solutions Multistate AIDS Projection Model provides this, ranging from eight to ten years depending on the age at seroconversion, which ranged from thirty-nine and above to below thirty, respectively. Finally, allowing for normal death, turnover with new employee replacements, non-HIV/AIDS-related health withdrawals, and retirement, the model can be run for each employee of a company

232   *AIDS and Business*

to estimate a company's HIV/AIDS incidence over ten years. Interestingly, the model assumes that new employee prospects are given a health examination and those who do have HIV/AIDS will be "less likely" to be employed by the company—an action that would contravene the Employment Equity Act of 1998. Yet, the model remains one of the few in the public domain and the only such that pertains to companies.

WHO SHOULD BE COVERED?

One difficulty in planning a company's HIV/AIDS policy is the choice, always implied, regarding who is to receive HIV/AIDS medical coverage or access to messages. There is anecdotal evidence of employees receiving antiretroviral treatments at work, then bringing them home and sharing them with the family—the chief executive officer of BIC in South Africa, Errol Sackstein, stated his observation that there are people who do not want to live if their spouse and children will die: "Some workers are getting the drugs and giving half of them to their spouse and children," thereby benefiting no one.[59] In such a case when an incorrect dose of antiretrovirals is taken, the risk of developing resistance to the drugs increases.[60] DaimlerChrysler in South Africa announced in 2003 that it would extend coverage to redundant employees as well as dependants. At Amalgamated Beverages Industries, the bottler for Coca-Cola in South Africa, the company HIV/AIDS policy covers antiretrovirals for each employee plus three dependents. The company refused to disclose the rate of HIV prevalence among its 4,500 workers, in order to "protect our employees and our company from the stigma," according to Lindi Brink, strategic affairs officer.[61] At Barclay's Bank, operating in several African countries, employees are offered free testing with the commitment of a "normal" working life in case of an HIV diagnosis, and antiretroviral treatment is extended to three family members if needed.[62]

Many companies provide coverage for full-time employees only. Woolworths South Africa is one of the few that has extended coverage to its part-time workers as well.[63] Should companies provide coverage only to their immediate employees, or should human resources along the supply chain be covered as well? Coca-Cola in Africa experienced the wrath of activists, public attacks in the media, demonstrations, and boycotts in 2002 for failing to extend HIV/AIDS coverage to its bottlers, who employed an estimated 60,000 people across Africa.[64]

WHAT SHOULD BE COVERED?

There are many possible components to a company HIV/AIDS program, such as the following:

Prevention
Workplace practices
Healthcare provision
Voluntary testing and counseling
Awareness programs
Provision of antiretroviral therapy
Treatment of sexually transmitted infections
Treatment of opportunistic infections

In South Africa, a country with exceptionally high prevalence and—unlike some of its poorer neighbors also suffering from high HIV/AIDS prevalence—a large number of companies operate at an international level, big and small. In South Africa, where one-fifth of the population is living with HIV, one-third of 130 South African companies had an HIV/AIDS budget, and less than half with a fully documented HIV/AIDS policy, according to a survey conducted by Markinor, a South African market research company. Employees often hide their status for fear of being refused normal health coverage by insurers. Approximately one-third of South African workers receive health coverage from their employer. Because their only health coverage comes to most people through their jobs, they will have no health insurance or health care benefits if they lose their job.[65] According to another survey conducted in South Africa, 90 percent of large companies (over 500 employees) and 13 percent of small companies (under 100 employees) had HIV/AIDS programs. This illustrates the immense difficulty for smaller companies to provide HIV/AIDS programs. In another study, Fraser et al. (2003) found that small businesses would only consider allocating resources for HIV/AIDS if they saw a direct effect of the pandemic on their business.[66]

GOALS AND PRINCIPLES FOR HIV/AIDS PROGRAMS

There is a wide range of possible aims and desired outcomes for a company HIV/AIDS program, as will be illustrated in the coming section. According to the German technical cooperation agency GTZ,[67] workplace policies have three primary goals:

1. To prevent the spread of HIV/AIDS by providing education and awareness programs, condom distribution, and voluntary testing and counseling.
2. To provide care and treatment for people with HIV/AIDS, namely, antiretrovirals and treatment of opportunistic infections.
3. To ensure that insurance provisions are made for the families of people with HIV/AIDS in case of death or disability.

The ILO in their Code of Practice[68] calls for ten principles in order to reduce disease transmission, assist people with HIV and those affected by it:

234　*AIDS and Business*

1. Recognition of HIV/AIDS as a workplace issue. Employers should acknowledge that HIV/AIDS is a workplace issue and that it should be managed in the same manner as any other serious illness or health condition. As a member of the community, the workplace has a role to play.
2. Nondiscrimination. There should be no discrimination against employees based on HIV status.
3. Gender equality. Gender equality and the empowerment of women are essential due to the biological, sociocultural, and economic factors that place women at a higher risk of being affected by HIV.
4. Healthy work environment. A healthy and safe work environment is necessary, in accordance with the Occupational Safety and Health Convention, 1981 (No. 155), to reduce HIV transmission risk and adapt to those who have HIV.
5. Social dialogue—Employers, workers, governments, and labor representatives should commit to trust and cooperation on the topic.
6. Screening for the purposes of exclusion from employment or work processes. Job applicants and employees should not be subject to mandatory HIV screening.
7. Confidentiality. Job applicants and employees should not be asked about their HIV status, and health records should be bound by rules of confidentiality.
8. Continuation of employment relationship. Continuation of health-appropriate work should be offered to people with HIV as long as they are medically fit.
9. Prevention. It is known that prevention is possible through changes in behavior and knowledge, provision of treatment, and fostering a nondiscriminatory environment. As a social partner, business is in a unique position to promote these.
10. Care and support. Workers with HIV and their dependants should not be discriminated against with regard to health services and benefits from public funds or workplace programs.[69]

The perspective of the ILO report is that businesses and employers' organizations have responsibilities in the epidemic, along with two other partners: (1) the government and competent authorities, and (2) workers and their organizations. According to the ILO, and in light of their Code of Practice, the primary specific responsibilities of employers are:

1. A workplace policy, developed with workers and their representatives.
2. National, sectoral, and workplace/enterprise agreements should be adhered to by employers, and elements of these should be integrated with the workplace policy.
3. Education and training should be delivered at the workplace regarding the employer's HIV/AIDS policy (including staff benefits and entitlements), and HIV/AIDS prevention, care, support, and nondiscrimination.

Designing a Company HIV/AIDS Program 235

4. Economic impact of HIV/AIDS on the sector and workplace should be monitored and a response formulated where possible.
5. Personnel policies should be nondiscriminatory and include provisions encouraging workers with HIV to continue working as long as medically fit, and allow for cessation of employment in accordance with antidiscrimination and labor laws with full benefits.
6. Grievance and disciplinary procedures.

According to a report authored by UNAIDS, the Prince of Wales Business Leaders' Forum, and the Global Business Council on HIV&AIDS, the business response to HIV/AIDS: impacts and lessons learned[70][71] corporate HIV/AIDS programs should include the following components:

1. Set of HIV/AIDS policies that are equitably applied, and are effectively communicated to everyone.
2. Condoms are available or are distributed.
3. Education and awareness programs provided for all.
4. Identification and treatment of STDs for employees and their partners.
5. Voluntary counseling and testing for all.[72]

WHAT SHOULD A COMPANY'S HIV/AIDS POLICY LOOK LIKE?

There are common criticisms of the early business response to AIDS that call for policies that avoid increasing stigma and fostering the spread of HIV/AIDS. As soon as they realize that HIV/AIDS increases company costs, companies have a range of responses to the increasing threat posed by HIV/AIDS. Some of these responses have had negative impacts on the epidemic, such as laying off workers found to be HIV positive, which in its least nasty form includes paying off employees who agree to "retire" early,[73] conducting HIV testing on potential new hires and turning away those who are HIV positive, reducing health and pension benefits, and outsourcing low-skilled jobs to avoid HIV/AIDS-related costs. Business has also been accused of fostering the spread of HIV through its use of migrant labor—known to be vulnerable for contracting HIV.[74] Other specific criticisms include the restriction of HIV/AIDS health coverage to a specific range of employees, or restricted provision of antiretrovirals. Other companies have been berated for not providing "reasonable accommodation" as would be expected for employees facing a catastrophic illness.

A Boston University School of Public Health study emphasized that treatment and prevention must work together: employees' risk of contracting HIV was lowered when treatment was provided for other sexually transmitted diseases in conjunction with education and counseling. According to Rosen et al. (2003), effective HIV/AIDS prevention programs at the workplace should include the following elements:

236   AIDS and Business

1. Education of employees and the community about HIV prevention.
2. Distribution of condoms at the workplace.
3. Treatment of other sexually transmitted diseases.
4. Offering free voluntary counseling and testing for employees and their families.[75]

There are a number of actions which have been successful in a variety of business sizes and situations. Many of these are well documented, and repeated in the advice of a number of international organizations such as the International Labor Organization, International Organization of Employers, and UNAIDS. It is worth summarizing and repeating them here in the context of effective company action against HIV/AIDS. One of the first steps for business leaders to take is to overcome an impression of helplessness: some may feel hopeless or powerless in the face of increasing HIV/AIDS caseload. This is often because they are unaware of the steps to take in conducting a situation analysis, and the steps for implementation that other companies have successfully taken.[76] The following paragraphs discuss some of these steps.

Fight Stigma

Companies need to address stigma at policy and management level. In effect, stigma is the enemy of workplace HIV/AIDS programs, just as it is for community programs. By implementing policies of nondiscrimination in hiring, promotion, and remuneration, companies take the first step towards reducing it. Of vital concern is maintaining employee confidentiality for testing and disclosure. Awareness programs for managers and employees are helpful in reducing stigma at the workplace.[77] Prevention, testing, and treatment programs will fail in a climate of HIV/AIDS stigma, as will any effort to establish the true number of people affected by HIV/AIDS—they will not disclose if they are HIV positive.

Unilever is concerned at global level by combating stigma. The corporation combines a tailored, locally adapted approach with a company-wide policy on HIV/AIDS.[78] Unilever has a nondiscriminatory policy for employees with HIV, and acts as the major health care supplier for its employees and their families in Africa. Brazilian Unilever subsidiary Gessy Lever won the Business Leaders Forum Award in 2002 for encouraging employees to support prevention programs in their communities, and AXE deodorant was used to promote safer sex and condom use among young males.[79] In Kenya, Unilever initiated "Neighbors against AIDS," an unofficial coalition of five companies that meet regularly to discuss HIV/AIDS-related issues.[80] In Nigeria, Unilever works with the British Department for International Development and the Liverpool Associates in Tropical Health to run an HIV and sexually transmitted disease management program.[81] The company states that transparency is an essential feature of its HIV/AIDS

Designing a Company HIV/AIDS Program 237

Box 10.2   A View from the Field:

The GBC's Dr. Neeraj Mistry on Corporate HIV/AIDS Programs

In November 2005 the Global Business Coalition on HIV/AIDS, Tuberculosis and Malaria (GBC) announced they had developed a business and AIDS measurement system termed Best Practice AIDS Standard (BPAS), the first of its kind. BPAS was based on GBC's Business AIDS Methodology, composed of four principles describing where companies can take action on HIV/AIDS. These principles are: core competency, workplace, community involvement, and advocacy and leadership. The system was developed in order to assist member companies to design their own workplace and supply chain management HIV/AIDS programs. According to Mistry, BPAS enables companies to "look at HIV in a comprehensive way, helping them to prioritize." BPAS is a "baseline" and can be used as a "monitoring tool, whereby at a given company each of the ten points is allocated a score from one to ten in a yearly assessment process." Assessments are done by the companies themselves, and as yet have not been made public by any member companies.

The ten points of BPAS comprise "all the possible ways companies can be involved," as follows:

1. Nondiscrimination.
2. Prevention, education, and behavior change.
3. Testing and counseling.
4. Care, support, and treatment.
5. Product and service donations.
6. Corporate philanthropy.
7. Community and government partnerships.
8. Business associates and supply chain engagement.
9. Advocacy and leadership.
10. Monitoring, evaluation, and reporting.

A GBC team assists member companies wishing to initiate the BPAS. The consulting process elaborated in the Business AIDS Methodology is essentially three steps, namely:

1. Situation analysis whereby the company's needs and goals are identified within the context of the business environment.
2. Elaboration of strategies.
3. Implementation of strategies, ongoing monitoring, and evaluation.

The AIDS Standard was developed using the best practices identified in case studies of member companies, and from its experience in helping companies develop their own AIDS programs. Trevor Nielson, then executive director of the GBC, stated his belief that using BPAS can give companies a

continued

238 *AIDS and Business*

> **Box 10.2 (continued)**
>
> competitive advantage over competitors that do not use it. BPAS will evolve as companies using it provide feedback to GBC. The BPAS is not aspirational: it is a workable set of practical points for companies.
>
> ### GBC Profile
>
> The Global Business Coalition on HIV/AIDS, Tuberculosis and Malaria grew from seventeen companies in 2001 to more than two hundred in 2006. In their own words, the mission of GBC is to "Harness the power of the global business community to end the HIV/AIDS, Tuberculosis and Malaria epidemics." GBC is headquartered in New York. GBC has piloted a number of initiatives, including high-profile awards ceremonies for company HIV/AIDS programs, and providing extensive publicity on the HIV/AIDS activities of its member companies through newsletters, an informative web site, and events.
>
> Source: Dr. Neeraj Mistry, technical director, Global Business Coalition on HIV/AIDS, Tuberculosis and Malaria (personal communication, 14 March, 2006) and the Global Business Coalition Web site http://www.businessfightsaids.org.

programs—relevant documents are available publicly and are written in a manner that is understandable for employees.[82]

Nestlé is also concerned with nondiscrimination of HIV-positive employees. Nestlé Nigeria stated in its HIV/AIDS workplace attitude document that the company "would make reasonable adjustment in the workplace or process for employees with HIV/AIDS if necessary to keep them in employment for as long as the person is medically fit for appropriate work" (p. 2).[83] In addition, the company commits to treating HIV-positive employees with "empathy and care" (p. 3), providing "all reasonable assistance which may include counseling, time off, sick leave, and information regarding the virus and its effects" (p. 3). Some require a preemployment or even a prebenefit HIV test (upon which positive result the employee is not hired or not provided with benefits if hired). In others, such as Unilever South Africa, pretesting practices have been declared unethical.[84] Due to the company's confidentiality policy, Nestlé Brazil has treatment expenses paid to employees through Nestlé's bank account managed by the Brazilian Department of Human Relations at Work.[85]

BUSINESSES SHOULD FIND PARTNERS

Although some companies have developed admirable programs, the effect of those, if shared, would be much greater on society and therefore even more effective long term. When companies work with an organization specialized in HIV/AIDS, such as the Business Coalition on HIV/AIDS, or the

Southern African Business Coalition on HIV/AIDS, the opportunities to have an impact are greater because these coalitions have broad experience in observing what is effective and what is not. For instance, Sony South Africa was a founding member of the South African Business Coalition on HIV/AIDS (SABCoHA), a leading business advocacy organization.[86] Businesses may partner with a nongovernmental organization, a health care provider, or even the government to benefit from economies of scale and shared experiences. A large number of multinational corporations have joined their efforts in fighting against AIDS in business coalitions.

One prominent international example is the Global Business Coalition (GBC) on HIV/AIDS, Tuberculosis and Malaria (www.businessfightsaids. org/). Their statement explaining "HIV/AIDS, TB and malaria are business issues" reads as follows:

> Business is doing a fraction of what it can do to address HIV/AIDS, TB and malaria. And yet it makes strong business sense for companies to respond to the epidemic. Increased costs, loss of productivity and overall threats to the foundations of the economies in which they operate threaten the bottom line. The workforce is placed at increasing risk, with the epidemic disproportionately affecting people during their most productive years. The GBC's strategy to increase business action in the workplace involves both advocacy with business leaders to convince them to act, and the identification of workplace "best practices" to help them implement proven initiatives. HIV/AIDS, TB and malaria are critical issues for every company in the world today. The disease has no boundaries. It penetrates borders and threatens the world's emerging economies (source: http://www.businessfightsaids.org/live/involved/respond.php).

Due to the multisectoral implications of an HIV/AIDS program, it is common to work with partners specialized in specific disciplines, or regions. In developing its HIV/AIDS policy, Siemens Limited southern Africa region worked with the following partners:

- HIV/AIDS Management Solutions, a consulting company subsidiary of the Wits Health Consortium of the University of the Witwatersrand for impact assessments and other program guidance.
- Personal Health Advisor Service, an independent health care organization.
- Aid for AIDS, a corporate disease management program provider for HIV/AIDS (not affiliated with the New York–based NGO Aid for AIDS).
- A health care provider which runs a free confidential twenty-four-hour helpline.
- Employee representatives.
- The labor union.
- External legal counsel.

240 *AIDS and Business*

The Transport Corporation of India has partnered with HIV/AIDS program Avahan to provide access to lorry drivers, who are key to stemming the tide of HIV/AIDS as it is spread geographically along major routes.[87] Business may also partner with government: as executive committee member of the National Corporate Council for HIV/AIDS Prevention, Nestlé Brazil supports the work of the Brazilian Ministry of Health, for example, by sponsoring and distributing prevention booklets.[88]

Companies can form partnerships to raise funds for HIV/AIDS research or treatment. One example is the Until There's a Cure Foundation, which partners with U.S. retail organizations to sell the bracelets that generate funds. Partners include Ben Bridge Jewelers, Kenneth Cole, The Body Shop, and Virgin Megastores, among others. A number of celebrities have joined the efforts of the foundation in public service announcements.[89]

Do not Reinvent the Wheel

In order to increase the effectiveness of HIV/AIDS programs, however, small, businesses should adapt an existing HIV/AIDS program model to their situation, rather than trying to develop their own. The experience of business coalitions has shown that companies can successfully adopt elements of programs that are known to work in other companies working in the same business environment.

An example from Kenya shows how a company can use partnerships as a way of learning from other organizations that may be more specialized and more experienced. Serena Hotels[90] in Kenya offers an extensive HIV/AIDS workplace program, designed with help from the Federation of Kenya Employers. There are two Serena Hotels in Kenya, and six safari lodges. The same is true of Tanzania. There are Serena Hotels in Mozambique, Uganda, Zanzibar, Afghanistan, and six in Pakistan. The company is run by Tourism Promotion Services,[91] a division of the Aga Khan Development Network.[92] In Kenya, where the company employs 1,200 people, there is an HIV/AIDS clinic run by a nurse at almost every property, who works also as the HIV/AIDS coordinator. Nurses work with community organizations and leaders to spread the word about HIV/AIDS prevention and education, and provide medical services free of charge to community members. Condoms are distributed at each work site to employees and the community, through a partnership with Family Health International, a nongovernmental organization. Serena Hotels has trained 120 employees as peer educators, and encourages them to attend HIV/AIDS conferences, all expenses paid. The hotel group works with Pharm Access Africa Ltd.[93] and Phillips Pharmaceuticals[94] to procure the medicines at cost price. Pharm Access Africa Ltd. works to negotiate the lowest prices with pharmaceutical companies.

Develop Awareness Programs

Hotel Novotel Bangna in Bangkok, Thailand, shows a public service announcement on its internal television system to raise awareness about child sex tourism and its legal consequences in both Thailand and one's country of origin. The announcement was developed by ECPAT International, a children's advocacy group, and used in the past on Air France long-haul flights. Other ACCOR properties in Thailand are planned to receive the announcement.[95] ACCOR hotels in Thailand, Cambodia, Laos, Indonesia, and a number of other places have instituted awareness training programs for five thousand employees likely at some point to be confronted with a child sex tourism issue.[96] Carlson Wagon-Lits, a division of ACCOR, distributed dissuasive child sex tourism information and warnings in its travel agent brochures in France, totaling half a million in 2003.[97]

At Sony Device Technology in Thailand, all new employees are exposed to a five- to ten-minute discussion of the company's policy and specifics of prevention. Drug-use-related risks are communicated along with sexual transmission risks, reflecting a social concern particularly relevant in the Thai context.[98] At the yearly JW Marriott Hotel Bangkok, HIV/AIDS awareness training sessions are voluntary, last for three hours, are offered during normal work times, form part of a general health promotion program, and use an interactive format.[99] The Body Shop has an HIV/AIDS staff-training program, and works to raise awareness of HIV in communities and suppliers in high-prevalence countries.[100] In Japan, a low-prevalence country, The Body Shop has targeted women, who are often excluded from HIV/AIDS awareness campaigns, for HIV information and cause-related marketing.[101]

Media companies have a special role in developing awareness of HIV/AIDS. In 2001, global media giant Viacom partnered with the Kaiser Foundation to launch the Know AIDS initiative. Viacom owns cable channels MTV, BET, Showtime, and others, and planned to use these different channels to disperse a consistent message.[102] MTV Networks, with a viewership of one billion, promotes HIV/AIDS awareness by offering free of charge to local broadcasters *Staying Alive*, an Emmy Award–winning series of documentaries, and other initiatives.[103]

Use Existing Corporate Social Responsibility Models

Companies attempt to cultivate a socially responsible image, in response to the expectations of their customers and the general public, and as such must be seen as active against the spread of HIV/AIDS or the treatment of those who have it. Companies are corporate citizens both at local and global levels, and as such are concerned about the wider stakeholders in their business, and the extent to which these may become affected by HIV/

242 *AIDS and Business*

AIDS. Some companies contribute to the wider efforts made to increase HIV/AIDS awareness and education. Top managers may be motivated to go beyond their companies' legal obligations for a number of reasons. They may feel social pressure—possibly from activists—to behave in a socially responsible manner, particularly if the company is highly visible in the media and society due to its size or other considerations. Another reason is that managers may opt to conform to voluntary regulation measures, such as a best practice code or a "responsible" stock exchange index. In addition, a risk management analysis may demonstrate the long-term benefits of a responsible HIV/AIDS policy. Whatever the case, it is expected today that companies of all sizes and sectors display concern for issues like HIV/AIDS that formerly were outside the realm of business.

Donations and Charitable Activities

Donations, and more generally charitable activities, are the most visible manifestation of corporate social responsibility. The Body Shop donates a portion of proceeds from the sale of condoms in Japan to people living with AIDS.[104] Nestlé Thailand donates milk and infant products in the context of prevention of mother-to-child transmission in Thailand, as part of its involvement with Her Royal Highness Princess Soamsawalee's program "Help reduce HIV/AIDS infection from mothers to their babies."[105] IKEA, the Swedish multinational, announced in 2003 an in-store campaign to raise money for UNICEF in twenty-two countries by donating £1.50 from the sale of each "Brum" bear. The "Brum" bear, a uniquely jointed teddy, largely exceeded its sales targets. The funds were used in Angola and Uganda, of which a portion will support HIV/AIDS education programs in the north of the country.[106]

Donation of drugs is a way for showing CSR on the part of pharmaceutical companies: Boehringer Ingelheim, through the PMTCT partnership, donates the antiretroviral Viramune to prevent transmission from mothers to babies.[107] A survey conducted in 2004 demonstrated the many ways in which pharmaceutical companies operating in low- and middle-income countries may be active in addition to developing and marketing medications. More than three-quarters of pharmaceutical companies developed partnerships with national health systems and implemented differential pricing in different markets to increase accessibility of their drugs. Half of the companies surveyed were active in encouraging governments to donate to the Global Fund for HIV, TB, and Malaria.[108] Abbott Laboratories donates its Determine HIV tests to pregnant women and mothers in resource-poor settings through a partnership, the PMTCT Donations Program.[109] Companies may also donate through their employees' generosity or by giving them time off to participate in an HIV/AIDS-related cause. The JW Marriott Hotel Bangkok has organized collective donations by its employees to benefit children with AIDS.[110] Levi Strauss & Co. employees are given time off to volunteer at HIV/AIDS organizations.[111]

Designing a Company HIV/AIDS Program 243

Box 10.3 A View from the Field:

Winners of GBC's "Outstanding Business Action on HIV/AIDS" in 2006

GBC 2006 Workplace Category Winner

Unilever Tea Kenya, which employs more than twenty thousand workers, operates twenty-two dispensaries, four health centers, and a hospital as well as mobile clinics. Unilever Tea Kenya is active in the following areas:
Awareness and education programs with multiple channels for HIV/AIDS messages.
Prevention programs including the distribution of male and female condoms, prevention of mother-to-child transmission, and postexposure prophylaxis.
Care and support that includes antiretroviral therapy, wellness program, voluntary counseling, and testing.
Capacity building includes community initiatives and active participation with the Kenya HIV/AIDS Business Council, Kenya Tea Growers Association, and others.For information: http://www.unilever.com.

Other winners in this category included:
Standard Bank (South Africa) http://www.standardbank.co.za.
PepsiCo (South Africa) http://www.pepsico.com.
Total (Burkina Faso) http://www.total.com.
SouthWest Railway (Ukraine) http://www.swrailway.gov.ua/en.

GBC 2006 "Community" Category Winner

National Basketball Association (NBA), which employs more than 1,100 people, was recognized for its "Basketball without Borders" program—part of the NBA Cares program. The program brought together young players from nearly one hundred countries in camps where they receive training in life skills in addition to HIV/AIDS awareness and prevention. In addition, the Basketball without Borders Legacy Project funded a recreation facility or a Reading and Learning Center in Beijing, Buenos Aires, Johannesburg, Rio de Janeiro, and Soweto. For information: http://www.nba.com.

Other winners in this category included:
Johnson & Johnson (Brazil) http://www.jnj.com.
Kerzner International (Bahamas) http://www.kerzner.com.
Abbott (Tanzania) http://www.abbott.com.

GBC 2006 "Core Competency" Category Winner

L'Oréal employs 52,403 people, and has seventeen global brands sold in 130 countries. In addition to its HIV/AIDS workplace program in South Africa, the company used its distribution channels to reach out to hairdressers for HIV/AIDS prevention, antistigma, and hygiene training through its "Train the Trainers" program in South Africa. In partnership with UNESCO, L'Oréal launched in 2005 "Hairdressers of the World against

continued

244 *AIDS and Business*

> *Box 10.3 (continued)*
>
> AIDS," which reached Brazil, Estonia, France, India, Indonesia, Latvia, Lithuania, Malaysia, Philippines, and the UK.
>
> Other winners in this category included:
> SSL International, which includes the Durex condom brand http://www.ssl-international.com.
> ZMQ Sofware Systems (India) http://www.zmqsoft.com.
> Black Entertainment Television (USA) http://www.rap-it-up.com.
>
> Source: Global Business Coalition Web site: http://www.businessfightsaids.org.

INTERNATIONALLY ACCEPTED FOUNDATIONS FOR CORPORATE SOCIAL RESPONSIBILITY

There is a growing body of work about corporate social responsibility (CSR), the notion that companies, like individuals, have responsibilities towards the community, region, or nation within which they operate. There are a number of philosophies, theories, and frameworks for designing and implementing corporate social responsibility programs, also referred to as "corporate citizenship" or "triple bottom line reporting." The first companies to be publicly involved in corporate social responsibility were large multinational corporations, partly due to the strict risk management guidelines of stock exchanges such as London Stock Exchange's Turnbull Guidelines, and the proliferation of corporate social responsibility indexes such as the FTSE4Good. Companies in South Africa like AngloAmerican and Eskom demonstrated this enlightened approach when they predicted the negative impact the epidemic would have, and proactively addressed HIV/AIDS in their workplaces and communities, although they did not refer to it at the time as CSR (Hamann, Agbazue, Kapelus, and Hein, 2005).[112] A variety of approaches may be used in defining, planning, and implementing corporate social responsibility. There are a range of existing frameworks for corporate social responsibility, which may guide businesses in the integration, implementation, and reporting of an HIV/AIDS program. Frameworks such as Global Compact, Global Reporting Initiative, and others can help imbue a proposal or budding program with legitimacy.

Some of the major internationally known organizations active in the field are described next to provide an overview of the range of ideas supporting corporate social responsibility as well as of the different perspectives on the issues. The AA1000 Assurance Standard framework was initiated to guide companies in the area of sustainability management systems and reporting.[113] FTSE4Good:[114] Excluded from the FTSE4Good are tobacco companies, companies involved with the manufacture of nuclear systems including

Designing a Company HIV/AIDS Program 245

nuclear power stations. FTSE4Good is based on an application process for companies that comply with three areas of corporate responsibility: (1) "working towards environmental sustainability"; (2) "developing positive relationships with stakeholders"; (3) "upholding and supporting universal human rights."[115]

The aim of the Global Reporting Initiative (GRI)[116] was to develop guidelines on how to measure, account for, and report corporate social responsibility initiatives in a manner consistent with globally accepted accounting standards. It is arguably the most useful of the CSR initiatives because it attempts to provide a common framework for several different initiatives. The GRI is an independent institution, working with the Global Compact and the active participation of accounting, environmental, investment, human rights, labor, and research organizations. Currently 707 companies use the GRI guidelines in their economic, environmental, and social reporting.

The ILO Core Labor Standards[117] were set out in 1919. This is the oldest set of standards relating to treatment of people in the workplace. In its modern incarnation, the Labor Standards in the Decent Work Agenda address the societal role of business more broadly as employment creation, social protection, and social dialogue in addition to specifically addressing the problems relating to decent workplace conditions and rights. The UN Global Compact:[118] The Compact consists of nine principles set out initially by UN Secretary-General Kofi Annan in 2000 in order to address development (such as the Millennium Development Goals) and corporate social responsibility issues. The compact incorporated a unique constellation of United Nations organizations, business associations, international nongovernmental organizations, and more than two thousand company members. The OECD Guidelines for Multinational Enterprises[119] are government-negotiated and multilaterally endorsed initiative regarding consumer interests, employee relations, environmental management, ethical practices, reporting, and diffusion of science and technology.

The International Standards Organization issued the ISO 14000 series[120] to aid companies in developing environmental management systems that improve performance without providing specific performance standards. Social issues are not specifically considered in the standards, although there is a reference to stakeholder engagement. Social Accountability International (SAI)[121] developed this standard and verification system focusing on workplace conditions, and to reduce sweatshops, "Promoting the human rights of workers around the world." In certain industries and sectors there are also codes of practice, guidelines, and certification systems. For example, the chemical industry has the Responsible Care program, the forestry industry has the Forest Stewardship Council (FSC) certification, the fishing industry has the Marine Stewardship Council, among many others.[122]

246 *AIDS and Business*

AN ARGUMENT FOR A BROADER BUSINESS PERSPECTIVE: THE UNITED NATIONS MILLENNIUM GOALS

It is often argued by leaders within the development community (notably the United Nations and nongovernmental organizations) and academics (such as C. K. Prahalad and S. L. Hart) alike that the private sector has a central role to play in development. Business leadership in complex societal problems like HIV/AIDS can set standards for action by governments and public sector organizations. Put simply by the World Business Council for Sustainable Development, "Business is good for development and development is good for business." The link between development, HIV/AIDS, and business becomes clearer when one considers the role played by poverty in the growth of the HIV/AIDS epidemic.

In the year 2000, the United Nations Millennium Goals were adopted by 189 nations as part of the Millennium Declaration. This was, according to UN Secretary-General Kofi Annan, an "unprecedented promise by world leaders . . . to address peace, security, development, human rights, and fundamental freedoms" (p. 3).[123] According to a report by the United Nations Development Program, the Millennium Development Goals (MDGs) are good for business in three ways:

1. Stable, secure, healthy societies are better business environments because of the quality of the workforce and the more lucrative consumption patterns of consumers
2. Ecological, health, and HIV/AIDS costs and risks, among others, may be reduced
3. The vast business opportunities of developing markets will be enhanced

Business has a key role to play by contributing to the achievement of these goals in their core business activities with customers, workers, and supply chains; in the community through their social responsibility programs; and they can advocate for structural change in their role as lobbyists and advocates on public policy.[124, 125]

The Millennium Development Goals included eight goals, eighteen targets, and forty-eight indicators. The eight goals are:

- Eradicate severe poverty and hunger.
- Achieve universal primary education.
- Promote gender equality and empower women.
- Reduce child mortality.
- Improve maternal health.
- Combat HIV/AIDS, malaria, and other diseases.
- Ensure environmental sustainability.
- Develop a global partnership for development.

Relating specifically to HIV/AIDS, the stated direction of the Millennium Development Goals was to halt, and begin to reverse, the spread of HIV/AIDS before 2015 by:

1. Adopting as an explicit goal the reduction of HIV infection rates in persons fifteen to twenty-four years of age—by 25 percent within the most affected countries before the year 2005, and by 25 percent globally before 2010.
2. Setting explicit prevention targets: by 2005 at least 90 percent, and by 2010 at least 95 percent, of young men and women must have access to the HIV-preventive information and services.
3. Urging every seriously affected country to have a national plan of action in place within one year of the Summit.[126]

Further health-related goals, specifically relating to malaria and tuberculosis, followed those relative to HIV/AIDS.

DISCUSSION QUESTION AND ASSIGNED TASK

Design a corporate HIV/AIDS program for a medium-sized South African company, or the country of your choice. The company, which employs approximately five hundred employees, deals with the bottling and distribution of soft drinks and other beverages. The HIV/AIDS policy guidelines for this company should be written on the basis of a discussion by groups of three to five members. The draft guidelines should be between five and ten pages long; they should be written in a clear, nonequivocal, and practical-minded manner. They should set both principles and practices, be understandable for all employees, and be as easy as possible to implement, after being approved and backed by top management and (possibly) other stakeholders in corporate decision making.

The guidelines should be practical and implementable, avoiding simply normative statements, and address the following issues:

- Prehiring policies (screening of job applicants, confidentiality issues, and soon).
- Testing of employees.
- Awareness programs.
- Continuation/discontinuation of employment relationships with HIV-positive employees.
- Prevention policies.
- Provision of treatment (To workers? To family members? Covering other sexually transmitted diseases in addition to HIV/AIDS? For free or against some form of participation-to-cost scheme for the employee?).

248   *AIDS and Business*

- Degree of involvement of workers and their representative in the process of drafting/implementing the HIV-AIDS corporate policy guidelines.

Where to Find Additional Information

The Web-based references used in this case are a good place to start for finding more information. There is a wealth of information on specific company actions and examples on the Internet, such as the following:

Asian Business Coalition on AIDS (Thailand): http://www.abconaids.org.

Asia Pacific Business Coalition on AIDS: http://www.apbca.com/.

Business Responds to AIDS/Labor Responds to AIDS (Centers for Disease Control, USA): http://www.hivatwork.org/.

Business Responds to AIDS/Labor Responds to AIDS (Centers for Disease Control, USA): Labor Leader's kit: http://www.hivatwork.org/tools/labor.cfm.

Global Business Coalition: http://www.businessfightsaids.org.

International Labor Organization: http://www.ilo.org/global/Themes/HIVAIDS/lang—en/index.htm.

International Organization of Employers: http://www.ioe-emp.org/.

South African Business Coalition on AIDS: http://www.sabcoha.org/.

UNAIDS: http://www.unaids.org/en/.

World Economic Forum's Global Health Initiative: http://www.weforum.org/en/initiatives/globalhealth/index.htm.

Glossary

GLOSSARY OF HIV/AIDS TERMS, PEOPLE, AND ORGANIZATIONS

Term	Explanation and Further Information
3 by 5 Initiative	Target announced by the World Health Organization (WHO) and UNAIDS in 2003 to provide antiretroviral treatment to three million people with HIV/AIDS living in low- and middle-income countries before 2005. See http://www.who.int/3by5/en/.
46664	Former South African president Nelson Mandela's foundation to raise funds for HIV/AIDS-related projects and conduct awareness campaigns, as well as "social mobilization" and other initiatives. 46664 notably conducted musical fund-raisers that featured international music stars. The foundation name was Mandela's prisoner number. http://www.46664.com.
Abbott	Pharmaceutical company. Abbott and its Abbott Fund set up the Global Care Initiatives with partners, such as the government of Tanzania, to improve health infrastructure and HIV/AIDS care. Worldwide, Abbott and its initiatives donated one million HIV/AIDS tests for pregnant women, as well as tests in 69 countries in 2004. The company's Step Forward program was founded to provide HIV/AIDS care to children in resource-poor settings such as India, Mexico, Romania, and Burkina Faso, notably increasing the life expectancy of children with HIV. Abbott is a member of the *Accelerating Access Initiative*. http://www.abbott.com/.
ABC	An HIV/AIDS prevention campaign first used by the government of Botswana in the 1990s. Loosely known as "Abstain, Be faithful, Use a Condom," the three steps have been adopted by the President's Emergency Plan for AIDS Relief (PEPFAR) and other governments. See http://www.state.gov/s/gac/partners/guide/abc/56567.htm.
Absenteeism	Employees being absent from work at a normally scheduled time for health or other reasons.
Abstinence	To refrain to participate in sex acts.

250 *Glossary*

Abstinence-only programs
Sex education programs that teach exclusively or mainly that people should abstain from all sex acts outside and before marriage. Such programs tend to omit information about condoms and other methods of contraception and usually promote strong religious or moral beliefs. See http://www.eldis.org/hivaids/prevention/abstinence.htm.

Academic journals dealing with HIV/AIDS
AIDS, official journal of the International AIDS Society, available at: http://www.aidsonline.com.
AIDS and Public Policy
AIDS Care (medical journal)
AIDS Education and Prevention
AIDS Patient Care and STDs
AIDS Research and Human Retroviruses
AIDS Science (Journal of the American Medical Association) available at: http://www.aidscience.com.
British Medical Journal
Journal of the American Medical Association
Reproductive Health Matters
The Lancet available at: http://www.thelancet.com.

Accelerating Access Initiative
An initiative of the International Federation of Pharmaceutical Manufacturers and Associations (IFPMA), UNAIDS UNICEF, UN Population Fund, World Bank, WHO, and seven pharmaceutical companies: Abbott Laboratories, Boehringer Ingelheim, Bristol-Myers Squibb, GlaxoSmithKline, Gilead Sciences, Hoffmann-La Roche, and Merck & Co. The initiative was founded in 2000 to increase access to affordable HIV medicines in resource-poor countries. http://www.ifpma.org/Health/hiv/health_aai_hiv.aspx.

Access
Whether a person in need of medical treatment can afford financially and in term of time or social strictures to take the treatment needed.

ACT UP NY (AIDS Coalition to Unleash Power, New York)
Active and vocal organization committed to raising awareness about HIV/AIDS and, in particular, about the response of government and other institutions to the HIV/AIDS epidemic. http://www.actupny.org/. See also ACT UP Paris (in French) http://www.actupparis.org.

Action plan
A management tool that sets out who will be responsible for the accomplishment of defined tasks, by which date.

Addiction
Compulsive and repeated use of psychoactive substances, such as drugs or alcohol, resulting in frequent intoxication and extreme difficulty to stop using the substance. See http://www.who.int/substance_abuse/terminology/who_lexicon/en/.

Adherence
To take medicines exactly according to the prescribed dosage, mode of administration, time of day, and length of time.

Adolescent Reproductive and Sexual Health
An initiative of UNESCO to provide holistic, targeted health and prevention information for adolescents. http://www.unescobkk.org/arsh.

Advocate *n.*
To be a party that argues for a particular position, idea, or cause.

Glossary 251

AEGIS (AIDS Education Global information System) "A nonprofit organization that was established in response to the growing HIV/AIDS pandemic. Our mission is aimed to facilitate access to current patient/clinician information specific to HIV/AIDS via our website and its specified services and preserve for future generations a global history of the pandemic with our historical news, scientific publications and treatment database . . . it has matured into the largest free-access virtual AIDS library on earth."http://www.aegis.com/.

AFESIP Cambodian organization offering assistance to sexually exploited children and women, including HIV/AIDS services. AFESIP fights against trafficking of women and children for sex commerce purposes. http://www.afesip.org/.

African Comprehensive HIV/ AIDS Partnership (Botswana) "A country-led, public-private development partnership between the Government of Botswana, the Bill & Melinda Gates Foundation, and Merck & Co., Inc/The Merck Company Foundation dedicated to supporting and enhancing Botswana's national response to HIV/AIDS through 2009." http://www.achap.org/.

AIDA model of communication Advertising and marketing communication Theory based on the concepts of attention, interest, desire, and action.

AIDES (France) Association de Lutte Contre le VIH-SIDA et les Hépatites French NGO whose "public health mission was recognized by the French government in 1990. AIDES directly supports persons living with HIV infection and their circle. AIDES informs the public . . . and institutions." http://www.aides.org/.

AIDS Acquired immunodeficiency syndrome: a disease that causes the immune system to function ineffectively. A person with AIDS is susceptible to opportunistic infections, infections that may be normally overcome by the immune system or treated in people without AIDS. AIDS is considered to be the active phase of HIV, human immunodeficiency virus. See www.stopaids.org/resources/std_info/aids_definition.html.

AIDS Official journal of the International AIDS Society http://www.aidsonline.com.

AIDS Alliance "A global partnership of nationally-based organisations working to support community action on AIDS in developing countries." See http://www.aidsalliance.org.

AIDSMAP Web site providing HIV-related news and patient information, searchable databases on treatment and care, and listings of HIV-related organizations worldwide. AIDSMAP is run by NAM, "an award-winning, community-based organisation, which works from the UK. We deliver reliable and accurate HIV information across the world to HIV-positive people and to the professionals who treat, support and care for them." See http://www.aidsmap.com.

AIDS Healthcare Foundation "AIDS Healthcare Foundation (AHF) is the nation's largest non-profit HIV/AIDS healthcare, research, prevention and education provider. AHF currently provides medical care and/or services to more than 65,000 individuals in 20 countries worldwide in the US, Africa, Latin America/Caribbean and Asia." See http://www.aidshealth.org.

252 *Glossary*

AIDSMark

A program of PSI, funded by USAID, that uses social marketing for behavior change and commercial marketing of health products, such as condoms, in the aim of reducing the spread of HIV/AIDS. AIDSMark notably uses branding techniques for social marketing of condoms, sending aspirational lifestyle messages in advertising and public relations for condom brands. Behavior change interventions are based on the ABC model, aiming to revalorize virginity among teenagers, address the cultural barriers to condom use, discourage risky relationships such as young women with older men more likely to have HIV/AIDS, and encourage testing. In addition, AIDSMark works with a range of faith-based organizations to spread its message. Source: www.aidsmark.org.

AIDS Portals and information sites

http://www.aidsportal.org. ELDIS: online database available at: http://www.eldis.org. HIVInsite (news compiled by the University of Southern California) available at: http://hivinsite.ucsf.edu/.

Alive and Well AIDS Alternatives

Organization that contends the validity of medical research into HIV/AIDS, the therapies currently proposed to people with HIV, and the very concepts of HIV and AIDS. http://www.aliveandwell.org/.

Alternative medicine

Also known as "complementary medicine." Approaches to health care that are outside conventional medicine as practiced by registered medical doctors. Examples include traditional Chinese, homeopathic, and naturopathic medicine. See www.nccam.nih.gov/health/whatiscam/.

AmfAR

American Foundation for AIDS Research, a nonprofit founded to support HIV/AIDS research, prevention and treatment programs as well as advocacy. See http://www.amfar.org.

Ansell International

Marketer of condoms.

Antenatal care

Health care for pregnant women.

Antenatal clinic

Clinic providing health care services for pregnant women.

Antenatal surveys

National or regional survey of HIV cases among pregnant women. Usually the women are administered an HIV test. For some countries these provide the best estimates of HIV infection.

Anthropology

The scientific study of human groups, cultures, language, and behavior.

Antibody

Protein manufactured by lymphocytes to combat foreign proteins in the body known as antigens.

Antigen

Proteins found on microorganisms that are foreign to the body, such as viruses and bacteria.

Antiretroviral treatment (ARV)

Drugs which slow the rate of replication of the human immunodeficiency virus (HIV), thereby delaying or preventing progression to AIDS, but which are not a "cure" for HIV.

Apartheid

Racial segregation policy, most notably enacted in South Africa until 1994.

Glossary 253

Appeal	An approach used in advertising to attract the attention of the targeted audience or influence their perceptions about a product, idea, or message.
Asian Business Coalition on AIDS (ABCON-AIDS)	A regional network of partnerships between businesses and not-for-profit organizations. http://www.abconaids.org.
Asian Development Bank	The Asian Development Bank has as its stated aim to promote sustainable economic growth, social protection aimed particularly at the poor, and governance. Membership includes 63 nations, from Afghanistan to Vietnam. The Asian Development Bank has been active in a number of HIV/AIDS projects. Source: http://www.adb.org.
AZT	Chemical name: Azidothymidin; generic name: Zidovudine; nickname: AZT; brand name: Retrovir® (Retrovis®); manufacturer: GlaxoSmithKline. See: http://www.virusmyth.com/aids/index/azt.htm.
Barrier method of contraception	Barrier methods of contraception are mechanical in their action, blocking contact between the penis and the vagina, such as male and female condoms, diaphragm, cap, and contraceptive sponge.
Bill and Melinda Gates Foundation	The foundation primarily works as an aide for existing organizations and programs through the provision of grants, with a focus on education, global health, libraries, and local (Pacific Northwest, U.S.) family programs. The foundation's stated global health priority is stopping the spread of HIV. With cumulative HIV-related funding of US$500 million, the foundation supports programs active in the areas of prevention, research funding, such as microbicide and vaccine research; support for orphans; and counseling and testing. Source: http://www.gatesfoundation.org.
Bioequivalent	Medicine containing the same active ingredient in the same amount and pharmaceutical form, and which has the same effect on the human body, as a medicine originated elsewhere, for example, a generic medicine versus a branded one.
Body fluids	Specifically blood, semen, urine, vaginal, and oral (mouth) fluids
Boehringer Ingelheim	Pharmaceutical company, *Member of Accelerating Access Initiative.*
Branched DNA test	One of two HIV laboratory tests that count the number of copies of the virus in a sample. See also the polymerase chain reaction test. For information, go to www.thebody.com/asp/septoct04/labs.html.
Brazil National Business Council	Conselho Empresarial Nacional Para Prevenção ao HIV/AIDS was founded by the Ministry of Health to "optimize efforts and resources" of company actions on HIV/AIDS. http://www.cenaids.com.br/eng.

254 *Glossary*

Brazil National STD and AIDS Program	Programa Nacional de DST e Aids, Minstério da Saúde. The Ministry of Health division responsible for monitoring, prevention, policymaking, and health care issues relating to HIV/AIDS. http://www.aids.gov.br.
Bristol-Myers Squibb	Pharmaceutical company. Member of Accelerating Access Initiative.
Campaign for Access to Essential Medicines	An initiative of Médecins Sans Frontières to lower barriers to access to treatment for HIV/AIDS and other diseases, support international trade rules that protect people's access to essential goods such as medicines, in addition to local production of such medicines; support and relaunch, if necessary, research and development into neglected communicable diseases, particularly tropical diseases. http://www.accessmed-msf.org.
Canadian HIV/AIDS Legal Network	Canada-based organization promoting a human rights and dignity basis for the care and of people affected by HIV in Canada and worldwide. The organization advocates the formulation of relevant laws and policies that support human rights for marginalized populations, workers, women, and others. http://www.aidslaw.ca.
CD4 count	HIV laboratory test that counts the number of CD4 cells in a sample, as an indicator of the strength of the immune system. For information, go to www.thebody.com/asp/septoct04/labs.html.
CDC	Center for Disease Control and Prevention (U.S. government agency). Online medical information. Available at: http://www.cdc.gov.
CSIS	Center for Strategic and International Studies (U.S.): www.csis.org.
Cipla	Indian pharmaceutical company manufacturing generic drugs. www.cipla.com/home.htm.
Combination therapy	HIV drug regimen that uses a combination of drugs, commonly three in number, hence the name "triple therapy" or drug "cocktail."
Complementary medicine	Healing system or technique used in addition to conventional medicine treatments.
Compulsory licensing	Patent law provision that allows a government to override the intellectual property right of a patent holder in case of a public health emergency. The company making the drug pays a royalty to the patent holder.
Condomi	German condom manufacturer known for its innovative marketing approaches, such as cobranding with MTV. Condomi condoms in a match-folder format have been used as a publicity medium by Hoffmann La Roche, Levis, Smart, Sony, Volkswagen, a number of cinemas, and several political parties across the spectrum, to name a few. Source: http://www.condomi.com.
Confederation of Indian Industry	India's oldest and most prominent business association, which has had several HIV/AIDS-related initiatives. http://www.ciionline.org.

Glossary 255

Constella Group U.S.-based multinational, provider of professional health services. http://www.constellagroup.com.

Crystal Meth See Methamphetamine.

Differential pricing Pricing of drugs differently according to the local market. See *Equity pricing*. See http://www.accessmed-msf.org.

DOTS Directly observed therapy: Five-point strategy to fight tuberculosis.

Doha Declaration 2001 World Trade Organization declaration allowing a nation with a medical emergency to nullify patents for relevant drugs in order to permit generic versions to be produced domestically to ease prices and shortages, placing public health above commercial gain as expressed in Trade Related Aspects of Intellectual Property Rights (TRIPS). http://www.wto.org/english/thewto_e/minist_e/min01_e/mindecl_trips_e.htm.

Drug In medicine, any substance that may cure or prevent a medical condition, or increase one's physical or mental well-being. Common usage refers to psychoactive substances, particularly those that are illegal. See http://www.who.int/substance_abuse/terminology/who_lexicon/en/.

Drug dependency Need for repeated doses of a drug, usually a psychoactive one.

ECPAT International End Child Prostitution, Pornography, and Trafficking for sexual purposes: An organization active in 70 countries that is committed to raising awareness among vulnerable children and adults seeking children for sex. http://www.ecpat.net.

Ecumenical Advocacy Alliance http://www.e-alliance.ch/.

Equity pricing Pricing strategy that aims to provide drugs at a price that is affordable and fair to specific markets defined as being in need. See http://www.accessmed-msf.org.

Essential drugs Drugs considered to be effective, safe, and necessary from a medical point of view. A drug with a high price may not be considered "essential." See the WHO Essential Drugs List. http://www.who.int/medicines/services/essmedicines_def/en/index.html.

Ethical Globalization Initiative Mary Robinson. http://www.realizingrights.org/.

Female circumcision Incorrect term for *female genital mutilation*.

Female genital mutilation Partial or total removal of external female genitalia. See www.who.int.

Full-blown AIDS Now commonly referred to as "AIDS."

Fusion inhibitors For example, Roche's Fuzeon.

Gay-Related Immunodeficiency Disease Commonly referred to by the acronym "GRID," used in the early days of the epidemic to describe a set of symptoms common to a number of self-declared homosexual men in the U.S.

GLBT Acronym for gay, lesbian, bisexual, and transsexual.

256 *Glossary*

Gender-related Development Index (GDI)	The United Nations Development Programme (UNDP) developed the GDI as an extension of the Human Development Index (HDI). The GDI is a composite index of "decent" life dimensions for females, resulting in a country ranking system.
Generic drug	A copy of a pharmaceutical product that is patented, or for which patent has expired. See: http://www.wto.org/English/tratop_e/trips_e/factsheet_pharm03_e.htm.
Grey market	Transactions conducted outside usual sales channels, as in the case of patented medicines sold by unauthorized distributors or online merchants.
GRID	See *gay-related immunodeficiency disease*.
HAART	Highly active antiretroviral therapy.
Harm reduction	Policies aiming to reduce harm associated with drug-taking, particularly syringe-exchange programs. See http://www.who.int/substance_abuse/terminology/who_lexicon/en/.
Heroin	One of a number of opioids that induce mood, psychomotor, and other changes in the user. It is a highly addictive substance with virulent withdrawal symptoms that set in relatively quickly. Heroin is commonly injected into a vein by users, thereby causing a number of health problems, including transmission of HIV, hepatitis B, hepatitis C, septicemia, and so on. See http://www.who.int/substance_abuse/terminology/who_lexicon/en/.
Human Development Index	The United Nations Development Programme (UNDP) developed the Human Development Index (HDI) to reflect the wider gains (or losses) related to the economic development process. See also the *Gender-related Development Index*.
Human Development Report	Report published annually by the United Nations Development Programme (UNDP) to analyze the process of economic development and its consequences on societies. For information go to: www.undp.org.
Human Immunodeficiency Virus (HIV)	HIV is the often symptom-free first stage of AIDS, which may last for years. People with HIV/AIDS generally need two categories of medications, antiretroviral drugs to boost the immune system and treatments for opportunistic infections.
Human Papillomavirus	Commonly known by its acronym, HPV, this virus is linked with a greater risk for genital and anal cancer and is the cause of some genital and anal warts
IDU	Injecting-Drug User. One who administers drugs, usually illicit substances like heroin, intravenously (by injection). See http://www.who.int/substance_abuse/terminology/who_lexicon/en/,
Infibulation (see also *female genital mutilation*)	The most extreme form of *female genital mutilation*. All external parts of the genitals are cut out. Remaining skin is sewn together or left to heal and a small opening is left for urine, menstrual fluids, sexual contact, and birth.

Glossary 257

Intellectual property	A product of intellectual activity that is innovative, has market value, and is unique. May be an idea, industrial process, or formulation and cumulate in a legal right such as a *patent* or *copyright*.
International Organizations dealing with HIV/AIDS	Asian Development Bank (ADB) (multilateral finance institution) available at: http://www.adb.org. Global Fund to fight AIDS, Malaria and Tuberculosis (international organization) available at: http://www.globalfund.org. International Federation of Red Cross and Red Crescent Societies (international organization) available at: http://www.ifrc.org. United Nations Children's Fund (UNICEF) (international organization) available at: http://www.unicef.org. United Nations Development Fund for Women (international organization) available at: http://www.unifem.org. United Nations Program on HIV/AIDS (UNAIDS) (international organization) available at http://www.unaids.org. World Bank (multilateral development agency) available at: http://www.worldbank.org. World Health Organization (WHO) (international organization) available at: http://www.who.int.
Intersexed	People born without distinguishable male or female genitals, or with genitals that have both male and female characteristics. The condition is sometimes referred to as the "third gender."
KAP survey	Knowledge, Attitudes and Perceptions survey.
Kothi	People who self-identify as male but who, in the context of a South Asian identity or culture, have "feminine" behaviors and may cultivate a "feminine" appearance. See also *Metis*.
Lazarus Effect	Name given to describe the sometimes dramatic and sudden improvement of patients who commence antiretroviral therapy after a steady AIDS-related decline.
License	Permission to manufacture, copy, use, or sell patented products or processes granted by the *patent* owner.
Lobbying	Influence over lawmakers to propose legislation, vote for or against proposed legislation, or change the emphasis in a legal document by offering cash payments, gifts, endorsements, or publicity.
Lube	Slang word for "lubrication."
Lymphocytes	A type of white blood cell that produces *antibodies*.
Malaria	A protozoan parasite infection spread primarily in poor settings by the anopheline mosquito. If untreated, malaria can be fatal.
Metis	Males who self-identify as male but who, in the context of a South Asian identity or culture, have "feminine" behaviors and may cultivate a "feminine" appearance. See also *Kothi*.
Missing women	A concept developed by the Noble Prize–winning economist Amartya Sen to account for the premature deaths of women, girls, and female fetuses due to various forms of discrimination.
Monitoring	Tests designed to guide antiretroviral treatments, such as the *CD4 count* and *viral load*.

258 *Glossary*

MSM	Men having sex with men.
MTCT or MCT (mother-to-child transmission)	Transmission of HIV from mother to child during pregnancy and birth, or through breast milk. The risk of MTCT may be reduced or nullified by antiretrovirals administered to the mother.
Multidrug- resistant tuberculosis	When the strains of bacteria responsible for tuberculosis infection are resistant to the usual first-line drugs, which they increasingly are, tuberculosis may be difficult or impossible to treat.
NACO	National AIDS Control Organisation (India).
Needle sharing	The use of syringes or other injecting equipment that has already been used by another person, usually in the context of injecting-drug use. http://www.who.int/substance_abuse/terminology/who_lexicon/en/.
NGOs (Non-governmental organizations) dealing with HIV/AIDS	Organizations that take upon themselves the kind of activity normally reserved for governments, such as medical care or education. Action AID UK available at: http://www.actionaid.org.uk. African Council of AIDS Service Organizations available at: http://www.africaso.net. Amnesty International available at: http://www.amnesty.org. Bill and Melinda Gates Foundation available at: http://www.gatesfoundation.org. Center for Reproductive Rights available at: http://www.crip.org. Engender Health available at: http://www.engenderhealth.org. François-Xavier Bagnoud Center for Health and Human Rights at Harvard University available at: http://www.hsph.harvard.edu/fxbcenter. Médecins Sans Frontières available at: http://www.msf.org and http://www.globaltreatmentaccess.org. International AIDS Economics Network available at: http://www.iaen.org. International AIDS Society available at: http://www.ias.se. International HIV/AIDS Alliance available at: http://www.aidsalliance.org. John Snow International available at: http://www.jsi.com. Kaiser Family Foundation available at: http://www.kff.org. Marie Stopes International available at: http://www.mariestopes.org.uk. Treatment Access Campaign available at: http://www.tac.org.za.
Nonoxyl-9	Spermicide
Opioids	Substances extracted from the opium poppy (*Papaver somniferum*) or produced synthetically that induce a number of changes in physical and mental states among users, most notably euphoria. The most well-known opioids include heroin, methadone, morphine, and pethidine. These are commonly injected by users. See http://www.who.int/substance_abuse/terminology/who_lexicon/en/.
Opportunistic infections	An infection or illness that may thrive on the weakened immune system of a person with HIV, but would have been fought off by an immune system free of HIV. If untreated, the infection may become fatal.

Glossary 259

Parallel imports Importing of goods often subject to industrial or intellectual property rights, conducted through unauthorized channels of distribution.

Patent Government-granted exclusive right to manufacture, use, or sell a medication granted to the inventor for a specific length of time, usually 20 years.

Penetrative sex Sex act where the penis enters the anus or vagina of the sex partner.

PWA or PLWA People Living with AIDS.

PEP Postexposure prophylaxis.

Polygyny The most common form of polygamy, when more than one woman is married by one man.

Polymerase chain reaction test One of two HIV laboratory tests that count the number of copies of the virus in a sample. See also the *branched DNA* test. For information, go to www.thebody.com/asp/septoct04/labs.html.

SIV Simian immunodeficiency virus.

STD Sexually transmitted disease.

STI Sexually transmitted infection.

Substance abuse Use of legal (e.g., alcoholic beverages, cigarettes) and illegal drugs (methamphetamine, heroin) to a harmful extent. See http://www.who.int/substance_abuse/terminology/who_lexicon/en/.

Syringe sharing Major component of a *harm reduction policy* that aims to reduce the medical consequences of the sharing of injecting equipment among injecting-drug users. See http://www.who.int/substance_abuse/terminology/who_lexicon/en/.

T cells Type of lymphocytes (white blood cells) that fight infected or cancerous cells and help coordinate an effective immune response.

Treatment Information Campaign South African group that disputes the link between HIV and AIDS, the validity of diagnostic tests, and the safety of antiretroviral drugs.

Triple therapy HIV drug regimen that uses a combination of drugs, commonly three in number, also known as *combination therapy* or drug "cocktail."

TRIPS Trade-related aspects of intellectual property (TRIPS) were agreed upon by World Trade Organization (WTO) members. It is the most important international law on intellectual property. It sets standards for national enforcement of intellectual property rights as well as sanctions for those who do not comply. See www.wto.org/english/tratop_e/trips_e/trips_e.htm.

Uruguay Round A series of trade negotiations under the auspices of the General Agreement on Tariffs and Trade (GATT), which began in Montevideo, Uruguay, in 1986 and was concluded in 1994, laying down most of the World Trade Organization (WTO)'s legal basis. See also *GATT: General Agreement on Tariffs and Trade.* For information go to: http://www.wto.org/English/docs_e/legal_e/legal_e.htm.

260 *Glossary*

Venereal disease	Sexually transmitted disease. Derived from the name *Venus*, goddess of love and now rarely used.
Viral load	Two types of HIV laboratory tests count the number of copies of the virus in a sample: the *polymerase chain reaction* test and *branched DNA* test. For information go to: www.thebody.com/asp/septoct04/labs.html.
World Trade Organization (WTO)	International organization based in Geneva, Switzerland. The WTO succeeded the General Agreement on Tariffs and Trade in 1995 and exists to regulate rules of trade between nations. See www.wto.org.

Notes

NOTES TO CASE STUDY 1

1. UNAIDS. (2006). *Spain*, countries and regions. Retrieved September 30, 2006, from http://www.unaids.org/en/Regions_Countries/Countries/spain.asp.
2. UNAIDS, UNICEF, WHO. (2004). *Epidemiological fact sheets: Spain*. Retrieved September 30, 2006, from http://data.unaids.org/Publications/Fact-Sheets01/Spain_EN.pdf.
3. Ibid.
4. UNAIDS. (2006). *2006 report on the global AIDS epidemic*. Geneva: UNAIDS.
5. UNAIDS. (2006). *2006 report on the global AIDS epidemic*. Geneva: UNAIDS.
6. Robalino, D. A., Jenkins, C., & El Maroufi, K. (2002). *Risks and macroeconomic impacts of HIV/AIDS in the Middle East and North Africa—why waiting to intervene can be costly*. Middle East and North Africa Working Paper series No. 26. Office of the Chief Economist, World Bank.
7. Obermeyer, C. M. (2006). HIV in the Middle East, analysis and comment. *British Medical Journal* 333, 851–54. Retrieved December 20, 2006, from http://www.bmj.com/cgi/content/full/333/7573/851?rss=1#REF12.
8. UNAIDS , op. cit.
9. Jenkins, op. cit.
10. UNAIDS. (2005). *AIDS epidemic update 2005*. Geneva: UNAIDS.
11. UNAIDS (2005). *AIDS epidemic update 2005 Middle East and North Africa*. Retrieved September 30, 2006, from http://www.unaids.org/epi/2005/doc/EPIupdate2005_html_en/epi05_11_en.htm.
12. Kingdom of Morocco, Ministry of Health. (2006). *Implementation of the declaration of commitment on HIV/AIDS, 2006 National Report*. Retrieved September 30, 2006, from http://data.unaids.org/pub/Report/2006/2006_country_progress_report_morocco_en.pdf#search=%22Morocco%2018%2C000%20HIV%20UNAIDS%22.
13. The Global Fund to Fight AIDS, Tuberculosis, and Malaria. (2005). *HIV/AIDS in Morocco*. Investing in our future. Retrieved September 30, 2006, from http://www.theglobalfund.org/en/in_action/morocco/hiv1/.
14. The Global Fund to Fight AIDS, Tuberculosis, and Malaria. (2005). *HIV/AIDS in Morocco*. Investing in our future. Retrieved September 30, 2006, from http://www.theglobalfund.org/en/in_action/morocco/hiv1/.
15. United Nations Development Programme. (2005). *Human development reports: Country sheet Morocco*. Retrieved September 30, 2006, from http://hdr.undp.org/statistics/data/countries.cfm?c=MAR.

262 *Notes*

16. UNAIDS, op. cit.
17. Hourani, A. (1991). *A history of the Arab peoples*. New York: Warner Books.
18. United Nations. (2002). *Western Sahara: MINURSO background*. UN Department of Peace Keeping Operations. Retrieved September 30, 2006, from http://www.un.org/Depts/DPKO/Missions/minurso/minursoB.htm.
19. UNAIDS. (2004). *Epidemiological fact sheets: Western Sahara*. Retrieved September 30, 2006, from http://www.who.int/GlobalAtlas/predefine-dReports/EFS2004/EFS_PDFs/EFS2004_EH.pdf.
20. UNAIDS, op. cit.
21. Gray, P. B. (2004). HIV and Islam: is HIV prevalence lower among Muslims? *Social Science and Medicine* 58(9), 1751–56.
22. El Ouali, A. (2006). Morocco: Civil war over condoms. Inter Press Service, January 26. Retrieved December 3, 2006, from http://www.aegis.com/news/ips/2006/IP060111.html.
23. Kelley, L. M., & Eberstadt, N. (2005). The Muslim face of AIDS. *Foreign Policy* 149, 42–48.
24. UNAIDS & WHO. (2007). *AIDS epidemic update*. Geneva: UNAIDS.
25. Jenkins, op. cit.
26. Jenkins, op. cit.
27. Policy Project. (2003). *Adolescent and youth reproductive health in Morocco: Status, issues, policies and programs*. Retrieved November 14, 2007, fromhttp://www.policyproject.com/pubs/countryreports/ARH_Morocco.pdf.
28. Jenkins, op. cit.
29. UNSTATS. (2003). *Population of capital cities and cities of 100,000 and more inhabitants: Latest available year*. Retrieved September 30, 2006, from http://unstats.un.org/UNSD/Demographic/products/dyb/DYB2003/Table08.pdf#search=%22morocco%20cities%20population%22.
30. Ibid.
31. Ibid.
32. Jenkins, op. cit.
33. Ministry of Communication Government of Morocco. (n.d.). *History of Morocco*. Retrieved October 7, 2006, from http://www.mincom.gov.ma/english/generalities/history/history.html.
34. Ibid.
35. Hourani, op. cit.
36. Ibn Khaldun. (2005) *The muqaddimah: An introduction to history* (Trans. F. Rosenthal). Princeton, NJ: Bollingen Series.
37. Hourani, op. cit.
38. Pawley, D. (1995). Coming up for air in Morocco. *Saudi Aramco World* 46(1), 8–13. Retrieved October 7, 2006, from http://www.saudiaramcoworld.com/issue/199501/coming.up.for.air.in.morocco.htm.
39. Tremlett, G. (2004, January 31). Morocco boosts women's rights. *The Guardian*. Retrieved October 7, 2006, from http://www.guardian.co.uk/international/story/0,3604,1127437,00.html.
40. UNDP Programme on Governance in the Arab Region. (2002). *Gender and citizenship initiative country profile: Morocco*. Retrieved October 7, 2006, from http://gender.pogar.org/countries/gender.asp?cid=12.
41. UNAIDS, op. cit.
42. U.S. State Department. (2006). *Morocco: Background note*. Retrieved September 30, 2006, from http://www.state.gov/r/pa/ei/bgn/5431.htm.
43. Ibid.
44. BBC News. (2005, March 10). *Madrid bombing suspects*. Retrieved September 30, 2006, from http://news.bbc.co.uk/2/hi/europe/3560603.stm.

Notes 263

45. UNDP Programme on Governance in the Arab Region, op. cit.
46. New York Times. (1991, February 4). War in the Gulf: Huge Morocco march supports Iraq in war. *New York Times*. Retrieved September 30, 2006, from http://www.nytimes.com.
47. Nichani, R. (2002). *Political parties, justice systems and the poor: The experience of the Arab states*. United Nations Development Programme Human Development Report Office Occasional Paper. Retrieved September 30, 2006, from http://hdr.undp.org/docs/publications/background_papers/2002/Richani_2002.pdf.
48. Campbell, P. J. (2003). Morocco in transition: Overcoming the democracy and human rights legacy of King Hassan II. *African Studies Quarterly* 7(1), 38–58. Retrieved September 30, 2006, from http://www.africa.ufl.edu/asq/v7/v7i1a3.htm.
49. U.S. Census Bureau (n.d.). *Population summary for Morocco*. Retrieved September 30, 2006, from http://www.census.gov/cgi-bin/ipc/idbsum.pl?cty=MO.
50. Ibid.
51. United Nations Development Programme, op. cit.
52. For more information go to SIDA Maroc (Association Marocaine des Jeunes Contre le SIDA) in English at http://www.sidamaroc.org/.
53. The Global Fund to Fight AIDS, Tuberculosis, and Malaria, op. cit.
54. Kingdom of Morocco, op. cit.
55. UNAIDS & WHO. (2006). *2006 report on the global AIDS epidemic*. Geneva: UNAIDS.
56. UNDP Programme on Governance in the Arab Region, op. cit.
57. Obermeyer, op. cit.
58. Gray, op. cit.
59. Obermeyer, op. cit.
60. Zuhur, S. (2005). *Gender, sexuality and the criminal laws in the Middle East and North Africa: A comparative study*. Istanbul, Turkey: Women for Women's Human Rights.
61. Inter Parliamentary Union. (n.d.). *Morocco*. Parliamentary campaign to stop violence against women, female genital mutilation: Legislative provisions. Retrieved September 30, 2006, from http://www.ipu.org/wmn-e/fgm-prov-m.htm.
62. Policy Project, op. cit.
63. Mellouk, O. (2006). *HIV prevention challenges facing MSM in the Middle East and North Africa: An NGO perspective*. XVI International AIDS Conference, Toronto, Canada. Retrieved September 30, 2006, from http://www.aids2006.org/Web/THBS0204.ppt#15.
64. D'Adesky, A.-C. (2004). *Moving mountains: The race to treat global AIDS*. New York: Verso.
65. Royaume du Maroc, Ministère de la Santé. (2006). *Third annual report: Appui de la mise en œuvre du plan stratégique de lutte national contre le SIDA*. Retrieved December 23, 2007, from http://www.programmesida.org.ma/dwn/Pulications/Rapport%20Annuel%20Mars%202005-Avril%202006.pdf.
66. The Global Fund to Fight AIDS, Tuberculosis, and Malaria, op. cit.
67. Royaume du Maroc, Ministère de la Santé, op. cit.
68. Zuhur, op. cit.
69. International HIV/AIDS Alliance. (2005). *Rapport de synthèse: Analyse rapide de situation des hommes ayant des relations sexuelles avec des hommes dans les pays du Maghreb et au Liban*. USAID and International HIV/AIDS Alliance.

264 Notes

70. Mellouk, O., op. cit.
71. Mellouk, O., op. cit.
72. International HIV/AIDS Alliance, op. cit.
73. D'Adesky, op. cit.
74. Francoeur, R. T., & Noonan, R. J. (eds.) (2001). *The international encyclopedia of sexuality*. New York: Continuum International.
75. Manhart, L. E., Dialmy, A., Ryan, C. A., & Mahjour, J. (2000). Sexually transmitted diseases in Morocco : Gender influences on prevention and health-care seeking behaviour. *Social Science and Medicine* 50(10), 1369–83.
76. Policy Project, op. cit.
77. Schoepf, B. G. (2001). International AIDS research in anthropology: Taking a critical perspective on the crisis. *Annual Review of Anthropology* 30, 335–61.
78. UNESCO/UNAIDS. (2001). A cultural approach to HIV/AIDS prevention and care: Culturally appropriate information/education/communication elaboration of delivery and care. *Methodological Handbooks, Special Series, Division of Cultural Policies, UNESCO, No. 1, 2001* (p. 25). Retrieved May 15, 2003, from http://unesdoc.unesco.org/images/0012/001255/125589e.pdf.
79. Piot, P. (2007). *To reduce HIV/AIDS globally, South Africa should succeed.* National AIDS Conference, Durban, South Africa, 5 June. Retrieved June 10, 2007, from http://data.unaids.org/pub/SpeechEXD/2007/20070605_sp_south%20africa_en.pdf.
80. UNAIDS. (2006). *Report on the global AIDS epidemic.* Retrieved September 1, 2006, from http://www.unaids.org/en/HIV_data/2006GlobalReport/default.asp.
81. Ibid.
82. Ibid.
83. UNFPA/UNAIDS/UNIFEM. (2004). *Women and AIDS: Confronting the crisis.* Retrieved May 30, 2007, from http://www.unfpa.org/hiv/women/report/chapter1.html.
84. UNAIDS, op. cit.
85. Epstein, B. G. (2004). The demographic impact of HIV/AIDS. In M. Haacker, *The Macroeconomics of HIV/AIDS* (pp. 1–40). Washington, DC: International Monetary Fund.
86. UNESCO/UNAIDS, op. cit.
87. Scalway, T. (2001). *Young men and HIV: Culture, poverty, and sexual risk.* Panos, London, 2001. Retrieved July 30, 2003, from http://www.panos.org.uk/resources/reportdetails.asp?id=1021.
88. UNESCO/UNAIDS, op. cit.
89. UNAIDS, op. cit.
90. National Intelligence Council. (2002). The next wave of HIV/AIDS: Nigeria, Ethiopia, Russia, India, and China, *Intelligence Community Assessment 2002–04 D*, September, 2002. Retrieved May 5, 2003, from http://www.fas.org/irp/nic/hiv-aids.html .
91. Taylor, J. J. (2006). Assisting or compromising intervention? The concept of "culture" in biomedical and social research on HIV/AIDS. *Social Science and Medicine* 64(4), 965–75.
92. United Nations General Assembly. (2006). *Uniting the world against AIDS.* Draft political declaration on high level meeting on HIV/AIDS, 31 May–2 June. Retrieved May 30, 2007, from http://www.un.org/ga/aidsmeeting2006/declaration.htm
93. Schaller, M., & Crandal, C. S. (eds.) (2004). *The psychological foundations of culture.* Mahwah, NJ: Lawrence Erlbaum Associates.

Notes 265

94. Parker, R. (2001). Sexuality, culture, and power in HIV/AIDS research. *Annual Review of Anthropology* 30, 163–79.
95. Singhal, A., & Rogers, E. M. (2003). *Combating AIDS: Communications strategies in action.* New Delhi: Sage Publications.
96. Garcia Abreu, A., Noguer, I., & Cowgill, K. (2003). *HIV/AIDS in Latin American countries: The challenge ahead.* Washington, DC: The World Bank.
97. Parker, op. cit.
98. Yinhe, L. (2001). Suppressing information in a country on the verge of an epidemic. *Media and sexuality: Between sensationalism and censorship.* Proceedings of the Sixth International Congress on AIDS in Asia and the Pacific, Melbourne, Australia, October 8, 2001.
99. McNeil, D. (2003). Sexy and smart: One sector that won't be left behind . . . *Japan, Inc.*, September, 2003. http://www.findarticles.com/p/articles/mi_m0NTN/is_47/ai_108722615/print.
100. Japan must fight HIV spread: Expert. (2005, July 22). *Japan Times.* Retrieved September 29, 2007, from http://search.japantimes.co.jp/print/news/nn07-2005/nn20050722b5.htm.
101. American Psychological Association. (n.d.). *Psychosocial issues over the spectrum of HIV disease: Psychosocial issues related to HIV/AIDS stigma.* APA Public Interest Directorate: Major HIV/AIDS topics and issues. Retrieved September 15, 2005, from http://www.apa.org/pi/aids/major.html#psychosocial.
102. Kidd, R., & Clay, S. (2003). *Understanding and challenging HIV stigma: Toolkit for action.* Washington, DC: Change Project.
103. American Psychological Association, op. cit.
104. McKee, N., Bertrand, J. T., & Becker-Benton, A. (2004). *Strategic communication in the HIV/AIDS epidemic.* New Delhi: Sage Publications.
105. Cogan, J., & Herek, G. (1998). In Raymond A. Smith (ed.), *The Encyclopedia of AIDS: A social, political, cultural, and scientific record of the AIDS epidemic.* Chicago: Fitzroy Dearborn Publishers.
106. Luchetta, T. (1999). Relationships between homophobia, HIV/AIDS stigma, and HIV/AIDS knowledge. In L. Pardie & T. Luchetta (eds.), *The construction of attitudes toward lesbians and gay men.* Binghamton, NY: The Haworth Press.
107. D'Adesky, op. cit.
108. D'Adesky, op. cit.
109. UNICEF. (2001). *Stigma, HIV/AIDS and mother-to-child transmission: A pilot study in Zambia, India, Ukraine, and Burkina Faso.* Retrieved September 15, 2007, from http://www.unicef.org/aids/aids_panosreportBS.pdf.
110. Kidd, R., & Clay, S., op. cit.
111. Pryor, J. B., Reeder G. D., & Landau, S., op. cit.
112. Pryor, J. B., Reeder G. D., Yeadon, C. & Hesson-McIness, M. (2004). A dual-process model of model of reactions to perceived stigma. *Journal of Personality and Social Psychology* 87(4), 436–52.
113. Luchetta, T. (1999). Relationships between homophobia, HIV/AIDS stigma, and HIV/AIDS knowledge. In L. Pardie & T. Luchetta (eds.), *The construction of attitudes toward lesbians and gay men.* Binghamton, NY: The Haworth Press.
114. Centers for Disease Control. (2005). *HIV/AIDS among men who have sex with men.* CDC. Retrieved October 27, 2005, from www.cdc.gov/hiv.
115. Silverman, M. (1998). In Raymond A. Smith (ed.), *The Encyclopedia of AIDS: A social, political, cultural, and scientific record of the AIDS epidemic.* Chicago: Fitzroy Dearborn Publishers.

266 Notes

116. Aggelton, P., & Parker, R. (2002). *A conceptual framework and basis for action: HIV/AIDS stigma and discrimination* (rev. ed.). UNAIDS (November). Retrieved April 30, 2007, from http://www.popcouncil.org/pdfs/horizons/sdcncptlfrmwrk.pdf.

117. Kidd, R., & Clay, S., op. cit.

118. Rabasca, L. (1998). Psychological barriers keep women from seeking care. *APA Monitor* 29(8). Retrieved September 15, 2005, from http://www.apa.org/monitor/aug98/hiv.html.

119. Scheer, R. (2005, June 6). A hypocritical church's sex lessons. *The Nation.* Retrieved October 31, 2005, from http://www.thenation.com/doc/20050606/scheer0524.

120. See the official proclamations at www.vatican.va.

121. Burke, K. (2003, April 2). Vatican's last word on safe sex—no. *Sydney Morning Herald.* Retrieved May 15, 2003, from http://www.smh.com.au/articles/2003/04/01/1048962756432.html.

122. International Planned Parenthood Federation at: www.ippfwhr.org.

123. Planned Parenthood Federation of America. (2003). *George W. Bush's war on women: A pernicious web.* Planned Parenthood Federation of America, January 14, 2003. Retrieved July 30, 2007, from http://www.plannedparenthood.org/news-articles-press/politics-policy-issues/public-affairs/George-W-Bushs-War-on-Women-A-Pernicious-Web.htm.

124. Northrup, N. (2003). Bush Administration urged to implement HIV/AIDS legislation without strings attached. *PLANetWire,* Center for Reproductive Rights, May 5, 2003. Retrieved July 30, 2003, from http://www.planetwire.org/details/4039.

125. Cohen, S. (2003). Bush Administration isolates US at international meeting to promote Cairo Agenda. *Guttmacher Report on Public Policy* 6(1), March, 2003. http://www.guttmacher.org/pubs/tgr/06/1/gr060103.html.

126. Anwar Ibrahim, former deputy prime minister of Malaysia, was released following the decision of an appeals court in 2004.

127. *Time Asia.* (2000, September 26). Homosexuality is a crime worse than murder: An interview with Malaysia's morality police. *Time Asia* Web exclusive. Retrieved August 20, 2006, from http://www.time.com/time/asia/features/interviews/2000/09/26/int.malay.gay2.html.

128. Internet Movie Database (2000). *Plot summary for Bukak Api.* Retrieved August 20, 2006, from http://www.imdb.com/title/tt0269027/plotsummary.

129. Crooks, R., & Barr, K. (1996). *Our sexuality.* Pacific Grove, CA: Brooks/Cole.

130. Watstein, S. B., & Stratton, S. E. (eds.) (2003). *The encyclopedia of HIV/AIDS.* New York: Facts on File, Inc.

131. Auvert, B., Taljaard, D., Lagarde, E., Sobngwi-Tambekou, J., Sitta, R., & Puren, A. (2005). Randomized, controlled intervention trial of male circumcision for reduction of HIV infection risk: The ANRS 1265 trial. *PloS Med* 2(11), e298. Retrieved January 27, 2007, from http://www.pubmedcentral.nih.gov/articlerender.fcgi?artid=1262556. Halperin, D. T., & Bailey, R. C. (1999). Male circumcision and HIV infection: 10 years and counting. *Lancet* 354(9192), 1813–15.

132. Schoofs, M., Lueck, S., & Phillips, M. M. (2005). Study says circumcision reduces AIDS risk by 70%. Findings from South Africa may offer powerful way to cut AIDS transmission. *The Wall Street Journal,* 5 July 2005, p. A1.

133. Paterson, G. (n.d.). *The church, AIDS, and stigma.* Ecumenical Advocacy Alliance, Switzerland. Retrieved April 30, 2003, from http://www.e-alliance.ch/media/media-3166.doc.

Notes   267

134. Barnett, T., & Whiteside, A. (2002). *AIDS in the twenty-first century: Disease and globalization.* New York: Palgrave Macmillan.
135. Oster, E. (2005). *HIV and sexual behaviour change: Why not Africa?* Chicago University and NBER Working Paper, April 17.
136. Reif, S., Lowe Geonnotti, K., & Whetten, K. (2006). HIV infection and AIDS in the Deep South. *American Journal of Public Health* 96(6), 970–73.
137. Messina, S. (1994). *A youth leader's guide to building cultural competence.* Advocates for youth, Washington, DC. Retrieved April 30, 2003, from http://www.advocatesforyouth.org/publications/guide/.
138. Hall, E. T. (1990 reissue). *The silent language.* New York: Anchor Books.
139. Hofstede, G., & Bond, M. H. (1988). The Confucian connection: From cultural roots to economic growth. *Organizational Dynamics* 16(4), 4–21.
140. Cournos, F., & Wainburg, M. L. (2001). HIV fact sheet: Promoting adherence to antiretroviral therapy. *Mental health treatment issues.* Retrieved May 30, 2003, from http://www.columbia.edu/~fc15/adherence.pdf.
141. Mascolini, M. (2002). *Barcelona 2002 (Parts I and II): The age of access begins* (conference report). International AIDS Society, August 14, 2002. Retrieved April 30, 2007, from http://www.ias.se/article/show.asp?article=1596.
142. Netherlands Development Assistance Research Council Round Table, preparers: Madeleen Wegelin and Françoise Jenniskens. (2001). *Research needs and priorities with respect to social and cultural aspects of HIV/AIDS.* Report on the Netherlands Development Assistance Research Council Round Table, Royal Tropical Institute, Amsterdam, The Netherlands, September 10 and 11, 2001. Retrieved June 1, 2003, from http://www.kit.nl/health/assets/images/finalreportRAWOO.doc.
143. Hernandez, E. E. H., Zepeda, S. J. Z., & Moncada, D. M. (2002). *Culturally specific peer support model addresses barriers to care, treatment adherence, and acculturation concerns in HIV positive Latino immigrants in San Francisco.* Conference abstract: XIV International AIDS Conference, San Francisco AIDS Foundation, San Francisco. Retrieved April 30, 2007, from http://www.ias.se.
144. Fredriksson, J., & Kanabus, A. (2003). HIV and AIDS in Botswana. *Avert.org* News, 2003. Retrieved May 15, 2007, from http://www.avert.org/aids-botswana.htm.
145. Fanon, F. (1965). *A dying colonialism.* London: Grove Press.
146. Campbell, C. (2003). *Letting them die: Why HIV/AIDS prevention programmes fail.* Oxford: James Currey.
147. Uganda Ministry of Health and IRD/Macro Systems, Inc. 1988/1989. (1989). Uganda demographic and health survey. In G. A. O'Sullivan, J. A. Yonkler, W. Morgan, & A. P. Merritt, A.P. (2003, March), *A field guide to designing a health communication strategy.* Baltimore: Johns Hopkins Bloomberg School of Public Health/Center for Communication Programs.
148. Scalway, op. cit.
149. United Nations. (2002). *Focus on the virgin myth and HIV/AIDS.* Integrated regional information network, April 25, 2002. Retrieved April 30, 2003, from http://www.aegis.com/news/irin/2002/IR020406.html.
150. Bogart, L., & Thorburn, S. (2005). Are HIV conspiracy beliefs a barrier to prevention among African Americans? *Journal of Acquired Immune Deficiency Syndromes* 38(2), 213–18.
151. Campbell, op. cit.
152. Campbell, op. cit.
153. Balk, D., & Lahiri, S. (1997). Awareness and knowledge of AIDS among Indian women from 13 states. *Health Transition Review,* Supplement to

268 Notes

Volume 7, 1997. Retrieved June 30, 2003, from http://htc.anu.edu.au/pdfs/Balk1a.pdf.

154. Reif, S., Lowe Geonnotti, K., & Whetten, K. (2006). HIV infection and AIDS in the Deep South. *American Journal of Public Health* 96(6), 970–73.

155. Gayle, H. D. (2003). *The global epidemiology of HIV/AIDS.* International AIDS Society, June 17, 2003. Retrieved June 30, 2003, from http://www.ias.se/article/show.asp?article=2210.

156. Lindsey, D. (2001). UN commits to AIDS reduction. Salon.com, June 28, 2001. Retrieved May 15, 2006, from http://dir.salon.com/news/feature/2001/06/28/aids/index.html.

157. UNAIDS. (2004). *AIDS epidemic update, sub-Saharan Africa.* December. Retrieved March 10, 2008, from http://www.unaids.org.

158. UNAIDS. (2001). *I Care . . . Do you? Men, culture, and HIV/AIDS.* Campaign documents, UNAIDS World AIDS Campaign 2001. Retrieved March 10, 2008, from http://www.thebody.com/unaids/wac/culture.html.

159. UNAIDS. (2004). *AIDS epidemic update.* December. Retrieved August 7, 2006, from http://www.unaids.org.

160. World Economic Forum. (2005). *Partnering for success: Business perspectives on multistakeholder partnerships.* Retrieved August 20, 2006, from http://www.weforum.org/pdf/ppp.pdf#search=%22Partnering%20for%20success%20%3A%20Business%20perspectives%20on%20multistakeholder%20partnerships%22.

161. Centers for Disease Control, op. cit.

162. UNAIDS. (2001). *Men, culture, and HIV/AIDS.* World AIDS Campaign 2001 documents (undated, 2001). Retrieved May 15, 2006, from http://www.thebody.com/unaids/wac/culture.html.

163. Barnett, T., & Whiteside, A., op. cit.

164. Narayanaswamy, L., & Sever, C. (2004). *Security and gender-based violence: What is the significance for development interventions?* BRIDGE Development-Gender. Retrieved September 15, 2006, from http://www.bridge.ids.ac.uk/docs/security-briefing.doc.

165. Elbe, S. (2003). *Strategic implications of HIV/AIDS.* Adelphi Paper 357. London: Oxford University Press.

166. UNFPA. (1999). *Empowering women.* UNFPA population issues. Retrieved August 9, 2006, from http://www.unfpa.org/6billion/populationissues/empower.htm.

167. UNICEF. (2005). *Female genital mutilation/cutting: A statistical exploration.* Retrieved August 9, 2006, from http://www.unicef.org/publications/files/FGM-C_final_10_October.pdf.

168. UNICEF, op. cit.

169. UNFPA, op. cit.

170. U.S. Department of State. (2001). *Nigeria: Report on female genital mutilation or female genital cutting.* Office of the Senior Coordinator of International Women's Issues. Retrieved August 9, 2006, from http://www.state.gov/g/wi/rls/rep/crfgm/.

171. Brady, M. (1999). Female genital mutilation: Complications and risk of HIV transmission. *AIDS Patient Care and STDs* 13(12), 709–16.

172. UNAIDS, op. cit.

173. Campbell, op. cit.

174. UNAIDS, op. cit.

175. Ahmed, S., & Khan, S. (2002). *Female partners of MSM.* Pukaar, April 2002. Retrieved October 30, 2005, from http://www.nfi.net.

176. Scalway, op. cit.

Notes 269

177. Campbell, op. cit.
178. UNDP Thailand. (2004). *Thailand's response to HIV/AIDS: Problems and challenges*. Retrieved 10 May, 2006, from http://www.undp.or.th/docs/HIV_AIDS_FullReport_ENG.pdf.
179. YouAndAIDS. (2000). *Thailand at a glance: HIV situation*. Retrieved July 8, 2006, from http://www.youandaids.org/Asia%20Pacific%20at%20a%20Glance/Thailand/index.asp.
180. Amnesty International. (2004). *Women, HIV/AIDS and human rights*. 24 November, 2004. Retrieved October 5, 2005, from http://www.web.amnesty.org/library/Index/ENGACT770842004.
181. Amnesty International, op. cit.
182. Gordon, P., & Crehan, K. (1999). *Dying of sadness: Gender, sexual violence and the HIV epidemic*. HIV and Development Programme, UNDP. Retrieved August 9, 2006, from http://www.undp.org/hiv/publications/gender/violence.htm.
183. Amnesty International, op. cit.
184. Global HIV Prevention Working Group. (2003). *Access to HIV prevention: Closing the gap* (May). Bill & Melinda Gates Foundation. Retrieved 30 April, 2006, from http://www.eldis.org/static/DOC12050.htm.
185. World Bank. (1997). *Confronting AIDS: Public priorities in a global epidemic*. Retrieved May 27, 2007, from http://www.worldbank.org/aids-econ/confront/confrontfull/.
186. Hope, Sr., R. H. (1999). The socio-economic context of AIDS in Africa: A review. In R. H. Hope, Sr. (ed.), *AIDS and development in Africa: A social science perspective*. Binghamton, NY: Haworth Press.
187. UNAIDS, op. cit.
188. Sen, A. (1998). Preface. In P. Farmer, *Pathologies of power: Health, human rights, and the new war on the poor*. Berkeley, CA: University of California Press.
189. D'Adesky, op. cit.
190. Garcia Abreu, A., Noguer I., & Cowgill, K., op. cit.
191. Galvan, A., Hare T., Voss, H., Glover, G., & Casey, B. J. (2007). Risk-taking and the adolescent brain: Who is at risk? *Developmental Science* 10(2), F8–F14.
192. McKee, N., Bertrand, J. T., & Becker-Benton, A. (2004). *Strategic communication in the HIV/AIDS epidemic*. New Delhi: Sage Publications.
193. UNICEF (n.d.). *HIV/AIDS and children: Prevention among young people*. Retrieved September 1, 2006, from http://www.unicef.org/aids/index_preventionyoung.html.
194. Kanabus, A. (2003). *HIV and AIDS in high income countries*. UNAIDS Fact Sheet 2000 High income countries. Avert.org. Retrieved 15 June, 2007, from http://www.avert.org/aidshighincome.htm.
195. UNAIDS, op. cit.
196. Centers for Disease Control, op. cit.
197. D'Adesky, A.-C. (2004). *Moving mountains: The race to treat global AIDS*. New York: Verso.
198. Centers for Disease Control, op. cit.
199. UNAIDS. (2001). *Men who have sex with men, and HIV/AIDS*. World AIDS campaign, 2001 documents (undated, 2001). Retrieved May 30, 2006, from http://www.thebody.com/unaids/wac/msm.html.
200. Lindsey, op. cit.
201. Amnesty International. (2001). *Crimes of hate, conspiracy of silence*. Amnesty International Library document 40/016/2001, June 22, 2001. Retrieved May 15, 2006, from http://web.amnesty.org/library/index/engact400162001.

270 *Notes*

202. Humphreys, B. (2003). *Briefing on Islam and homosexuality.* Gay and Lesbian Humanist Association (March 30). Retrieved May 15, 2006, from http://www.galha.org/briefing/2003_03.html.
203. Amnesty International. (2005). *Stonewalled: Police abuse against gay, lesbian, bisexual and transgender people in the USA.* Retrieved October 17, 2005, from http://www.amnestyusa.org/outfront/stonewalled/report.pdf.
204. UNAIDS, op. cit.
205. Farmer, P. (2002). *Pathologies of power: Health, human rights, and the new war on the poor.* Berkeley, CA: University of California Press.
206. Centers for Disease Control, op. cit.
207. Aegis-UNAIDS. (2006). *UNAIDS statement on access to HIV treatment, prevention, and care in prison settings.* Retrieved September 1, 2006, from http://www.aegis.org/news/UNAIDS/2006/UN060805.html.
208. National Intelligence Council, op. cit.
209. Scalway, op. cit.
210. Garcia Abreu, A., Noguer I., & Cowgill, K., op. cit.
211. National Intelligence Council, op. cit.
212. International HIV/AIDS Alliance (n.d.). *Alliance's national anti-retroviral treatment work threatened by Ukraine committee move to ban methadone.* Latest news International HIV/AIDS Alliance. Retrieved September 29, 2005, from http://synkronweb.aidsalliance.org/sw29122.asp.
213. Jenkins, op. cit.
214. Kanabus, op. cit.
215. U.S. Department of Health and Human Services. (2002). Further details of heterosexual exposure of HIV and AIDS (table). *HIV/AIDS Surveillance Report,* U.S. HIV and AIDS cases reported through December 2001, End Year Edition Vol. 13 , No.2. Retrieved May 30, 2003, from http://www.cdc.gov/hiv/stats/hasrlink.htm.
216. Jenkins, op. cit.
217. Elbe, op. cit.
218. Scalway, op. cit.
219. Elbe, op. cit.
220. Elbe, op. cit.
221. Scalway, op. cit.
222. Elbe, op. cit.
223. Cheek, R. (2001). Playing God with HIV: Rationing HIV treatment in South Africa. *African Security Review.* In Stefan Elbe (2003), *Strategic implications of HIV/AIDS.* Adelphi Paper 357. London: Oxford University Press.
224. UNESCO/UNAIDS, op. cit.
225. Anonymous. (2003, May 21). Philippines proud of its low infection rate, number of cases. *San Francisco Chronicle.* Retrieved May 15, 2006, from http://www.aegis.com/news/sc/2003/SC030519.html.
226. Flamm, M. (2003). Exploited, not educated: Trafficking of women and children in South East Asia. *United Nations Chronicle,* 3 February. Retrieved June 21, 2006, from http://www.un.org/Pubs/chronicle/2003/issue2/0203p34.html.
227. United Nations Office on Drugs and Crime. (2006). *Trafficking in persons: Global patterns.* Retrieved June 21, 2006, from http://www.unodc.org/pdf/traffickinginpersons_report_2006ver2.pdf.
228. Quitkin, M. (2006). Risky business. *Business and AIDS* (Winter). Retrieved June 21, 2006, from http://www.businessfightsaids.org/atf/cf/<4AF0E874-E9A0-4D86-BA28-96C3BC31180A>/W06RiskyBusinessPages.pdf.
229. Ainsworth, M., Beyrer, C., & Soucat, A. (2003). AIDS and public policy . . . The lessons and challenges of "success" in Thailand. *Health Policy* 64(1), 13–37.

Notes 271

230. Dworkin, S. L., & Ehrhardt, A. A. (2007). Going beyond ABC to include GEM: Critical reflections on progress in the HIV/AIDS epidemic. *American Journal of Public Health* 97(1), 13–18.
231. UNESCO/UNAIDS, op. cit.
232. Narayanaswamy, L., & Sever, C. (2004). *Security and gender-based violence: What is the significance for development interventions?* BRIDGE Development-Gender. Retrieved September 15, 2006, from http://www.bridge.ids.ac.uk/docs/security-briefing.doc
233. Gordon, P., & Crehan, op. cit.
234. Goldstein, D. E. (2004). *Once upon a virus: AIDS legends and vernacular risk perception.* Logan, UT: Utah University Press.
235. UNESCO/UNAIDS, op. cit.
236. Scalway, op. cit.
237. Scalway, op. cit.
238. Kaiser Family Foundation. (2005). *Media leaders commit resources to addressing HIV/AIDS in India.* News release, Heroes Project, January 6. Retrieved September 1, 2006, from http://www.kff.org/hivaids/phip010605nr.cfm.
239. Balk, D., & Lahiri, S. (1997). Awareness and knowledge of AIDS among Indian women from 13 states. *Health Transition Review*, Supplement to Volume 7. Retrieved June 30, 2003, from http://htc.anu.edu.au/pdfs/Balk1a.pdf.
240. Transatlantic Partners Against AIDS. (2005). *Survey shows Russians want greater media attention and education on HIV/AIDS.* News Release, STOP-SPID, October 27. Retrieved September 1, 2006, from http://www.kff.org/entpartnerships/russia/phip102705nr.cfm.
241. Scalway, op. cit.
242. Monzon, O. T., & Sciortino, R. (2002). Media and sexuality: Between sensationalism and censorship. Preface and introduction to proceedings of the Sixth International Congress on AIDS in Asia and the Pacific, Melbourne, Australia, October 8, 2001. Retrieved May 30, 2003, from http://www.rockmekong.org/pubs/lab-pubs/media%20%20sexuality.pdf.
243. Human Rights Watch. (2005). *Restrictions on AIDS activists in China.* New York: Human Rights Watch. Retrieved June 21, 2006, from http://hrw.org/reports/2005/china0605/.
244. Kakuchi S. (2005). HIV breeds on complacent attitudes among youth. *Inter Press Service News Agency*, November 30. Retrieved June 21, 2006, from http://www.ipsnews.net/news.asp?idnews=31235.
245. Lindsey, op. cit.
246. Rafique, E. M. (2002). A company's policy on HIV/AIDS in the workplace. *Indian Journal of Medical Ethics*, October. Retrieved June 21, 2006, from http://issuesinmedicalethics.org/104di094.html.
247. Baldrini, F., & Trimble, C. (2006). *Beyond big business: Are your distributors and suppliers ready to fight AIDS?* World Economic Forum. Retrieved June 21, 2006, from http://www.weforum.org/pdf/Business_AIDS.pdf.
248. UNAIDS. (2002). *Report on the global HIV/AIDS epidemic. Focus: AIDS and the world of work.* UNAIDS Update, July 2002. Retrieved May 30, 2003, from http://libdoc.who.int/unaids/2002/global_report_2002.pdf .

NOTES TO CASE STUDY 2

1. World Bank. (2005). *HIV/AIDS in Latin America and the Caribbean.* Retrieved October 2, 2006, from http://web.worldbank.org/WBSITE/EXTERNAL/COUNTRIES/LACEXT/EXTLACREGTOPHEANUT-

272 *Notes*

POP/EXTLACREGTOPHIVAIDS/0,,contentMDK:20560003~menuPK:841626~pagePK:34004173~piPK:34003707~theSitePK:841609,00.html. Sekles, F. (2005). *Au Brésil, les politiques en matière de SIDA lient étroitement la prévention et le traitement.* Population Reference Bureau (March). Retrieved October 2, 2006, from http://www.prb.org/FrenchTemplate.cfm?Section=Accueil&template=/ContentManagement/ContentDisplay.cfm&ContentID=12581.

2. World Health Organization. (2004). *Treatment works: Scaling up antiretroviral treatment.* Retrieved October 2, 2006, from http://www.who.int/3by5/en/treatmentworks.pdf.

3. World Bank.(2006). *Brazil country brief,* July. Retrieved October 2, 2006 from http://web.worldbank.org/WBSITE/EXTERNAL/COUNTRIES/LACEXT/BRAZILEXTN/0,,menuPK:322351~pagePK:141132~piPK:141107~theSitePK:322341,00.html.

4. World Health Organization. (2005). *Developing countries and free access fact sheet,* December. Retrieved October 2, 2006, from http://www.who.int/hiv/countries_freeaccess.pdf.

5. Nogueira, S. A., Abreu, T. F., Pinheiro, T. C., Oliveira, R. H., Araujo, L., et al. (2001). Successful prevention of HIV transmission from mother to infant in Brazil using a multidisciplinary team approach. *Brazilian Journal of Infectious Diseases, 5,* 78–86. Retrieved October 2, 2006, from http://www.scielo.br/scielo.php?pid=S1413–86702001000200006&script=sci_arttext.

6. Singhal, A., & Rogers, E. M. (2003). *Combating AIDS: Communications strategies in action.* New Delhi: Sage Publications.

7. Nogueira, S. A., Abreu, T. F., Pinheiro, T. C., Oliveira, R. H., Araujo, L., et al., op. cit.

8. UNAIDS/WHO. (2004). *HIV/AIDS epidemic update.* Geneva: UNAIDS.

9. World Bank, op. cit.

10. Ministerio da Saude Programa Nacional de MST e AIDS. (2004). *Boletim Epidemiologico: AIDS et DST,* Ano I, no. 1. Retrieved October 2, 2006, from http://www.aids.gov.br/data/documents/storedDocuments/%7BB8EF5DAF-23AE-4891-AD36–1903553A3174%7D/%7B4DCE69E5-BE5F-43EC-A715-C593FC6B21C8%7D/boletim_marco_2005.pdf.

11. Okie, S. (2006). Fighting HIV—lessons from Brazil. *New England Journal of Medicine, 354*(19), 1977–81. Retrieved October 30, 2006, from http://content.nejm.org/cgi/reprint/354/19/1977.pdf.

12. World Bank, op. cit.

13. United Nations Development Programme. (2006). *Adult literacy rate per cent.* Human development reports. Retrieved September 30, 2006, from http://hdr.undp.org/statistics/data/indicators.cfm?x=3&y=1&z=1.

14. United Nations Development Programme. (2005). Brazil: Country data. *Human Development report 2005.* Retrieved September 30, 2006, from http://hdr.undp.org/statistics/data/countries.cfm?c=BRA.

15. United Nations Development Programme. (2005). Commitment to health: Resources, access and services (table). *Human development report.* Retrieved September 30, 2006, from http://hdr.undp.org/statistics/data/pdf/hdr05_table_6.pdf.

16. UNAIDS/WHO. (2007). *AIDS epidemic update.* Retrieved December 13, 2007, from http://www.unaids.org/en/KnowledgeCentre/HIVData/EpiUpdate/EpiUpdArchive/2007default.asp

17. United Nations Development Programme. (2005). *Human development report 2005.* Retrieved September 30, 2006, from http://hdr.undp.org/reports/global/2005/.

18. World Bank, op. cit.

Notes 273

19. Messias, E. (2003). Income inequality, illiteracy rate, and life expectancy in Brazil. *American Journal of Public Health* 93(208), 1294–96. Retrieved September 30, 2006, from http://www.ajph.org/cgi/content/full/93/8/1294.
20. United Nations Development Programme. (2005). Brazil: Country data. *Human Development report 2005*. Retrieved September 30, 2006, from http://hdr.undp.org/statistics/data/countries.cfm?c=BRA. .
21. National Geographic. (2004). *People and places: Brazil*. Retrieved October 23, 2006, from http://www3.nationalgeographic.com/places/countries/country_brazil.html.
22. United Nations Habitat. (2001). *Statistical overview: Brazil*. Retrieved September 30, 2006, from http://www.unhabitat.org/categories.asp?catid=140.
23. UNAIDS. (2002). *Illustrative menu of partnership options in Brazil*. Retrieved September 30, 2006, from http://data.unaids.org/Topics/Partnership-Menus/PDF/brazilinserts_en.pdf.
24. The Pew Forum on Religion and Public Life. (2006). *Historical overview of Pentecostalism in Brazil*. Retrieved October 23, 2006, from http://pewforum.org/surveys/pentecostal/countries/?CountryID=29.
25. The Pew Forum on Religion and Public Life. (2006). *Brazil: Religious demographic profile*. Retrieved October 23, 2006, from http://pewforum.org/world-affairs/countries/?CountryID=29.
26. Ministerio do Planejamento Orçamento et Gestão. (2000). Território Brasileiro e povoamiento, *500 anos de povoamento*. Retrieved September 30, 2006, from http://www.ibge.gov.br/brasil500/index2.html.
27. Ministerio do Planejamento Orçamento et Gestão. (2000) Presença negra, *500 anos de povoamento*. Retrieved October 23, 2006, from http://www.ibge.gov.br/brasil500/index2.html.
28. Ministerio do Planejamento Orçamento et Gestão. (2000). População Escrava no Brasil, *500 anos de povoamento*. Retrieved October 23, 2006, from http://www.ibge.gov.br/brasil500/index2.html.
29. Secretaría de MERCOSUR (n.d.). *Antecedentes del MERCOSUR*. Retrieved October 23, 2006, from http://www.mercosur.int/msweb/principal/contenido.asp.
30. International Trade Administration. (1999). *Assistant secretarial business development mission*. Retrieved October 23, 2006, from http://www.ita.doc.gov/doctm/mercosur.html.
31. For more information go to the Brazilian government National STD and AIDS Program site, available partially in English, French, Russian, and Spanish and completely in Portuguese (http://www.aids.gov.br).
32. UNAIDS. (2006). *Fact sheet: Latin America*. Retrieved October 30, 2006, from http://www.unaids.org.
33. UNAIDS. (2006). *2006 report on the global AIDS epidemic*. Geneva: UNAIDS.
34. Ibid.
35. UNAIDS/WHO. (2007). *AIDS epidemic update*. Retrieved December 13, 2007, from http://www.unaids.org/en/KnowledgeCentre/HIVData/EpiUpdate/EpiUpdArchive/2007default.asp.
36. Chamas, C. (2005). Developing innovative capacity in Brazil to meet health needs. In MIHR Report to Commission on intellectual property rights, innovation and public health (2005). *Innovation in developing countries to meet health needs: Experiences of China, Brazil, South Africa, and India* (pp. 75–107). Retrieved October 30, 2006, from http://www.who.int/intellectual-property/studies/MIHR-INNOVATION%20EXPERIENCES%20OF%20South%20Africa,%20CHINA,%20BRAZIL%20AND%20INDIA%20MIHR-CIPIH%20REPORTS%2014–04–05.pdf.

274 *Notes*

37. Ibid.
38. Garcia Abreu, A., Noguer I., & Cowgill, K. (2003). *HIV/AIDS in Latin American countries: The challenge ahead.* Washington, DC: The World Bank.
39. UNAIDS. (2006). *2006 report on the global AIDS epidemic.* Geneva: UNAIDS.
40. Ibid.
41. UNAIDS. (2006). *Fact sheet: Latin America.* Retrieved October 30, 2006, from http://www.unaids.org.
42. Garcia Abreu, A., Noguer I., & Cowgill, op. cit.
43. Nogueira, S. A., Abreu, T. F., Pinheiro, T. C., Oliveira, R. H., & Araujo, L., op. cit.
44. Cowley, G. (2003, July 14). Hope for Africa. *Newsweek.* Retrieved July 15, 2006, from http://www.globalfundatm.org/journalists/inthenews/news_030714.html.
45. World Health Organization. (2004). *Treatment works: Scaling up antiretroviral treatment.* Retrieved October 2, 2006, from http://www.who.int/3by5/en/treatmentworks.pdf.
46. World Health Organization. (2005), op. cit.
47. Cohen, J. (2006). Brazil. Free drugs do not equal quality care. *Science* 313(5786), 486.
48. Gupta, G. R. (2002). How men's power over women fuels the HIV epidemic: It limits women's ability to control sexual interactions. *British Medical Journal* 324(7331), 183–84.
49. Francoeur, R. T., & Noonan, R. J. (eds.) (2001). *The international encyclopedia of sexuality.* New York: Continuum International.
50. Ibid.
51. Pan American Health Organization. (n.d.). *Involving men in sexual and reproductive health: Fact sheet.* Gender and Health Unit, Pan American Health Organization. Retrieved September 30, 2006, from http://www.paho.org/English/AD/GE/MenSRHFactSheet.pdf.
52. Francoeur, R. T., & Noonan, R. J., op. cit.
53. Flood, M. (2003). *Addressing the sexual cultures of heterosexual men: Key strategies in involving men and boys in HIV/AIDS prevention.* United Nations Expert Group Meeting on "The role of men and boys in achieving gender equality," 21–24 October 2003, Brasilia, Brazil.
54. Monteiro de Andrade, L. O., & de H. C. Barreto, I. C. (2004). Health promotion and the unified National Health System. *Ciência & Saúde Coletiva* 9(3), 539–41. Retrieved September 16, 2006, from http://www.scielo.br/scielo.php?pid=S1413–81232004000300007&script=sci_arttext.
55. D'Adesky, A.-C. (2004). *Moving mountains: The race to treat global AIDS.* New York: Verso.
56. http://www.aids.gov.br.
57. *The Economist.* (2005, July 28). Roll out, roll out: What can the world learn from Brazil's experience of dealing with AIDS? Retrieved September 30, 2006, from http://www.economist.com/science/displaystory.cfm?story_id=E1_QNNTQSV.
58. *The Economist,* op. cit.
59. Knowledge @ Wharton. (2006). Generic drugs in Brazil are a hard pill for big pharma to swallow. *Knowledge @ Wharton,* March 1. Retrieved October 30, 2006, from http://knowledge.wharton.upenn.edu/createpdf.cfm?articleid=1338.
60. Chamas, op. cit.
61. Okie, op. cit.
62. Knowledge @ Wharton, op. cit.

Notes 275

63. Chamas, op. cit.
64. BBC News. (2007). *Brazil to break AIDS drug patent*. Retrieved December 20, 2007, from http://news.bbc.co.uk/2/hi/americas/6626073.stm.
65. Press office, National STD and AIDS Programme, Government of Brazil. (2007). *Brazil issues compulsory license for Efavirenz*. Retrieved December 21, 2007, from http://www.aids.gov.br/main.asp?View=%7BE77B47C8%2D3436%2D41E0%2DAC19%2DE1B215447EB9%7D&Team=&params=itemID=%7B9382FADF%2D025E%2D4533%2DB7DA%2D7CF63CA44115%7D%3B&UIPartUID=%7BD90F22DB%2D05D4%2D4644%2DA8F2%2DFAD4803C8898%7D.
66. Press Office, National STD and AIDS Programme, Government of Brazil. (2007). *Brazilian government declares Efavirenz to be of public interest*. Retrieved December 21, 2007, from http://www.essentialdrugs.org/edrug/archive/200704/msg00085.php.
67. D'Adesky, op. cit.
68. World Health Organization. (2005), op. cit.
69. Chamas, op. cit.
70. Homedes, N., & Ugalde, A. (2005). Multisource drug policies in Latin America: Survey of 10 countries. *Bulletin of the World Health Organisation* 83(1). Retrieved October 30, 2006, from http://www.scielosp.org/scielo.php?script=sci_arttext&pid=S0042-96862005000100016.
71. World Health Organization. (2005), op. cit.
72. Oliveira-Cruz, V., Kowalski, J., & McPake, B. (2004). Viewpoint: The Brazilian HIV/AIDS "success story"—can others do it? *Tropical Medicine and International Health* 9(2), 292–97.
73. Garcia Abreu, A., Noguer I., & Cowgill, K., op. cit.
74. *The Economist*. (2005, July 28). Roll out, roll out: What can the world learn from Brazil's experience of dealing with AIDS? Retrieved September 30, 2006, from http://www.economist.com/science/displaystory.cfm?story_id=E1_QNNTQSV.
75. Okie, op. cit.
76. Oliveira-Cruz, V., Kowalski, J., & McPake, B. (2004). Viewpoint: The Brazilian HIV/AIDS "success story"—can others do it? *Tropical Medicine and International Health* 9(2), 292–97.
77. D'Adesky, op. cit.
78. Human Rights Watch. (2004). *Access to condoms and HIV/AIDS information: A global health and human rights concern*. Retrieved December 12, 2007, from http://hrw.org/backgrounder/hivaids/condoms1204/condoms1204.pdf.
79. Medical News Today. (2007, March 16). *Brazil officials say condom distribution effective part of HIV prevention campaign; Church officials criticize policy*. Retrieved January 8, 2008, from http://www.medicalnewstoday.com/articles/65276.php.
80. Bendell, J. (2003). *Waking up to risk: Corporate responses to HIV/AIDS in the workplace*. Geneva: UNRISD & UNAIDS. Retrieved April 30, 2008, http://www.unrisd.org/unrisd/website/document.nsf/d2a23ad2d50cb2a280256eb300385855/8836d5e635b2d234c1256dd6004ee8c1/$FILE/bendell2.pdf.
81. World Economic Forum Global Health Initiative. (2003). *Volkswagen Brazil: HIV/AIDS workplace program overview*. Retrieved September 30, 2006, from http://www.weforum.org/en/initiatives/globalhealth/Case%20Study%20Library/Volkswagen.
82. World Economic Forum Global Health Initiative. (2003). *Case study Nestlé*. Retrieved September 30, 2006, from http://www.weforum.org/pdf/Initiatives/GHI_HIV_CaseStudy_Nestle.pdf.

276 Notes

83. World Economic Forum Global Health Initiative. (2003). *Case study Varig.* Retrieved September 30, 2006, from http://www.weforum.org/pdf/Initiatives/GHI_HIV_CaseStudy_Varig.pdf.
84. *The Economist.* (2005, July 28). Roll out, roll out: What can the world learn from Brazil's experience of dealing with AIDS? Retrieved September 30, 2006, from http://www.economist.com/science/displaystory.cfm?story_id=E1_QNNTQSV.
85. Beyrer, C., Gauri, V., & Vaillancourt, D. (2006). *Evaluation of the World Bank's assistance in responding to the AIDS epidemic: Brazil case study.* Washington, DC: The World Bank.
86. AVSC International and IPPFWHR. (1998). *Male participation in sexual and reproductive health: New paradigms.* Symposium report, October 10–14, 1998, Oaxaca, Mexico. Retrieved September 30, 2006, from http://www.ippfwhr.org/publications/download/monographs/mi_symp_report_e.pdf.
87. UNAIDS. (1999). *Comfort and hope: Six case studies on mobilizing family and community care for and by people with HIV/AIDS.* UNAIDS Best Practice Collection. Retrieved September 30, 2006, from http://data.unaids.org/Publications/IRC-pub01/JC099-Comfort_Hope_en.pdf.
88. Arco Iris (in Portuguese only): http://www.arco-iris.org.br.
89. UNAIDS. (2002). *Illustrative menu of partnership options in Brazil.* Retrieved September 30, 2006, from http://data.unaids.org/Topics/Partnership-Menus/PDF/brazilinserts_en.pdf.
90. D'Adesky, op. cit.
91. Berkman, A., Garcia, J., Munoz-Laboy, M., Paiva, V., & Parker, R. (2005). A critical analysis of the Brazilian response to HIV/AIDS: Lessons learned for controlling and mitigating the epidemic in developing countries. *American Journal of Public Health* 95(7), 1162–72.
92. Oliveira-Cruz, V. (2002). Capacity issues in the Brazilian health system in providing HIV/AIDS prevention and care. *Int Conf AIDS*, July 7–12.
93. Berkman, A., Garcia, J., Munoz-Laboy, M., Paiva, V., & Parker, R., op. cit.
94. de Avila Vitoria, M. A. (2002). Model of success, universal access to treatment in Brazil. *ID21 Insights* Health Issue No. 2, February 2002. Retrieved January 12, 2008, from http://www.id21.org/insights/insights-h02/insights-issh02-art07.html.
95. Beyrer, C., Gauri, V., & Vaillancourt, D. (2006). *Evaluation of the World Bank's assistance in responding to the AIDS epidemic: Brazil case study.* Washington, DC: The World Bank.
96. Ibid.
97. Berkman, A., Garcia, J., Munoz-Laboy, M., Paiva, V., & Parker, R., op. cit.
98. UNAIDS. (2006). *Global facts and figures.* Retrieved January 13, 2008, from http://data.unaids.org/pub/GlobalReport/2006/200605-FS_global-factsfigures_en.pdf.
99. International HIV/AIDS Alliance. (2002). *Improving access to HIV/AIDS-related treatment.* International HIV/AIDS Alliance, London, June, 2002, p. 24. Retrieved January 13, 2008, from http://synkronweb.aidsalliance.org/graphics/secretariat/publications/att0602_Improving_access_to_ARV_treatment.pdf.
100. World Health Organisation (2003). Senegal contains the spread of HIV. *Health a key to prosperity: Success stories in developing countries* (undated, 2003). Retrieved January 15, 2008, from http://www.who.int/inf-new/index.html.
101. UNAIDS. (2000). *Social marketing.* Retrieved January 15, 2008, from http://data.unaids.org/Publications/IRC-pub04/Social_Marketing_en.pdf#search=%22UNAIDS%20(2000).'Social%20marketing'%22.

Notes 277

102. Rhodes, T., & Simic, M. (2005). Transition and the HIV risk environment. *British Medical Journal* 331, 220–23. Rhodes, T., Singer, M., Bourgois, P., Friedman, S. R., & Strathdee, S. A. (2005). The social structural production of HIV risk among injecting drug users. *Social Science and Medicine* 51(5), 1026–44.

103. Nolte, E., & McKee, C. M. (2008). Measuring the health of nations: Updating an earlier analysis. *Health Affairs* 27(1), 58–71.

104. World Health Organization, UNAIDS, UNICEF. (2007). *Towards universal access: Scaling up priority HIV/AIDS interventions in the health sector: Progress report, April, 2007.* Retrieved June 30, 2007, from http://www. who.int/hiv/mediacentre/universal_access_progress_report_en.pdf.

105. Oster, E. (2005). Sexually transmitted infections, sexual behavior and the HIV/AIDS epidemic. *Quarterly Journal of Economics* 120(2), 467–515.

106. Cohen, J. (2007). India slashes estimates of HIV-infected people. *Science* 317(5835), 179–81. Retrieved July 30, 2007, from http://www.sciencemag. org/cgi/content/full/317/5835/179?rss=1.

107. Whiteside, A. (2005). The economic, social and political drivers of HIV/ AIDS in Swaziland: A case study. In A. Stephenson Patterson (ed.), *The African state and the AIDS crisis* (pp. 97–126). Aldershot, UK: Ashgate.

108. Kingdom of Swaziland. (2002). *Kingdom of Swaziland 8th sentinel serosurveillance report.* Retrieved July 30, 2007, from http://www.fhi.org/NR/ rdonlyres/e3ce637nxcwectxyxmmg7fznofqyq6viarycufbcbs73bxvzbbp-bi73x57jbxfrosc6c5fvo4d4a6n/swazilandaidsreport1.pdf.

109. Groenewald, P., Nannan, N., Bourne, D., Laubscher, R., & Bradshaw, D. (2005). Identifying deaths from AIDS in South Africa. *AIDS* 19(7), 744–5.

110. For in-depth information on the process of calculating HIV/AIDS estimates, read the "Q & A" on the topic by UNAIDS at http://data.unaids.org/pub/ GlobalReport/2006/2006_Epi_backgrounder_on_methodology_en.pdf.

111. Oster, op. cit.

112. Cohen, op. cit.

113. National Intelligence Council. (2002).The next wave of HIV/AIDS: Nigeria, Ethiopia, Russia, India, and China. *Intelligence Community Assessment* 2002–04 D, September 2002. Retrieved May 30, 2003, from http://www. fas.org/irp/nic/hiv-aids.html.

114. Epstein, B. G. (2004). The demographic impact of HIV/AIDS. In M. Haacker, *The Macroeconomics of HIV/AIDS* (pp. 1–40). Washington, DC: International Monetary Fund.

115. National Intelligence Council. (2002). The next wave of HIV/AIDS: Nigeria, Ethiopia, Russia, India, and China. *Intelligence Community Assessment* 2002–04 D, September, 2002. Retrieved May 30, 2006, from http://www. fas.org/irp/nic/hiv-aids.html.

116. CDC site: http://www.cdc.gov/.

117. USAID site: http://www.usaid.gov/.

118. NIH site: http://www.nih.gov/.

119. Smolinski, M. S., Hamburg, M. A., & Lederberg, J. (eds.) (2003). *Microbial threats to health: Emergence, detection and response*, Institute of Medicine of the National Academies, 2003. Retrieved August 30, 2003, from http:// www.nap.edu/books/030908864X/html.

120. Barnett, A., & Pryns, T. (2006). HIV/AIDS and security: Fact, fiction and evidence. A report to UNAIDS. *International Affairs* 82(2), 359–68.

121. Dare, L., Kim, J. Y., & Farmer, P. (2006). Where AIDS efforts lag: Shortages of health workers undermine advances. *Washington Post*, December 1, p. A29. Retrieved December 29, 2006, from http://www.washingtonpost.com/ wp-dyn/content/article/2006/11/30/AR2006113001164_pf.html.

278 Notes

122. Swarns, R. (1999, November 25). Safety of common AIDS drug questioned in South Africa. *New York Times*. Retrieved June 15, 2003, from http://www.virusmyth.net/aids/news/rsmbeki.htm.
123. Associated Press. (2003). *AIDS activists file manslaughter charges against government minister*. Retrieved July 30, 2007, from http://ww2.aegis.org/news/ap/2003/AP030319.html.
124. Burroughs Wellcome (now GSK) site: http://www.bwfund.org.
125. South Africa National HIV and AIDS and Tuberculosis Unit: http://www.doh.gov.za/aids/index.html.
126. Chaya, N., Amen, K. A., & Fox, M. (2002). *Condoms count: Meeting the need in the era of HIV/AIDS*. Washington, DC: Population Action International.
127. Clark, S. (2004). Early marriage and HIV risks in sub-Saharan Africa. *Studies in Family Planning* 35(3), 149–60.
128. Dworkin, S. L., & Ehrhardt, A. A. (2007). Going beyond ABC to include GEM: Critical reflections on progress in the HIV/AIDS epidemic. *American Journal of Public Health*, 97(1), 13–18.
129. Chaya, N., Amen, K. A., and Fox, M., op. cit.
130. WHO (2009). *Governance of WHO*. Retrieved January 12, 2009 from http://www.who.int/about/governance/en/index.html.
131 Adapted from WHO (2009). *The WHO agenda*. Retrieved January 12, 2009 from http://www.who.int/about/agenda/en/index.html.
132. WHO site: http://www.who.int
133. World Health Organization, UNAIDS, UNICEF. (2007). *Towards universal access: Scaling up priority HIV/AIDS interventions in the health sector. Progress report 2007*. Retrieved June 21, 2007, from http://www.who.int/hiv/mediacentre/universal_access_progress_report_en.pdf.
134. WHO. (2005). *Progress on global access to antiretroviral therapy: An update on "3 by 5."* Retrieved July 30, 2007, from http://www.who.int/3by5/fullreportJune2005.pdf.
135. For a report on the much-criticized 3 by 5 program, go to http://www.who.int/3by5/fullreportJune2005.pdf.
136. ILO site: http://www.ilo.org/.
137. Global Fund site: http://www.theglobalfund.org/en/.
138. World Bank site: http://www.worldbank.org/.
139. World Bank. (2007). *The World Bank: HIV/AIDS*. Retrieved July 30, 2007, from http://web.worldbank.org/WBSITE/EXTERNAL/TOPICS/EXTHEALTHNUTRITIONANDPOPULATION/EXTHIVAIDS/0,,menuPK:376477~pagePK:149018~piPK:149093~theSitePK:376471,00.html.
140. Médecins Sans Frontières/Doctors Without Borders site: http://www.msf.org/.
141. Bill and Melinda Gates Foundation site: http://www.gatesfoundation.org.
142. Gates, B. (2002). *UN secretary general's luncheon* (speech). New York (May 9). Retrieved June 30, 2003, from http://www.unicef.org/media/media_9465.html.
143. Cowley, op. cit.
144. For a description of Volkswagen do Brasil HIV/AIDS program go to: http://www.ilo.org/public/english/protection/trav/aids/examples/brazil.htm.
145. UNAIDS and WHO. (2005). *AIDS epidemic update: Intensifying prevention*. Geneva, Switzerland: UNAIDS.
146. World Economic Forum site: http://www.weforum.org.
147. Global Business Coalition site: http://www.businessfightsaids.org.
148. Global Business Coalition on HIV/AIDS (2006). *The state of business and HIV/AIDS (2006): A baseline report*. New York: Booz Allen Hamilton.
149. Viacom site: http://www.viacom.com/.

Notes 279

150. Global Business Coalition on HIV/AIDS. (2003). *Nelson Mandela tackles controversial world issues on MTV.* Global Business Coalition on AIDS press release (June 23). Retrieved June 30, 2003, from http://www.businessfightsaids.org/news_read.asp?sct=3&ID=9093.
151. Plumley B., Bery, P., & Dadd, C. (2002). *Beyond the workplace: Business participation in the multi-sectoral response to HIV/AIDS.* The XIV International Conference on AIDS, Barcelona (discussion paper), July, 2002. Retrieved June 30, 2003, from http://www.businessfightsaids.org/pdf/beyond_wrkplace.pdf.
152. Global Business Coalition on HIV/AIDS. (2006). *The state of business and HIV/AIDS (2006): A baseline report.* New York: Booz Allen Hamilton.
153. The Global Fund to Fight AIDS, Tuberculosis and Malaria site: www.theglobalfund.org.
154. World Bank (2003). *World Bank intensifies action against HIV/AIDS.* DevNews Center, World Bank (April). Retrieved June 30, 2003, from http://web.worldbank.org/WBSITE/EXTERNAL/NEWS/0,,contentMDK:20040236~menuPK:34480~pagePK:34370~theSitePK:4607,00.html.
155. ACT UP site: http://www.actupny.org/.
156. Act Up New York. (2000). *Global manifesto.* Retrieved June 30, 2008, from http://www.actupny.org/reports/durban-access.html.
157. International HIV/AIDS Alliance. (2002). *Improving access to HIV/AIDS-related treatment.* International HIV/AIDS Alliance, London (June). Retrieved August 30, 2003, from http://www.eldis.org/static/DOC11065.htm.
158. Patterson, A. S. (2005). Introduction: The African state and the AIDS crisis. In A. S. Patterson (ed.), *The African state and the AIDS crisis* (pp. 1–16). Aldershot, UK: Ashgate.
159. UNAIDS Regional Support Team for Eastern and Southern Africa. (2006). *Regional profile for Eastern and Southern Africa.* Retrieved July 21, 2007, from http://www.unaidsrstesa.org/regional_charts.html.
160. UNAIDS. (2006). *2006 report on the global AIDS epidemic.* Geneva: UNAIDS.
161. Southern African Development Community was established in 1980 and consists of: Angola, Botswana, Democratic Republic of Congo, Lesotho, Madagascar, Malawi, Mauritius, Mozambique, South Africa, Swaziland, Tanzania, Zambia, and Zimbabwe. For information go to: http://www.sadc.int/.
162. Southern African Development Community. (2006). *Expert think tank meeting on HIV prevention in high-prevalence countries in Southern Africa.* Maseru, Lesotho, 10–12 May. Retrieved July 30, 2007, from http://data.unaids.org/pub/Report/2006/20060601_sadc_meeting_report_en.pdf.
163. Maharaj, P. (2001). Male attitudes to family planning in the era of HIV/AIDS. *Journal of Southern African Studies* 27(2), 246–57.
164. Iwuagwu, S. C., Ajuwon, A. J., & Olaseha, I. O (2000). Sexual behavior and negotiation of the male condom by female students at the university of Ibadan, Nigeria. *Journal of Obstetrics and Gynecology* 20(5), 507–13.
165. Amuyunzu-Nyamongo, M., Biddlecom, A. E., Ouedraogo, C., & Woog, V. (2005). *Qualitative evidence on adolescents' views of sexual and reproductive health in sub-Saharan Africa.* Guttmacher Institute Occasional Report No. 16 (January).
166. Uganda Ministry of Health and IRD/Macro Systems, Inc. 1988/1989. (1989). *Uganda Demographic and health survey.* In G. A. O'Sullivan, J. A. Yonkler, W. Morgan, & A. P. Merritt, *A field guide to designing a health communication strategy.* Baltimore: Johns Hopkins Bloomberg School of Public Health/Center for Communication Programs.

280 *Notes*

167. Fleischmann, J. (2002). *The links between human rights abuses and HIV transmission in Zambia.* Human Rights Watch. Retrieved May 15, 2003, from http://www.hrw.org/reports/2003/zambia/.
168. Ibid.
169. UNAIDS. (2002). *AIDS epidemic update.* UNAIDS/World Heath Organisation (December). Retrieved July 30, 2003, from http://www.who.int/hiv/pub/epidemiology/epi2002/en/.
170. Race, K., McInness, D., Kleinert, V., Wakeford, E., McMurchie, M., & Kidd, M. (2001). *Adherence and communication: Reports from a study of HIV general practice.* National Centre in HIV Social Research Monograph No.8. Retrieved May 30, 2003, from http://www.synergyaids.com/documents/adherence&communication.pdf.
171. Other relevant magazines include: *Genre*: targeting affluent gay men in the United States, and "intends to be the ultimate lifestyle resource for gay men" at http://www.genremagazine.com. *The Advocate*, the oldest magazine for the lesbian, gay, and transgender community at http://www.advocate.com.
172. Young, I. (n.d.). *The folklore of the AIDS culture.* Health, Education AIDS Liaison (HEAL), Toronto. Retrieved September 7, 2003, from http://www.healtoronto.com/buythis.html.
173. Koblin, B. A., Husnik, M., Colfax, G., et al. (2006). Risk factors for HIV infection among MSM. *AIDS* 20(5), 732–39.
174. *International Herald Tribune.* (2008, January 16). Silence still equals death. Retrieved February 1, 2008, from http://www.iht.com.
175. Van de Ven, P., Rawstorne, P., Crawford, J., & Kippax, S. (2001). *Facts and figures: 2000 male out survey* (monograph 2). National Centre in HIV research, University of New South Wales. Retrieved April 30, 2003, from http://www.glrl.org.au/publications/major_reports/age_of_consent/age_of_consent_13.htm.
176. Altman, D. (2006). Taboos and denial in government responses. *International Affairs* 82(2), 257–68.
177. For exposure to these views go to: http://www.reviewingaids.com/.
178. Specter, M. (2007, March 12). The denialists. *New Yorker*, pp. 32–38.
179. Ross, M. W., Essien, J. E., & Torres, I. (2006). Conspiracy beliefs about the origin of HIV/AIDS in four racial/ethnic groups. *Journal of Acquired Immune Deficiency Syndromes* 41(3), 342–44.
180. Sengupta, S., Strauss, R. P., Devellis, R., Crouse Quinn, S., Devellis, B., & Ware, W. B. (2000). *Factors affecting African American participation in AIDS research.* University of California, San Francisco AIDS Research Institute. Retrieved June 15, 2006, from http://www.caps.ucsf.edu/publications/sengupta.pdf.
181. Signorile, M. (2001). AIDS at 20, complacency returns. Gay.com (June 6). Retrieved April 30, 2006, from http://www.signorile.com/articles/gca20.html.
182. Scarce, M. (1998, August 21). Back to barebacking. *New York Blade.* Retrieved June 15, 2006, from http://www.managingdesire.org/scarcebtb.html.
183. Jaffe, H. W., Valdiserri, R. O., & De Cock, K. M. (2007). The re-emerging HIV/AIDS epidemic in men having sex with men. *Journal of the American Medical Association* 298, 2412–14.
184. Public Broadcasting Service. (2006). *Frontline: The age of AIDS: Country profile United States* (June 19). Retrieved June 29, 2007, from http://www.pbs.org/wgbh/pages/frontline/aids/countries/us.html.

Notes 281

185. Specter, M. (2005). Higher risk: Crystal meth, the Internet, and dangerous choices about. *The New Yorker I.* Retrieved May 28, 2007, from http://www.newyorker.com/archive/2005/05/23/050523fa_fact?printable=true.
186. Scott, H. (2001). Splitting image: Reflections on the newest cracks in the looking glass. *POZ magazine* (July). Retrieved June 29, 2007, from http://www.poz.com/articles/190_1205.shtml.
187. Lane, T. (2002). HIV-related stigma falls, but misperceptions about transmission persist. *Perspectives on sexual and reproductive health* 34(4). Retrieved June 29, 2007, from http://www.guttmacher.org/pubs/journals/3421502.html.
188. World Bank, Thailand. (2000). Thailand response to AIDS success and confronting the future. *Thailand Social Monitor* (November 3). Retrieved September 1, 2006, from http://siteresources.worldbank.org/INTTHAILAND/Resources/Social-Monitor/2000nov.pdf.
189. VanLandingham, M., & Trujillo, L. (2002). Recent changes in heterosexual attitudes, norms and behaviors among unmarried Thai men: A qualitative analysis. *International Family Planning Perspectives* 28(1). Retrieved August 15, 2006, from http://www.guttmacher.org/pubs/journals/2800602.html.
190. World Bank, Thailand. (2000). Thailand response to AIDS success and confronting the future. *Thailand Social Monitor* (November 3). Retrieved September 1, 2006, from http://siteresources.worldbank.org/INTTHAILAND/Resources/Social-Monitor/2000nov.pdf.
191. Ibid.
192. Cohen, J. (2003). Two hard-hit countries offer rare success stories: Thailand and Cambodia. *Science* 301(5640). Retrieved October 1, 2006, from http://aidscience.org/Science/Cohen301(5640)1658.htm.
193. VanLandingham, M., & Trujillo, L., op. cit.
194. Ainsworth, M., Beyrer, C., & Soucat, A. (2003). AIDS and public policy . . . The lessons and challenges of "success" in Thailand. *Health Policy* 64(1), 13–37.
195. World Bank, Thailand, op. cit.
196. VanLandingham, M., & Trujillo, L., op. cit.
197. Cohen, J. (2003). Two hard-hit countries offer rare success stories: Thailand and Cambodia. *Science* 301(5640). Retrieved October 1, 2006, from http://aidscience.org/Science/Cohen301(5640)1658.htm.
198. Lakhaney, A. (2002). *Self-reliance key to anti-AIDS efforts: Museveni.* International Information Programs, U.S. Department of State (February 27). Retrieved June 15, 2006, from http://usinfo.state.gov/regional/af/usafr/a2022710.htm.
199. Global HIV Prevention Working Group. (2003). *Access to HIV prevention: Closing the gap.* Bill and Melinda Gates Foundation. Retrieved April, 30, 2006, from http://www.kaisernetwork.org/health_cast/hcast_index.cfm?display=detail&hc=868.
200. Rosenberg, M. (2003). As Bush prepares to visit Africa, questions surround his commitment to democracy. *AEGiS-Associated Press* (July 4). Retrieved July 30, 2006, from http://www.aegis.com/news/ap/2003/AP030707.html.
201. UNESCO/UNAIDS. (2001). A cultural approach to HIV/AIDS prevention and care: Culturally appropriate information/education/communication elaboration of delivery and care. *Methodological Handbooks, Special Series, Division of Cultural Policies, UNESCO.* Retrieved July 30, 2006, from http://unesdoc.unesco.org/images/0012/001255/125589e.pdf.
202. Singhal, A., & Rogers, E. M., op. cit.
203. Timberg, C. (2007, March 29). Uganda's early gains against HIV eroding. *The Washington Post*, p. A1.

282 Notes

204. Whiteside, A. (2001). Demography and economics of HIV/AIDS. *British Medical Bulletin* 58, 73–88.
205. U.S. Agency for International Development. (2003).*Country Profile HIV/AIDS: Uganda*. USAID Bureau for Global Health, June 2003. Retrieved June 25, 2003, from http://pdf.usaid.gov/pdf_docs/PNACT355.pdf.
206. Timberg, C. (2007, March 29). Uganda's early gains against HIV eroding. *The Washington Post*, p. A1.
207. U.S. Agency for International Development. (2003).*Country Profile HIV/AIDS: Uganda*. USAID Bureau for Global Health, June 2003. Retrieved June 25, 2003, from http://pdf.usaid.gov/pdf_docs/PNACT355.pdf.
208. Hogle, J. A. (ed.) (2002). *Project lessons learned case study: What happened in Uganda*. USAID. Retrieved July 30, 2007, from http://pdf.usaid.gov/pdf_docs/PNACQ623.pdf.
209. Oster, E. (2007). *Routes of infection: Exports and HIV incidence in sub-Saharan Africa*. University of Chicago and NBER Working Paper, June 8. Retrieved August 17, 2007, from http://home.uchicago.edu/~eoster/hivexports.pdf.
210. UNAIDS/WHO. (2006). *AIDS epidemic update* (December). Geneva : UNAIDS.
211. Shafer, L. A., Biraro, S., Kamali, A., Grosskurth, H., Kirungi, W., Madraa, E., & Opio, A. (2006). *HIV prevalence and incidence are no longer falling in Uganda—a case for renewed prevention efforts: Evidence from a rural population cohort 1989–2005, and from ANC surveillance*. Sixteenth International AIDS Conference, Toronto, August 13–18.
212. Timberg, C. (2007, March 29). Uganda's early gains against HIV eroding. *The Washington Post*, p. A1.
213. Human Rights Watch. (2005). *HRW honors Ugandan AIDS activist, outspoken defender of women with AIDS* (25 October). Retrieved July 21, 2007, from http://hrw.org/english/docs/2005/10/25/uganda11920.htm.
214. Altman, L. K. (2005, August 30). US Blamed for condom shortage in fighting AIDS in Uganda. *New York Times*. Retrieved October 31, 2006, from http://www.nytimes.com.

NOTES TO CASE STUDY 3

1. For more information go to NGO site Mexicovivo: http://www.mexicovivo.org/ or the Government of Mexico Ministry of Health: http://www.salud.gob.mx/.
2. UNAIDS. (2002). Epidemiological fact sheets. *Global HIV/AIDS and STD Surveillance*, UNAIDS, and WHO, undated, 2002. Retrieved July 30, 2003, from http://www.unaids.org.
3. Caro, D. (2002). *An evaluation of participatory, multisectoral planning for HIV/AIDS in key states in Mexico*. POLICY, USAID. Retrieved April 30, 2006, from http://www.futuresgroup.com/abstract.cfm/2714.
4. Pan American Health Organization. (n.d.). *Health situation analysis and trends summary: Mexico*. Retrieved March 15, 2006, from http://www.paho.org/English/DD/AIS/cp_484.htm.
5. UNAIDS/WHO. (2006). *AIDS epidemic update*. Retrieved January 17, 2008, from http://data.unaids.org/pub/EpiReport/2006/08-Latin_America_2006_EpiUpdate_eng.pdf.
6. Family Health International. (2007). *Mexico final report October 1997 to January 2007*. Retrieved January 30, 2008, from http://www.fhi.org/NR/rdonlyres/ep53mvqacgtfazo3xhilmxmxahj56eofe4z4lcj6ptclhrmfwbl2ni7f-n45unllspbyjfy3cv3iyrk/IMPACTFinalReportMexicoHV.pdf.

Notes 283

7. Bautista, S. A., Dmytraczenko, T., Kombe, G., & Bertozzi, S. M. (2003). *Costing of HIV/AIDS treatment in Mexico.* Technical Report 020 (June). Bethesda, MD: Partners for Health Reform Plus Project. Retrieved July 30, 2002, from http://www.phrplus.org/Pubs/Tech020_fin.pdf.

8. Secretaría de Salud. (2004). *Salud: Mexico 2004.* Retrieved 2 March, 2006, from http://evaluacion.salud.gob.mx/saludmex2004/sm2004.pdf.

9. Brouwer, K. C., Strathdee, S. A., Magis-Rodriguez, C., Bravo-Garcia, E., Gayet, C., Patterson, T. L., Bertozzi, S. M., & Hogg, R. S. (2006). Estimated numbers of men and women infected with HIV/AIDS in Tijuana. *Journal of Urban Health* 83(2), 299–307.

10. Comisión Nacional para el Desarrollo de los Pueblos Indígenas. (2005). *Lenguas Indígenas: Diversidad etnolingüística.* Retrieved 7 April, 2005, from http://cdi.gob.mx/index.php?id_seccion=90.

11. UNESCO Institute for Statistics. (2003). *Education in Mexico.* Education in brief. Retrieved March 2, 2008, from http://www.uis.unesco.org/profiles/EN/EDU/countryProfile_en.aspx?code=4840.

12. *Agence France Presse.* (2003. May 9). Mexico-Religion-Sex: Mexican Bishops attack First Lady for advocating condom use against AIDS. Retrieved April 27, 2008, from http://www.aegis.com/NEWS/AFP/2003/AF030522.html.

13. Smallman, S. (2007). *The AIDS pandemic in Latin America.* University of North Carolina Press.

14. UNAIDS/WHO. (2007). *Report on the global AIDS epidemic.* Retrieved December 15, 2007, from http://www.unaids.org/en/KnowledgeCentre/HIVData/GlobalReport/.

15. Smallman, S. (2007). *The AIDS pandemic in Latin America.* Chapel Hill, NC: University of North Carolina Press.

16. Pulerwitz, J., et al. (2001). Extrarelational sex among Mexican men and their partners' risk of HIV and other sexually transmitted diseases. American Journal of Public Health 91(10), 1650–52.

17. Baral, S., Sifakis, F., Cleghorn, F., & Beyrer, C. (2007). Elevated risk for HIV infection among men who have sex with men in low- and middle income countries 2000–2006: A systematic review. *PLoS Med* 4(12), e339. Retrieved January 19, 2008, from http://www.plos.org/press/plme-04-12-beyrer.pdf.

18. American Foundation for AIDS Research. (2002). *AIDS in Latin America and the Caribbean.* Global Initiatives, American Foundation for AIDS Research Special Reports. Retrieved April 30, 2006, from http://www.amfar.org/cgi-bin/iowa/programs/globali/record.html?record=139.

19. Cevallos, D. (2002). Rural women with AIDS suffer ostracism. *Inter Press Service*, AEGIS (September 19). Retrieved January 30, 2008, from http://www.aegis.com/news/ips/2002/IP020913.html.

20. Mexico Child Link. (2003). *Mexico street children statistics.* Mexico Child Link. Retrieved July 20, 2008, from http://www.mexico-child-link.org/street-children-definition-statistics.htm.

21. U.S. Centers for Disease Control and Prevention. (2003). Mexico: Street children at high risk of HIV/AIDS. *The Body.* Retrieved February 20, 2008, from http://www.thebody.com/content/world/art29534.html.

22. Casa Alianza (2000). *Worldwide statistics: Exploitation of children, a global outrage.* Hilton Foundation, September 2000. Retrieved December 15, 2006, from http://www.hiltonfoundation.org/press/16-pdf3.pdf.

23. U.S. Department of Justice. (2007). *Child sex tourism.* Child exploitation and obscenity section (November). Retrieved May 14, 2008, from http://www.usdoj.gov/criminal/ceos/sextour.html.

284 *Notes*

24. U.S. Agency for International Development. (2003). *Country profile HIV/AIDS: Mexico,* Country Profiles (June 2003). Retrieved Decenber 15, 2006, from http://www.usaid.gov.
25. American Foundation for AIDS Research. (2002). *Global Initiatives Mexico.* American Foundation for AIDS Research Special Reports, undated, 2002. Retrieved July 30 from http://www.amfar.org.
26. Lacey, M. (2007, July 18). Back from the US, and spreading HIV in Mexico. *International Herald Tribune.* Retrieved May 2, 2008, from http://www.iht.com/articles/2007/07/16/news/mexico.php?page=1.
27. Hofmann, R. (2007). Precious stone. *POZ* (December). Retrieved January 19, 2008, from http://www.poz.com/archive/2007_Dec_2111.shtml.
28. YouthAIDS site: http://projects.psi.org/site/PageServer?pagename=home_homepageindex.
29. Usdin, S. (2000). Soul City. *Urban Health and Development Bulletin,* Medical Research Council of South Africa 3(2), 15–24.
30. LoveLife site: http://www.lovelife.org.za/.
31. See http://www.stopaids.ch/.
32. World Health Organization. (2002). *Infectious diseases report 2002.* World Health Organization, 2002. Retrieved June 30, 2003, from http://www.who.int.
33. Ministry of Health, Government of Mexico. (n.d.). Vete sano, regresa sano. Retrieved June 1, 2008, from http://www.saludmigrante.salud.gob.mx/acciones/slideshow.htm.
34. See an example of *MTV*'s work in the area by viewing the CNN-MTV news special on HIV/AIDS at http://eu.staying-alive.org/stayingalive/shells/inline_watch.jhtml?article=30113633.
35. For a recent example of a fund-raising campaign, see information about the product (red) campaign: http://joinred.com/products/.
36. Grover, R., & Vriens, M. (2006). *The handbook of marketing research: Uses, misuses, and future advances.* Thousand Oaks, CA: Sage.
37. The theory of cognitive dissonance (CD), by Festinger (1957), explains that individuals, when confronted with new information that questions their established beliefs, will experience cognitive dissonance and consequently a psychological loss of balance. They will try to reduce the gap. Dissonance is especially activated by (1) exposure to new information incompatible with former established beliefs and (2) exposure to new circumstances and a modified social environment which questions deeply ingrained behavior consistent with individual values.
38. Cooper, J., & Croyle, R. T. (1984). Attitudes and attitude change. *Annual Review of Psychology* 35, 395–426.
39. Campbell, C. (2003). Letting them die: Why HIV/AIDS prevention programmes fail. Oxford: James Currey.
40. This literature is mostly concerned with antitobacco campaigns (AT), but a large part of its conceptual approach and empirical findings can be transferred *mutatis mutandis* to AIDS prevention campaigns.
41. Janis, I. L., & Mann, I. (1965). Effectiveness of emotional role playing in modifying smoking habits and attitudes. *Journal of Experimental Research in Psychology* 1, 84–90. Janis I. L. (1967). Effects of Fear Arousal on Attitude: Recent Developments in Theory and Research. *Advances in Experimental Psychology* 4, 166–224.
42. Floyd, D., & Prentice-Dunn, S. (2000). A Meta-Analysis of Research on Protection Motivation Theory. *Journal of Applied Social Psychology* 30(2), 407–30. Rogers, R.-W. (1975). A protection motivation theory of fear appeals and attitude change. *The Journal of Psychology* 91, 93–114.

Keller, P.A., & Block, L. G. (1996). Increasing the persuasiveness of fear appeals: The effect of arousal and elaboration. *Journal of Marketing Research* 22, 448–59.

43. Tanner, J. F., Hunt, B., & Eppright, D. R. (1991). The protection motivation model: A normative model of fears appeals. *Journal of Marketing* 55, 36–45.

44. Leventhal, H., & Watts, J. C. (1966). Sources of resistance to fear arousing communications on smoking and lung cancer. *Journal of Personality* 34 (June), 155–75.
Keller, P. A.(1999). Converting the unconverted. The effects of inclination and opportunity to discount health related fear appeals. *Journal of Applied Psychology* 84(3), 403–15.

45. Bandura, A. (1994). Social cognitive theory and exercise of control over HIV infection. In R. J. DiClemente & J. L. Peterson (eds), *Preventing AIDS: Theories and methods of behavioral interventions.* New York: Plenum Press.

46. Bandura, A. (2004). Health promotion by social cognitive means. *Health Education and Behavior* 31(2), 143–64.

47. Bandura, A. (1997). *Self-efficacy: The exercise of control.* New York: Freeman.

48. UNAIDS. (1999). *Communications framework for AIDS: A new direction.* Retrieved March 23, 2005, from http://www.unaids.org/NetTools/Misc/DocInfo.aspx?LANG=en&href=http%3a%2f%2fgva-doc-owl%2fWEBcontent%2fDocuments%2fpub%2fPublications%2fIRC-pub01%2fJC335-CommFramew_en%26%2346%3bpdf.

49. UNAIDS. (1999). *Communications framework for AIDS: A new direction.* Retrieved March 23, 2005, from http://www.unaids.org/NetTools/Misc/DocInfo.aspx?LANG=en&href=http%3a%2f%2fgva-doc-owl%2fWEBcontent%2fDocuments%2fpub%2fPublications%2fIRC-pub01%2fJC335-CommFramew_en%26%2346%3bpd.

NOTES TO CASE STUDY 4

1. Christian Viladent is coauthor of this case. We thank him for reprinting permission.

2. For information about PEPFAR, go to: http://www.whitehouse.gov/infocus/hivaids/.

3. Confirmatory tests are usually performed on the same sample if the sample itself is of good enough quality.

4. Bill and Melinda Gates Foundation is a private foundation that aims to reduce inequities in the areas of health care libraries, education, and specific actions in the Pacific Northwest of the United States. For information, go to: http://www.gatesfoundation.org.

5. The William J. Clinton Foundation works to build capacity in four areas: health security, economic empowerment, leadership development and citizen service, racial, ethnic, and religious reconciliation. For information go to: http://www.clintonfoundation.org/mission.htm.

6. The "3 by 5" initiative was launched in 2003 with the stated goal of providing three million people living with HIV/AIDS in low- and middle-income countries with antiretroviral treatments. Approximately one-third (one million) people were reached by 2005, according to the WHO's progress report: http://www.who.int/3by5/progressreportJune2005/en/. For information, go to: http://www.who.int/3by5/en/.

7. Richard Holbrooke is currently president of the Global Business Coalition on HIV/AIDS, and a former U.S. ambassador to the United Nations.

286 *Notes*

8. Holbrooke, R. (2005). AIDS: The strategy is wrong. *GBC & Member News*, accessed 18 January, 2006, from http://www.businessfightsaids.org/site/apps/nl/content2.asp?c=gwKXJfNVJtF&b=1009023&ct=1638199.
9. Ibid.
10. Ibid.
11. Mechoulan, S. (2004). HIV testing: A Trojan horse? *Topics in Economic Analysis and Policy*, 4(1), 1261.
12. Ibid.
13. Leaty, S., Sherr, L., Wells, H., Evans, A., et al. (2000). Repeat HIV testing: High-risk behavior or risk reduction strategy? *AIDS* 14, 547–52.
14. Weinhardt, L. S., Carey, M. P., Johnson, B. T., et al. (1999). Effects of HIV counseling and testing on sexual risk behavior: A meta-analytic review of published research, 1985–1997. *American Journal of Public Health* 89, 1397–40.
15. For the latest guidelines on tests that are recommended go to: http://www.aidsinfo.nih.gov/guidelines/.
16. John Snow, Inc./Deliver. (2003). *Guidelines for managing the HIV/AIDS supply chain*. Arlington, VA: John Snow, Inc./Deliver.
17. World Health Organisation. (2004). *Rapid HIV tests: Guidelines for use in HIV testing and counselling services in resource-constrained settings*. Geneva: World Health Organisation. Accessed March 15, 2008, from http://www.unicef.org/aids/files/rapidhivtestsen.pdf.
18. Cardo, D. M., Culver, D. H., Ciesielski, C. A., et al. (1997). A case-control study of HIV seroconversion in health care workers after percutaneous exposure. Centers for Disease Control and Prevention Needlestick Surveillance Group. *New England Journal of Medicine* 337, 21, 1485–90.
19. International Labour Office. (n.d.). *Know your status* (pamphlet issued with the cooperation of UNAIDS). Accessed 25 October, 2008, from http://www.ilo.org/aids.
20. Centers for Disease Control and Prevention. (2001). *HIV counseling and testing in publicly funded sites: Annual report 1997 and 1998*. Atlanta: U.S. Department of Health and Human Services. Accessed March 15, 2006, from http://www.cdc.gov/hiv/pubs/cts98.pdf.
21. FDA. (2006). *Testing yourself for HIV-1, the virus that causes AIDS*. Center for Biologics Evaluation and Research. Accessed March 15, 2007, from http://www.fda.gov/cber/infosheets/hiv-home2.htm.
22. Ibid.
23. World Health Organization. (2004), op. cit.
24. Gostin, Lawrence O. (2004). *The AIDS pandemic: Complacency, injustice, and unfulfilled expectations*. Chapel Hill: University of North Carolina Press.
25. California Senate. (2006). *SB699 Senate Bill (Soto)*. Third reading as amended March 7. Accessed March 15, 2006, from http://info.sen.ca.gov/pub/bill/sen/sb_0651–0700/sb_699_cfa_20060307_155457_asm_floor.html.
26. Selection and Procurement of HIV/AIDS Diagnostics (PAHO Technical Advisory Committee on HIV/AIDS, January, 2005), presentation delivered during the Technical Advisory Committee on HIV/AIDS/STI, Boca Chica, República Dominicana, 22–24 January 2005. Accessible at: http://www.paho.org/english/ad/fch/ai/Clinton%20HIV%20Initiative-Selection%20&%20Procurement.pdf.
27. Schoofs, M. (2004, January 14). HIV-Test makers agree to discounts for poorer nations. *Wall Street Journal*. Accessed October 20, 2005, from http://proquest.umi.com.
28. William J. Clinton Foundation. (2006). *Press release: New agreements to lower prices of HIV/AIDS rapid tests and second-line drugs*. Accessed

Notes 287

March 15, 2008, from http://www.clintonfoundation.org/011206-nr-cf-hs-ai-isr-ind-chn-zaf-bra-pr-new-agreements-to-lower-prices-of-hiv-aids-rapid-tests-and-second-line-drugs.htm.

29. John Snow, Inc./Deliver. (2005). *Building blocks for inventory management of HIV tests and ARV drugs.* Arlington, VA: John Snow, Inc./Deliver.
30. Schoofs, op. cit.
31. Holmes, E. C. (2001). On the origin and evolution of the human immunodeficiency virus. *Biological Reviews* 76, 239–54.
32. Schoofs, op. cit.
33. Family Health International. (n.d.). *Issues in diagnostics for VCT.* Accessed January 30, 2006, from http://www.fhi.org/en/HIVAIDS/pub/fact/vctissues.htm.
34. USAID/Deliver. (2003). *Guide for quantifying HIV test requirements.* Arlington, VA: John Snow, Inc./Deliver. Accessed January 30, 2006, from http://www.jsi.com/JSIInternet/Publications/hiv-aids.cfm.
35. John Snow, Inc./Deliver. (2003). *Guidelines for managing the HIV/AIDS supply chain.* Arlington, VA: John Snow, Inc./Deliver.
36. World Health Organisation Regional Office for South East Asia. (2003). *Standard operating procedures for diagnosis of HIV infection.* Guidelines on standard operating procedures for diagnosis of HIV opportunistic infections. Accessed February 21, 2006, from http://w3.whosea.org/bct/332/diagnosis1.htm.
37. Family Health International. (n.d.). *Issues in diagnostics for VCT.* Accessed January 30, 2008, from http://www.fhi.org/en/HIVAIDS/pub/fact/vctissues.htm.
38. John Snow, Inc./Deliver (2003), op. cit.
39. Family Health International, op. cit.
40. Klitzman, R., & Bayer R. (2003). *Mortal secrets: Truth and lies in the age of HIV/AIDS.* Baltimore: Johns Hopkins University Press.
41. UNAIDS Best Practice Collection. (2005). *HIV stigma, discrimination and human rights violations.* Retrieved May 4, 2007, from http://data.unaids.org/publications/irc-pub06/JC999-HumRightsViol_en.pdf.
42. D'Adesky, A.-C. (2004). Moving mountains: The race to treat global AIDS. New York: Verso.
43. Rabasca, L. (1998). Psychological barriers keep women from seeking care. *APA Monitor,* American Psychological Association 29:8, August 1998. Retrieved September 15, 2005, from http://www.apa.org/monitor/aug98/hiv.html.
44. Gostin, op. cit.
45. National HIV Testing Resources. (n.d.). *Frequently asked questions about HIV and HIV testing.* A service of the National Centers for Disease Control and Prevention. Accessed October 20, 2007, from http://www.hivtest.org/subindex.cfm?FuseAction=FAQ.
46. McCauley, A. P. (2004). *Equitable access to HIV counseling and testing for youth in developing countries: A review of current practice.* Horizons Program/International Center for Research on Women. Accessed October 25, 2007, from http://www.popcouncil.org/pdfs/horizons/vctythrvw.pdf.
47. Sheon, N. (2006). *Theory and practice of client-centered counseling and testing,* HIV InSite Knowledge Base Chapter, June 2004. Accessed March 20, 2008, from http://hivinsite.ucsf.edu/InSite?page=kb-07–01–04.
48. World Health Organisation. (2004), op. cit.
49. World Health Organisation/UNAIDS. (2005). *Scaling up HIV testing and counselling services: A toolkit for program managers.* Geneva: World Health Organisation. Retrieved March 29, 2008, from http://www.who.int/hiv/pub/vct/counsellingtestingtoolkit.pdf.

288 *Notes*

50. The Global Health Council is an international membership alliance composed of health organisations, professionals, government agencies, and research institutions. For information go to: http://www.globalhealth.org.
51. Chapman, S. (n.d.). *A new way in HIV prevention: Research techniques use evidence for making decisions in India campaign*. Field notes, PSI International. Accessed March 20, 2008, from http://www.globalhealth.org/reports/text.php3?id=229.
52. AIDSMark is a cooperative agreement with USAID that is implemented by Population Services International to use social marketing to reduce the spread of HIV/AIDS and other sexually transmitted diseases. For information go to: http://www.psi.org.
53. AIDSMark. (1999). *Achieving results in HIV/AIDS prevention*. Population Services International. Retrieved March 29, 2008, from http://www.popline.org/docs/274978.
54. All information in this section is from CDC & NAPWA (2005). *National HIV Testing Day Campaign Kit 2005*. Accessed October 25, 2007, from http://www.cdcnpin.org/scripts/display/MatlDisplay.asp?MatlNbr=33510.
55. The National Association of People with AIDS (NAPWA) is the oldest HIV/AIDS membership organization in the world, being founded in 1983. It is composed of people living with HIV/AIDS in the United States. For information go to: http://www.napwa.org.
56. The Centers for Disease Control and Prevention (CDC) is part of the U.S. government Department of Health and Human Services, and the principal agency for protecting health and safety. For information go to: http://www.cdc.gov.
57. CDC & NAPWA, op. cit. Information in the booklet was based on CDC reports.

NOTES TO CASE STUDY 5

1. The Love Life Stop AIDS campaign features innovative and attention-grabbing advertisements that can be viewed at http://www.stopaids.ch.
2. Condoms are essential wear campaign (UK Department of Health): http://www.condomessentialwear.co.uk.
3. Michael Stich Foundation: http://michael-stich-stiftung.de/.
4. Hindustan Latex: http://www.hindlatex.com.
5. Krishnakumar, R. (1998). Public sector undertakings: A question of quality. *Frontline*, 15(7), 4–17 April. Retrieved June 20, 2006, from http://www.hinduonnet.com/fline/fl1507/15070960.htm.
6. Hindustan Latex. (2006). *Business unit home: Condoms*. Retrieved June 20, 2006, from http://www.hindlatex.com/BusinessUnitHome.aspx?idVal=12&type=3.
7. SGS moving towards bioanalysis, biotech: Official. (2005, July 2), *Deepika Kerala News*. Retrieved June 20, 2006, from http://www.deepika.com.
8. For a view of Hindustan Latex Moods site, go to: http://www.moodsplanet.com/home.asp.
9. Go to www.condomania.com for information and measurement kit for They-Fit condoms.
10. Jaffe, H. W., Valdiserri, R. O., & De Cock, K. M. (2007). The re-emerging HIV/AIDS epidemic in men having sex with men. *Journal of the American Medical Association* 298, 2412–14.
11. Vasagar, J. (2000, June 2). More gays disregard safe-sex warnings. *The Guardian*. Retrieved July 4, 2003, from http://www.guardian.co.uk/gay-rights/story/0,12592,838530,00.html.

Notes 289

12. *New York Times*. (2008, January 14). HIV rises among young gay men. Retrieved January 28, 2008, from http://www.nytimes.com/2008/01/14/opinion/14mon2.html?_r=1&oref=slogin.
13. For information about the female condom, which is, as the company points out, the "only new prevention technology invented" sine the beginning of the HIV/AIDS epidemic, go to the Female Health Company at: http://www.femalehealth.com/.
14. Chaya, N., Amen, K. A., & Fox, M. (2002). *Condoms count: Meeting the need in the era of HIV/AIDS*. Washington, DC: Population Action International.
15. Haeberle, N. J. (2006). *Human sexuality: An encyclopedia*. Humboldt-University Berlin. Retrieved January 30, 2007, from http://www2.hu-berlin.de/sexology/GESUND/ARCHIV/SEN/INDEX.HTM.
16. Chaya, N., Amen, K. A., & Fox, M. (2002). *Condoms count: Meeting the need in the era of HIV/AIDS*. Washington, DC: Population Action International.
17. Youssef, H. (1993). The history of the condom. *Journal of the Royal Society of Medicine* 86, 226–28.
18. Durex (n.d.). *Condom history*. Retrieved June 16, 2005, from http://www.durex.com/cm/condomHistory.asp?intHistoryStep=14&intMenuOpen=4.
19. Chaya, N., Amen, K. A., and Fox, M., op. cit.
20. Roper, W. L., Peterson, H. B., & Curran, J. W. (1993). Commentary. Condoms and HIV/STD prevention: Clarifying the message. *American Journal of Public Health*, 83(4), 501–3.
21. Altman, D. (2006). Taboos and denial in government responses. *International Affairs* 82(2), 257–68.
22. Holmes, K. K., Levine, R., & Weaver, M. (2004). Effectiveness of condoms in preventing sexually transmitted infections. *Bulletin of the World Health Organisation* 82, 6, 454–61. Retrieved April 30, 2006, from http://www.who.int/bulletin/volumes/82/6/454.pdf.
23. Catholics for Choice: http://www.catholicsforchoice.org.
24. Human Rights Watch. (2005). *Uganda : Abstinence-only programs hijack AIDS success story*. Retrieved June 20, 2006, from http://hrw.org/english/docs/2005/03/30/uganda10380.htm .
25. Bruckner, H., & Bearman, P. (2005). After the promise: The STD consequences of adolescent virginity pledges. *Journal of Adolescent Health* 36, 271–78.
26. Levy, D. (1994, August 12). AIDS programs to spur global condom demand. *USA Today*. p. 1D. Retrieved April 30, 2006, from http://www.aegis.com/news/ads/1994/AD941408.html.
27. Zhang, H., Stanton, B., Li, X., Mao, R., Sun, Z., et al. (2004). Perceptions and attitudes regarding sex and condom use among Chinese college students: A qualitative study. *AIDS and Behavior* 8(2), 105–17.
28. Uchida, Y. (1981). Male acceptance of condoms in Japan. *Concern*, January–March, 20:35. http://www.ncbi.nlm.nih.gov/entrez/query.fcgi?cmd=Retrieve&db=PubMed&list_uids=12338297&dopt=Abstract.
29. Agence France Presse. (2004, December 6). Japan: Condom sales shrivel as Japanese log on to cyber porn. Retrieved March 20, 2008, from http://www.aegis.com/news/ads/2004/AD042476.html.
30. USTI Net News. (2005, February 4). Japan AIDS infection rate on the rise. United Press International. Retrieved April 30, 2006, from http://news.usti.net/home/news/cn/?/world.asia+oceania/1/wed/dg/Ujapan-aids.RiNV_FF4.html.
31. Elford, J., Bolding, G., Davis, M., Sherr, L., & Hart, G. (2004). Trends in sexual behaviour among London homosexual men 1998–2003: Implications for HIV prevention and sexual health promotion. *Sexually Transmitted Infections*, 80, 451–54.

290 Notes

32. Hart, G. J., & Williamson, L. M. (2005). Increase in HIV sexual risk behaviour in homosexual men in Scotland, 1996–2002: Prevention failure? *Sexually Transmitted Infections* 81, 367–72.
33. Mansergh, G., & Marks, G. (1998). Age and risk of HIV infection in men who have sex with men. *AIDS* 12, 1119–28.
34. Wolitski, R. J., Valdiserri, R. O., Denning, P. H., & Levine, W. C. (2001). Are we headed for a resurgence of the HIV epidemic among men who have sex with men? *American Journal of Public Health* 91(6), 883–88.
35. Specter, M. (2005). Higher risk: Crystal meth, the Internet, and dangerous choices about. *The New Yorker I*. Retrieved May 28, 2007, from http://www.newyorker.com/archive/2005/05/23/050523fa_fact?printable=true.
36. Bareback.com. (2006). *Hi studs* . . . Retrieved October 12, 2007, from http://www.bareback.com/#.
37. Clatts, M. C., Goldsamt, L. A., & Yi, H. (2005). An emerging risk environment: A preliminary epidemiological profile of a POZ party in New York City. *Sexually Transmitted Infections* 81, 373–76.
38. Hi+Five. (n.d.). *History*. Hi+Five: So Cal's monthly POZ party. Retrieved October 12, 2007, from http://www.hi-five.org/history.htm.
39. For an example, see the Durex Play range at http://www.lovehoney.co.uk/brands/durex-play/.
40. World Health Organisation. (n.d.). *Research and studies: Male condom*. Retrieved May 15, 2008, from http://www.who.int/reproductive-health/stis/male_condom.html.
41. Roberts, C., Kippax, S., Waldby, C., & Crawford, J. (1995). Faking it: The story of "Ohhh!" *Women's Studies International Forum* 18 (5/6), 523–32.
42. See for instance: http://www.condomx.com/home/okamoto/index.htm.
43. Durex worldwide Web site: http://www.durexworld.co
44. For an example, see the Swiss Love Life Stop AIDS campaign at http://www.lovelive.ch/stopaids.php.
45. For more information see: http://www.doetschgrether.ch/de/brands.asp.
46. In order to view the advertisement, go to http://www.adc.ch.
47. Association for the Condom Quality Seal: http://www.guetesiegel.ch/.
48. Excerpts from an interview with Doetsch Grether AG, Basel (J.-C. Usunier, July 12, 2005).
49. See http://www.doetschgrether.ch/de/Health_Care_Inhalt.asp.
50. For a presentation of condom social marketing programs, see http://www.unfpa.org/hiv/programming.htm.

NOTES TO CASE STUDY 6

1. UNAIDS. (2006). *Fact sheet: Sub-Saharan Africa*. Retrieved December 15, 2007, from http://data.unaids.org/pub/GlobalReport/2006/200605-FS_Sub-SaharanAfrica_en.pdf.
2. Panel on Antiretroviral Guidelines for Adult and Adolescents. (2008). *Guidelines for the use of antiretroviral agents in HIV-1-infected adults and adolescents*. Department of Health and Human Services (January 29), 1–128. Retrieved February 25, 2008, from http://www.aidsinfo.nih.gov/ContentFiles/AdultandAdolescentGL.pdf
3. Medical guidelines may change frequently. For the latest from the National Institutes of Health (U.S.) AIDSinfo site, go to http://AIDSinfo.nih.gov.
4. Arias, E., & Smith, B. L. (2003). *Deaths: Preliminary data for 2001 51(5)*. Centers for Disease Control. Retrieved November 20, 2007, from http://0-www.cdc.gov.pugwash.lib.warwick.ac.uk/NCHS/data/nvsr/nvsr51/nvsr51_05.pdf.

Notes 291

5. Lloyd-Smith, E., Brodkin, E., Wood, E., Kerr, T., Tyndall, M. W., Montaner, J. S. G., & Hogg, R. S. (2006). Impact of HAART and injection drug use on life expectancy of two HIV-positive cohorts in British Columbia. *AIDS* 20(3), 445–50.

6. Morgan, D., Mahe, C., Mayanja, B., Okongo, J. M., Lubega, R., & Whitworth, J. A. G. (2002). HIV-1 infection in rural Africa: Is there a difference in median time to AIDS and survival compared with that in industrialized countries? *AIDS* 16(4), 597–603.

7. UNDP. (2005). *Human development report 2005: International cooperation at a crossroads.* Retrieved January 12, 2006, from http://hdr.undp.org/reports/global/2005/pdf/HDR05_complete.pdf.

8. Gaffeo, E. (2003). The economics of HIV/AIDS: A survey. *Development Policy Review* 21(1), 27–49.

9. Stop TB Partnership. (2007). *TB HIV facts at a glance.* Retrieved January 9, 2007, from http://www.stoptb.org/wg/tb_hiv/assets/documents/TBHIV%20 Facts%20and%20figures_27%2007%2006_last%20version.ppt.

10. Abu-Raddad, L. J., Patnaik, P., & Kublin, J. G. (2006). Dual infection with HIV and malaria fuels the spread of both diseases in sub-Saharan Africa. *Science* 314(5805), 1603–06.

11. Centers for Disease Control. (n.d.). *The role of STD detection and treatment in HIV prevention.* Retrieved January 9, 2007, from http://www.cdc.gov/std/hiv/STDFact-STD&HIV.htm.

12. Glied, S. (1998). From *The encyclopedia of AIDS, a social, political, cultural, and scientific record of the AIDS epidemic* by Raymond A. Smith (ed.). Chicago: Fitzroy Dearborn Publishers.

13. Over, M. (2004). Impact of HIV/AIDS on the health sector of developing countries. In M. Haacker, *The macroeconomics of HIV/AIDS* (pp. 311–44). Retrieved November 20, 2007, from http://www.imf.org/external/pubs/ft/AIDS/eng/chapter10.pdf.

14. Bell, C., Devarajan, S., & Gersbach, H. (2003). *The long-run economic cost of HIV/AIDS: Theory and application to South Africa.* Retrieved November 20, 2007, from http://www1.worldbank.org/hiv_aids/docs/BeDeGe_BP_total2.pdf.

15. Gilmore, K. (2003). AIDS slowly eroding food security. *UN Chronicle* (July 8). Retrieved September 30, 2003, from http://www.un.org/Pubs/chronicle/2003/webArticles/070803_aids.html.

16. Food, Agriculture, and Natural Resources Policy Action Network. (2006). *Silent hunger: Policy options for effective responses to the impact of HIV and AIDS on agriculture and food security in the SADC region.* Retrieved January 15, 2008, from http://www.fanrpan.org/documents/d00351/.

17. Topouzis, D. (2003). *Assessing the impact of HIV/AIDS on ministries of agriculture: Focus on Eastern and Southern Africa.* UNAIDS/Food and Agricultural Organization, Rome. Retrieved June 15, 2008, from http://www.fao.org/hivaids/publications/moa.pdf.

18. Food, Agriculture, and Natural Resources Policy Action Network. (2006). *Silent hunger: Policy options for effective responses to the impact of HIV and AIDS on agriculture and food security in the SADC region.* Retrieved January 15, 2008, from http://www.fanrpan.org/documents/d00351/.

19. UNAIDS/WHO. (2002). *Global summary of the HIV/AIDS epidemic.* UNAIDS, December 2002. Retrieved June 15, 2003, from http://www.who.int/hiv/pub/epidemiology/epi2002/en/.

20. Topouzis, op. cit.

21. World Bank. (2003). World Bank intensifies action against HIV/AIDS. *DevNews Center* (April). Retrieved June 30, 2008, from http://web.world-

292 *Notes*

bank.org/WBSITE/EXTERNAL/NEWS/0,,contentMDK:20040236~menu PK:34480~pagePK:34370~theSitePK:4607,00.html.

22. United Nations Development Program. (2001). *HIV/AIDS, implications for poverty reduction.* Background paper, UN Special Assembly Special Session on HIV/AIDS, 25–27 June, 2001.

23. International Labour Organization. (2006). *HIV/AIDS and work: Global estimates, impact on children and youth, and response.* Retrieved June 1, 2007, from http://www.ilo.org/public/english/protection/trav/aids/.

24. Bell, C., Devarajan, S., & Gersbach, H. (2004). Thinking about the long-run economic costs of AIDS. In M. Haacker, *The macroeconomics of HIV/AIDS* (pp. 96–133). Washington, DC: International Monetary Fund.

25. Bloom, D., Reddy Bloom, L., Steven, D., & Weston, M. (2006). *Business and HIV/AIDS: A healthier partnership?* Geneva: World Economic Forum.

26. Smolinski, M. S., Hamburg, M.A., & Lederberg, J. (eds) (2003). *Microbial threats to health: Emergence, detection and response.* Institute of Medicine of the National Academies. Retrieved August 15, 2003, from http://www.nap.edu/books/030908864X/html/index.html.

27. United Nations Development Program. (2001). *HIV/AIDS, implications for poverty reduction.* Background paper, UN Special Assembly Special Session on HIV/AIDS, June 25–27, 2001.

28. International Labor Organization. (2005). *World AIDS Day: HIV/AIDS and work in a globalizing world.* Retrieved January 9, 2008, from http://www.ilo.org/global/About_the_ILO/Media_and_public_information/Press_releases/lang—en/WCMS_075519/index.htm.

29. Schneider, M., & Moodie, M. (2001). *The destabilizing impacts of HIV/AID'*, p. 5, Center for Strategic and International Studies, Washington, DC. Retrieved October 30, 2007, from http://www.kaisernetwork.org/health_cast/uploaded_files/Destabilizing_impacts_of_AIDS.pdf.

30. Ibid.

31. Harris, P. G., & Siplon, P. (2001). *International ethics, environmental change, and the global AIDS crisis: Precedents and arguments for action.* Oxford Center for the Environment, Ethics, and Society research paper (September).

32. Glied, op. cit.

33. Sen, A. (2001). Health and human freedom. *Medicus Mundi International Newsletter* 66. Retrieved May 30, 2008, from http://www.medicusmundi.org/E/news/news%2066.htm.

34. Smith, M. (2002, July 10). AIDS orphans toll mounting. *UPI Science News.* Retrieved September 10, 2007, from http://www.aegis.com/news/upi/2002/UP020712.html.

35. Goliber, T. (2002). *The status of the HIV/AIDS epidemic in sub-Saharan Africa.* Population Reference Bureau. Retrieved November 11, 2007, from http://www.prb.org/Articles/2002/TheStatusoftheHIVAIDSEpidemicinSub-SaharanAfrica.aspx.

36. Frith, M. (2003, July 10). Bush takes AIDS message to Botswana, a nation sitting on an HIV time bomb. *The Independent* (UK).

37. World Bank. (2002). *Social capital and health, nutrition, and populatio.* (October 10). Retrieved October 15, 2007, from http://www.worldbank.org/poverty/scapital/topic/health1.htm.

38. UNAIDS/WHO. (2002). *Global summary of the HIV/AIDS epidemic.* UNAIDS (December). Retrieved June 15, 2008, from http://www.who.int/hiv/pub/epidemiology/epi2002/en/.

39. Waddington, J. (2002). Children orphaned by HIV/AIDS in sub-Saharan Africa. *The EID Review* 6. Retrieved November 30, 2006m from http://ioewebserver.ioe.ac.uk/ioe/schools/leid/docs/eidreview/EIDRev6P09to15.pdf,

Notes   293

40. Law Research Services. (2002). *The Code of Hammurabi* (Web page) .Law Research Services. Retrieved September 30, 2007, from http://www.lawresearchservices.com/firms/admin/CodeHam.htm.

41. Direction Générale de la Coopération Internationale et du Développement. (n.d.). *French policy on international cooperation in the fight against HIV/AIDS in developing countries.* Direction Générale de la Coopération Internationale et du Développement, Ministry of Foreign Affairs, France.

42. Anonymous. (2002). *Clinton, Mandela call for AIDS action.* Reports from the 14th International AIDS Conference, Barcelona, *Body Positive* (October). Retrieved October 15, 2007, from http://www.thebody.com/bp/sept02/aids2002.html.

43. Thompson, D. F. (2005). *Restoring responsibility: Ethics in government, business, and healthcare.* Cambridge: Cambridge University Press.

44. World Bank Group. (2003). *Millennium development goals.* World Bank Group (September 23). Retrieved October 15, 2007, from http://www.developmentgoals.org/Hiv_Aids.htm.

45. Haerry, D., Lemmen, K., & Wiessner, P. (2005). *Travel and residence regulations for people with HIV and AIDS: Material for counsellors in AIDS service organisations.* Deutsche AIDS-Hilfe e.V. Retrieved July 25, 2006, from http://doc.ilga.org/ilga/publications/other_publications/hiv_aids_regulations.

46. Gostin, L., & Mann, J. (1994). Toward the development of a human rights assessment for the formulation and assessment of public health policies. *Health and human rights: An international journal* 1, 1. Retrieved July 30, 2006, from http://www.hsph.harvard.edu/fxbcenter/V1N1gostin.htm.

47. Bayer, R. (1998). From *The encyclopedia of AIDS, a social, political, cultural, and scientific record of the AIDS epidemic* by Raymond A. Smith (ed.). Chicago: Fitzroy Dearborn Publishers.

48. WHO. (2006). *Millennium development goals: Goal 6.* Retrieved July 30, 2006, from http://www.who.int/mdg/goals/goal6/en/index.html.

49. Lange, Joep M. A. (2002). *Access to antiretroviral therapy in resource-poor settings.* International AIDS Society (December 1). Retrieved June 15, 2008, from http://www.impactaids.org.uk/IAS%20Access3.htm.

50. Ibid.

51. United Nations General Assembly. (1948). *The International Bill of Human Rights*, General Assembly Resolution 217A (III), 10 December, 1948.

52. Ibid.

53. Mann, J. M., & Tarantola, D. (eds.) (1996). *AIDS in the World II.* New York: Oxford.

54. United Nations Economic and Social Council. (1997). *Further promotion of human rights and fundamental freedoms . . .* Second International Consultation on HIV/AIDS and Human Rights, Geneva, 23–27 September, 1996. Accessed January 31, 2008, from http://www.unhchr.ch/huridocda/huridoca.nsf/(Symbol)/E.CN.4.1997.37.En?Opendocument#guidelines.

55. Council of Europe. (1997). Convention for the Protection of Human Rights and Dignity of the Human Being . . . , Council of Europe, 4 April, 1997.

56. Gostin, op. cit.

57. United Nations Economic and Social Council, op. cit.

58. International HIV/AIDS Alliance. (2002). *Improving access to HIV/AIDS-related treatment.* International HIV/AIDS Alliance, London, June, 2002.

59. African Programme for Onchocerciasis control. (2005). *The curative tool (Ivermectin): What does it do?* Retrieved July 27, 2006, from http://www.apoc.bf/en/ivermectine.htm.

294　*Notes*

60. Okie, S. (2006). Fighting HIV—lessons from Brazil. *New England Journal of Medicine*, 354,19, 1977–81. Retrieved July 27, 2006, from http://content. nejm.org/cgi/content/full/354/19/1977.
61. Lindsey, D. (2001). A pandemic fueled by poverty. Salon.com, 27 June, 2001. Retrieved May 15, 2003 from http://dir.salon.com/news/feature/2001/06/27/ aids_poverty/index.html.
62. Mascolini, M. (2002). *Barcelona 2002: The age of access begins.* International AIDS Society (August 14). Retrieved June 15, 2003, from http://www. ias.se/article/show.asp?article=1596.
63. Friedman, M. (1970). The social responsibility of business is to increase its profits. *New York Times* magazine, 13 September. Reprinted in T. Donaldson & P. Werhane (1983), *Ethical issues in business: A philosophical approach* (2nd ed.). Englewood Cliffs, NJ: Prentice Hall.
64. UNAIDS. (2003). *HIV/AIDS: It's your business.* Retrieved July 27, 2006, from http://data.unaids.org/Publications/IRC-pub06/JC1008-Business_en.pdf.
65. Booz Allen and Global Business Coalition. (2006). *The state of business and HIV/AIDS 2006: A baseline report.* Retrieved July 27, 2007, from http:// www.boozallen.com/media/file/State_of_Business_and_HIVAIDS_2006_ v2.pdf.
66. World Health Organization. (2006). Progress on global access to HIV antiretroviral therapy: A report on "3 by 5" and beyond. Geneva: World Health Organization.
67. The WHO Prequalification Project medicines list and information may be viewed at: http://mednet3.who.int/prequal.
68. Cipla is a leading Indian pharmaceutical company, producing 1,300 products in thirty manufacturing facilities, and is an approved supplier for the WHO. For information go to www.cipla.com.
69. *Ranbaxy* is one of the top ten producers of generic medications worldwide, with manufacturing facilities in seven countries including its Indian headquarters. For information go to http://www.ranbaxy.com.
70. Strides Arcolab is a newer Indian pharmaceutical company with twelve manufacturing facilities worldwide. For information go to www.stridesarco.com.
71. Aspen Pharmacare is the largest manufacturer of generic pharmaceutical products in South Africa. For information go to http://www.pharmacare.co.za.
72. William J. Clinton Foundation. (2006). *Press release: New agreements to lower prices of HIV/AIDS rapid tests and second-line drugs.* Accessed March 15, 2006, from http://www.clintonfoundation.org/011206-nr-cf-hs-ai-isr-ind-chn-zaf-bra-pr-new-agreements-to-lower-prices-of-hiv-aids-rapid-tests-and-second-line-drugs.htm.
73. Bahadur, C. (2001) *TRIPS, HIV/AIDS, and access to drugs.* United Nations Development Project, trade and sustainable human development policy (background paper). September, 2001.
74. IMS Health. (2003). 2002 world pharma sales growth: Slower but still healthy. *Market Insight* (28 February). Retrieved June 30, 2006, from http:// www.ims-global.com/insight/news_story/0302/news_story_030228.htm.
75. McNeil, D. G. (2000, May 21). Drug companies and the third world. *New York Times.* Retrieved June 30, 2007, from http://query.nytimes.com/gst/ abstract.html?res=F70C1FF73B5E0C728EDDAC0894D8404482.
76. Pharmaceutical Research and Manufacturers' Association of America. (2003). *The issues: Research and development.* (March 26).
77. Pharmaceutical Research and Manufacturers of America. (2002). *2002 industry profile.* Pharmaceutical Research and Manufacturers of America, Washington, D.C. Retrieved June 30, 2003, from http://www.phrma.org/ publications/publications/profile02/index.cfm.

Notes 295

78. Martin, G., Sorenson, C., & Faunce, T. (2007). Balancing intellectual monopoly privileges and the need for essential medicines. *Global Health* 3(4). Retrieved May 18, 2008, from http://www.pubmedcentral.nih.gov/articlerender.fcgi?artid=1904211.

79. Leisinger, K. M. (2005). The corporate social responsibility of the pharmaceutical industry: Idealism without illusion and realism without resignation. *Business Ethics Quarterly* 15(4), 577–94.

80. Oxfam. (2001). *Oxfam briefing paper on GlaxoSmithKline. Dare to lead: Public health and company wealth.* . Oxfam (February). Retrieved June 30, 2007, from http://www.oxfam.org.uk/what_we_do/issues/health/downloads/daretolead.pdf.

81. Lobbying Disclosure Act of 1995: Public Law 104–65. December 19, 1995. Retrieved April 30, 2006, from http://www.senate.gov/reference/resources/pdf/contacting10465.pdf.$.

82. Public Citizen. (2002). The other drug war. *Public Citizen Congress Watch Reports* (June). Retrieved June 30, 2007, from http://www.citizen.org/documents/Drug_War_II.pdf.

83. McNeil, D. G. (2000). Medicine merchants: Patents and patients. As devastating epidemics increase, nations take on drug companies. *New York Times,* July 9, 2000. Retrieved August 30, 2007, from http://query.nytimes.com/gst/abstract.html?res=F60B15F93F5C0C7A8CDDAE0894D8404482.

84. Katz, D., Caplan, A. L., & Merz, J. F. (2003). All gifts large and small: Toward an understanding of the ethics of pharmaceutical industry gift-giving. *The American Journal of Bioethics*, 3(3), 39–46.

85. Wazana, A. (2000). Physicians and the pharmaceutical industry: Is a gift ever just a gift? *Journal of the American Medical Association*, 283(3), 373–80.

86. Katz, D., Caplan, A. L., & Merz, J. F., op. cit.

87. Wazana, op. cit.

88. Vachani, S. (2002). *South Africa and the AIDS Epidemic: Case study.* (October 14), Retrieved June 30, 2003, from http://cetai.hec.ca.

89. Mintzes, B., Barer, M. L., Kravitz, R. L., Kazanjian, A., Bassett, K., Lexchin, J., Evans, R. G., Pan, R., & Marion, S. A. (2002). Influence of direct to consumer pharmaceutical advertising and patients' requests on prescribing decisions: Two site cross sectional survey. *British Medical Journal* 324, 278–79.

90. Mintzes, B., Barer, M. L., Kravitz, R. L., Bassett, K., et al., op. cit.

91. Porter, Michael E. (1986). Changing patterns of international competition. *California Management Review* XXVIII(2), 9–39.

92. World Economic Forum Global Corporate Citizenship Initiative. (2005). *Partnering for success: Business perspectives on multistakeholder partnerships.* Retrieved March 16, 2005, from http://www.weforum.org/pdf/ppp.pdf.

93. Porter, M., & Kramer, M. R. (2006). Strategy and society. *Harvard Business Review* 84(12), 78–92.

94. Abbott Laboratories. (2004). *Touching lives: Global citizenship report 2003.* Accessed March 8, 2005, from http://www.abbott.com/en_US/content/document/2003_gc_report.pdf.

95. Corporate profile of Ranbaxy is found on http://www.Ranbaxy.com/profile.htm.

96. United Nations Least Developed Countries office site: http://www.un.org/ohrlls/.

97. William Jefferson Clinton Foundation site: http://www.clintonfoundation.org.

98. U.S. Food and Drug Administration site: http://www.fda.gov.

99. U.S. President's Emergency Plan for AIDS Relief (PEPFAR) site: http://www.state.gov/s/gac/.

100. World Health Organization site: http://www.who.int.

296   *Notes*

101. For the Agreement on Trade Related Aspects of Intellectual Property Rights, Including Trade in Counterfeit Goods, see http://www.wto.org/english/docs_e/legal_e/ursum_e.htm#nAgreement.
102. http://www.wto.org/english/thewto_e/minist_e/min01_e/mindecl_trips_e.htm.
103. http://www.wto.org/english/tratop_e/trips_e/factsheet_pharm02_e.htm#compulsorylicensing.
104. For more information see: http://www.inhousepharmacy.com/generics/*Cipla*-information.html.
105. AIDS Healthcare Foundation. (2008). *Drug patent decision "A victory for the Thai people," says AHF*. Retrieved May 18, 2008, from http://www.aidshealth.org/index.php?option=com_content&task=view&id=1254&Itemid=193.
106. Martin, G., Sorenson, C., & Faunce, T., op. cit.
107. WTO. (2007). Canada is first to notify use of compulsory licensing to export generic AIDS drug. Retrieved May 23, 2008, from http://www.wto.org/english/news_e/news07_e/trips_health_notif_oct07_e.htm.
108. Palia, Aspy P., & Keown, Charles F. (1991). Combating parallel importing: Views of US exporters to the Asia-Pacific region. *International Marketing Review* 8(1), 47–56.
109. Myers, Matthew B. (1999). Incidents of grey market activity among US exporters: Occurrences, characteristics and consequences. *Journal of International Business Studies* 30(1), 105–26.
110. Clarke, I., & Owens, M. (2000). Trademark rights in grey markets. *International Marketing Review* 17(3), 272–86.
111. Chaudry, P. E., & Walsh, M. J. (1995). Managing the grey market in the European Union: The case of the pharmaceutical industry. *Journal of International Marketing* 3(3), 11–33.
112. Tan, Soo J., Lim, Guan H., & Lee, Khai S. (1997). Strategic responses to parallel importing. *Journal of Global Marketing* 10(4), 45–66.
113. Narayandas, D., Quelch, J., & Swartz, G. (2000). Prepare your company for global pricing. *MIT Sloan Management Review* 42(1), 61–70.
114. Weigand, R. E. (1991). Parallel import channels: Options for preserving territorial integrity. *Columbia Journal of World Business* 26(1), 53–60.
115. *K Mart Corporation v. Cartier*, 486 US 281 (1987).
116. http://www.wto.org/english/news_e/pres03_e/pr350_e.htm.
117. http://www.wto.org/english/tratop_e/trips_e/implem_para6_e.htm.
118. http://www.wto.org/english/tratop_e/trips_e/factsheet_pharm02_e.htm#compulsorylicensing.
119. "All WTO member countries are eligible to import under this decision, but 23 developed countries are listed in the decision as voluntarily announcing that they will not use the system for imports: Australia, Austria, Belgium, Canada, Denmark, Finland, France, Germany, Greece, Iceland, Ireland, Italy, Japan, Luxembourg, the Netherlands, New Zealand, Norway, Portugal, Spain, Sweden, Switzerland, the United Kingdom and the United States" (source: WTO Web page on TRIPS and pharmaceutical patents).
120. Usunier, Jean-Claude. (2000). *Marketing across cultures*. Harlow, UK: Pearson.
121. Attaran, A. (2004). How do patents and economic policies affect access to essential medicines in developing countries? *Health Affairs* 23(3), 155–66. Attaran, A., & Gillespie-White, L. (2001). Do patents for antiretroviral drugs constrain access to AIDS treatment in Africa? *Journal of the American Medical Association* 286(15), 1886–92.
122. Bate, R. (2004). *Poverty, not patents*. American Enterprise Institute for Public Policy Research Short Publications, May 18. Retrieved August 20, 2006, from https://www.aei.org/publications/filter.all,pubID.20548/pub_detail.asp.

123. Davey, S. (2001). Medicines for all, not just the rich. *Bulletin of the World Health Organization* 79(4). Retrieved August 23, 2006, from http://www.scielosp.org/scielo.php?script=sci_arttext&pid=S0042–96862001000400019&lng=en&nrm=iso.

124. Thurow, R., & Miller, S. (2003, June 2). As US balks on medicine deal, African patients feel the pain. *Wall Street Journal*. Retrieved June 30, 2007, from http://www.aegis.com/news/wsj/2003/WJ030601.html.

125. For more about the Doha Declaration, go to the WTO page: http://www.wto.org/english/tratop_e/trips_e/public_health_e.htm.

126. Médecins Sans Frontières. (2002). *US trade position threatens access to medicines in Latin America and the Caribbean.* Press release (October 31). Retrieved June 30, 2007, from http://www.msf.org/msfinternational/invoke.cfm?objectid=78A53306–2B31–4462-BBC4F02A6C9B996F&component=toolkit.pressrelease&method=full_html.

127. Phillips, M. M. (2002, December 23). US Eases Drug-Patent Rules. *Wall Street Journal*. Retrieved June 30, 2007, from http://www.aegis.com/news/ads/2002/AD022477.html.

128. Brown, D. (2004). Bush's AIDS program balks at foreign generics: US insistence on more tests complicates rollout. *The Washington Post* (March 27). Retrieved August 23, 2006, from http://www.washingtonpost.com. Lueck, S. (2004). Activists, drug firms duel over use of funds for generic combination drugs in Africa: White House gets pressure on AIDS plan. *The Wall Street Journal* (March 25), p. A4

129. Baker, B. K. (2002). *Four lies post-Doha.* Health GAP Coalition (December 23). Retrieved June 15, 2007, from http://www.healthgap.org/press_releases/02/122302_HGAP_BP_TRIPS_exp.html.

130. World Trade Organization. (2003). *Patents.* The Agreements: Intellectual property, protection and enforcement (Web page), World Trade Organization, undated, 2003. Retrieved June 30, 2007, from http://www.wto.org/english/tratop_e/trips_e/trips_e.htm.

131. Baker, B. K. (2002). *Four lies post-Doha.* Health GAP Coalition (December 23). Retrieved June 15, 2007, from http://www.healthgap.org/press_releases/02/122302_HGAP_BP_TRIPS_exp.html.

132. Congressional Black Caucus Foundation. (2003). African trade bloc to lobby United States, pharmaceutical firms for right to produce generic antiretrovirals. *CBCF Health*, (July 7). Retrieved July 8, 2003, from http://www.cbcf-health.org/content/contentID/1980.

133. Shacinda, S. (2002). Africa wants to produce AIDS drugs. *Reuters Health*, Reuters Limited (November 15). Retrieved July 8, 2003, from http://www.reuters.com.

134. Kobori, Shinzo. (2002). TRIPS and the primacy of public health. *Asia-Pacific Review* 9 (1). Retrieved June 30, 2007, from http://unpan1.un.org/intradoc/groups/public/documents/apcity/unpan010594.pdf.

135. World Bank. (2003). *Drug patents draw scrutiny in Africa.* DevNews Center, World Bank Web site (July 10). Retrieved June 30, 2007, from http://web.worldbank.org/WBSITE/EXTERNAL/NEWS/0,,date:2003–07–10~menuPK:34461~pagePK:34392~piPK:64256810~theSitePK:4607,00.html.

136. ACT UP Paris. (2002). *Accelerating Access serves pharmaceutical companies while corrupting health organizations.* ACT UP Paris press release (May 15). Retrieved July 30, 2007, from http://www.globaltreatmentaccess.org/content/press_releases/02/051502_APP_PS_WHO_ACC_ACC.html.

137. Thomas, J. R. (2001). *HIV/AIDS drugs, patents, and the TRIPS agreement.* CRS Report for Congress (July 27). Retrieved July 30, 2007, from http://www.law.umaryland.edu/marshall/crsreports/crsdocuments/RL31066.pdf .

298 *Notes*

138. Boseley, S. (2003). Yusuf Hamied, generic drugs boss. *The Guardian* (February 18). Retrieved June 30, 2007, from http://www.guardian.co.uk/aids/story/0,7369,898056,00.html.
139. Borchardt, J. K. (2000). More than altruism behind donations of AIDS drugs to Africa. *The Scientist* (December 8). Retrieved October 30, 2007, from http://www.biomedcentral.com/news/20001208/03.
140. World Trade Organization. (2003). Decision removes final patent obstacle to cheap drug imports. WTO News Press Releases (August 30). Retrieved September 30, 2007, from http://www.wto.org/english/news_e/pres03_e/pr350_e.htm.
141. WTO. (2005). *Members OK amendment to make health flexibility permanent.* Retrieved May 13, 2008, from http://www.wto.org/english/news_e/pres05_e/pr426_e.htm.
142. Anonymous. (2003). Go-ahead for global cheap drugs. *BBC WORLD* online (August 30). Retrieved August 30, 2007, from http://news.bbc.co.uk/2/hi/health/3193723.stm.
143. Médecins Sans Frontiéres. (2003). Flawed drugs deal. Médecins Sans Frontières Press Releases (August 30). Retrieved September 30, 2003, from http://www.msf.org/content/page.cfm?articleid=C1540425–7F56–4D60-A6CB-9D7ABA6D627F.
144. McNeil, D. G., Jr. (2004). Plan to battle AIDS worldwide is falling short. *New York Times* (March 28). Retrieved August 23, 2006, from http://www.newyorktimes.com.
145. The Body. (2003). *South Africa: Glaxo, Boehringer allow more copying of AIDS drugs*, December 10. Retrieved August 23, 2006, from http://www.the-body.com/cdc/news_updates_archive/2003/dec10_03/aids_drug_copying.html.
146. Merck. (2004). Merck & Co., Inc. grants license for HIV/AIDS drug Efavirenz to South African Company, Thembalami Pharmaceuticals, in effort to accelerate access to life-saving treatment. Press release from Merck, 13 July. Retrieved August 23, 2006, from http://www.socialfunds.com//news/release_save.cgi?sfArticleId=2882.
147. Kaiser Network Daily HIV/AIDS report. (2006). *Drug access: Gilead signs license agreements with generic drug makers in India to produce antiretroviral drug Viread*, August 15. Retrieved August 23, 2006, from http://www.kaisernetwork.org/daily_reports/rep_index.cfm?hint=1&DR_ID=39164.
148. Anonymous. (2002). *TAC and MSF import generic ARV drugs into South Africa in defiance of patent abuse.* Treatment Access Campaign, Médecins Sans Frontières, and Oxfam joint press release (29 January). Retrieved October 20, 2007, from http://www.essentialdrugs.org/edrug/archive/200201/msg00090.php.
149. Lange, Joep, op. cit.
150. Lange, Joep, op. cit.
151. Anonymous. (2002). Model of success, universal access to treatment in Brazil. *ID21 Insights* Health Issue No. 2 (February). Retrieved June 30, 2007, from http://www.id21.org/insights/insights-h02/insights-issh02-art07.html.
152. International HIV/AIDS Alliance. (2002). *Improving access to HIV/AIDS-related treatment.* International HIV/AIDS Alliance, London (June). Retrieved June 30, 2007, from http://synkronweb.aidsalliance.org/graphics/secretariat/publications/att0602_Improving_access_to_ARV_treatment.pdf.
153. Ibid.
154. Kapczinski, A. (2002). Strict international patent laws hurt developing countries. *YaleGlobal* online (16 December). Retrieved July 30, 2003, from http://www.yaleglobal.yale.edu.
155. Oxfam, op. cit.

Notes 299

156. Médecins Sans Frontières. (2001). *A matter of life and death*. Médecins Sans Frontières, Campaign for Access to Essential Medicines (November). Retrieved June 30, 2007, from http://www.doctorswithoutborders.org/publications/reports/2001/doha_11–2001.pdf.
157. The Brazilian HIV/AIDS program is covered in detail in Case Study 2.
158. Anonymous (2002), op. cit.
159. Cowley, M. (2003). Brazil threatens to break AIDS drugs patents. *CDC Updates* (August 1). Retrieved August 30, 2007, from http://www.thebody.com/cdc/news_updates_archive/2003/aug4_03/brazil_patents.html.
160. Meldrum, J. (2003). Latin America to set lower prices for HIV treatments. *AIDSMAP* (June 10). Retrieved October 10, 2007, from http://www.aidsmap.com/news/newsdisplay2.asp?newsId=2109.
161. Lee, K., & McInness, C. (2006). Health, security and foreign policy. *Review of International Studies* 32, 5–23.
162. Ibid.
163. Bahadur, op. cit.
164. Ouedraogo, B. (2003). Burkina Faso to purchase generic AIDS drugs from Indian company. Associated Press (April 22). Retrieved June 30, 2007, from http://www.thebody.com/cdc/news_updates_archive/2003/apr23_03/generic_drugs.html.
165. Boseley, op. cit.
166. Arackaparambil, R. (2003). India's anti-AIDS drugs look for more takers. National AIDS Information Clearing House (March 24). Retrieved June 10, 2007, from http://www.aidsinfobbs.org/library/cdcsums/2003/003.mar/2549.
167. Bahadur, op. cit.
168. AsiaSource. (2007). *Q & A AsiaSource interview with Mongkol Na Songkhla* (May 24). Retrieved May 17, 2008, from http://www.asiasource.org/news/special_reports/thai_health.cfm.
169. Médecins Sans Frontières, (2002). *Untangling the web of price reductions*. Médecins Sans Frontières (December) Retrieved June 30, 2007, from http://www.accessmed-msf.org.
170. Bahadur, op. cit.
171. Ibid.
172. Abarca, D., et al. (2003). *Letter from 65 NGO's*. Published by CPTech (June 30). Retrieved October 15, 2007, from http://www.cptech.org/ip/health/ngos06302003.html.
173. Holmer, A. F. (2002). *The case for innovation: The role of intellectual property*. The Economist's Second Annual Pharmaceuticals Roundtable (speech) (November 20). Retrieved July 30, 2003, from http://www.phrma.org/issues/intprop/index.cfm?archive=intellprop.
174. Kobori, S. (2002). TRIPS and the primacy of public health. *Asia-Pacific Review* 9(1).
175. Donnelly, J. (2001). Africa may skirt patent to get AIDS drugs. *Boston Globe* (August 25). Retrieved July 30, 2007, from http://www.cid.harvard.edu/cidinthenews/articles/Globe_082501.html.
176. Holmer, A. F. (2002). *The case for innovation: The role of intellectual property*. The Economist's Second Annual Pharmaceuticals Roundtable (speech) (November 20). Retrieved July 30, 2003, from http://www.phrma.org/mediaroom/press/releases/20.11.2002.628.cfm.
177. Borchart, op. cit.
178. Anonymous. (2000). Cheaper AIDS drugs for Africa. Health Afrol.com (July 10). Retrieved July 30, 2007, from http://www.afrol.com/Categories/Health/health006_aids_drugs_cheaper.htm.

300 *Notes*

179. Anonymous. (2003). Clinton secures AIDS drugs deal. *SBS World News* (October 24). Retrieved October 30, 2003, from http://www9.sbs.com.au/theworldnews/region.php?id=71439&region=4.
180. Boseley, S. (2003). Investors pressure drug firms on pricing. *The Guardian* (March 25). Retrieved October 15, 2007, from http://www.guardian.co.uk/uk_news/story/0,3604,921328,00.html.
181. A Investment Office. (2003). *Agenda Item 8d* CalPERS (September 15). Retrieved October 15, 2003, from http://www.calpers.ca.gov/whatshap/calendar/board/invest/200309/Item08d-00.doc.
182. Anonymous. (2003). *CalPERS to reopen GSK's AIDS pricing issue.* Media Releases AIDS Healthcare Foundation (November 18). Retrieved November 20, 2007, from http://www.aidshealth.org/index.php?option=com_content&task=view&id=858&Itemid=193.
183. View the letter from the US senators at: http://www.cptech.org/ip/health/aids/senate06132003.html.
184. View the investor statement from *ISIS* and its good practice guidelines in full at: http://www.isisam.com/uploadfiles/pharmaceuticalper cent-20companiesper cent20andper cent20publicper cent20healthper cent-20crisis.pdf.
185. View, for instance, GlaxoSmithKline's corporate social responsibility report at: http://www.gsk.com/financial/reps02/CSR02/GSKcsr-5.htm.
186. Roth, G. Y. (2003). *Top 20 pharmaceutical companies.* ContractPharma (July–August). Retrieved October 15, 2007, from http://www.contract-pharma.com/articles/2007/07/2007-top-20-pharmaceutical-companies-report.
187. Velasquez, G. (2003). Unhealthy profits. *Le Monde Diplomatique* (July). Retrieved September 30, 2007, from http://mondediplo.com/2003/07/10velasquez.
188. Dinh, K. (2002). Linking local to the global in promoting access to medicines. *Campaign for Essential Medicines*, Médecins Sans Frontières. Retrieved July 30, 2007, from http://www.public-policy.unimelb.edu.au/events/health_policy.html.
189. Anonymous. (2001). Patent nonsense. *Financial Times* (editorial) (August 24). Retrieved July 30, 2003, from http://www.ft.com.
190. Zimmerman, R. (2002). *Roche is faulted.* Médecins Sans Frontières Articles, Médecins Sans Frontières (15 November). Retrieved July 30, 2007, from http://www.msf.org/content/page.cfm?articleid=7A49233B-8D3E-4754-A515AACD59B7AAEA.
191. Anonymous. (2003). Roche fuels HIV drugs debate. BBC News (February 24). Retrieved September 30, 2007, from http://news.bbc.co.uk/1/hi/business/2793953.stm.
192. Anonymous. (2003). Anxiety over cost of new AIDS drug. CBS News (March 13). Retrieved October 1, 2007, from http://www.cbsnews.com/stories/2003/03/13/health/main543887.shtml.
193. Associated Press. (2003, February 13). Roche cuts prices of its AIDS drugs to poor countries. Retrieved September 30, 2007, from http://www.thebody.com/cdc/news_updates_archive/2003/feb18_03/roche_prices.html.
194. Anonymous. (2003). Roche fuels HIV drugs debate. BBC News (February 24). Retrieved September 30, 2007, from http://news.bbc.co.uk/1/hi/business/2793953.stm.
195. Roth, Gil, op. cit.
196. *Businessweek.* (2005). Pfizer's funk. Retrieved July 30, 2007, from http://www.businessweek.com/magazine/content/05_09/b3922001_mz001.htm.
197. Ibid.

Notes 301

198. Corporatewatch UK. (2001). *Pfizer, Inc. corporate crimes*. Company profiles, undated. Retrieved July 30, 2007, from http://www.corporatewatch.org/?lid=330.
199. Kaiser Daily HIV/AIDS report. (2007). *HIV/AIDS group reacts to new Viagra ad campaign* (July 25). Retrieved May 17, 2008, from http://www.aidshealth.org/index.php?option=com_content&task=view&id=1114&Itemid=194.
200. Donohue, J. M., Cevasco, M., & Rosenthal, M. B. (2007). A decade of direct-to-consumer advertising of prescription drugs. *New England Journal of Medicine* 357, 673–81.
201. Swearingen, S. G., & Klausner, J. D. (2005). Sildenafil use, sexual risk behaviour, and risk for sexually transmitted diseases, including HIV infection. *American Journal of Medicine* 118(6), 571–77.
202. For more information on drug price and marketing advocacy by the U.S. AIDS Healthcare Foundation, go to : http://www.aidshealth.org/.

NOTES TO CASE STUDY 7

1. Kouteya, S. (2006, July 29). 29 per cent of HIV+ve people refused loans. *The Times of India Online*. Retrieved October 13, 2006, from http://www.undp.org.in/MEDIA/2006/july/TimesofIndia.pdf.
2. Sudha, R. T., Vihay, D. T., & Lakshmi, V. (2005). Awareness, attitudes, and beliefs of the general public towards HIV/AIDS in Hyderabad, a capital city from South India. *Indian Journal of Medical Sciences* 59(7), 307–16. Retrieved 13 October, 2006, from http://www.indianjmedsci.org/article.asp?issn=0019-5359;year=2005;volume=59;issue=7;spage=307;epage=316;aulast=Sudha.
3. Wonacott, P., & Chase, M. (2006, August 9). In India, call centers warn young workers about HIV risk. *Wall Street Journal*. Retrieved October 13, 2006, from http://www.aegis.com/news/wsj/2006/WJ060801.html.
4. NAZ Foundation. (2005). *Development manual. Developing community-based organisations addressing HIV/AIDS, sexual health, welfare and human rights issues for males-who-have-sex-with-males, their partners, and families*. Retrieved October 13,, 2006, from http://www.nfi.net/NFI per cent20Publications/Manuals/Contents per cent20Manual1.pdf.
5. Jenkins, C. (2004). HIV/AIDS and culture: Implications for policy. In V. Rao & M. Walton (eds.), *Culture and public action* (pp. 260–81). Stanford, CA: Stanford Social Sciences.
6. Pelzer, K., Nzewi, E., & Mohan, K. (2004). Attitudes towards HIV antibody testing and people with AIDS among university students in India, South Africa, and the United States. *Indian Journal of Medical Sciences* 58(3), 95–108. Retrieved October 13, 2006, from http://www.indianjmedsci.org/article.asp?issn=0019-5359;year=2004;volume=58;issue=3;spage=95;epage=108;aulast=Peltzer;type=0.
7. Ibid.
8. Sudha, R. T., Vihay, D. T., & Lakshmi, op. cit.
9. National Institute of Allergy and Infectious Diseases. (2005). HIV *infection and AIDS*. Fact sheet, March. Retrieved October 13, 2006, from http://www.niaid.nih.gov/factsheets/hivinf.htm.
10. NASSCOM is the trade body for information technology firms and sourcing companies in India (http://www.nasscom.in).
11. Gautam, V., & Arora, C. (2007, July 27). HIV test to join a BPO? *The Times of India*. http://timesofindia.indiatimes.com/Cities/City_Supplements/Delhi_Times/HIV_test_to_join_a_BPO_/articleshow/2151695.cms.

302 *Notes*

12. NACO. (2007). *India launches world's largest social mobilisation campaign.* (Press release, December 1). Retrieved January 8, 2008, from http://www.nacoonline.org/NACO_Action/Media__Press_Release/.
13. Global Business Coalition. (2006). *GBC launches call center initiative to confront India's growing HIV/AIDS crisis* (March 20). Retrieved November 30, 2007, from http://www.businessfightsaids.org/live/media/news/article.php?id=524.
14. Sudha, R. T., Vihay, D. T., & Lakshmi, op. cit.
15. Prasad, T. L., & Damayanti, K. (2004). *Prevalence of viral markers, HIV, HBV, HCV.* International AIDS Conference, Bangkok, Thailand, July 11–16. Retrieved January 6 2008 from http://www.aegis.com/conferences/iac/2004/C11887.html.
16. Business Process Industry Association of India. (2006). *Human resources challenges.* Retrieved January 6 2008 from http://www.bpiai.org/hr-challenges.html bpiai.org/hr-challenges.html.
17. Dash, D. K. (2007, December 11). BPO's to prepare employee database to counter attrition. *Times of India.* Retrieved January 6, 2008, from http://www.bpiai.org/images/Employee-Database-19dec07.jpg.
18. *Wall Street Journal.* (2006, October 6). Dell, Inc.: Call center in India to expand to 2,500 workers from 800. Retrieved October 13, 2006, from http://www.proquest.com.
19. *International Contact Center Magazine.* (2006, May). Foreign accents most significant call center frustration among US respondents to poll. Retrieved October 13, 2006, from http://www.iccmnewsline.com/News/05–04–06c.htm.
20. NAZ Foundation, op. cit.
21. Babu, V. (2006). From voice to value: Call centers still account for 82 per cent of the ITES industry revenue. *Business Today* (New Delhi), October 8, p. 118.
22. *CFO Magazine.* (2003, October). The China syndrome. Retrieved October 13, 2006, from http://www.cfo.com/article.cfm/3010459/3/c_3046600?f=related.
23. Indian Business Trust for HIV/AIDS. (n.d.). *Board of trustees for Indian Business Trust for HIV/AIDS.* Retrieved October 13, 2006, from http://www.indianbusinesstrust.org/board_of_trusties.htm.
24. Confederation of Indian Industry and Indian Business Trust for HIV/AIDS. (2003). *Business for life: Industry response to HIV/AIDS in India.* New Delhi: Confederation of Indian Industry.
25. Blake, R. O. (2005). *Workplace interventions for the prevention of HIV/AIDS.* U.S. Embassy, New Delhi, July 9. Retrieved October 13, 2006, from http://newdelhi.usembassy.gov/ipr071105a.html.
26. Cohen, J. (2007). India slashes estimates of HIV-infected people. *Science* 317(5835), 179–81. Retrieved July 30, 2007, from http://www.sciencemag.org/cgi/content/full/317/5835/179?rss=1.
27. Moses, S., Blanchard, J. F., Kang, H., Emmanuel, F., Reza Paul, S., et al. (2006). *AIDS in South Asia: Understanding and responding to a heterogenous epidemic.* Washington, DC: The World Bank. Retrieved October 13, 2006, from http://www-wds.worldbank.org/external/default/WDSContentServer/WDSP/IB/2006/08/24/000160016_20060824174441/Rendered/PDF/370930SAR0Aids01PUBLIC1.pdf.
28. Kumar, R., Jha, P., Arora, P., Mony, P., Bhatia, P., et al. (2006). Trends in HIV-1 in young adults in south India from 200 to 2004: A prevalence study. *The Lancet* 367(9517), 1164–72.
29. Moses, S., Blanchard, J. F., Kang, H., Emmanuel, F., Reza Paul, S., et al., op. cit.

Notes   303

30. India National AIDS Control Organisation. (2005). *Annual report, 2002–2003, 2003–2004 (Up to 31 July, 2004)*. Retrieved October 13, 2006, from http://www.nacoonline.org/annualreport/annulareport.pdf.
31. Global Business Coalition. (2005). AIDS in emerging economies. *Business and AIDS* 2(1), 31. Retrieved October 13, 2006, from http://www.businessfightsaids.org/atf/cf/ per cent7B4AF0E874-E9A0–4D86-BA28–96C3BC31180A per cent7D/GBC per cent20Summer per cent2005.pdf.
32. Global Business Coalition. (2005). AIDS in emerging economies. *Business and AIDS* 2(1), 31. Retrieved October 13, 2006, from http://www.businessfightsaids.org/atf/cf/ per cent7B4AF0E874-E9A0–4D86-BA28–96C3BC31180A per cent7D/GBC per cent20Summer per cent2005.pdf.
33. Moses, S., Blanchard, J. F., Kang, H., Emmanuel, F., Reza Paul, S., et al., op. cit.

NOTES TO CASE STUDY 8

1. The International Labor Organization (ILO) is the United Nations agency charged with the "world of work." The agency initiated ILOAIDS, in 2000, as an initiative to study the impacts of the epidemic on business, support government and company efforts in the area, and fight HIV discrimination and stigma. For information: http://www.ilo.org/aids.
2. BBC News. (2004). *End workplace AIDS bias, UN says*. (12 July). Retrieved October 28, 2007, from http://news.bbc.co.uk/2/hi/asia-pacific/3885331.stm.
3. Mechai Viravaidya founded the Population and Community Development NGO in 1974 with the primary aim of reducing the number of children per family. He has served as cabinet member and senator, and remains a flamboyant public figure who stages attention-grabbing events and publicly rebukes members of the government who he says do not do enough to fight HIV/AIDS. He uses humor to reduce potential embarrassment surrounding the topic, also in a way that everyone can understand. Viravaiydia owns the Cabbages and Condoms restaurant and hotel chain, as well as free vasectomy clinics that are responsible for 30 percent of the procedures in Thailand. He runs a number of companies that generate revenue for NGO activities. For information: http://www.cabbagesandcondoms.co.th/. Gayle, H. (2006). Mechai Viravaidya: By preaching safe sex, Thailand's condom king became a legend. *TIME*, November. Retrieved November 6, 2006, from http://www.time.com/time/asia/2006/heroes/in_viravaidya.html. Johnson, C. (2004). *Cabbages and condoms: Business innovation for social change*. Retrieved October 31, 2006, from http://worldbenefit.cwru.edu/inquiry/feature_cc.cfm.
4. IRIN News. (2006). *Thailand: Increased HIV/AIDS awareness campaings needed: UNAIDS* (31 May). Retrieved July 2, 2007, from http://www.irin-news.org/report.aspx?reportid=34361.
5. Brown, A. D., Jejeebhoy, S. J., Shah, I., & Yount, K. M. (2001). *Sexual relations among young people in developing countries: Evidence from WHO case studies*. Geneva: Department of Reproductive Health and Research, World Health Organization.
6. Revenga, A., Over, M., Masaki, E., Peerapatanapokin, W., Gold, J., et al. (2006). *The economics of effective AIDS treatment: Evaluating policy options*. Retrieved June 17, 2007, from http://web.worldbank.org/WBSITE/EXTERNAL/COUNTRIES/EASTASIAPACIFICEXT/EXTEAPREG-TOPHEANUT/EXTEAPREGTOPHIVAIDS/0,,contentMDK:21024879~pagePK:34004173~piPK:34003707~theSitePK:503157,00.html.

304　*Notes*

7. IRIN News. (2006). *Thailand: Increased HIV/AIDS awareness campaigns needed: UNAIDS* (31 May). Retrieved July 2, 2007. from http://www.irinnews.org/report.aspx?reportid=34361.

8. Population Services International (PSI) uses social marketing tactics to promote health services and products in more than sixty countries, in four action areas (child survival, HIV, malaria, and reproductive health). Its HIV focus is on abstinence, fidelity, and condom use. For information: http://www.psi.org.

9. The Body Shop. (2007). *Stop HIV: Spray to change attitudes.* Retrieved December 19, 2007, from http://www.thebodyshopinternational.com/Values+and+Campaigns/Our+Campaigns/Stop+HIV+Spray+to+Change+Attitudes/Home.htm.

10. Asian Business Coalition on AIDS & UNAIDS. (2002). *Business taking action to manage HIV/AIDS.* Retrieved December 19, 2007, from http://data.unaids.org/Topics/Partnership-Menus/PDF/asianbusinesssummary_en.pdf.

11. For information about PepsiCo's HIV/AIDS initiatives worldwide, go to http://www.pepsico.com/PEP_Citizenship/HIVAIDSInitiatives/PolicyandInitiatives/Programs/index.cfm#thailand.

12. Pepsico. (2008). *Citizenship HIV/AIDS initiatives. Thailand.* Retrieved February 7, 2008, from http://www.pepsico.com/PEP_Citizenship/HIVAIDSInitiatives/PolicyandInitiatives/Programs/index.cfm#thailand.

13. GTZ is the German technical cooperation angency, *Gesellschaft für Wirtschaftliche Zusammenarbeit.*

14. Mukherjee, P. (2007). Pepsi makes the right choice. *Business-Standard* (December 11) Retrieved December 19, 2007, from http://www.business-standard.com/general/storypage_general.php?&autono=307117.

15. The Global Business Coalition on HIV/AIDS (GBC). The GBC has four main goals: increase the number of companies committed to fighting the pandemic, increase and improve business actions, develop business competencies for HIV/AIDS programs, and use the power of business as advocate. In 2006, GBC had approximately 200 member companies such as Coca-Cola, L'Oréal, Luckystar China, and Volkswagen, Walmart, among others. For information: http://www.businessfightsaids.org.

16. ECPAT UK. (n.d.). *Child sex tourism in Thailand.* Retrieved May 13, 2008, from http://www.thetravelfoundation.org.uk/ecpat_tools.asp.

17. Thailand Business Coalition on AIDS (TBCA) was in 1993 the first organization of its type. TBCA provides technical assistance on HIV/AIDS workplace and community programs to 1,300 companies in Thailand. Some members include: American International Assurance, Honda, Hilton, Nestlé, Pan Pacific, Toshiba, and 3M. For information: http://www.abconaids.org.

18. These "reasons" were based on the eleven objections in the article: Van der Borght, S., Rinke de Wit, T. F., Janssens, V., et al. (2006). HAART for the HIV-infected employees of large companies in Africa. *The Lancet* 368(9534), 547–50.

19. Anonymous. (1999). Condoms should be as easily available as Coca-Cola. *BBC News Health,* November 24. Retrieved October 28, 2007, from http://news.bbc.co.uk/1/hi/health/221114.stm.

20. Morgan, R. (2000). *Equity Map.* Research International, February 17. Retrieved November 8, 2007, from http://www.research-int.com/library/library.asp?id=162.

21. Harris Interactive. (2007). Coca-Cola on top for first time in annual "best brands" Harris Poll. *The Harris Poll 71* (July 17). Retrieved November 30, 2007, from http://www.harrisinteractive.com/harris_poll/index.asp?PID=787.

Notes   305

22. Grande, C. (2007). Ethical consumption makes mark on branding. *Financial Times*. Retrieved November 17, 2007, from http://www.ft.com/cms/s/2/d54c45ec-c086–11db-995a-000b5df10621.html.

23. Davison, L. (2003). *Finding the elusive "cool factor."* Research International, August 28. Retrieved November 8, 2007, from http://www.research-int.com/library/library.asp?id=432.

24. Taylor, H. (2003). Sony tops the list. *Harris Poll 2003*, Harris Interactive, July 23. Retrieved November 17, 2007, from http://www.harrisinteractive.com/harris_poll/index.asp?PID=388.

25. Spencer, J. (2003) Healthy scores in consumer survey. *Wall Street Journal*, November 19. Retrieved November 30, 2007, from http://www.cfigroup.com/resources/wsj/wsj_11_19_03.htm.

26. Borja, R. R. (2003). Coca-Cola plays both sides of the school marketing game. *Education Weekly*, November 5, 2003. Retrieved November 15, 2007, from http://www.edweek.org/ew/newstory.cfm?slug=10Cokebiz.h23.

27. BBC. (2001). Coke sued over death squad claims. *BBC News*, 20 July. Retrieved November 15, 2006, from http://news.bbc.co.uk/2/hi/business/1448962.stm. See also activist site: http://www.killercoke.org/crimes.htm.

28. BBC. (2001). *Coke sued over death squad claims.* (20 July). Retrieved November 15, 2006, from http://news.bbc.co.uk/2/hi/business/1448962.stm.

29. Thomsen, M. (2000). Coke settles racial discrimination suit. *Social Funds*, November 17. Retrieved November 15, 2006, from http://www.socialfunds.com/news/article.cgi/article430.html.

30. *The Economist*. (2006). Face Value: The real thing. Sunita Narain, an Indian environmentalist, has dented two of the world's glossiest brand, August 24–September 1, 49.

31. Simons, C. (2007). Coca-Cola, Indian village in dispute. *Statesman* (December 25) Retrieved January 3, 2008, from http://www.statesman.com/news/content/news/stories/world/12/25/1225indiacoke.html.

32. Lamont, J., & Liu, B. (2002). Coca-Cola to face worldwide demonstrations. *Financial Times*, October 17. Retrieved July 30, 2006, from http://www.thebody.com/content/art18426.html.

33. White, B. (2002). Black Coca-Cola workers still angry. *Washington Post* (April 18). Retrieved November 5, 2006, from http://thebody.com/cdc/news_updates_archive/apr18_02/04_18_02.html.

34. Additional information may be found on the following sites: Coca-Cola's membership page at www.businessfightsaids.org. Global Business Coalition on HIV/AIDS: http://www.businessfightsaids.org. A corporate "watchdog" site: http://www.cokewatch.org.

35. Health GAP Web site: http://www.healthgap.org.

36. For a description of the site, which no longer exists, go to: http://www.comminit.com/strategicthinking/stdigitalpulse/sld-1625.html.

37. AIDS Coalition to Unleash Power (ACT UP) New York Web site: http://www.actupny.org/.

38. Weinert, L. (2002). Can Coke prevent AIDS? *The Nation*, October 24. Retrieved December 6, 2006, from http://www.thenation.com/doc/20021111/weinert20021024.

39. Lynch, S. (2003). *Health GAP on Coke's AIDS programs in Africa.* Health GAP Press release (27 October). Retrieved November 15, 2007, from http://www.healthgap.org/press_releases/03/102703_HGAP_PR_KO_12mos.html.

40. ACT UP NY. (2002). *Barcelona AIDS Conference reports: AIDS activists protest Coke's deadly neglect of workers in developing countries* (10 July).

306 Notes

Retrieved November 13, 2007, from http://www.actupny.org/reports/bcn/BCNcoke.html.

41. Health GAP. (2003). *Show real corporate responsibility: Treat your workers, corporate complicity and the HIV/AIDS workplace programs.* Health GAP position paper (February 27). Retrieved November 15, 2007, from http://www.globaltreatmentaccess.org/content/press_releases/03/022803_HGAP_PP_MNC_2003.html.

42. U.S. Centers for Disease Control and Prevention. (2003). *England—activists question faith in PepsiCo* (May 28). Retrieved November 6, 2007, from http://www.thebody.com/content/living/art29697.html.

43. McNeil, D. G. (2001). Coca-Cola joins AIDS fight in Africa. *New York Times* (21 June). Retrieved November 15, 2006, from http://query.nytimes.com/gst/fullpage.html?res=9C05E1D71F31F932A15755C0A9679C8B63&scp=1&sq=coca%20cola%20HIV&st=cse.

44. The Coca-Cola Company. (2001). *The Coca-Cola Company 2001 Annual Report.* Retrieved December 6, 2006, from http://www2.coca-cola.com/investors/annualreport/2001/pdf/ko_ar_2001_our_building_blocks.pdf.

45. Mbogo, S. (2003). Islamic Coke arrives in East Africa: Coke boycott called. *CNS News* (October 17). Retrieved November 30, 2006, from http://www.cnsnews.com/ForeignBureaus/archive/200310/FOR20031017b.html.

46. Sachs, J. D., McArthur, J. W., Schmidt-Traub, G., Kruk, M., et al. (2004). Ending Africa's poverty trap: Comments and discussion. *Brookings Papers on Economic Activity* 1, 117–41.

47. International Finance Corporation/World Bank Group. (2007). *The business of health in Africa: Partnering with the private sector to improve people's lives.* Retrieved May 18, 2008, from http://siteresources.worldbank.org/INTAFRHEANUTPOP/PublicationsandReports/21630695/IFC_HealthinAfrica_Final.pdf.

48. Cone. (2007). *Research report: Cone cause evolution and environmental survey.* Retrieved May 17, 2008, from http://www.coneinc.com/stuff/contentmgr/files/0/a8880735bb2e2e894a949830055ad559/files/2007_cause_evolution_survey.pdf.

49. Domini Web site: http://www.domini.com.

50. *Ethical Corporation* Web site: http://www.ethicalcorp.com/.

51. *CSR-Asia* (weekly) Web site: http://www.csr-asia.com.

52. UNAIDS Web site: http://www.unaids.org.

53. PharmAccess International Web site: http://www.pharmaccess.org.

54. Coca-Cola Africa Foundation page: http://www2.coca-cola.com/citizenship/foundation_local.html.

55. Coca-Cola Africa Foundation. (n.d.) *The Coca-Cola Africa Foundation HIV/AIDS programs in Africa facts sheet.* Coca-Cola Africa Foundation. Retrieved November 30, 2006, from http://www.businessfightsaids.org/pdf/cocacola_africa_fact.pdf.

56. Coca-Cola Africa–Kenya. (n.d.). *Coca-Cola Africa-Kenya: Citizenship* (Web page). Coca-Cola Africa. Retrieved October 28, 2003, from http://www.kenya.Coca-Cola.com/citizenship.html.

57. Global Compact site: http://www.unglobalcompact.org/.

58. Global Reporting Initiative site: http://www.globalreporting.org.

59. Unilever corporate values: http://www.unilever.com/ourvalues/.

60. WEF case study on the Namibia Business Coalition: http://www.weforum.org/pdf/GHI/Namibia.pdf.

61. Global Business Coalition on HIV/AIDS, Tuberculosis and Malaria site: http://www.businessfightsaids.org.

Notes   307

62. WEF Global Health Initiative site: http://www.weforum.org/en/initiatives/globalhealth/index.htm.
63. Global Fund to Fight HIV/AIDS, Tuberculosis and Malaria: http://www.theglobalfund.org.
64. Volkswagen Sustainability site: http://www.volkswagen-sustainability.com.
65. World Wildlife Fund site: http://www.worldwildlife.org.
66. Lafarge site : http://www.lafarge.fr.
67. PSI (Population Services International) Web site: http://www.psi.org/.
68. Population Services International. (n.d.). *PSI Profile: What is social marketing?* (Web page). Population Services International. Retrieved October 28, 2007, from http://www.psi.org/resources/pubs/what_is_SM.html.
69. Population Services International. (n.d.) *Experience social marketing* (Web presentation). Population Services International. Retrieved October 28, 2007, from http://www.psi.org/experience_social_marketing/index.html.
70. U.S. Agency for International Development. (2003). *PSI partners with Coca-Cola to market AIDS prevention and awareness.* Bureau for Global Health, October. Retrieved August 26, 2006, from http://www.psi.org/news/zimbabwe.pdf#search= per cent22condom per cent20coca per cent20cola per cent22.
71. Coca-Cola. (2003). *Coca-Cola Africa Foundation.* Retrieved July 30, 2003, from http://www2.Coca-Cola.com.
72. Anonymous. (2001). UNAIDS signs up Coca-Cola in battle against AIDS. *Corporate Social Responsibility Wire* (June 20). Retrieved November 8, 2007, from http://www.socialfunds.com/news/release_print.cgi?sfArticleId=671.
73. PharmAccess International. (2003). *PharmAccess International organizes HIV/AIDS treatment program in collaboration with the Coca-Cola Africa Foundation and Coca-Cola bottlers in 56 countries in Africa.* PharmAccess International, September 26, 2003. Retrieved November 30, 2003, from http://www.pharmaccess.org/documents/Press per cent20release per cent20Coca per cent20Cola per cent2026 per cent20sept per cent202002.pdf.
74. Global Business Coalition. (2003). *HIV/AIDS threatens our workers, our customers and our communities.* Retrieved November 7, 2007, from http://www.kintera.org/atf/cf/%7BEE846F03-1625-4723-9A53-B0CDD2195782%7D/GBC%20Brochure%202003.pdf.
75. Coca-Cola Company. (2003). *Africa's Coca-Cola bottlers to provide HIV/AIDS healthcare benefits to employees, their spouses and children. HIV/AIDS healthcare benefits include antiretroviral treatment* (April 15). Retrieved October 19, 2007, from http://www.thecoca-colacompany.com/presscenter/pdfs/2003_news_releases.pdf.
76. Ibid.
77. Henry J. Kaiser Family Foundation. (2007). *Coca-Cola distributes HIV, TB, Malaria prevention playing cards among Chinese migrant workers* (May 29). Retrieved October 19, 2007, from http://www.thebody.com/content/news/art41173.html.
78. Henry J. Kaiser Family Foundation. (2007). GBC president says Russia is losing battle against AIDS because of government inaction, lack of awareness. Retrieved October 19, 2007, from http://www.thebody.com/content/news/art43685.html.
79. AngloAmerican (2008). *Responsible mining.* Retrieved October 28, 2008 from http://www.angloamerican.co.uk/aa/development/performance/miningbriefs/mb_hivaids/mb_hivaids.pdf.
80. Global Business Coalition (2008). *Member profile: AngloAmerican.* Retrieved October 28, 2008 from http://www.gbcimpact.org/live/members/members.php?id=151.

308 *Notes*

81. AngloAmerican (2008). *Responsible mining.* Retrieved October 28, 2008 from http://www.angloamerican.co.uk/aa/development/performance/miningbriefs/mb_hivaids/mb_hivaids.pdf
82. Ibid.
83. Global Business Coalition (2008). *Member profile: AngloAmerican.* Retrieved October 28, 2008 from http://www.gbcimpact.org/live/members/members.php?id=151.
84. AngloAmerican, op. cit.
85. Van der Borght, S. (2003) *Heineken HIV/AIDS policy*, Heineken, EMS Roundtable on Development (March 17). Retrieved November 1, 2008 from http://europa.eu.int/comm/enterprise/csr/documents/20030317/csrdevheineken.pdf.
86. Ibid.
87. Rijckborst, H., Wesseling, J. L. , Van der Borght, S. F., Van Mameren, J. H., et al. (2004). Heineken's HIV/AIDS policy, the contribution of a private company. *International Conference on AIDS* Bangkok, Thailand, July 11–16.
88. Sansoni, S. (2003). Keeping alive. *Forbes*, February 3. Retrieved November 18, 2003 from http://www.forbes.com/forbes/2003/0203/064.html.
89. Global Business Coalition (2008). Member profile: Heineken NV. Retrieved November 5, 2008 from http://www.gbcimpact.org/live/members/members.php?id=179.
90. The Coca-Cola Company (2008). *HIV/AIDS.* http://www.thecoca-colacompany.com/citizenship/hiv_aids.html.
91. Coca-Cola Africa Foundation (2006). *The Coca-Cola Africa Foundation HIV/AIDS Report.* Retrieved October 28, 2008 from http://www.gbcimpact.org/documents/members/cocacola/Coke%20HIV%20Report%202006.pdf.
92. Global Health Initiative (2002). *Coca Cola Africa Workplace Prevention Programme Community Outreach Manual 4.* Retrieved October 28, 2008 from http://www.weforum.org/pdf/Initiatives/GHI_HIV_CocaCola_AppendixE.pdf.
93. Coca-Cola Africa Foundation, op. cit.
94. The Coca-Cola Company, op. cit.
95. World Economic Forum (2006) *Global Health Initiative, Private sector case example: BMW*, World Economic Forum Global Health Initiative. Retrieved September 30, 2008 from http://www.weforum.org/fweblive/groups/public/documents/wef_webpage/05.09.06_ghi_hiv_case_study_bm.pdf.
96. BMW ZA (undated). *BMW's drive against HIV/AIDS.* Retrieved November 5, 2008 from http://www.bmwplant.co.za/Content/people/aids_brochure.pdf.
97. World Economic Forum (2006), op. cit.
98. World Economic Forum (2003) *Global Health Initiative, Private sector case example: ChevronTexaco*, World Economic Forum Global Health Initiative. Retrieved November 5, 2008 from http://www.weforum.org/pdf/Initiatives/GHI_%20HIV_CaseStudy_Chevron.pdf.
99. Global Business Coalition (2008). *Member profile: Chevron Corporation.* Retrieved November 5, 2008 from http://www.gbcimpact.org/live/members/members.php?id=49.
100. TPAA (2004). *ChevronTexaco contributes $25,000 to fight HIV/AIDS in Russia and Ukraine.* Retrieved November 5, 2008 from http://www.tpaa.net/news/pressreleases/?id=546

NOTES TO CASE STUDY 9

1. This case study was written based on communications with Katy Hayes, National HIV/AIDS coordinator, Woolworths, Cape Town, South Africa.

Notes 309

2. Woolworths site: http://www.woolworths.co.za.
3. Marks & Spencer site: http://www2.marksandspencer.com/thecompany/.
4. Country Road Australia site: http://www.countryroad.com.au.
5. Woolworths. (2005). Annual Report 2005.
6. French-owned supermarket/hypermarket chain at http://www.auchan.ru/en/home/.
7. Supermarket chain owned by Marta (Russia) and Rewe (Germany) at http://www.marta.ru/en1/billa.php.
8. Ramstore supermarket, owned by Ramenka, a Turkish-based retail group.
9. United Nations Development Program. (2004). *Human Development Report: South Africa.* Accessed August 16, 2005, from http://hdr.undp.org/statistics/data/cty/cty_f_ZAF.html.
10. Woolworths Holdings. (2004). Investor relations: Corporate citizenship (Web page). Accessed August 12, 2005, from http://www.Woolworthsholdings.co.za/corp_citizenship/corp_citizenship5.html.
11. Woolworths. (n.d.). Franchise welcome: Our most important asset (Web page). Accessed August 12, 2005, from http://www.Woolworths.co.za/caissa2asp.asp?Page=ITB_Context&Post=FAT_ImportantAsset.
12. Woolworths. (n.d.). Franchise welcome: Where we are today (Web page). Accessed August 12, 2005, from http://www.Woolworths.co.za/caissa2asp.asp?Page=ITB_Context&Post=FAT_AreToday.
13. Woolworths. (2004). *HIV/AIDS position paper* (unpublished, internal document).
14. Woolworths. (2004). *HIV/AIDS position paper* (unpublished, internal document).
15. International Organisation of Employers. (2002). *Employers handbook on HIV/AIDS: A guide for action.* International Organisation of Employers/UNAIDS, Geneva. Accessed August 15, 2005, from http://data.unaids.org/Publications/IRC-pub02/JC767-EmployersHandbook_en.pdf#search=%22International%20Organisation%20of%20Employers%20(2002).%20Employers%20handbook%20on%20HIV%2FAIDS%3A%20A%20guide%20for%20action%22.
16. International Organisation of Employers. (2002). *Employers handbook on HIV/AIDS: A guide for action.* International Organisation of Employers/UNAIDS, Geneva. Accessed August 15, 2005, from http://data.unaids.org/Publications/IRC-pub02/JC767-EmployersHandbook_en.pdf#search=%22International%20Organisation%20of%20Employers%20(2002).%20Employers%20handbook%20on%20HIV%2FAIDS%3A%20A%20guide%20for%20action%22.
17. Woolworths. (2005). *Standing in the retail arena: A look at how Woolworths is addressing HIV/AIDS.* Unpublished advertorial drafted by Woolworths.
18. For more information on QUALSA, go to http://www.qualsa.co.za/page.asp?page=hiv.
19. Hayes, K. (2005). Personal communication, 11 December 2005.
20. For more information on the GRI, go to http://www.globalreporting.org/.
21. Woolworths. (2005). *Standing in the retail arena: A look at how Woolworths is addressing HIV/AIDS.* Unpublished advertorial drafted by Woolworths.
22. For more information on Occupational Care SA, go to http://www.ocsa.co.za.
23. International Organisation of Employers. (2002). *Employers handbook on HIV/AIDS: A guide for action.* International Organisation of Employers/UNAIDS, Geneva. Accessed August 15, 2005, from http://data.unaids.org/Publications/IRC-pub02/JC767-EmployersHandbook_en.pdf#search=%22International%20Organisation%20of%20Employers%20(2002).%20Employers%20handbook%20on%20HIV%2FAIDS%3A%20A%20guide%20for%20action%22.

310 Notes

24. Burt, S. L., Mellahi, K., Jackson, T. P., & Sparks, L. (2002). Retail internationalisation and retail failure: Issues from the case of Marks and Spencer. *International Review of Retail, Distribution, and Consumer Research* 12(2), 191–219.
25. http://www.Woolworths.co.za/caissa2asp.asp?Page=ITB_ConText&Post=FAT_Home.

NOTES TO CASE STUDY 10

1. United Nations (2001). *The UN works to stop the spread of HIV/AIDS: Business leaders take up the fight*. UN General Assembly Special Session on HIV/AIDS. Retrieved October 23, 2007, from http://www.un.org/works/aidssession/feature6.html.
2. Rosen, S., Feeley, R., Connelly, P., & Simon, J. (2006). *The private sector and HIV/AIDS in Africa: Taking stock of six years of applied research.* Health and Development discussion paper No. 7 (June). Retrieved May 3, 2008, from http://www.sabcoha.org/images/stories/hddp_7-private_sector_and_aids_in_africa.pdf.
3. World Economic Forum Global Corporate Citizenship Initiative. (2005). *Partnering for success: Business perspectives on multistakeholder partnerships.* Retrieved March 16, 2007, from: http://www.weforum.org/pdf/ppp.pdf.
4. EurActiv.com. (2005). Survey: Business do too little about the HIV/AIDS epidemic. World Business Council for Sustainable Development News Articles. Retrieved March 12, 2007, from: http://www.wbcsd.ch/plugins/DocSearch/details.asp?type=DocDet&ObjectId=MTI5NTU.
5. UNAIDS. (2001). *Top businesses pledge to act on HIV/AIDS*. Press release, June 26, 2001. Retrieved on October 31, 2007, from http://www.thebody.com/unaids/businesses.html.
6. Bendell, J. (2003). *Waking up to risk: Corporate responses to HIV/AIDS in the workplace*. Geneva: UNRISD & UNAIDS. Retrieved November 7, 2007, from: http://www.unrisd.org/unrisd/website/document.nsf/d2a23ad2d50cb2a280256eb300385855/8836d5e635b2d234c1256dd6004ee8c1/$FILE/bendell2.pdf.
7. Rosen, S., Simon, J., MacLeod, W., Fox, M., Thea, D. M., & Vincent, J. R. (2003). AIDS is your business. *Harvard Business Review* 81(1).
8. Whiteside, A. (2001). Demography and economics of HIV/AIDS. *British Medical Bulletin* 58, 73–88.
9. Rosen, S., Vincent, J. R., Macleod, W., Fox, M., Thea, D. M., & Simon, J. (2004). The cost of HIV/AIDS to businesses in Southern Africa. *AIDS* 18, 317–24.
10. International Labor Organization. (2005). *HIV/AIDS and work: Global estimates, impact, and response*. Retrieved March 23, 2005, from http://www.ilo.org/public/english/protection/trav/aids/publ/global_est/.
11. International Labor Organization. (2005). *HIV/AIDS and work: Global estimates, impact, and response*. Retrieved March 23, 2005, from http://www.ilo.org/public/english/protection/trav/aids/publ/global_est/.
12. Morgan, D., Mahe, C., Mayanja, B., Okongo, J. M., Lubega, R., & Whitworth, J. A. G. (2002). HIV-1 infection in rural Africa: Is there a difference in median time to AIDS and survival compared with that in industrialized countries? *AIDS* 16(4), 597–603.
13. Barnett, T., & Whiteside, A. (2002). *AIDS in the twenty-first century: Disease and globalization*. New York: Palgrave Macmillan.

Notes   311

14. Rosen, S., Simon, J. L., Thea, D. M., & Vincent, J. R. (2000). Care and treatment to extend the working lives of HIV positive employees: Calculating the benefits to business. *South African Journal of Science* (July). Retrieved November 30, 2006, from http://sph.bu.edu/images/stories/scfiles/cih/Businessbenefitsofcareandtreatmentsajs.pdf.

15. International Organisation of Employers. (2002). *Employers' Handbook on HIV/AIDS—a guide for action.*

16. International Labor Organization. (2005). *HIV/AIDS and work: Global estimates, impact, and response.* Retrieved March 23, 2005, from http://www.ilo.org/public/english/protection/trav/aids/publ/global_est/.

17. International Labor Organization. (2005). *HIV/AIDS and work: Global estimates, impact, and response.* Retrieved March 23, 2005, from: http://www.ilo.org/public/english/protection/trav/aids/publ/global_est/.

18. International Organisation of Employers. (2004). *Employer's Guide: Employment relationships.* Geneva: International Organisation of Employers.

19. World Economic Forum Global Corporate Citizenship Initiative. (2005). *Partnering for success: Business perspectives on multistakeholder partnerships.* Retrieved March 16, 2005, from: http://www.weforum.org/pdf/ppp.pdf.

20. Sengupta, J., & Sinha, J. (2004). Battling AIDS in India. *The McKinsey Quarterly* 4. Retrieved February 15, 2005, from http://www.mckinseyquarterly.com/article_page.aspx?ar=1430&L2=12#foot4up.

21. World Economic Forum Global Health Initiative. (2003). *Focusing on prevention through behaviour change for nearly two decades, contributing to a reduction of more than 50 per cent of workers partaking in high-risk behaviour: Nestlé.* Global Health Initiative private sector intervention case example. Retrieved March 23, 2005, from http://www.weforum.org/site/homepublic.nsf/Content/Global+Health+Initiative%5CGHI+Case+Studies+and+Supporting+Documents.

22. Kotler, P., & Lee, N. (2005). *Corporate social responsibility: Doing the most good for your company and your cause.* Hoboken, NJ: John Wiley and Sons, Inc.

23. Ibid.

24. World Economic Forum Global Health Initiative. (2003). *A hotel in Thailand ensures nondiscrimination through a life threatening disease policy while providing employee access to HIV/AIDS education as part of a health promotion program: JW Marriott Hotel Bangkok.* Global Health Initiative private sector intervention case example. Retrieved March 23, 2005, from: http://www.weforum.org/site/homepublic.nsf/Content/Global+Health+Initiative%5CGHI+Case+Studies+and+Supporting+Documents.

25. Stone, G. (2004). *Remarks by Dr. Greg Stone at Ford Motor Company media conference on HIV/AIDS.* Ford Motor Company, December 6, 2004. Accessed 15 February, 2006, from: http://media.ford.com/newsroom/release_display.cfm?release=19740.

26. Ford Motor Company. (2004). *Sustainability report 2003–2004: Global Reporting Initiative HIV/AIDS Program.* Retrieved January 30, 2006, from: http://www.ford.com/NR/rdonlyres/esoskte3tjujzvqnvcezsqdjyftvfkglfb-dtpthdwbv3fkvxch5yzt7rngr466bjzacjajiqmzhixkocqabituoytyg/hiv_aids_report.pdf.

27. Moore, S. (2002). A way to foster employees health: How some southern African firms are taking on the costs of fighting AIDS for their workers. *Los Angeles Times.* Accessed February 14, 2006, from http://www.aegis.org/news/lt/2002/LT021210.html.

312 Notes

28. World Economic Forum Global Health Initiative. (2004). *A leading electronics company with operations in South Africa developed and sustained a comprehensive prevention and treatment programme to address the threat of a potential 13% workplace HIV-prevalence rate in 2009: Siemens.* Global Health Initiative private sector intervention case example. Retrieved March 23, 2005, from http://www.weforum.org/site/homepublic.nsf/Content/Global+Health+Initiative%5CGHI+Case+Studies+and+Supporting+Documents.
29. American Express: http://www.americanexpress.com.
30. Apple: http://www.apple.com/ipodnano/red/.
31. Converse: http://www.converse.com.
32. GAP: http://www.gapinc.com/red.
33. Giorgio Armani: http://www.emporioarmaniproductred.com.
34. Motorola: http://direct.motorola.com/hellomoto/red/.
35. World Economic Forum. (2005). *South African companies at cutting edge of HIV/AIDS programs.* Retrieved October 31, 2005, from http://www.weforum.org/site/homepublic.nsf/Content/South+African+Companies+At+Cutting+Edge+Of+HIV%2FAIDS+Programmes.
36. International Labour Organisation. (2005). *World employment report 2004–2005.* Geneva: International Labour Organisation.
37. SABCoHA/BER. (2008). *The impact of HIV/AIDS on selected companies in South Africa.* Retrieved May 3, 2008, from http://www.ber.ac.za/Knowledge/pkDownloadDocument.aspx?docid=4132.
38. Rosen, S., Feeley, R., Connelly, P., & Simon, J. (2006). *The private sector and HIV/AIDS in Africa: Taking stock of six years of applied research.* Health and Development discussion paper No. 7 (June). Retrieved May 3, 2008, from http://www.sabcoha.org/images/stories/hddp_7-private_sector_and_aids_in_africa.pdf.
39. International Finance Corporation. (2005). *Projects: Work with small and medium-sized enterprises.* Accessed on 14 February, 2006, from: http://www.ifc.org/ifcext/aids.nsf/Content/Projects?OpenDocument&ExpandSection=18.
40. International Labor Organization. (2003). *Workplace action on HIV/AIDS: Identifying and sharing best practice.* Retrieved January 23, 2005, from http://www.ilo.org/public/english/protection/trav/aids/bpreport.pdf.
41. World Economic Forum. (2005). *South African companies at cutting edge of HIV/AIDS programs.* Press releases, 28 October, 2005. http://www.weforum.org/site/homepublic.nsf/Content/South+African+Companies+At+Cutting+Edge+Of+HIV%2FAIDS+Programmes.
42. Barnett, T., & Whiteside, A. (2002). *AIDS in the twenty-first century: Disease and globalization.* New York: Palgrave Macmillan.
43. Rafique, M. (2002). A company's policy on HIV/AIDS in the workplace. *Indian Journal of Medical Ethics* 10(4). Retrieved March 8, 2005, from http://www.issuesinmedicalethics.org/104di094.html.
44. World Economic Forum Global Health Initiative. (2003). *Integrating HIV/AIDS prevention into existing induction and health and safety training programmes: PT Ricky Putra Globalindo.* Global Health Initiative private sector intervention case example. Retrieved March 23, 2005, from http://www.weforum.org/site/homepublic.nsf/Content/GHI_Case_Studies_Details?OpenDocument&docID=63167CF6EB1F9749C1256E00004A1725&DB=site%5CGHI%5CGHI.nsf. .
45. World Economic Forum Global Health Initiative. (2003). *Focusing on prevention through behaviour change for nearly two decades, contributing to a reduction of more than 50 percent of workers partaking in high-risk behaviour: Nestlé.* Global Health Initiative private sector intervention case

Notes 313

example. Retrieved March 23, 2005, from http://www.weforum.org/site/homepublic.nsf/Content/Global+Health+Initiative%5CGHI+Case+Studies+and+Supporting+Documents.

46. Spicer, A. (2004). South Africa tries to cut AIDS's costs. *The Wall Street Journal*, January 28, 2004. Retrieved on October 31, 2005, from http://www.wsj.com.

47. Bendell, op. cit.

48. Rosen, S., Simon, J., MacLeod, W., Fox, M., Thea, D. M., & Vincent, J.R. (2003). AIDS is your business. *Harvard Business Review* 81(1).

49. World Economic Forum Global Health Initiative. (2004). *A leading electronics company with operations in South Africa developed and sustained a comprehensive prevention and treatment programme to address the threat of a potential 13% workplace HIV-prevalence rate in 2009: Siemens.* Global Health Initiative private sector intervention case example. Retrieved March 23, 2005, from: http://www.weforum.org/site/homepublic.nsf/Content/Global+Health+Initiative%5CGHI+Case+Studies+and+Supporting+Documents.

50. German Technical Cooperation GTZ is a private company owned by the German federal government offering services in the transfer of knowledge that helps people to work towards development goals. GTZ employs approximately 10,000 employees in 130 countries. For more information on GTZ go to: http://www.gtz.de.

51. German Technical Cooperation GTZ, Global Business Coalition, et al. (2005). *Making Co-Investment a Reality.* Accessed on February 14, 2006, from: http://www.gtz.de/de/dokumente/en-gtz-gbc-co-investment-2005–12.pdf.

52. World Economic Forum Global Health Initiative. (2003). *Integrating HIV/AIDS prevention into existing induction and health and safety training programmes: PT Ricky Putra Globalindo.* Global Health Initiative private sector intervention case example. Retrieved March 23, 2005, from: http://www.weforum.org/site/homepublic.nsf/Content/GHI_Case_Studies_Details?OpenDocument&docID=63167CF6EB1F9749C1256E00004A1725&DB=site%5CGHI%5CGHI.nsf. .

53. World Economic Forum. (2005). *Business and HIV/AIDS in Asia: Pushing back the tide.* Retrieved October 31, 2005, from http://www.weforum.org/pdf/Initiatives/GHI_Asia_Aids_Report05.pdf.

54. Seitz, B., Staber, U., & Jonczyk, C. (2002).DaimlerChrysler South Africa: Dealing with the effects of HIV/AIDS on human and social capital. In United Nations Global Compact, *Case Studies Series HIV/AIDS everybody's business* (pp. 41–62). Retrieved March 30, 2007, from http://www.unglobalcompact.org/docs/news_events/8.1/HIV_AIDS.pdf.

55. Rosen, S., Simon, J. L., Thea, D. M., & Vincent, J. R. (2000). Care and treatment to extend the working lives of HIV positive employees: Calculating the benefits to business. *South African Journal of Science* (July). Retrieved November 30, 2006, from http://sph.bu.edu/images/stories/scfiles/cih/Businessbenefitsofcareandtreatmentsajs.pdf.

56. World Economic Forum Global Health Initiative. (2003). *Focusing on prevention through behaviour change for nearly two decades, contributing to a reduction of more than 50 percent of workers partaking in high-risk behaviour: Nestlé.* Global Health Initiative private sector intervention case example. Retrieved March 23, 2005, from: http://www.weforum.org/site/homepublic.nsf/Content/Global+Health+Initiative%5CGHI+Case+Studies+and+Supporting+Documents.

57. Barnett, T., Fantan, T., Mbakile, B., & Whiteside A. (2002). *The private sector responds to the epidemic: Debswana—a global benchmark.* UNAIDS

314 *Notes*

case study. Retrieved May 30, 2008, from http://data.unaids.org/Publications/IRC-pub02/JC769-Debswana_en.pdf.

58. Kalavakonda, V. (2005). *Managing HIV/AIDS risk: An enterprise risk management model*. Washington, DC: World Bank. Retrieved February 27, 2007, from: http://siteresources.worldbank.org/INTAFRREGTOPHIVAIDS/Resources/HIV-AIDS-Enterprise-Risk-Management-Model.doc.

59. Moore, S. (2002). A way to foster employees' health: How some southern African firms are taking on the costs of fighting AIDS for their workers. *Los Angeles Times*. Accessed 14 February, 2006, from http://www.aegis.org/news/lt/2002/LT021210.html.

60. Karpf, T. (2005). Interview.

61. Moore, S., op. cit.

62. Wilson, B. (2006). Business faces up to AIDS challenge. *BBC News*, 11 January 2006. Accessed 14 February, 2006, from http://news.bbc.co.uk/2/hi/business/4601628.stm.

63. Faulk, S., & Usunier, J. C. (2005). *Woolworths South Africa case*.

64. Faulk, S., & Usunier, J. C. (2005). *Coca Cola case*.

65. Spicer, A. (2004). South Africa tries to cut AIDS's costs. *Wall Street Journal*, January 28, 2004. Retrieved October 31, 2005 ,from http://www.wsj.com.

66. AICC. (2004). *Corporate social responsibility (CSR): Implications for an ISO standard*. Retrieved October 31, 2005, from http://www.stansa.co.za/pdf/AICC.pdf.

67. German Technical Cooperation GTZ. (2005). *HIV/AIDS workplace policies and programs for the public and private sector*. International Symposium, Dar-es-Salaam, Tanzania, 26–28 May, 2004. Retrieved January 30, 2006, from http://www2.gtz.de/dokumente/bib/05-0196.pdf.

68. To access the ILO Code of Practice online, go to: http://www.ilo.org/public/english/protection/trav/aids/publ/code.htm.

69. Source: International Labor Office. (2001). *An ILO code of practice on HIV/AIDS and the world of work*, Geneva: ILO (pp. 3–4).

70. To access the UNAIDS report online go to: http://www.unaids.org/DocOrder/OrderForm.aspx.

71. UNAIDS. (2000). The business response to HIV/AIDS: Impacts and lessons learned. Retrieved March 23, 2005 from: http://www.unaids.org/NetTools/Misc/DocInfo.aspx?href=http%3A%2F%2Fgva%2Ddoc%2Dowl%2FWEBcontent%2FDocuments%2Fpub%2FPublications%2FIRC%2Dpub05%2FJC445%2DBusinessResp%5Fen%2Epdf.

72. Source: UNAIDS (2000). *The business response to HIV/AIDS: impacts and lessons learned*, Geneva and London: UNAIDS, PWBLF, and Global Business Council on HIV&AIDS.

73. Karpf, op. cit.

74. Bendell, op. cit.

75. Rosen, S., Simon, J., MacLeod, W., Fox, M., Thea, D. M., & Vincent, J. R., op. cit.

76. World Economic Forum. (2005). *Business and HIV/AIDS in Asia: Pushing back the tide*. Retrieved October 31, 2005, from http://www.weforum.org/pdf/Initiatives/GHI_Asia_Aids_Report05.pdf.

77. World Economic Forum. (2005), op. cit.

78. Global Business Coalition on HIV/AIDS (n.d.). Unilever. Retrieved on October 23, 2005, from http://www.businessfightsaids.org/site/apps/nl/content2.asp?c=gwKXJfNVJtF&b=1009053&ct=1365329.

79. Global Business Coalition on HIV/AIDS. (n.d.). *Awards for business excellence 2000–2001*. Retrieved October 23, 2005, from http://www.businessfightsaids.org/site/pp.asp?c=gwKXJfNVJtF&b=1008781.

Notes 315

80. Unilever. (2005). *Case studies: Kenya Fighting HIV/AIDS.* Retrieved October 23, 2005, from http://www.unilever.com/ourvalues/environmentandsociety/casestudies/health/kenyahivaids.asp.
81. Unilever. (2005). *Case studies: Nigeria AIDS management project.* Retrieved October 23, 2005, from: http://www.unilever.com/ourvalues/environmentandsociety/casestudies/health/nigeria.asp.
82. Global Business Coalition on HIV/AIDS. (n.d.). Unilever. Retrieved October 23, 2005, from: http://www.businessfightsaids.org/site/apps/nl/content2.asp?c=gwKXJfNVJtF&b=1009053&ct=1365329.
83. Nestlé Nigeria. (2003). *HIV/AIDS workplace attitude.* Supporting document in the Global Health Initiative Case Study and Supporting Document Library. Retrieved March 23, 2005, from: http://www.weforum.org/site/homepublic.nsf/Content/Global+Health+Initiative%5CGHI+Case+Studies+and+Supporting+Documents.
84. Unilever South Africa. (n.d.). *Unilever HIV/AIDS strategic roadmap. World Economic Forum case studies.* Retrieved March 8, 2005, from: http://www.weforum.org/pdf/Initiatives/GHI_HIV_Unilever_AppendixF.pdf.
85. World Economic Forum Global Health Initiative. (2003). *Focusing on prevention through behaviour change for nearly two decades, contributing to a reduction of more than 50 percent of workers partaking in high-risk behaviour: Nestlé.* Global Health Initiative private sector intervention case example. Retrieved March 23, 2005, from: http://www.weforum.org/site/homepublic.nsf/Content/Global+Health+Initiative%5CGHI+Case+Studies+and+Supporting+Documents.
86. Sony Global. (2005). *Activities to combat HIV/AIDS.* Retrieved March 23, 2005, from http://www.sony.net/SonyInfo/Environment/people/employees/human/#block12.
87. Sengupta, J., & Sinha, J. (2004). Battling AIDS in India. *The McKinsey Quarterly* 4. Retrieved February 15, 2005, from http://www.mckinseyquarterly.com/article_page.aspx?ar=1430&L2=12#foot4up.
88. Nestlé. (2004). *Nestlé in the community: Brazil National Corporate Council for HIV/AIDS.* Retrieved April 11, 2005, from http://www.community.nestle.com/activity.asp?a=6&c=8&p=0.
89. Until There's a Cure Foundation. (2008). *About Until There's a Cure.* Retrieved October 12, 2005, from http://www.until.org/about.shtml.
90. For more information on Serena Hotels, go to http://www.serenahotels.com/.
91. Tourism Promotion Services owns and operates hotels as part of the Aga Khan Development Network that offer world-class accommodation in a manner that is environmentally compatible and culturally sensitive. For more information, go to http://www.akdn.org/agency/akfed_tourpromo.html.
92. The Aga Khan Development Network is active in development projects relating to cultural heritage, education, health, microfinance, and others with a focus on Africa and Asia. For more information, go to http://www.akdn.org/.
93. PharmAccess was founded to expand access to HIV care and treatment products. For more information, go to http://www.pharmaccess.org.
94. Phillips Pharmaceuticals is a Kenyan distributor of medicines, medical information, and training.
95. ECPAT International. (2005). Novotel Bangna, Bangkok, Thailand. Retrieved October 27, 2005, from http://www.ecpat.net/eng/ECPAT_news/novotel.htm.
96. ACCOR (n.d.). Lutte *contre le tourisme sexuel impliquant des enfants,* Developpement durable. ACCOR. Retrieved October 12, 2005, from http://www.accor.com/fr/groupe/dev_durable/tourisme.asp.

316 *Notes*

97. ACCOR, op. cit.
98. World Economic Forum Global Health Initiative. (2003). *Promoting workplace HIV/AIDS awareness and prevention through awareness and worker training at an electronics company in Thailand: Sony Device Technology.* Global Health Initiative private sector intervention case example. Retrieved March 23, 2005, from: http://www.weforum.org/site/homepublic.nsf/Content/Global+He alth+Initiative%5CGHI+Case+Studies+and+Supporting+Documents.
99. World Economic Forum Global Health Initiative. (2003). *A hotel in Thailand ensures nondiscrimination through a life threatening disease policy while providing employee access to HIV/AIDS education as part of a health promotion program: JW Marriott Hotel Bangkok.* Global Health Initiative private sector intervention case example. Retrieved March 23, 2005, from http://www.weforum.org/site/homepublic.nsf/Content/Global+Health+Initi ative%5CGHI+Case+Studies+and+Supporting+Documents.
100. United Nations. (2001). *The UN works to stop the spread of HIV/AIDS: Business leaders take up the fight.* UN General Assembly Special Session on HIV/AIDS. Retrieved October 23, 2005, from http://www.un.org/works/ aidssession/feature6.html.
101. American Chamber of Commerce. (2004). *AmCham HIV/AIDS resource book.* Retrieved October 23, 2005, from http://asp.amcham.org.sg/hiv-aids/ success%20stories_new.htm.
102. Gail, C. (2003). Media assets support a powerful campaign. *Best Practices on Philanthropy.* Retrieved March 10, 2005, from http://www.onphilan- thropy.com/bestpract/bp2003–11–07.html.
103. UNAIDS. (2001). *Top businesses pledge to act on HIV/AIDS.* Press release, June 26, 2001. Retrieved October 31, 2005, from http://www.thebody.com/ unaids/businesses.html.
104. Asian Business Coalition on AIDS. (2002). *Business taking action to manage HIV/AIDS: A selection of business practices responding to HIV/AIDS in- and outside the Asian workplace.* Retrieved October 23, 2005, from http:// www.ksg.harvard.edu/cbg/hiv-aids/Business%20taking%20action%20 to%20manage%20AIDS.pdf.
105. Nestlé. (2004). *Nestlé in the community: Thailand HIV/AIDS.* Retrieved April 11, 2005, from http://www.community.nestle.com/activity.asp?a=6&c=60&p=0.
106. UNICEF. (2005). *IKEA sales for UNICEF far exceed expectations.* News, June 9. Retrieved October 29, 2003, from http://www.unicef.org/press/ news_detail.asp?news _id+ 459.
107. Abbott Laboratories. (2004). *Touching lives: Global citizenship report 2003.* Accessed March 8, 2005, from http://www.abbott.com/citizenship/ gcr_2003/4_5.htm.
108. World Economic Forum Global Corporate Citizenship Initiative. (2005). *Partnering for success: Business perspectives on multistakeholder partnerships.* Retrieved March 16, 2005, from http://www.weforum.org/pdf/ppp.pdf.
109. Abbott Laboratories, op. cit.
110. World Economic Forum Global Health Initiative. (2003). *A hotel in Thailand ensures nondiscrimination through a life threatening disease policy while providing employee access to HIV/AIDS education as part of a health promotion program: JW Marriott Hotel Bangkok.* Global Health Initiative private sector intervention case example. Retrieved March 23, 2005, from http://www.weforum.org/site/homepublic.nsf/Content/Global+Health+Initi ative%5CGHI+Case+Studies+and+Supporting+Documents.
111. Kotler, P., & Lee, op. cit.
112. Hamann, R., Agbazue, T., Kapelus, P., & Hein, A. (2005). Universalizing corporate social responsibility? South African challenges to the International

Organization for Standardization's new social responsibility standard. *Business and Society Review* 110(1), 1–19.

113. For more information on the AA1000 Assurance Standard, go to: http://www.accountability.org.uk.
114. For more information on FTSE4Good, go to: http://www.ftse.com/ftse-4good/FTSE4GoodCriteria.pdf.
115. FTSE. (2003). *FTSE4Good Index Series: Inclusion criteria.* Retrieved October 23, 2005, from http://www.ftse.com/ftse4good/FTSE4GoodCriteria.pdf.
116. For more information on the GRI, go to: http://www.globalreporting.org/.
117. For more information on the ILO Core Labour Standards, go to: http://www.ilo.org/public/english/standards/norm/introduction/need.htm.
118. For more information on the UN Global Compact, go to: http://www.unglobalcompact.org.
119. For more information on the OECD Guidelines, go to: http://www.oecd.org/department/0,2688,en_2649_34889_1_1_1_1_1,00.html.
120. For more information on the ISO 14000 series, go to: http://www.iso14000-iso14001-environmental-management.com/iso14000.htm.
121. For more information on the SA 8000, go to: http://www.sa-intl.org.
122. For more information on Responsible Care, go to: http://www.responsible-care.org/. For more information on Forest Stewardship Council, go to: http://www.fsc.org. For more information on the Marine Stewardship Council, go to: http://www.msc.org/.
123. Kofi Annan. (2004). *The Millennium Development Goals Report 2005.* United Nations. Retrieved October 12, 2005, from http://unstats.un.org/unsd/mi/pdf/MDG%20Book.pdf.
124. United Nations Development Programme. (2003). *Business and the Millennium Development Goals.* Retrieved October 12, 2005, from http://www.undp.org/business/docs/mdg_business.pdf.
125. Global Reporting Initiative. (2004). *Communicating business contributions to the Millennium Development Goals.* Retrieved October 12, 2005, from http://www.globalreporting.org/about/MDG_Final.pdf.
126. Kofi Annan. (2004). *The Millennium Development Goals Report 2005: Key proposals.* United Nations. Retrieved October 12, 2005, from http://www.un.org/millennium/sg/report/key.htm.

Index

A

Abarca, D., 299
Abbott, 53, 60, 120–125, 158, 171, 242, 243, 250
ABC model, 18, 66, 252
Abreu, T.F., 272, 274
Abu-Raddad, L.J., 42, 291
Academic journals, 250
ACCOR, 241
ACT UP, 70, 150, 202–203, 250
Activists, 31, 56, 70, 104, 105, 109, 127–129, 138, 142, 146, 157, 162, 166, 169, 176, 177, 180, 181, 201–206, 232
Adari, J.S., 42
Addiction, 250
Afghanistan, 6, 183, 240, 253
African American, 26, 33, 116, 117
Agadjanian, V., 42
Agbazue, T., 244, 316
Aggelton, P., 266
Ahmed, S., 268
AIDS risk-reduction model, 95
Ainsworth, M., 37, 42, 270, 281
Airhihenbuwa, C.O., 42
Ajuwon, A.J., 279
Albania, Belarus, Bulgaria, China, Lithuania, 37
Algeria, 3–9, 23
Allen, T., 42, 76
Altman, D., 73, 131, 280, 289
Altman, L.K., 282
Amen, K.A., 278, 289
Amnesty International, 30, 258
Amuyunzu-Nyamongo, M., 279
Anal sex, 11, 13, 16, 34
Anglo American, 208
Angola, 24, 36, 183, 242
Annan, K., 27, 85, 245, 246, 317

Antenatal care, 252
Antibodies, 101, 111, 113, 124, 258
Antiretroviral Treatment, 24, 31, 48, 53, 66–68, 82, 109, 112, 151, 152, 164, 165, 179, 227, 229-232, 249, 252, 258
Arab, 3, 4, 8–11, 29, 133, 152
Arackaparambil, R., 299
Araujo, L., 272, 274
Arias, E., 290
Armed forces, 27, 34–36
Armenia, 147, 183
Arora, C., 301
Arora, P., 302
Arrindel, W.A., 42
Aspen Pharmacare, 153
Attaran, A., 296
Austin, W., 44
Australia, 62, 73, 152, 187, 189, 212, 218
Auvert, B., 266
Aventis, 153
Awareness program, 38, 69, 90, 93, 194, 199, 208, 209, 225, 233, 235, 236, 241, 247
AZT (zidovudine), 51, 53, 63, 64, 106, 154, 169, 174, 253

B

Babu, V., 302
Bagés, N., 42
Bahadur, C., 173, 294, 299
Bahamas, 152, 243
Bahrain, 3, 152, 212, 218
Bailey, R.C., 266
Baker, B.K., 167, 297
Baldrini, F., 271
Balk, D., 267, 271
Bandura, A., 42, 93, 96, 97, 285

320 *Index*

Baral, S., 283
Barer, M.L., 295
Barnett, A., 63, 277
Barnett, T., 42, 60, 61, 231, 267, 268, 310, 312, 313
Barr, K., 266
Basabe, N., 42
Bassett, K., 295
Bate, R., 296
Bautista, S.A., 283
Bayer, R., 287, 293
Bearman, P., 289
Becker-Benton, A., 16, 32, 265, 269
Belgium, 37
Belize, 51, 81
Bell, C., 143, 144, 291, 292
Benatar, S.R., 13, 42
Bendell, J., 54, 275, 310, 313, 314
Berber, 8–11
Berkman, A., 276
Bertozzi, S.M., 283
Bertrand, J.T., 16, 32, 265, 269
Bery, P., 279
Beyrer, C., 37, 42, 270, 276, 281, 283
Bhatia, P., 302
BIC, 227, 232, 253
Biddlecom, A.E., 279
Biraro, S., 282
Blake, R.O., 302
Blanchard, J.F., 302, 303
Block, L.G., 93, 285
Bloom, D., 144, 221, 292
BMW, 208
Body fluids, 253
Boehringer Ingelheim, 158, 167, 169, 177, 178, 183, 242, 250
Bogart, L., 267
Bolding, G., 289
Bolivia, 49, 162, 174
Bond, M.H., 22, 44, 45, 267
Borchardt, J.K., 298
Borja, R.R., 305
Boseley, S., 298, 299, 300
Botswana, 23, 48, 68, 107, 145, 197, 198, 218, 222, 229, 231, 249, 251
Bourgois, P., 45, 277
Bourne, D., 43, 277
Bradford, J., 44
Bradshaw, D., 43, 277
Brady, M., 268
Brands, 135–140, 164, 196, 200–202, 243, 252
Braun, K.L., 45

Bravo-Garcia, E., 283
Brazil, 15, 18, 35, 48–80, 81–96, 108, 138, 150, 151, 161–163, 167, 168, 170–172, 174–176, 180–183, 208, 220, 226, 229, 231, 236, 238, 240, 243, 244, 254, 255
Breastfeeding, 13, 114, 141, 253
Bredstrom, A., 42
Bristol-Myers-Squibb, 167, 177, 250, 254
Brodkin, E., 291
Brothel, 37, 75, 197
Brouwer, K.C., 283
Brown, A.D., 297, 303
Bruckner, H., 289
Brunei, 152
Buddhism, 75
Burke, K., 266
Burkina Faso, 71, 172, 174, 183, 243, 249
Burt, S.L., 310

C

Caballo, V.E., 42
Cabezas, A.L., 37, 42
Caesarian section, 114
Caldwell, J.C., 42
Caldwell, P., 42
Cameroon, 24, 183
Campbell, C., 25, 26, 30, 43, 93, 267, 268, 269, 284
Campbell, C.A., 43
Campbell, P.J., 263
Canada, 62, 81, 142, 152, 156, 162, 165, 180, 254
Cape Verde, 174
Caplan, A.L., 295
Cardo, D.M., 286
Carey, M.P., 119, 286
Caro, D., 282
Casey, B.J., 269
Castilla, E.J., 43
Castro, A., 14, 43
Catholicism, 54, 132
CD4 tests, 109
Centers for Disease Control and Prevention (CDC), 63, 108, 115, 116, 119, 132, 254
Central Asia, 57, 58, 152
Cevallos, D., 283
Cevasco, M., 301
Chacham, A.S., 27, 43
Chamas, C., 53, 273, 274, 275

Chapman, S., 288
Chase, M., 301
Chassler, D., 43
Chastang, J.F., 43
Chaudry, P.E., 162, 163, 296
Chaya, N., 278, 289
Cheek, R., 270
ChevronTexaco, 203
Child, 1, 5, 9, 26, 29, 38, 48, 51, 64, 84, 114, 154, 199, 241, 246, 255
China, 16, 37, 39, 40, 49, 50, 62, 68, 134, 137, 147, 190, 207, 220, 227
Choi, K., 44
Ciesielski, C.A., 286
Cipla, 153, 161, 164, 171, 172, 183, 254
Circumcision, 5, 10, 15, 21, 29, 71, 256
Clark, S., 43, 278
Clarke, I., 162, 296
Clatts, M.C., 290
Clay, S., 265, 266
Cleghorn, F., 283
Coca-Cola, 70, 195, 199, 201, 202–210, 225, 232
Cocaine, 35
Cogan, J., 265
Cohen, J., 119, 192, 274 277, 281, 302
Cohen, S., 266
Colfax, G., 280
Colombia, 30, 51, 174, 202
Communication, 14, 23, 27, 32, 33, 37, 38, 51, 60, 66, 69, 77, 79, 81–99, 104, 116, 117, 140, 154, 155, 160, 175, 189, 193, 195, 198, 201, 204–209, 216, 225, 226, 238, 251
Compulsory licensing, 53, 58, 70, 152, 159, 161–167, 170, 173, 180, 254
Condom, 5, 6, 10–20, 26–40, 51–55, 58, 65, 66, 70–86, 88, 91, 94–99, 116, 127–140, 141, 170, 186, 194, 195, 197, 200, 202, 206, 208, 209, 216, 217, 225, 229–236, 240–244, 249, 250–253, 260
Confidentiality, 55, 107–108, 118–119, 208, 234–238, 247
Congo, 30, 36, 72, 183
Connelly, P., 220, 310, 312
Coon, H.M., 45
Cooper, J., 92, 284

Corporate social responsibility (CSR), 118, 151, 158–159, 201, 204, 210, 217, 241–245
Cost-benefit analysis, 229
Costs of HIV/AIDS, 142, 143, 150
Cournos, F., 267
Cowgill, K., 31, 32, 265, 269, 270, 274, 275
Cowley, G., 274, 278
Cowley, M., 299
Crandal, C.S., 15, 46, 264
Crawford, J., 280, 290
Crehan, K., 269, 271
Crooks, R., 266
Crouse Quinn, S., 280
Croyle, R.T., 92, 284
Cultural value systems, 16
Culture Shock, 37
Culver, D.H., 286
Curran, J.W., 289
Cyprus, 152
Czech Republic, 190

D

D'Adesky, A.-C., 10, 11, 263, 264, 265, 269, 274, 275, 276, 287
Dadd, C., 279
Daimler Chrysler, 197
Damayanti, K., 302
Dare, L., 63, 277
Dash, D.K., 302
Davey, S., 297
Davis, M., 289
Davison, L., 305
de Avila Vitoria, M.A., 276
De Cock, K.M., 280, 288
de H.C. Barreto, I.C., 274
Deaton, A., 43
Denning, P.H., 290
Devarajan, S., 143, 144, 291, 292
Devellis, B., 280
Devellis, R., 280
Devine, P.G., 43
Dialmy, A., 264
DiClemente, R.J., 42, 95, 285
Diener, E., 42
Differential pricing, 104, 158, 172–177, 183, 242, 255
Diffusion of innovations, 96
Dinh, K., 300
Discrimination, 10, 14, 18–19, 30, 31, 66, 99, 115, 123, 125, 126, 146–151, 184, 202, 208, 222, 234–236, 258

322 Index

DiStefano, J.J., 45
Dmytraczenko, T., 283
Dominican Republic, 38, 174
Donaldson, T., 294
Donnelly, J., 299
Donohue, J.M., 301
Dorfman, P.W., 44
Dovidio, J.F., 44
Drug prequalification, 152
Drug users, 1, 3, 7, 12, 18, 20, 27, 35,
      40–41, 48, 51, 54–56, 61, 76,
      81, 84, 91, 114, 115, 146, 147,
      184, 192, 259
Dunkle, K.L., 27, 43
Dworkin, S.L., 27, 37, 43, 65, 271, 278

E
Eagley, A.H., 15, 27, 47
East Timor, 174
Eberstadt, N., 43, 262
Ecstasy, 34
Egypt, 3, 6, 21, 29, 34, 131
Ehrhardt, A.A., 27, 37, 43, 65, 271,
      278
Eisenmann, M., 42
El Maroufi, K., 1, 2, 261
El Ouali, A., 262
El Salvador, 174
Elbe, S., 268, 270
Elford, J., 289
ELISA (enzyme linked immunosorbent
      assay), 111, 113, 121–126
Elliott, J.R., 19, 27, 43
Emmanuel, F., 302, 303
Eppright, D.R., 94, 285
Epstein, B.G., 12, 62, 264, 277
Equitable pricing, 152, 173–176
Eritrea, 36, 183
Essien, J.E., 280
Ethics, 141–183, 201
Ethiopia, 48, 62, 183
Ethnic groups, 21, 26, 49, 146, 217
EU (European Union), 162, 180
Evans, A., 286
Evans, R.G., 295
Extended Parallel Processing Model, 93
Ezio, S., 42

F
Fanon, F., 23, 267
Fantan, T., 231, 313
Far-Manguinhos, 171, 174
Farmer, P., 14, 43, 63, 269, 270, 277
Fatalism, 23, 117

Faulk, S., iii, v, 314
Faunce, T., 295, 296
Fear appeals, 93, 129
Feeley, R., 220, 310, 312
Feldmann, L., 42
Female genital mutilation (FGM), 10,
      15, 29, 30, 72, 256, 257
Fertility, 28, 61
Fitzgerlad, T., 43
Flamm, M., 270
Fleischmann, J., 280
Flood, M., 274
Floyd, D., 93, 284
Food and Drug Administration (FDA),
      106, 118, 132, 138, 155, 160,
      176, 182
Football, 30, 85, 86, 89, 91
Ford, 199, 203, 226, 227
Forsythe, S., 43
Foulis, C.A., 43
Fox, M., 46, 221, 222, 278, 289, 310,
      313, 314
France, 6, 8, 12, 35, 62, 67, 128, 130,
      131, 139, 211, 241, 244, 251
Francoeur, R.T., 264, 274
Fredine, H.G., 45
Fredriksson, J., 267
Freedman, J., 43
Friedman, M., 150, 294
Friedman, S.R., 45, 277
Frith, M., 292
Fuhrer, R., 43

G
Gaertner, S.L., 44
Gaffeo, E., 14, 43, 291
Gail, C., 316
Galvan, A., 269
Garcia Abreu, A., 31, 32, 265, 269,
      270, 274, 275
Garcia, J., 276
Gates, B., 68, 103, 193, 251, 253, 258,
      269, 278, 281, 285
Gauri, V., 276
Gausset, Q., 14, 43, 72
Gautam, V., 301
Gay, 11, 19, 27, 33, 34, 48, 55, 73, 74,
      82, 84, 89, 90, 96, 127–131,
      135, 139, 185, 186, 256
Gayet, C., 283
Gayle, H.D., 268, 303
Gender, 12, 14, 15, 16, 19, 27–28, 31,
      37, 52, 71, 84, 98, 115, 137,
      189, 230, 231, 234, 246, 256

Generic, 53, 54, 118, 141, 142, 150, 152, 156–159, 160–178, 180–181, 253–256
Germany, 37, 128, 129, 139
Gersbach, H., 143, 144, 291, 292
Gillespie, S., 32, 43
Gillespie-White, L., 296
Gilmore, K., 291
Glass, D.C., 19, 44
Glaxo-SmithKline (GSK), 177–178
Glied, S., 291, 292
Global Business Coalition on HIV/AIDS (GBC), 69–70, 85, 105, 151, 159, 180, 186, 199, 205–207, 237–239, 243, 244, 248
Global Fund to Fight AIDS, Tuberculosis and Malaria, 66, 70, 205, 227
Glover, G., 269
Gold, J., 210, 303
Goldsamt, L.A., 290
Goldstein, D.E., 271
Goliber, T., 292
Gomez, C.B., 45
Gonzalez, J.L., 42
Gordon, P., 269, 271
Gostin, L.O., 119, 148, 286, 287, 293
Grande, C., 305
Gray, P.B., 5, 262, 263
Greco, D.B., 27, 43
Greco, M., 27, 43
Greece, 37, 139, 228
Grenada, 152
Grey market, 162, 163, 175, 183
Groenewald, P., 43, 61, 277
Grosskurth, H., 282
Grover, R., 92, 284
GTZ, 197, 230, 233
Guatemala, 24, 81, 82, 99, 178
Guinea-Bissau, 174, 183
Gupta, G.R., 27, 43, 274
Gupta, V., 44

H

HAART (highly active antiretroviral therapy), 142, 208, 256
Hadler, M., 44
Haeberle, N.J., 289
Haerry, D., 293
Hall, E.T., 22, 44, 267
Hall, M.L., 44
Haller, M., 44
Halperin, D.T., 266
Hamann, R., 244, 316

Hamburg, M.A., 277, 292
Hampton, N.Z., 44
Hanges, R.J., 44
Hare, T., 269
Harris, P.G., 292
Harrison, K., 43
Hart, G.J., 289, 290
Härtel, C.E.J., 44
Härtel, G.F., 44
Harvey, P.W., 44
Hashem, F., 45
Hass, R.G., 44
Haughton, L.T., 44
Hayes, K., xiii, 213, 215, 308, 309
Heald, S., 42, 76
Health belief model, 95
Health insurance, 108, 165, 167, 229, 233
Hein, A., 244, 316
Heineken, 191, 197, 206, 208, 225
Hendricks, M., 44
Herek, G., 265
Herek, G.M., 44
Hernandez, E.E.H, 267
Hesson-McIness, M.S., 45, 265
Heterosexual, 3, 4, 13, 23, 33, 35, 48, 73, 84, 117, 132, 137, 185, 192
Hierarchy of effects, 91, 96
Hispanic, 33
HIV prevalence, 1–7, 11–12, 16, 21, 35–37, 48, 50, 51, 60–62, 71, 75–76, 79, 81–82, 119, 133–134, 144, 155, 156, 165, 173, 186, 191–192, 201, 213–217, 220–233, 241
HIV/AIDS campaigns, 10, 12, 14, 40, 41, 52, 54, 55, 56, 69, 71, 72, 75, 77, 80–89, 90–100, 116, 117, 129, 133, 135, 137, 142, 151, 156, 165, 170, 171, 185–187, 195–198, 206, 209, 216, 230, 241, 249
Hofmann, R., 284
Hofstede, G., 22, 42, 44, 267
Hogg, R.S., 283, 291
Hogle, J.A., 282
Holbrooke, R., 105, 108, 285, 286
Holmer, A.F., 176, 299
Holmes, E.C., 109, 287
Holmes, K.K., 289
Home-brew tests, 118
Homedes, N., 275
Homosexuality, 6, 10, 16, 17, 19, 20, 33, 34, 73, 83, 185

324 Index

Honduras, 24, 51
Hope, R.H., 269
Hourani, A., 262
House, R.J., 44
Human Development Index, 173
Human Rights, 8, 14, 16, 18, 30, 54, 56, 63, 76, 105, 133, 147, 148–149, 151, 203, 245, 246, 254, 258
Humphreys, B., 270
Hungary, 190
Hunt, B., 94, 285
Husnik, M., 280
Hydroxybutyrate (GHB), 34

I

Ibn Khaldun, 8, 262
Income distribution, 31
India, 17, 26, 33, 38–40, 49, 50, 59, 62, 85, 86, 96, 99, 120, 123, 128, 130, 137, 150, 151, 153, 160, 161, 163, 164, 167, 169–172, 176, 180, 183, 184–193, 198, 202, 208, 227, 229, 240, 244, 249, 253–255, 258
Injecting Drug User (IDU), 1, 3, 7, 12, 20, 35, 48, 51, 54, 56, 61, 81, 91, 147, 192, 257, 259
International Labor Organization (ILO), 66, 144–145, 194, 222, 224, 228, 233–236, 245, 248
International organizations, 12, 57, 58, 60, 65, 66, 68, 70, 79, 86, 117, 119, 141, 146, 147, 148, 150, 155, 201, 236, 257
Iran, 3, 6, 9, 34, 35
Ireland, 190
Islam, 21, 132
Israel, 3, 4, 37, 152
Italy, 37, 131
Ivory Coast, 30
Iwuagwu, S.C., 279

J

Jackson, T.P., 310
Jaffe, H.W., 280, 288
Jamaica, 34, 132
Janis, I.L., 93, 284
Janssens, V., 304
Japan, 16, 37, 40, 130–135, 137, 138, 152, 241, 242
Jarama, S.L., 44
Javidan, M., 44
Jejeebhoy, S.J., 303

Jenkins, C., 1, 2, 32, 61, 261, 262, 270, 301
Jha, P., 302
Johnson, B.T., 119, 286
Johnson, C., 303
Jonczyk, C., 230, 313
Jonsson, P.O., 19, 44
Jordan, 3, 6, 49, 176

K

Kakuchi, S., 271
Kalavakonda, V., 231, 314
Kamali, A., 282
Kanabus, A., 267, 269, 270
Kang, H., 302, 303
Kapczinski, A., 298
Kapelus, P., 244, 316
Karpf, T., xiii, xxi, xxii, 64, 65, 78, 154, 207, 314
Katz, D., 295
Katz, I., 19, 44
Kawachi, I., 46
Kazanjian, A., 295
Keefe, J., 45
Keller, P.A., 93, 96, 285
Kelley, L.M., 262
Kemmelmeier, M., 45
Kennamer, J.D., 44
Kenya, 25, 40, 70, 71, 101, 145, 183, 204, 206, 218, 222, 236, 240, 243, 252
Keown, C.F., 162, 296
Kerr, T., 291
Ketamine, 34
Khan, S., 193, 268
Kidd, M., 280
Kidd, R., 265, 266
Kikuyu, 21
Kim, J.Y., 63, 277
Kinzie, J.D., 45
Kippax, S., 280, 290
Kirungi, W., 282
Klausner, J.D., 301
Kleinert, V., 280
Klitzman, R., 287
Knight, K., 45
Koblin, B.A., 280
Kobori, S., 297, 299
Kombe, G., 283
Korea, 152, 161, 183
Kothi, 185, 257, 258
Kotler, P., 226, 311, 316
Kouteya, S., 301

Kowalski, J., 275
Kramer, M.R., 158, 295
Kravitz, R.L., 295
Kreuter, M., 44
Krishnakumar, R., 288
Kruk, M., 306
Kublin, J.G., 42, 291
Kumar, R., 302
Kuwait, 3, 152

L

L'Oréal, 243
Lacey, M., 284
Lafarge, 205
Lagarde, E., 266
Lahelma, E., 44
Lahiri, S., 267, 271
Lakhaney, A., 281
Lakshmi, V., 301, 302
Lamont, J., 305
Landau, S., 17, 45, 265
Lane, T., 281
Lange, J.M.A., 293, 298
Laos, 24, 194, 241
Latin America, 12, 23, 32, 48, 49, 51,
    55, 57, 87, 102, 117, 132, 133,
    152, 163, 171, 252
Laubscher, R., 43, 277
Leaty, S., 286
Lebanon, 3, 4, 33
Lederberg, J., 277, 292
Lee, K.S., 296, 299
Lee, N., 226, 311, 316
Leisinger, K.M., 155, 295
Lemmen, K., 293
Lesbian, 34, 55, 256
Lesotho, 107, 183
Leventhal, H., 96, 285
Levine, R., 289
Levine, W.C., 290
Levy, D., 289
Lexchin, J., 295
Li, X., 289
Libya, 3, 6, 9, 203, 208
Life expectancy, 12, 21, 49, 50, 142,
    145, 249
Lim, G.H., 296
Lindsey, D., 268, 269, 271, 294
Link, B.G., 13, 44
Literacy, 8, 9, 31, 48, 82, 84
Liu, B., 305
Liu, J.X., 44
Lloyd-Smith, E., 291

Lowe Geonnotti, K., 21, 267, 268
Low-income countries, 2, 139, 168,
    169, 173, 177, 178, 183
Lubega, R., 45, 291, 310
Lucero, J., 45
Luchetta, T., 44, 265
Lueck, S., 266, 297
Lundgren, L., 43
Luo, 21
Luskewane ceremony, 38
Lynch, S., 305

M

Machismo, 33, 52, 81, 82
Macleod, W., 46, 221, 222, 310, 313,
    314
Macroeconomic Impacts of HIV/AIDS,
    144, 221, 223
Madraa, W., 282
Magis-Rodriguez, C., 283
Maharaj, P., 279
Mahe, C., 45, 291, 310
Mahjour, J., 264
Maia, M.B., 27, 43
Maimaine, S., 43
Malaria, 6, 13, 17, 30, 51, 66, 70,
    143–147, 150, 158, 160, 168,
    179, 205, 227, 237–239, 242,
    246, 247, 257, 258
Malawi, 67, 71, 107, 183
Malaysia, 20, 41, 51, 137, 162, 212,
    218, 244
Mali, 6, 29, 183, 203
Malnutrition, 13, 31, 74, 149
Manhart, L.E., 264
Mann, I., 93, 284
Mann, J.M., 148, 293
Mansergh, G., 290
Mao, R., 289
Marianismo, 52
Marion, S.A., 295
Marks, G., 290
Marmot, M., 14, 45
Marshall, A., 44
Martin, G., 295, 296
Martinkainen, P., 44
Masaki, E., 210, 303
Mascolini, M., 267, 294
Mauritania, 5, 6, 9, 183
Mayanja, B., 45, 291, 310
Maznevski, M.L., 45
Mbakile, B., 231, 313
Mbogo, S., 306

326 *Index*

Mboi, N., 45
McArthur, J.W., 306
McCauley, A.P., 115, 287
McInness, C., 299
McInness, D., 280
McIntosh, W.A., 45
McKee, C.M., 277
McKee, N., 16, 32, 265, 269
McLaughlin, L., 45
McMurchie, M., 280
McNeil, D.G., 265, 294, 295, 298, 306
McPake, B., 275
Mechoulan, S., 105, 286
Médecins Sans Frontières (MSF), 22,
    24 -25, 67, 68, 165, 169, 171,
    173, 177, 178, 254, 255, 258
Media, 9, 10, 16, 38, 39–40, 52,
    74–76, 81, 86, 87, 89, 90, 91,
    99, 100, 101, 104, 108, 129,
    156, 195, 198, 199, 204, 218,
    220, 226, 232, 241
Meldrum, J., 299
Mellahi, K., 310
Mellouk, O., 263, 264
Men having Sex with Men (MSM), 1,
    2, 8, 9, 11, 12, 13, 16, 17, 20,
    28, 29, 33–35, 39, 52, 56, 61,
    81, 83, 84, 90, 105, 117, 128,
    130, 135, 182, 258
MERCOSUR, 49
Merritt, A.P., 267, 279
Merz, J.F., 295
Messias, E., 273
Messina, S., 267
Methamphetamine ("crystal meth"),
    34, 35, 73, 74, 182, 255, 259
Mexico City Policy, 20
Mexico, 51, 81–84, 88, 98–99, 249,
Middle East, 2, 3, 5, 6, 9, 32, 35, 57,
    152
Migration, 2, 5, 6, 12, 16, 31, 32, 51,
    63, 204, 230
Miller, S., 45, 297
Miners, 25, 26, 30, 197
Mintzes, B., 156, 295
Missildine, W., 45
Moffic, H.S., 45
Moghadam, M.R., 42
Mohan, K., 301
Moldova, 28, 37, 183
Moncada, D.M., 267
Montaner, J.S.G., 291
Monteiro de Andrade, L.O., 274
Mony, P., 302

Monzon, O.T., 271
Moodie, M., 292
Moore, S., 311, 314
Morgan, D., 45, 142, 291, 310
Morgan, R., 304
Morgan, W., 267, 279
Morocco, 1–41
Moses, S., 302, 303
Mother-to-child transmission, 76, 110,
    141, 169, 206, 208, 242, 243,
    258
Mozambique, 24, 67, 174, 183, 240
Mukherjee, P., 304
Munoz-Laboy, M., 276
Muslim, 5, 6, 8, 10, 20, 77, 203
Myanmar (Burma), 24, 183
Myers, M.B., 162, 296

N

Namibia, 36, 197, 205, 218, 307
Nannan, N., 43, 277
Narayanaswamy, L., 268, 271
Narayandas, D., 296
National Institutes of Health (NIH), 63,
    132, 251
Nestlé, 55, 203, 226, 229, 231, 238,
    240, 242
New Zealand, 152, 156, 189, 212, 218
Nichani, R., 263
Niger, 6, 183
Nigeria, 37, 62, 183, 192, 203, 209,
    218, 236, 238
Nitrate inhalants ("poppers"), 34, 73
Nogueira, S.A., 272, 274
Noguer, I., 31, 32, 265, 269, 270, 274,
    275
Nolte, E., 277
Nonnucleoside reverse transcriptase
    inhibitors (NNRTI's), 142
Noonan, R.J., 264, 274
Noorderhaven, N.G., 45
North Africa, 2–9, 32, 35, 57, 152
Northrup, N., 266
Novartis, 191
Nzewi, E., 301

O

O'Connell, J., 45
O'Sullivan, G.A., 267, 279
Obermeyer, C.M., 1, 2, 5, 10, 261, 263
Obregon, R., 42
Oei, T.P.S., 42
Okie, S., 48, 272, 274, 275, 294
Okongo, J.M., 45, 291, 310

Olaseha, I.O., 279
Oliveira, R.H., 272, 274
Oliveira-Cruz, V., 56, 275, 276
Oman, 4
Opio, A., 282
Opportunistic infections, 17, 22, 24, 40, 51, 111, 141, 144, 146, 150, 170, 179, 209, 229, 233, 251, 257, 259
Ortiz-Torres, B., 45
Oster, E., 21, 60, 62, 79, 267, 277, 282
Ouedraogo, B., 299
Ouedraogo, C., 279
Over, M., 210, 291, 303
Owens, M., 162, 296
Oyserman, D., 45

P

Paez, D., 42
Paiva, V., 276
Palia, A.P., 162, 296
Pan, R., 295
Panthi, 185
Paraguay, 49, 174
Parallel imports, 161, 162, 175, 183, 259
Parallel testing, 109, 110
Pardie, L., 44, 265
Parik, 185
Parker, R., 13, 15, 45, 265, 266, 276
Parsons, J.T., 45
Patent, 52, 53, 70, 141, 152–159, 161, 165–168, 171, 172, 174, 176, 177, 180, 182, 183, 254, 255–257, 259
Paterson, G., 266
Patnaik, P., 42, 291
Patterson, A.S., 277, 279
Patterson, T.L., 283
Pawley, D., 262
Peerapatanapokin, W., 210, 303
Pelzer, K., 301
PepsiCo, 196, 198, 201, 202, 203, 243
Peterson, H.B., 289
Peterson, J.L., 42, 285
Pfizer, 156, 171, 178, 181–183, 301
Pharmaceutical companies, 52, 58, 74, 118, 141, 142, 152, 153, 155, 156, 157, 159, 163–169, 171, 172, 173, 175–178, 179, 182, 183, 191, 225, 240, 242, 250
Pharmaceutical Research and Manufacturers of America (PhRMA), 176, 177
Phelan, J., 13, 44

Philippines, 36, 170, 190, 244
Phillips, M.M., 266, 297
Pinheiro, T.C., 272, 274
Piot, P., xii, xiii, 16, 143, 145, 220, 264
Plant, E.A., 43
Pliskin, K.L., 45
Plumley, B., 279
Poku, N., 43
Poppen, P.J., 44
Porter, M.E., 140, 157, 158, 295
POZ, 73, 136, 156
Prasad, T.L., 302
Prentice-Dunn, S., 93, 284
President's Emergency Plan for AIDS Relief (PEPFAR), 101, 103, 160, 166, 179, 249
Press, 6, 39, 56, 70, 73, 85, 185, 191, 204, 226
Prison, 3, 11, 20, 30, 34–35
Productivity, 51, 144, 150, 190, 213, 215, 221, 222, 231, 239
Prostitutes, 30, 75, 83, 212
Protection Motivation Model, 93
Pryns, T., 63, 277
Pryor, J.B., 17, 45, 265
Public health system, 48, 53, 150, 176
Puerto Rico, 34
Pulerwitz, J., 283
Puren, A., 266

Q

Qatar, 4, 152
Quelch, J., 296
Quiggin, P., 42
Quitkin, M., 270

R

Rabasca, L., 266, 287
Race, K., 280
Radio, 10, 13, 39, 82, 84, 85, 88, 90, 91, 95, 99, 100
Rafique, E.M., 271, 312
Rahkonen, O., 44
Rahman, M.R., 45
Ranbaxy, 153, 160
Rao, V., 301
Rau, B., 43
Rawstorne, P., 280
Reddy Bloom, L., 144, 221, 292
Reeder, G.D., 17, 45, 265
Reif, S., 21, 267, 268
Research and development (R&D), 103, 153, 155, 159, 163–167, 171, 175, 176, 182

328 *Index*

Revenga, A., 210, 303
Reza Paul, S., 302, 303
Rhodes, T., 45, 277
Rimé, B., 42
Rinke de Wit, T.F., 304
Risk-taking, 31
Robalino, D.A., 1, 2, 32, 61, 261
Roberts, C., 290
Roche, 53, 107, 108, 118, 167, 171, 178–183, 256
Rodgers, G.B., 45
Rogers, E.M., 37, 265, 272, 281
Rogers, R.-W., 93, 96, 284
Romania, 34, 37, 249
Romero, L., 45
Roos, E., 44
Roper, W.L., 289
Rosen, S., 46, 220, 221, 222, 228, 229, 231, 235, 310, 311, 312, 313, 314
Rosenberg, M., 281
Rosenthal, F., 262
Rosenthal, M.B., 301
Ross, M.W., 280
Roth, G.Y., 300
Russia, 13, 35, 37, 39, 49, 50, 58, 62, 147, 207–209, 211–215, 217, 218, 220, 227
Russian Federation, 37, 49
Ryan, C.A., 264

S

Saastamoinen, P., 44
Sachs, J.D., 306
Safe-sex, 74, 94, 115
São Tomé and Principe, 174, 183
Satel, S., 43
Saudi Arabia, 4, 9, 34, 147
Scalway, T., 30, 264, 267, 268, 270, 271
Scarce, M., 280
Schaller, M., 15, 46, 264
Scheer, R., 266
Schmaus, A., 43
Schmidt-Traub, G., 306
Schneider, M., 292
Schoepf, B.G., 11, 264
Schoofs, M., 266, 286, 287
Sciortino, R., 271
Scott, H., 281
Seitz, B., 230, 313
Sekles, F., 272
Sen, A., 257, 269, 292
Senegal, 39, 48, 58, 183, 203

Sengupta, J., 311, 315
Sengupta, S., 280
Serial testing, 109
Serostatus, 110
Serrano-Garcia, I., 45
Sever, C., 268, 271
Severe acute respiratory syndrome (SARS), 17, 150
Sex workers, 1, 3, 6, 9, 10–12, 16–18, 20, 25, 27, 30, 36, 39–41, 55, 56, 75, 81, 88, 115, 132, 147, 184–186, 191, 192, 195, 199
Sexually transmitted infections (STIs), 4, 32, 40, 52, 90, 128, 132, 208, 233
Shacinda, S., 297
Shafer, L.A., 282
Shah, I., 303
Sheon, N., 115, 287
Sherr, L., 286, 289
Shipley, M.J., 43
Shtarkshall, R.A., 46
Sica, C., 42
Siemens, 4–6, 11
Sifakis, F., 283
Sigiya, Z., 43
Signorile, M., 280
Silva, A.P., 27, 43
Silverman, M., 265
Simic, M., 45, 277
Simon, J.L., 46, 220, 221, 222, 231, 309, 310, 311, 312, 313, 314
Simons, C., 305
Singapore, 152, 212, 218
Singer, M., 45, 277
Singhal, A., 37, 265, 272, 281
Sinha, J., 311, 315
Siplon, P., 292
Sitta, R., 266
Smallman, S., 283
SME (Small and Medium-sized Enterprises), 220, 228, 230
Smith, B.L., 290
Smith, M., 292
Smith, R.A., 19, 27, 43, 265, 291, 293
Smolinski, M.S., 277, 292
Sobngwi-Tambekou, J., 266
Social cognition theory, 93
Social marketing, 54, 57, 58, 77–80, 82, 86–88, 96, 116, 139, 206, 225, 226, 252, 255
Sodomy, 20
Somalia, 4, 183
Sorenson, C., 295, 296

Soskolne, V., 46
Soucat, A., 37, 42, 270, 281
South Africa, 40, 48, 49, 61, 63, 64, 70, 71, 85, 86, 90, 130, 150–154, 160, 169, 177, 178, 182, 191, 192, 198, 211–219, 220, 222, 226–230, 231, 232–233, 238–239, 243, 244, 247, 253
Southeast Asia, 17, 103, 152, 163
Spain, 1, 6, 8, 9, 12, 35
Sparks, L., 310
Specter, M., 280, 281, 290
Spencer, J., 305
Spicer, A., 313, 314
Sri Lanka, 190
Staber, U., 230, 313
Standard Chartered Bank, 197, 198
Stanton, B., 289
Starnes, C.N., 42
Steptoe, A., 42
Stereotypes, 15, 17, 18, 27, 97
Sternberg, P., 46
Steven, D., 144, 221, 292
Stigma, 2, 10, 14, 16–18, 21, 22, 34, 35, 56, 61, 66, 71, 74, 82–84, 90, 91, 99, 105, 107, 108, 112, 115, 117, 186, 208, 229, 232, 235, 236
Stone, G., 226, 311
Strathdee, S.A., 45, 277, 283
Stratton, S.E., 266
Strauss, R.P., 280
Strides Arcolab, 153
Subramanian, S.V., 46
Sub-Saharan Africa, 1, 5, 9, 12, 27, 28, 31, 57, 62, 70–72, 114, 141, 143, 152, 175, 179, 180, 204, 220
Sudan, 2, 4, 24, 29, 30, 183, 203
Sudha, R.T., 186, 301, 302
Sun, Z., 289
Swarns, R., 278
Swartz, G., 296
Swaziland, 39, 192
Swearingen, S.G., 301
Switzerland, 18, 60–69, 78, 86, 94, 107, 128, 138, 139, 154, 157, 178, 179, 198, 205, 207, 227, 260
Syrian Arab Republic, 4

T

Taljaard, D., 266
Tan, S.J., 163, 296

Tangwa, G.B., 46
Tanner, J.F., 94, 285
Tarantola, D., 293
Tattooing, 13
Taylor, B.M., 46
Taylor, H., 305
Taylor, J.J., 14, 46, 264
Television, 10, 13, 39, 69, 84, 85, 88, 90, 91, 95, 99, 128, 129, 165, 204, 211, 226, 241, 244
Testing kit, 102, 106, 107
Testing, 2, 4, 11, 14, 17, 20, 23, 34, 40, 41, 55, 57, 58, 61, 66, 77, 82–85, 91, 94, 101–126, 128, 139, 141, 147, 164, 170, 174, 186, 207–209, 215–217, 225, 229–238, 243, 247, 252, 253, 260
Thailand, 23, 30, 37, 39, 48, 53, 58, 63, 75–76, 137, 142, 150, 161, 171, 173, 182, 194–196, 199, 201, 204, 209, 227, 241, 242
The Netherlands, 23, 62
Thea, D.M., 46, 221, 222, 231, 310,311, 313, 314
Theory of reasoned action and planned behavior, 95
Thomas, J.K., 45
Thomas, J.R., 297
Thompson, D.F., 293
Thomsen, M., 305
Thorburn, S., 267
Thurow, R., 297
Timberg, C., 281, 282
Topouzis, D., 291
Torres, I., 280
Torres-Burgos, N., 45
Trademark, 159, 161, 162, 164
Tremlett, G., 262
Trimble, C., 271
TRIPS (Trade Related Industrial Property rightS), 161, 162, 164, 166, 169, 170, 180, 255, 260
Tropical diseases, 149, 168, 254
Truck drivers, 36, 38, 186, 192
Trujillo, L., 281
Tuberculosis, 6, 13, 22, 32, 35, 50–52, 61, 63, 66, 70, 110, 112, 115, 142, 145, 147, 205, 227, 230, 237–239, 247, 255, 257, 258
Tunisia, 4, 6, 8
Turkey, 4, 37, 49, 228
Turmen, T., 46
Turner, D., 46
Tyndall, M.W., 291

330 *Index*

U

U.S. Agency for International Development (USAID), 63, 77, 79, 88, 89, 132, 252
Uchida, Y., 289
Ugalde, A., 275
Uganda, 23, 58, 71, 72, 76–80, 133, 142, 165, 183, 222, 240, 242
Ukraine, 28, 35, 37, 207, 209, 243
UNAIDS, 1–9, 12, 16, 28, 33, 34, 36, 41, 51, 54, 57–62, 65, 66, 69, 70, 81, 83, 85, 98, 115, 145, 151, 178, 191, 196, 198, 204, 206, 220, 231, 235, 236, 248, 249, 250, 257
UNDP, 30, 65, 142, 256
UNESCO, 12, 13, 36, 38, 65, 243, 250
Unilever, 191, 198, 205, 228, 236, 238, 243
United arab Emirates, 4, 152
United Nations (UN), 5, 14, 27, 37, 40, 65, 66, 85, 143, 148, 150, 182, 245, 246
United Nations Children's Fund (UNICEF), 28, 65, 85, 242, 250, 257
United Nations Development Fund for Women (UNIFEM), 66, 257
United Nations Education, Scientific and Cultural Organization(UNESCO), 12, 13, 36, 38, 65, 243, 250
United Nations International Drug Control Program (UNDCP), 65
United Nations Population Fund (monitoring and reporting) (UNFPA), 20, 65, 133
United States, 8, 12, 21, 23, 26, 28, 31–38, 40, 41, 51, 58, 62, 70, 73–74, 81–84, 85, 86, 102, 103, 106, 108, 109, 112, 116, 130–133, 138, 142, 147, 148, 150, 152, 153, 156, 162–168, 176, 181, 188, 190, 192, 202, 204, 211, 218, 228
Usdin, S., 284
Usunier, J.C., iii, v, 165, 290, 296, 314
Utilitarianism, 150

V

Vachani, S., 295
Vaillancourt, D., 276
Valdiserri, R.O., 280, 288, 290
Valencia, J., 42

Van de Ven, P., 280
Van der Borght, S., 304, 308
VanLandingham, M., 281
Vasagar, J., 288
Veenstra, N., 46
Velasquez, G., 300
Vietnam, 183, 190, 194, 195, 253
Vihay, D.T., 301, 302
Vincent, J.R., 46, 221, 222, 231, 310, 311, 313, 314
Virginity, 15–16, 33, 52, 252
Volkswagen, 40, 55, 69, 191, 205, 228, 255
Voss, H., 269
Vriens, M., 92, 284

W

Wackenhut, J., 44
Waddington, J., 292
Wainburg, M.L., 267
Wakeford, E., 280
Waldby, C., 290
Wallerstein, N., 45
Walsh, M.J., 162, 163, 296
Walton, M., 301
Wardle, J., 42
Ware, W.B., 280
Watstein, S.B., 266
Watts, J.C., 96, 285
Wazana, A., 156, 295
Weaver, M., 289
Weigand, R.E., 163, 296
Weinert, L., 305
Weinhardt, L.S., 119, 286
Wells, H., 286
Werhane, P., 294
Western Blot, 111, 113
Western Europe, 12, 29, 130, 152
Western Sahara, 5, 9
Weston, M., 144, 221, 292
Whetten, K., 21, 267, 268
White, B., 305
Whiteside, A., 42, 46, 60, 61, 222, 223, 231, 267, 268, 277, 282, 310, 312, 313
Whitworth, J.A.G., 45, 291, 310
Wiessner, P., 293
Williamson, L.M., 290
Wilson, B., 314
Wolitski, R.J., 290
Wonacott, P., 301
Wood, E., 291
Wood, W., 15, 27, 47
Woog, V., 279

Index 331

Worchel, S., 44
World Bank, 31, 48, 55, 67, 69, 70, 76, 103, 143, 144, 179, 183, 231, 250, 257
World Economic Forum's Global Health Initiative, 69, 201, 248
World Health Organization (WHO), 2, 41, 48, 51, 59, 60, 65–68, 86, 101–105, 107, 109, 115, 119, 130, 133, 136, 148, 150, 151–154, 160, 166, 172, 175, 182, 218, 249, 250, 255, 257
World Intellectual Property Organization (WIPO), 53
World Trade Organization (WTO), 53, 141, 157, 159, 161, 164, 166–170, 172, 180, 255, 260
World Wildlife Fund (WWF), 205
Wu, Pei-Chan, 45

Y

Yeadon, C., 45, 265
Yemen, 4, 183
Yi, H., 290
Yinhe, L., 265
Yonkler, J.A., 267, 279
Young, I., 280
Yount, K.M., 303
Youssef, H., 289

Z

Zambia, 36, 48, 70, 80, 107, 183, 206, 218
Zepeda, S.J.Z., 267
Zhang, H.X., 47, 289
Zimbabwe, 49, 71, 104, 183, 206, 215, 218
Zimmerman, R., 300
Zuhur, S., 263